American Travel Literature, Gendered Aesthetics, and the Italian Tour, 1824–1862

Edinburgh Critical Studies in Atlantic Literatures and Cultures
Series Editors: Andrew Taylor, Colleen Glenney Boggs and Laura Doyle

Modern global culture makes it clear that literary study can no longer operate on nation-based or exceptionalist models. In practice, American literatures have always been understood and defined in relation to the literatures of Europe and Asia. The books in this series work within a broad comparative framework to question place-based identities and monocular visions, in historical contexts from the earliest European settlements to contemporary affairs, and across all literary genres. They explore the multiple ways in which ideas, texts, objects and bodies travel across spatial and temporal borders, generating powerful forms of contrast and affinity. The Edinburgh Critical Studies in Atlantic Literatures and Cultures series fosters new paradigms of exchange, circulation and transformation for Atlantic literary studies, expanding the critical and theoretical work of this rapidly developing field.

Available titles
Sensational Internationalism: The Paris Commune and the Remapping of American Memory in the Long Nineteenth Century
J. Michelle Coghlan

American Travel Literature, Gendered Aesthetics, and the Italian Tour, 1824–1862
Brigitte Bailey

Forthcoming titles
Emily Dickinson and Her British Contemporaries: Victorian Poetry in Nineteenth-Century America
Páraic Finnerty

Following the Middle Passage: Currents in Literature Since 1945
Carl Plasa

www.edinburghuniversitypress.com/series/ECSALC

American Travel Literature, Gendered Aesthetics, and the Italian Tour, 1824–1862

Brigitte Bailey

EDINBURGH
University Press

Edinburgh University Press is one of the leading university presses in the UK. We publish academic books and journals in our selected subject areas across the humanities and social sciences, combining cutting-edge scholarship with high editorial and production values to produce academic works of lasting importance. For more information visit our website: edinburghuniversitypress.com

Edinburgh University Press Ltd
The Tun – Holyrood Road
12 (2f) Jackson's Entry
Edinburgh EH8 8PJ

Typeset in 11/13 Adobe Sabon by
IDSUK (DataConnection) Ltd, and
printed and bound in Great Britain.

A CIP record for this book is available from the British Library

ISBN 978 1 4744 3283 2 (hardback)
ISBN 978 1 4744 3286 3 (webready PDF)
ISBN 978 1 4744 3285 6 (epub)

Contents

Illustrations

Acknowledgments

As my parents downsized in retirement, they handed on to me a scrapbook of their honeymoon: a collection of black and white photographs and postcards of their trip through Italy in the 1950s. In those pictures of my young parents, one German and one American, standing in the ruins of Pompeii or before a vista into the Italian countryside, I recognized both the book I was writing and what I was leaving out: the individual, aspirational aspects of traveling. And I was reminded that, in spite of the illusion of independence one has as a scholar, each book has a long cultural, professional, and personal history.

It is a pleasure, at last, to be able to thank all those who have contributed to this book, which has been long in the making. Thanks to the following institutions, which gave me access to their archives of texts and images: the American Antiquarian Society; the Cleveland Museum of Art; Dimond Library, at the University of New Hampshire; the Houghton Library and the Harvard College Library, at Harvard University; the print collection at the Museum of Fine Arts, Boston; and the Fenimore House Museum of the New York State Historical Association (now the Fenimore Art Museum). My home institution, the University of New Hampshire, provided financial support: a Faculty Development Grant brought me to art museums, Summer Faculty Fellowships and a Liberal Arts Faculty Research Fellowship supported research and writing over three summers, and a Writing Academy grant supported the book's completion. Special thanks to UNH's Center for the Humanities for a Gustafson Fellowship and a Senior Faculty Research Fellowship, which gave me two much needed semesters to write. The Center and the English Department helped with publication costs. And the National Endowment for the Humanities gave me an encouraging Summer Stipend, early in the project.

My thinking about travel, nineteenth-century writings, gender, and visual culture has benefitted enormously from many conversations with colleagues at conferences and in various collaborations. Of special note are the collaboration with Beth L. Lueck and Lucinda Damon-Bach in shaping the first Transatlantic Women conference and editing the ensuing collection of essays, and the opportunities and collegiality offered by the Margaret Fuller Society during its first twenty-five years, including collaborating with Jeffrey Steele on a number of conference panels.

Mentors, colleagues, friends, and students have lent support and enriched my understanding of nineteenth-century literature and culture. Long ago, Alan Heimert supported my decision to write a dissertation on travel writing, and Elizabeth McKinsey gave me the interdisciplinary tools to do so. Rudolph Martinez and I helped each other through doctoral studies and our early careers. At UNH, I have been lucky in my colleagues and students. David Watters, always enthusiastic about interdisciplinary work, saw the potential in this project. Sarah Sherman offered a model of thoughtful scholarship, read a chapter, and brought her considerable experience as a series editor to a reading of my book proposal. Others read early drafts of chapters with insight and interest: Michael Ferber, Romana Huk, Dan Reagan, Mary Rhiel, Sandhya Shetty, Doris Sommer, and Susan Walsh. Michele Dillon gave the manuscript a supportive reading toward the end of the process. Of those who, over the years, read drafts and provided collegial support I especially want to thank Lisa MacFarlane, from whom I learned much during our team teaching in American Studies and whose friendship has been a sustaining presence, and Rachel Trubowitz, who never let me forget that I am a scholar. Jan Golinski read a chapter and gave excellent advice along the path to publication, even as his friendship became important to me in many other ways. My undergraduate students have asked great questions about the meanings of literature and have connected texts with images and history in insightful projects. Graduate seminars have been rich and inventive places, and I am grateful to UNH's graduate students for making them so. Those students from whom I've learned are too numerous to list, but I do want to thank four doctoral students with whom I have worked the most closely and whose work I admire: Nancy von Rosk, Laura Smith, Christina Healey, and James Finley.

Parts of the book have appeared in earlier versions. I have found this sustained development of an interdisciplinary project invaluable; the earlier publications proved to be mutually illuminating, as their conjunction revealed a broader cultural narrative. The book has benefitted from the earlier editorial reviews, and I thank the editors and publishers of the following essays for permission to republish material: "Irving's

Italian Landscapes: Skepticism and the Picturesque Aesthetic," *ESQ: A Journal of the American Renaissance* 32.1 (1986), reprinted in *Short Story Criticism*, vol. 210, ed. Lawrence J. Trudeau (Farmington Hills, MI: Gale, 2015); "The Protected Witness: Cole, Cooper, and the Tourist's View of the Italian Landscape," in David C. Miller (ed.), *American Iconology: New Approaches to Nineteenth-Century Art and Literature* (New Haven: Yale University Press, 1993); "The Panoptic Sublime and the Formation of the American Citizen in Cooper's *Wing-and-Wing* and Cole's *Mount Etna from Taormina, Sicily*," in Hugh MacDougall (ed.), *James Fenimore Cooper: His Country and His Art—Papers from the 1997 Cooper Seminar* (Oneonta: James Fenimore Cooper Society and SUNY College at Oneonta, 1999); "Representing Italy: Fuller, History Painting, and the Popular Press," in Fritz Fleischmann (ed.), *Margaret Fuller's Cultural Critique: Her Age and Legacy* (New York: Peter Lang, 2000); "Fuller, Hawthorne, and Imagining Urban Spaces in Rome," in Robert K. Martin and Leland S. Person (eds), *Roman Holidays: American Writers and Artists in Nineteenth-Century Italy* (Iowa City: University of Iowa Press, 2002), reprinted in *Nineteenth-Century Literature Criticism*, vol. 176, ed. Kathy D. Darrow and Russel Whitaker (Detroit: Gale, 2007); "Gender, Nation, and the Tourist Gaze in the European 'Year of Revolutions': Kirkland's *Holidays Abroad*," *American Literary History* 14.1 (2002); "Tourism and Visual Subjection in *Letters from Abroad* and 'An Incident at Rome,'" in Lucinda Damon-Bach and Victoria Clements (eds), *Catharine Maria Sedgwick: Critical Perspectives* (Boston: Northeastern University Press, 2003); and "Religious Icons, National Iconography, and Female Bodies in Hawthorne and Stowe," in Derek Rubin and Hans Krabbendam (eds), *Religion in America* (Amsterdam: Vrije Universiteit Press, 2004).

Thanks as well to the anonymous readers and the series editors of Edinburgh Critical Studies in Atlantic Literatures and Cultures – Andrew Taylor, Colleen Glenney Boggs, and Laura Doyle – for their fruitful suggestions. And thanks to those through whose adroit hands the manuscript passed, including my copy-editor, Cathy Falconer.

This book is dedicated, with love, to my family: to my smart and beautiful daughter, Wei Marley; my creative and world-traveled sister, Christine Bailey; my pastor-philosopher father, Theodore Bailey; and to the memory of my intellectual and fiercely independent mother, Gunda Gabcke Bailey. They have nurtured, challenged, and inspired me – as I know they will continue to do.

Introduction

In 1844 a nineteen-year-old farmer's son, printer's apprentice, and aspiring poet – Bayard Taylor – sailed for Liverpool with two friends and with commissions for travel essays from the *Saturday Evening Post* and the *United States Gazette*. Taylor grew up in a society that linked European travel with cultural aspirations; as he says, "An enthusiastic desire of visiting the Old World haunted me from early childhood."[1] However, his limited means led him to design "a more humble method of seeing the world [that] would place within the power of almost every one what has hitherto been deemed the privilege of the wealthy few" (15). And so, drawing on the precedent of German journeymen and university students, Taylor became perhaps the first young American tourist to backpack through Europe. His two-year travels on foot through Britain, Germany, France, and Italy resulted in periodical essays, which he collected in his first and quite popular travel book: *Views A-Foot; or, Europe seen with Knapsack and Staff* (1846). They also resulted in a career as a professional travel writer, newspaper correspondent, lecturer, poet, novelist, translator, and finally ambassador to Prussia.[2]

This trajectory – from his father's substantial Pennsylvania farm through travel and travel writing to the U.S. embassy in Berlin – maps out one route toward class and gender formation in the antebellum United States. The conjunction of travel and print culture offered the possibility of gaining and demonstrating cultural authority, and Taylor's democratic extension of the means of travel ensured that this possibility was available to "almost every one," that is, most literate citizens in the post-Jacksonian era of universal white male adult suffrage. One crucial demonstration of cultural authority in these travel writings was the caliber of affective and aesthetic responses to the scenes of tourism. Although *Views A-Foot* also engages other implications of European tourism, my interest is in the role of aesthetic responses in the tourist's performance of a culturally elite subjectivity. As was the case with most Americans, Taylor experienced and composed particularly heightened responses to landscapes in Italy. It was important for Taylor to articulate both Italy's content (its history, artistic achievements, and literary past) and his relationship to its visual presence. In a sojourn in Tuscany, he needs to know about ancient Etruscan cities to experience the depth of the historical vista, about the intellectual achievements of the Renaissance to refer to Dante and Galileo, and about art to view the galleries of Florence and to visit the American expatriate sculptor Hiram Powers. But, in order to perform a cultivated masculinity, he also needs to adore the landscape – to idealize, even to apostrophize the scene that contains and exceeds this content.

As Taylor describes his explorations around Florence, he is repeatedly "enraptured" (313) by the "grand panorama, around which the Apennines stretch with a majestic sweep, wrapped in a robe of purple air" (300); or by views of "mountains and valleys all steeped in that soft blue mist which makes Italian landscapes more like heavenly visions than realities" (310); or by the "brilliant yet mellow glow . . . lighting up the houses of Tosi and the white cottages half seen among the olives, while the mountain of Vallombrosa stretched far heavenward like a sunny painting, with only a misty wreath floating . . . around its summit"; or by "the current of the Arno flashing like a golden belt through the middle of the picture" (313). The pictorial language culminates in an emotional and archaically phrased[3] address to Italy as landscape: "Sweet, sweet Italy! I can feel now how the soul may cling to thee, since thou canst thus gratify its insatiable thirst for the Beautiful. . . . In the twilight more radiant than light, and the stillness more eloquent than music, . . . there is a silent, intense poetry that stirs the soul through all its impassioned depths" (314). Using the common trope of the solitary spectator alone with "Italy" (although he is touring with friends), Taylor invokes the silent and feminized Italy that elicits just those qualities in the cultivated male tourist that seem cast aside by the "restless eagerness" and "activity" of American life (435): "With warm, blissful tears . . . and a heart overflowing with its own bright fancies, I wander in the solitude and calm . . . and love thee as if I were a child of thy soil" (314). If, as Liam Corley has demonstrated, "the purpose of travel writing" for Taylor "was to secure his position in literate society" (51), then how did this discourse of aesthetic idealization and emotional (if provisional) attachment function to accomplish this social task? In this book, I explore the significance of such loaded images and language and explain the importance of cultivating and publishing an aesthetic appreciation of Italy in pre-Civil War American culture.

American Travel Literature examines tourists' aesthetic responses in the context of U.S. nation formation; it brings perspectives from the history of art, theories of aesthetic response, and the study of tourism to a reading of the many published American travel accounts of Italy from 1824 to 1862, the period when modern forms of tourism emerged.[4] Italy had been associated with aesthetic perception, and especially with the training of foreign artists, in the previous century.[5] However, "Italy" took on particular national configurations for Americans. By the late eighteenth century, U.S. artists, travelers, and readers perceived Italy in at least three ways: as the classical site of republican values, as the Gothic site of violence and sexual danger, and as Arcadian landscape.[6] And all three associations would remain in play in the nineteenth century. However, by the 1820s tourist interest in classical Rome as a precedent for the U.S. experiment in republican government had waned. An ensuing vogue for Gothic Italy, running from the 1790s to the 1820s and fed by English novels and pictures, revealed a shift from an ideal of rational revolution to a post-revolutionary anxiety about the threat of lower-class disorder and revolt. During the 1820s tourists, artists, and writers decided to push the Gothic image of Italy into the background and to foreground the Arcadian landscape as a complementary counterpoint to the republican ideal: a locus of apolitical, feminized, noncommercial values – a timeless and silent "other" whose aesthetic contemplation solidified the contrasting definition of the U.S. as the current site of linguistic, political, and economic activity (coded as masculine) and of U.S. citizens as historical agents. As the land of the aesthetic, "Italy" offered American elites a controlled space for temporarily submitting to and, thereafter, appropriating the "feminine" and historically transcendent cultural forces of aesthetic insight, art, and public iconography to educate and manage the emergent energies of democratic society at home.

In a period of unsettled yet often strident U.S. nationalism, the Italian tour and its textual (and visual) expressions were forms through which predominantly white, northeastern, middle- and upper-class Americans dreamed their way into national identity and cultural authority. This book takes seriously the large number of published antebellum travel accounts as a revealing episode in U.S. literary and cultural history and seeks to answer the following questions: why did so many Americans write about their trip to Italy and publish their accounts in book form, or as travel sketches worked into fiction, or as essays, poems, and sketches in periodicals? Why was there a market – a reliable appetite – for these accounts? What functions did they serve? These allegedly personal writings add up to a veiled public discussion, a public playing with national, class, gender, religious, and ethnic identity – displaced from the fraught debates on U.S. soil and pleasurably refracted through the prism of leisure and aesthetic contemplation.

Focusing on representations of Italy in this period enables me to analyze what's at stake in American tourists' acquisition of an aesthetic gaze. The wealth of textual and visual images of Italy in books and periodicals signals its pivotal role as a site on which tourists practiced forms of visual response and reproduced, in print, what they saw. Scholars have argued that key literary and artistic genres, such as novels and landscape paintings, furthered the emergence of modern forms of nationalism and national subjectivity; nations depended for their cultural identities on the circulation of these literary forms and visual images – marked by shared conventions – among their citizens.[7] Tourism became a similar nation-forming ritual of consensus: the circulation of citizens among conventional images. The genre of tourist writing that emerged from this practice and that, in turn, was consumed by a wide middle-class readership, then, was also a modern nation-producing genre.

Although I examine a range of texts, I focus on U.S. writers who were well known at the time they published travel writings on Italy (unlike Taylor), who expected and received a wide readership for their tourist accounts, and who were therefore consciously performing as national representatives. Chapters concentrate on Washington Irving, whose "The Italian Banditti" (1824) appeared four years after *The Sketch Book* made him famous; James Fenimore Cooper, whose *Gleanings in Europe: Italy* (1838) appeared after the transatlantic success of *The Last of the Mohicans*; Catharine Maria Sedgwick, whose *Letters from Abroad to Kindred at Home* (1841) appeared after her similarly successful *Hope Leslie; or, Early Times in the Massachusetts*; Caroline Kirkland, whose *Holidays Abroad; or, Europe from the West* (1849) played off of her renown as the author of the book on the Michigan frontier *A New Home, Who'll Follow?*; Margaret Fuller, whose internationally read feminist work *Woman in the Nineteenth Century* and front-page column for the *New-York Tribune* gave her a wide readership for her foreign correspondence (1846–50); Nathaniel Hawthorne, whose *The Marble Faun* (1860) appeared a decade after *The Scarlet Letter* had made him instantly canonical in the newly arranged body of American literature; and Harriet Beecher Stowe, whose *Agnes of Sorrento* (1862) appeared, similarly, a decade after *Uncle Tom's Cabin* made her an international celebrity.

These writers combined national visibility with transatlantic travel. The artists discussed here, whose work most of these writers knew, also followed this pattern. Thomas Cole, whose two sojourns in Italy and many Italian paintings make him central to this project, went abroad after his early U.S. landscapes launched (according to his fellow painters) the school of American landscape painting.[8] All of these figures clearly saw their Italian works in dialogue with their American works. While Irving and Fuller have often been read as transatlantic writers, many of the antebellum writers and artists most identified with U.S. national subjects and landscapes have pronounced transatlantic careers, as recent scholarship on Stowe has confirmed.[9] Transatlantic approaches ask us to pay attention to American authors' and artists' investments in their European travels, sojourns, and works – to decide, for example, what we make of the fact that Cooper wrote as many travel books about Europe as he wrote Leatherstocking novels.

The shape of the argument below follows the consolidation, exploration, and – at times – revision of the picture of Italy in U.S. representations. In the 1820s and 1830s, Irving's and Cooper's Italian works (and paintings by Cole and others) reveal the process by which an aristocratic English landscape aesthetic, based on land ownership, was adapted to bourgeois and American uses. In picturesque travel, the proprietary gaze became metaphorical; the act of aesthetic possession rendered to the observer a provisional property – what I have called the "tourist's estate" – and defined a normative subjectivity for the male citizen, the variety of "liberal" gentleman that Cooper called the "American democrat." In the context of nineteenth-century representative democracy, the supervisory gaze of northeastern elites shifted from a more explicitly authoritative to a managerial mode; in support of this shift, the Italian tour trained observers to perceive aesthetic harmonies in diverse landscapes and, analogously, to use cultural means to harmonize social landscapes.

Antebellum projects of forming a national identity through culture also invited participation by women; in the 1840s several women published accounts of their Italian tours. Accepting, for the most part, the coding of Italy as feminine, women writers found that inhabiting the gap between being a tourist – an aesthetic subject – and being an aesthetic object (themselves objects of a similar gaze) could become intellectually productive. Travel books by Sedgwick and Kirkland examined the gentleman's gaze and experimented with other perspectives (Kirkland alternates between aestheticism and iconoclasm); more radically, Fuller's Roman journalism during the revolutions of 1848–9 critiqued tourists' reductive views of Italy and reconnected visual with political forms of representation.

Fuller's efforts to re-masculinize Italy in the service of revolutionary republicanism produced fervent support for the short-lived Roman Republic in the U.S.; however, it is striking that *travel* accounts, both during and after the revolutionary period, defaulted to the paradigm of Italy as silent, feminine, pastoral, and apolitical. Clearly the tourist's need for an aesthetic training ground outweighed the desire to recognize an emerging modern nation. Therefore, in two final syntheses of the antebellum lessons of this "Italy," Hawthorne and Stowe published novels incorporating tourist writing in 1860 and 1862 that reasserted the aesthetic uses of Italy and the link between national identity and aesthetics. Their romances explored the uses of art and visual response in reforming the self and in shaping nations, even as the ability of "culture" to sustain a vision of ideological coherence – the aesthetic capacity for imagining unity in a diverse landscape – was called into question by the advent of the Civil War.

In tracing this story of U.S. representations of Italy, I am historicizing aesthetic practices. This approach allows me to analyze the constitution of national subjectivities more precisely – in this case, to examine the conflation of public performance and private sensibility that tourist writing entailed as a significant means of defining a normative U.S. subjectivity. The image of a serene, feminized Italy, bathed in the glow of an Arcadian nostalgia, furthered the invention of a class perspective that, in turn, stood in for a national subjectivity. "Italy" helped to create a culturally elite vision – normalized through print culture as an American middle-class gaze – that sought not only to preside over others in the social landscape but also to manage aspects of the self.

Tourism and Atlantic World Circulations

The growth of elite U.S. practices of European tourism took place in a wider context of movements within the Atlantic world. This period is defined in part by patterns of migration triggered by endemic poverty and by the economic crises of the 1830s and 1840s, such as the arrival of Irish and Italian immigrants in U.S. and British cities; of political exile, including the presence of Italian and Hungarian refugees in London and New York, Polish and German refugees in Paris, and U.S. fugitive slaves in Britain; and of increased professional, educational, and commercial travel, as the modern global economy took shape.[10] These other circulations of people appear in antebellum print culture alongside the tourist accounts examined here. Lydia Maria Child's "Letters from New-York" in the *National Anti-Slavery Standard*, for example, describe European immigrants drawn into the city by the international labor market and coming to rest in one of its graveyards, with its "predominance of foreign epitaphs."[11]

Usually defined by privilege, leisure, and choice, antebellum tourism created transatlantic patterns of travel markedly different from the sometimes involuntary movements, often associated with labor and loss, listed above. Tourists sought out sites that offered self-culture through the pleasure of visual consumption, sites that had no permanent claim on them. Nevertheless, there were intersections between tourist routes and other circulations that characterized the period. Sedgwick refers to Italian political exiles in New York as she describes visits to their relations in Italy.[12] Fuller meets the Italian political exile Giuseppe Mazzini in London and converses with German travelers and a "Bengalese" student "in England for his education" on an English canal boat.[13] Two travel books of the Black Atlantic illustrate striking intersections of labor, loss, and even bondage with the mobility and leisurely self-cultivation of tourism: William Wells Brown's *The American Fugitive in Europe* (1855) and David Dorr's *A Colored Man Round the World* (1858). Brown sojourns in England to escape the Fugitive Slave Act and works as a lecturer on the abolitionist circuit; his book, however, pointedly claims the elite white tourist's sensibility and cultural authority by describing visits to such historical, literary, and cultural sites as Westminster Abbey, Sir Walter Scott's home, and the British Museum.[14] On the other hand, Dorr travels as an enslaved man; he is making the European tour as the property of a New Orleans slaveholder, and his book at once claims his owner's elite perspective in his commentary on the sights and resists it in his contrasts between European nations and the U.S.: "of all the German kingdoms, the most despotic is Austria; but she hates slavery more than the 'freest government in the world.'"[15]

Finally, as scholars have increasingly documented, the North Atlantic world was defined less by the unilateral gaze of tourists than by fluid and dialogic exchanges.[16] It was shaped by transnational migrations and their impact on national cultures, including, for example, the multilingual publishing environment in New York, which offered such foreign language newspapers as *Die Deutsche Schnellpost*.[17] The Atlantic world was networked through its print cultures and the ubiquitous habits of translating and reprinting works, just as it was through other forms of exchange and travel.[18]

And it was shaped by international reform movements. Reformers in northern Europe – especially Britain – and the U.S. met and corresponded on issues of slavery, poverty, temperance, women's rights, and peace; and writers incorporated reform perspectives in literary texts.[19]

By focusing on tourist writing, I am highlighting a particular form of transatlantic movement and its characteristic expression: in this case, a form of writing which often resisted a dialogic engagement with another nation – indeed, which often idealized silence and stasis in the other in order to develop a comprehensive vision in the self. Recovering the function of this genre, especially as Americans practiced it in Italy, demands an interdisciplinary approach.

Travel Writing and Interdisciplinary Methodologies

Travel writing has been a growing area of analysis in recent decades, a field formalized by the founding of the International Society for Travel Writing in 1997. Literary scholars – such as James Buzard, Mary Louise Pratt, and Sara Mills – have fruitfully examined British and European accounts of Europe, the Americas, Africa, and the Pacific from national, postcolonial, and feminist perspectives. And later U.S. travel writers, such as Henry James, have also received sustained attention.[20] Antebellum American writings on Europe, including Italy, have drawn scholarly discussion since the mid twentieth century, but much of this work has been descriptive or biographical.[21] Other discussions of travel writing on Italy occur within broader contexts, such as Americans in Europe (William W. Stowe), the American experience of Rome over the centuries (William L. Vance), or the growth of American women's travel writing on a global stage (Mary Suzanne Schriber). However, tourism and its expressions existed at the juncture of visual experience and written communication; therefore, antebellum tourist writings on Italy – especially – need a more interdisciplinary approach to explain their popularity and function in the era of the cultural invention of the U.S.

Developments in several disciplines have made such a reading possible. Art historians – such as Angela Miller, Alan Wallach, Elizabeth Johns, and David Morgan – have grounded discussions of antebellum visual genres in social and historical contexts, while both literary critics and art historians, such as Malcolm Andrews, have unpacked the social and political implications of the British aesthetics that shaped American responses. Sociologists, such as John Urry, have contributed important definitions of tourist practices and the

"tourist gaze."[22] National theorists, following Benedict Anderson, have analyzed the ways in which literary genres generate nations, even as, more recently, transatlantic scholars have complicated this argument and have emphasized the inherently transnational process of defining nations and national literary traditions (see, for example, Paul Giles, Meredith McGill, and Colleen Glenney Boggs). Literary scholars focusing on writers such as Hawthorne, Fuller, and Stowe have increasingly examined their engagement with Europe or their careers and writings abroad (see Larry J. Reynolds, Charles Capper and Cristina Giorcelli, Leslie Elizabeth Eckel, Robert K. Martin and Leland S. Person, and Denise Kohn et al.), while at least one literary critic, Paola Gemme, has developed a genuinely transnational reading of American and Italian reactions to the central Italian political movement in this period, the Risorgimento.

This book synthesizes these developments to analyze antebellum tourist writings on Italy. What it especially attempts is a sustained attention to connections between tourist writing and visual culture. Studying this conjunction clarifies the trope of Italy as woman, the American turn toward visual iconography in articulating social and national identities, and the uses of tourist writing not only to convey visual impressions but also to model the process of aesthetic response. Rehearsing this process on Italy's aesthetic ground and reproducing and disseminating it through print culture enabled tourists to develop a broader middle-class embrace of the ameliorative, "feminine" iconographical route toward social harmony and even (they hoped) a more binding national union. Therefore, given the importance of aesthetic language in tourist writings, I draw on the conventions of antebellum visual arts – especially of landscape, history, and genre paintings – to analyze the habits of visual perception tourists carried with them.

However, travel writing grew from and shaped the broader field of antebellum culture. And so I also pay attention to the burgeoning popular print culture in this period, in which periodicals frequently printed travel writing, fiction, poetry, bits of biography, and so on, along with visual images. I discuss Italian representations in such annuals, magazines, and newspapers as *Friendship's Offering*, the *United States Magazine and Democratic Review*, and the *New-York Tribune*. I refer to other writers and artists from both sides of the Atlantic in my analysis, including Germaine de Staël, Byron, Anna Jameson, Samuel Rogers, Henry Wadsworth Longfellow, James Jackson Jarves, Washington Allston, J. M. W. Turner, Harriet Hosmer, and Daniel Gabriel Rossetti. And I connect travel writing with other discourses in the period, such as republicanism, anti-Catholic Nativism, and spiritualism. Fleshing out the ways in which tourist writing was embedded in all these aspects of antebellum culture explains why readers habitually bought and read what often strikes modern readers as formulaic accounts of the beaten track of the Italian tour.

Chapters

The period from the 1820s to the 1860s corresponds with significant eras in both Italian and U.S. history and in the history of tourism in Italy. The end of the Napoleonic occupation of Italy in 1814 triggered the return first of English and then American tourists and artists, while during the ensuing decades the Italian movement for independence culminated in the unification of most Italian states in 1860 (and Rome in 1870).[23] The same period in the U.S. – from the end of the War of 1812 to the start of the Civil War in 1861 – is marked by rapid population growth and geographical expansion and by the cultural nation-building meant to make the burgeoning nation cohere.[24] These histories intersect in several ways, including American sympathy for Italian nationalism,[25] but the primary point of intersection in U.S. print culture is tourist writing in the service of the cultural building of self and nation.

Chapter 1, "Irving's Landscapes: Aesthetics, Visual Work, and the Tourist's Estate," examines his southern European landscape descriptions over three decades to trace the adaptations of eighteenth-century English patterns of visual response to an emerging American tourist class and to chart the evolution of depictions of Italy through the revolutionary threat of bandits toward the pastoral feminine space that harmonizes and thereby disarms such lower-class threats. Irving's Italian sketches in 1804–5 show his pursuit of British aesthetic perspectives, especially the prospect view and the picturesque, as a supervisory gaze, concerned with harmonizing disparate elements of both natural and social scenes. The Italian sketches in *Tales of a Traveller* (1824), however, reveal a crisis of confidence in the capacity of aesthetic perception to sustain an ideologically coherent vision. In Part III, "The Italian Banditti," Irving uses the early nineteenth-century banditti vogue to question the social efficacy of aesthetic perception and representation. This under-analyzed work remarkably illuminates the hopes and weaknesses of the tourist's aesthetic project. While the Italian paintings of Washington Allston, whom Irving met in Rome, are visual analogies for strategies of managing the world of the senses and the centrifugal forces of American democracy, Irving's hyper-masculine banditti prove unmanageable; the "images" their violent tales produce overwhelm his central character – a painter – just as their predatory acts devastate pastoral scenes and kill women, the symbols of pastoral and cultural harmony. Finally, in Irving's last sketch book, the collection of Spanish tales and sketches *The Alhambra* (1832), he does achieve the aesthetic integration of a divided, and previously violent, landscape. However, he does so by lapsing into the explicitly fantastic and thus redefines the tourist gaze as a withdrawal from the desire to manage landscapes and their inhabitants. *The Alhambra* completes the trajectory of Irving's Italian exploration of aesthetics.

Chapter 2, "The Protected Witness: Cooper, Cole, and the Male Tourist's Gaze," argues that in the 1820s and 1830s writers and artists embraced the option Irving avoids: the faith in aesthetic response as a basis for elite identity and cultural oversight. Tourists endorsed the integrating techniques of the picturesque and insisted on an image of Italy as a feminized and idealized landscape: the repository of the values which the commercial and pragmatic U.S. seemed to marginalize. This phase of American tourism coincided with an English vogue for representations of Italy,[26] a vogue that similarly supported the construction of a national subjectivity in England. As Anglo-Americans toured a feminized Italy – a counterpoint to the normative, masculine world identified with Britain or the U.S. – their depictions of this encounter drew on an analogous cultural opposition between word and image. Associating the visual with the feminine, U.S. travelers, including Cooper and Cole, found the meaning of "Italy" in an aesthetic scrutiny of its landscape and valorized a model of cultural authority that aimed to create social harmony by enlisting those traits associated with the feminine – traits visible in "Italy." In the gendered aesthetics of the Italian tour, "England" functions as cultural superego: the locus of regulative power and patriarchal authority. As Americans move from England to Italy, they go from "the head of civilization . . . – a country that all respect, but few love," Cooper notes, toward a mute but visually powerful territory associated with the heart or the unconscious, one that feels "like another wife." The tourist's status as an invisible "protected witness" (Emerson's phrase) offers the viewer the illusion of being the solitary, privileged observer – as in Cole's painting *View of Florence from San Miniato* (1837) and Cooper's travel book *Gleanings in Europe: Italy* (1838) – while a later Cooper novel, *The Wing-and-Wing* (1842), synthesizes the lessons of "Italy" in a panoramic view of the Bay of Naples.

Chapter 3, "Gazing Women, Unstable Prospects: Sedgwick and Kirkland in the 1840s," foregrounds women's travel writing on this strongly gendered landscape. Although men and women shared the nationalist and class-based project of tourist perception, women used their gendered positions to begin a critique of the tourist gaze. The chapter compares Sedgwick's, Kirkland's, and Fuller's aesthetic gazes and critiques of looking and then analyzes Sedgwick's and Kirkland's travel books. Like many accounts, Sedgwick's *Letters from Abroad* (1841) is informed by the tension between the pleasurable visual submission to the foreign scene and the need to put the spectacle of otherness into the service of U.S. ideology. Even as the visual experience of Italy enables an elite, supervisory sensibility, it threatens the formation of rational republican subjects by drawing tourists away from the nation-constructing activities both of "domestic" pursuits and of "political economy" into a pre-modern, pre-linguistic past in which the image dominates. In her book Sedgwick gives a sympathetic account of the male gaze on Italy by describing a poet's aesthetic response. However, in the story "An Incident at Rome" she reads the spectacle of the male submission to "Italy" ironically; the male figure loses his sanity in a delusional wandering that parodies the tourist's sightseeing. This split subjectivity appears in Kirkland's *Holidays Abroad* (1849). The 1848 revolutions evoked support in the U.S., as they seemed to follow an American model of iconoclastic republicanism. But elite Americans continued to visit Europe for lessons in consolidating national identities through images. Touring in 1848 heightened the tension between these iconoclastic and iconophilic tendencies, especially in women, given their double status as icons and spectators. Aware that the tourist's pleasure depends on "rite[s]" of projection and "illusion" but alert to other ways of looking – the heterogeneous visual field formed by political graffiti and a non-canonical, newspaper culture – Kirkland both invokes and undermines the conventions of the silent, feminine Italian scene and, so, sometimes parallels the visual strategies of Martin Johnson Heade's painting *Roman Newsboys* (1848), whose wall of posters and caricatures blocks any vista into an imagined landscape mirroring the tourist's cultivated interiority.

In Chapter 3, I discuss Fuller briefly in conjunction with other women travelers and thereby follow critics who argue for connecting her work with that of other women.[27] But Fuller was unusual among travelers, women or men, in remaining in Rome through the revolutionary period of 1847–9 and in performing as a transnational public intellectual.[28] Her dialectical work as a gender theorist in *Woman in the Nineteenth Century* (1845)[29] produced strategies for deconstructing such mutually constitutive ideological categories as male/female or United States/Italy. Fuller's *New-York Tribune* dispatches transform a tourist site into an emergent capital city of a modern republic. Chapter 4, "Fuller and Revolutionary Rome: Republican and Urban Imaginaries," focuses on two features usually absent from the U.S. picture of Italy – contemporary history and the city; it reads one of Fuller's dispatches as a history painting and contrasts her depictions of Roman urban space with her friend Hawthorne's urban descriptions in *The Marble Faun*. Disturbed that Americans see Italians through the perspectives of genre painting, which turned its subjects into types,[30] and aware that she may be witnessing originating moments in the national narrative of a unified Italy, Fuller tries to move her readers from genre perspectives to that of history painting, from static pastoral images to a narrative image of history in the making. Her depiction of Garibaldi's departure from Rome after the defeat of republican forces uses strategies similar to Emanuel Leutze's in *Washington Crossing the Delaware*, painted in Germany as the 1848 revolutions were failing there. In addition to seeing Rome as a re-masculinized space of political activity, she sees it as an urban space: a republican polis. On the other hand, Hawthorne's Rome consists of tourist spaces – galleries, ruins, churches – visited after the Roman Republic's fall and before Italy's unification. *The Marble Faun* acknowledges yet recontains women's bid for participation in the informing gaze onto cities, as both revolution and women's gazes – indeed, Fuller herself – are evoked and repressed. Referring to Harriet Hosmer's statue of the captive queen *Zenobia* (1859), Hawthorne describes Rome as the site of revolution repressed; potential historical agents – the Italian man and the urban woman – return to the gallery of images Italy offers, and, in a reversal of Fuller's project, the paradigm of the tourist's vision returns.

Hawthorne and Stowe conflated travel writing with the novel in the romances they wrote ten years after Fuller's coverage of the Roman Republic: Hawthorne's *The Marble Faun* (1860) and Stowe's historical romance *Agnes of Sorrento* (1862). Chapter 5, "National Spaces, Catholic Icons, and Protestant Bodies: Instructing the Republican Subject in Hawthorne and Stowe," returns to the relationship between tourist writing and fiction. While in 1824 Irving's "Italian Banditti" sought and failed to imagine aesthetic culture as a means of managing the predatory energies of a rising class of "self-made men," Hawthorne's and Stowe's novels examine national consolidation through cultural iconography – a project threatened by the approaching Civil War – as they consider the role of national spaces and images in ordering affect and belief in a republic. In spite of habitually contrasting a Catholic Italy and a Protestant U.S.,[31] tourist writings suggest that Catholicism's attempt to consolidate a community through aesthetic experiences offered a model to the U.S. Stowe and Hawthorne follow Protestant culture in appropriating and revising Catholic visual experience by substituting sentimental icons for religious ones. In these romances, the heroines Agnes and Hilda (both have saints' names) replace religious images and become national Protestant icons: icons which organize the emotional life of modern national subjects and yet "Protestant" bodies whose physical presences are dispersed, sublimated, into national life. These women parallel the national artist's concern with making images and managing subjects. While Hawthorne features expatriate artists, Stowe emphasizes the national and spiritual virtues of Christian art in Pre-Raphaelite and spiritualist language. However, both books leave unincorporated into the tourist imaginary sites of excess in the landscape: Stowe the pagan, fertile gorge at Sorrento and Hawthorne a mythical abyss, under the Forum, of historical violence. Unlike George Healy's painting *The Arch of Titus* (1871), which put prominent American artists in the Forum, Hawthorne's romance implies that this monumental space cannot be revived for U.S. purposes. Both novels flag portions of the matter of Italy which remain unmanageable in the tourist imagination and indicate the limits of the aesthetic program of nation-building.

The conclusion maps out the implications of this study and its methodology. It focuses on two areas – Italy-as-woman in the transatlantic construction of the U.S. and the genre of tourist writing – and reiterates the importance of interdisciplinary research for understanding tourism as visual work. As John Urry has argued, analyzing "how social groups construct their tourist gaze" is an important avenue to understanding "what is happening in the 'normal society.'"[32] European tourism in its modern form began for Americans in the antebellum era. The writers and artists discussed here fashioned the normative gaze that shaped the post-Civil War era of mass tourism and influenced the growing investment in national iconography in the last third of the century. Travel writing and tourism – as the nexus of visual work, transatlantic travel, national imagining, and print culture – remain capacious fields for research.

Chapter 1

Irving's Landscapes: Aesthetics, Visual Work, and the Tourist's Estate

> If . . . the admirer of nature can turn his amusements to a higher purpose; if it's [*sic*] great scenes can inspire him with religious awe; . . . it is certainly the better. . . . It is so much into the bargain; for we dare not *promise* him more from picturesque travel, than a rational and agreeable amusement.
>
> William Gilpin[1]

In the period when modern tourism developed, from the late eighteenth to the mid nineteenth centuries, a variety of "higher purpose[s]" fueled its language and practice. These purposes included not only the investment of "religious awe" in nature but also the formation of class, gender, and national identities – the focal points of this study. Despite the modest claims of William Gilpin, the eighteenth-century English popularizer of "picturesque travel," tourists' perceptions of aesthetic order became the vehicle of their constructions of ideological order. Italy's status within the culture of tourism as the land of the eye, the home of the aesthetic, elicited travelers' efforts to pictorialize social agendas in terms of foreign landscapes. Washington Irving's repeated engagements with the landscapes of southern Europe over the course of three decades make his work a useful case study of the adaptations of eighteenth-century British patterns of aesthetic response and their social implications to an emerging American tourist class.

The importance of cultivating an aesthetic gaze – of "practicing" aesthetics – drove U.S. landscape tourism by the 1820s. Kenneth John Myers argues that this decade represents a turning point in the habituation of the process by which "natural environments were . . . objectified as visually integrated aesthetic wholes," a process by which both "elites and the emerging middle class" distinguished themselves from lower-class observers. The cultural authority, or even the religious insight (as Gilpin indicates), that aesthetic responses to landscapes implied was secured by naturalizing these responses, as Myers shows: by suppressing the collective memory of learning such "skills" and thereby forgetting "the labor of admiring." The ostensibly democratic promise of defining "landscape appreciation" as a "natural ability" that transcended class status "obscure[d]" the history of its acquisition and thus naturalized the cultural authority of "northeastern elites".[2] Tourism, then, was visual work that suppressed its own labor trail.[3] Irving's exercises in landscape tourism lay bare this history and recover the labor of acquiring an aesthetic gaze.

As the origins of many of these aesthetic conventions lay in seventeenth-century Italian landscape art, as the following discussion notes, touring Italy could feel like engaging the source of one's own perceptions. Irving's three forays into tourist writing on the landscapes of Italy and Spain demonstrate three stages of engaging these conventions: his early travel journal labors to acquire them; the "Italian Banditti" section of *Tales of a Traveller* critiques their claims to insight, social control, and the production of property; and *The Alhambra* naturalizes aesthetic vision – but merely as a pleasurable fantasy. Irving's descriptions make visible the work that aesthetic response does in nineteenth-century tourism but resist the naturalization of this response; his example reveals the uses, ethics, and limitations of tourist aesthetics at the beginning of nineteenth-century U.S. travel in Europe.

Irving first composed literary sketches of the Italian landscape in 1804–5, before middle-class tourism became widespread. His journal shows his acquisition of British cultural tools, especially the picturesque, whose adaptability made it, as John Conron says, "the first American aesthetic" (xvii). Irving develops an elite U.S. identity by adapting older perspectives of landownership to bourgeois sensibilities. His responses to landscape rehearse the process by which the proprietary gaze of the landowner became metaphorical as the tourist momentarily appropriated each landscape through the controlling filter of aesthetic conventions; this act of aesthetic possession rendered to the observer a provisional property, what I have called the "tourist's estate." Twenty years later, however, Irving's Italian sketches in his collection of fiction, *Tales of a Traveller* (1824), reveal a crisis of confidence in the ability of aesthetic perception to sustain an ideologically coherent vision. As Gilpin hinted, Irving now found picturesque travel and the form of property it conveyed too fragile a basis for either elite identity or social understanding. Just at the moment when most U.S. tourists seized on landscape aesthetics as a way to acquire a socially authoritative gaze, Irving expressed doubt in this cultural project. For his contemporary, the painter Washington Allston, whom Irving met in Rome in 1805 and whose work he knew,[4] the aesthetic gaze promised transcendent and social unities; Allston's harmonious Italian paintings highlight the fractures in Irving's natural and social landscapes in "The Italian Banditti." In a final sketch book, the collection of Spanish tales and sketches *The Alhambra* (1832) (only briefly treated here), Irving capitalizes on this uncertainty by embracing it; perceived harmonies become explicit exercises in wish fulfillment. He presides over a preternaturally integrated scene in which geographical, racial, historical, and class divisions are magically healed in the willed projections of the tourist's gaze. The trajectory of Irving's career as a sketcher of southern European scenes maps out and implicitly critiques the contours of the U.S. tourist's project abroad.

"The Luxury of the Prospect": The 1804–1805 Journal

Not long before the publications of Goethe's *Italienische Reise* (1816–17), Staël's *Corinne, ou l'Italie* (1807), and Byron's *Childe Harold's Pilgrimage* (1812–18) – texts that influenced later travelers – Irving traveled to Italy with Addison in his luggage. His first European tour (1804–6), for which Italy served as the centerpiece, produced his first sustained effort at sketching landscapes. In his detailed journal, he develops his posture with respect to landscape from readings in eighteenth-century British literature. The journal records a rite of passage for the twenty-one-year-old upwardly mobile Grand Tourist; written in part for his family, it is an exercise in acquiring and reproducing an elite cultural perspective through the "mechanism"[5] of aesthetic response. As it did for English followers of the Grand Tour, "Italy" functioned as a middle term in the cultural exchange at home – in New York. It is not simply that the fact of travel to Italy conferred status; it was also the form of the traveler's response to this landscape that determined the trip's success, that is, its conversion into the currency of social or cultural authority. Irving makes his tour before Goethe and Staël provide an alternative model of the Italian journey as a destabilizing, transformative experience. He bases the form of his response on two eighteenth-century perspectives on landscape – the prospect and the picturesque – that posit a stable relationship between the perceiving subject and the object of its gaze. The nature of this relationship reveals the nature of the self Irving is attempting to produce.

The social context of Irving's tour – his ties and ambitions in New York – illuminates the dynamics behind the writing of the journal. His biographer, Stanley T. Williams, describes the late eighteenth-century Irvings as a family in the process of moving upwards from the status of "tradesmen" and "shopkeepers" to that of merchants, "a common experience in New York families of this day."[6] Irving's older brothers continued the family ascent by moving into such professions as medicine, law, and politics. Their concomitant literary pursuits – literary clubs, journalism, poetry, and political essays – were an aspect of this social project. As Williams says, "To write well in the New York of 1800 was evidence of a gentlemanly origin" (25). Turn-of-the-century periodicals, according to David Paul Nord, offered themselves as republican mediators between aspiring shopkeepers and the merchant class. They provided an "arena for popular participation . . . in the formerly elite culture of . . . arts and letters, . . . cultivation and character."[7] By participating both in the reading of this print culture and in its production, the Irving brothers at once adapted themselves to the values of an elite culture and commented on those values.[8]

Their social aspirations may have prompted the frequently parodic nature of their publications. The aim of their satire was not to advocate social reform or to inculcate republican virtue in their readers but rather to signal their fluency within the discourse of this elite culture. In the first number of their periodical *Salmagundi*, co-written by Irving, his brother William, and their brother-in-law James Kirke Paulding, they explicitly satirized reformist motives: "Our intention is simply to instruct the young, reform the old, correct the town and castigate the age; this is an arduous task, and therefore we undertake it with confidence."[9] Parody – the dominant mode of the texts which Irving wrote or co-wrote during the first, amateur phase of his career (1802–9) – served both as a detached, Olympian position from which to survey and "castigate" New York and as a sign of the writer's off-hand intimacy with the social and literary forms he so casually ridiculed. The aristocratic ease – the *brio* – with which Irving lampooned his milieu advertised the degree to which he had internalized elite culture.

Critics have pointed out how thoroughly Irving at once drew on and parodied the eighteenth-century British writers who formed the canon, or at least the fashionable reading, of New York literary culture: Addison, Pope, Swift, Fielding, Goldsmith, Gray, Smollett, Sterne, Radcliffe.[10] As Andrew Burstein points out, Irving's early periodical writings were "awfully close" to Joseph Addison and Richard Steele's influential essays of social commentary in *The Spectator* (24, 21).[11] *Salmagundi*'s comments on subjects from the theater to gender relations dissected both the targeted institution and the persona of the cultivated commentator: "We are critics, amateurs, dillitanti, and cognoscenti; . . . every opinion which we advance in either of these characters will be correct" (50). Irving's adroitness at this type of parodic intimacy with the forms of elite literary and social culture gained him both popular and critical recognition.[12]

Given that his European tour was flanked by this parodic literary activity, the general absence of parody from the travel journal is striking.[13] Nathalia Wright, the journal's editor, emphasizes the polished quality of these notebooks; Irving rewrote portions of his notes into more "finished" entries and into letters to his brothers which he suggested, futilely, they might further revise and publish: "If you find anything in [my letters] . . . that you think proper to publish, I beg you will arrange and finish [them] *handsomely*."[14] In the care with which he develops an informal genre – the travel journal – and in his offering his letters to the collaborative efforts of his brothers, Irving follows the pattern of his parodic writings. But in this work he aligns himself more respectfully with the literary tradition; he quotes Pope, Gray, Sterne, and especially Addison to provide an authorizing context for his reactions to European sights. His shift in tone may stem from the fact that his primary audience is his family, specifically the brothers who are paying for this traditional Grand Tour through France, Italy, and England. Wright says that "the entire journal is addressed to William" (32). The journal addresses, in effect, his family's social aspirations.

One of the journal's principal internal forms is the landscape sketch. Irving's sketches are repeated attempts to master both a genre and a stance. This concern with articulating a correct subject position echoes the Irvings' approach to parody. It also informs the cultural project of the Grand Tour, which served as the "finish to a gentleman's upbringing."[15] If the tour shaped "manners," it proceeded by naturalizing ideology into gesture. In his study of the eighteenth-century Tour as practiced by the English aristocracy, Christopher Hibbert implies that to be educated meant to preside over and manage physical and social landscapes. The young tourist was advised to begin his visit to each town with a comprehensive view from a steeple; in parallel activities, he was to learn other languages, collect "prints" of sites and of works of art as well as biological and mineralogical "specimens," look for hints to improve his own estate, and keep a "note-book" on other cultures' handling of social issues, such as "the pay of the clergy, military training, . . . grounds for divorce, water supplies, . . . corporal punishment at the university or the care of paupers in the workhouse."[16] In this training of the ruling class, the tourist's perspective on the landscape – the view from the steeple – reinforces the Tour's social function: its inculcation of a managerial view of social institutions.[17]

In the last third of the century, with the increase of upper-middle-class tourism, landscape aesthetics took up an increasing portion of the tourist's energy; Charles L. Batten notes the emergence of the "picturesque traveler" in writings of this period.[18] As the orientation of tourists shifted from aristocratic paternalism toward a bourgeois paradigm, their aesthetic responses took over the function of more explicitly managerial activities in establishing their relationship to physical and social landscapes. Ann Bermingham discusses one appropriation of aristocratic aesthetics in mid to late eighteenth-century paintings of rising bourgeois landowners and their families on the grounds of their estates. The English "outdoor conversation piece," she observes, conflates natural and social landscapes; it "confer[s] status on its subjects while naturalizing" this status. She points to the informality – the "'natural ease'" – of "the figures' gestures." This informality of manners within a landscape which is the subject's property implies the "derivation of social . . . practice . . . from the natural structure of the world" and posits a "mutual justification" between "nature" and "'bourgeois culture.'"[19] Her discussion of these paintings sheds light on turn-of-the-century tourism and on the needs of U.S. tourists. As travelers without as much real estate at home – not landowners but members of professional and merchant classes – adapt these perspectives to their own ends, they turn their visual appreciation of landscape into a form of property: the tourist's estate. Situating oneself within a landscape by means of a "sketch" becomes an extension of what Bermingham might call the "gestures" of privilege.

Irving's descriptive exercises are such performances: the staging of an upper-class self for the benefit of his socially aspiring family. The sketches are the means by which he holds up his end of the deal; they, together with his inveterate instinct of making social contacts even on the road, are for him the most congenial means of developing a gentleman's point of view. William's letters occasionally berate him for not putting enough energy into the other aspects of his *Bildung* abroad: acquiring languages, reading histories, assiduous sightseeing.[20] But Irving seems to know that it is the form of the tourist's response, rather than the contents of his knowledge, that produces class identity. The sketches are gestures by which the privileged traveler surveys the foreign scene much as the parodist surveys the social landscape at home.

The term Irving uses most often in his landscapes is "prospect." The views which merit this word are far-reaching and require either the observer's literal elevation – "never did I see a prospect that gave me more dilight. . . . The view from the top of the hill . . . baffles all discription. . . . The eye embraced a vast extent of country" – or a breadth of perspective which implies a psychologically analogous point of view: "the eye wandered enraptured along the lovely coast of Baia . . . to the beautifully situated town of Puzzuoli . . . [then to the] villages that skirt the feet of Vessuvius. . . . [We] admir[ed] this enchanting prospect."[21] Carole Fabricant argues that eighteenth-century prospects "possessed important ideological and symbolic overtones, due largely to the prospect viewer's lofty position and his consequent relationship to all objects within his scope of vision."[22] She uses Addison's writings to demonstrate the bourgeois adaptation of this aristocratic aesthetic, primarily through the addition of breadth to the prospect; by emphasizing "'wide and undetermined Prospects,'" Addison "combines the grandeur . . . linked to a traditional aristocracy with the liberty and mobility more congenial to the nouveaux riches" (55).[23] Irving's views proceed in part from the *Spectator* essays;[24] his eye participates in the totalizing gaze from the heights – it "embraced" or "commanded" (76, 101) – as well as in the ranging movement of the horizontal glance – it "wandered." He solidifies this connection by quoting Addison's poem "A Letter from Italy" in his sketches.

Irving externalizes the source of the aesthetic order he sees by emphasizing his passivity as a spectator and thus naturalizing his commanding position. The views offer themselves: "as we rode along we were presented with . . . charming prospects" (117); "the most romantic views continually present[ed] themselves" (59). His other favorite activity during the tour was attending the theater, a lifelong compulsion.[25] The journal makes the parallel between these types of spectacle explicit; "we had a fine view of Aetna at a vast distance. . . . The prospect reminded me of the scenery of a theatre – rows of olives planted each side of the road served for side scenes" (196). Irving's approach to landscape is related to his position as theater-goer.[26] He is exercising here the privileged vision of the "critics, amateurs, dillitanti, and cognoscenti" that he will again parody on his return.

However, Irving often combines the Addisonian prospect with the subtler conventions of the picturesque. This more recent aesthetic, which Gilpin disseminated through his English travel books and theories,[27] encouraged tourists to reproduce landscapes in visual or textual sketches. Although at this early date Irving mentions neither Gilpin nor other writers that promote this aesthetic, he seems to have absorbed it through the fiction and tourist writing he read before or during his tour: Ann Radcliffe's *The Mysteries of Udolpho* (1794) and *The Italian* (1797), or Patrick Brydone's *Tour Through Sicily and Malta* (1773).[28] Brydone, according to Batten, helped to shift travel descriptions from "blueprints" to "rough sketches like those of Claude Lorrain" (102–7), a painter favored by proponents of the picturesque sketch. Irving follows both aspects of the vogue; Wright's edition of his journal reproduces a number of faint pencil sketches together with his more fully realized prose sketches.

The picturesque became central to tourist aesthetics; indeed, critics have periodically renewed their discussion of its persistence in nineteenth-century culture. Following earlier, more descriptive critics, literary scholars and art historians in the 1980s and 1990s analyzed its ideological functions in eighteenth and early nineteenth-century British literature and art.[29] Transatlantic and postcolonial scholars have traced the perspectives of the picturesque into U.S. culture and British imperial texts and images throughout the nineteenth century: John Conron demonstrates its pervasiveness in the arts in the U.S., Beth Lueck examines its workings in U.S. travel writing, while David Bunn views the picturesque landscape as "a system of aesthetic . . . and ideological ordering useful in the management of political contradictions" in European colonial writing.[30] Carrie Tirado Bramen summarizes many of these developments and the critical debates on the picturesque's ideological implications: on the unethical nature of the "distance between the pictorial gaze and the picturesque object," especially when that object is human, and on "the picturesque as a mode of social control," an attempt to "contain . . . and master otherness." As critics find this language in both liberal and conservative expressions, Bramen argues for "multiple picturesques" and states that its study brings scholars to the heart of crucial issues in the nineteenth century: "the criticism of the picturesque continues to grapple with some of the most challenging questions surrounding the ethical implications of aesthetic practice" (7, 15, 16).

The picturesque scene as Gilpin defines it and Irving practices it embodies a contained complexity – a diversity of shapes and textures, and juxtapositions of light and shade; "contrast" and "variety" make a sketch picturesque (Gilpin, 20). This variety is then unified by a harmonious tone pervading the whole[31] or by internal frames within the sketch (either supplied by nature or added by the tasteful sketcher), much as Irving's theatrical prospect is framed by the olive trees. In "The Art of Sketching Landscape," Gilpin says that a well-shaped foreground is "essential . . . in *forming a composition*" and recommends that sketchers enhance a scene's structure: "nature is most defective in composition; and *must* be a little assisted. Her ideas are too vast for picturesque use, without the restraint of rules" (69, 67). Malcolm Andrews explains that these "rules" enabled a "leisured connoisseur elite" (236) to give "stability" to "new experiences":

> The Picturesque tourist is . . . a gentleman or gentlewoman engaged in an experiment in controlled aesthetic response to . . . new . . . visual experiences. The . . . vocabulary [of the picturesque], the . . . classification of . . . scenery, the development of technical skills in drawing . . . to enable the viewer to "fix" a landscape . . . formed a subtle psychological protection to the tourist freshly exposed to . . . disorienting landscapes. (67)

As does the prospect, the picturesque view puts the observer in a position of authority, here based on the viewer's ability to see aesthetic unity in a complex scene and to participate in "nature's" act of composition. If the prospect offers an analogy to aristocratic power and scope of knowledge, the picturesque implies a bourgeois ability to absorb various, even contradictory, elements in one point of view, sanctioned by nature. As Sidney Robinson explains, the picturesque "stands at the hinge between 'estate culture' and 'bourgeois culture.'"[32] Uvedale Price, an advocate of the picturesque in the 1790s, implies its ideological implications, as Andrews notes, when he compares a "good landscape," where contrasting elements of "rough" and "polished" are subsumed into a general "harmony," with a "good government."[33] The shift in this ideal of government parallels the picturesque's revisions of the prospect's point of view.

In spite of Gilpin's insistence that the sketcher is only after "*general shapes*" (64), the picturesque requires a steadier focus on a specific place than the prospect. Although Addison's eye is already alive to the ingredients of the picturesque – he delights in a varied and rugged landscape, a "broken and interrupted scene"[34] – he rarely composes sketches. Instead, especially in the prefatory poem to *Remarks on Italy*, "A Letter from Italy," to which Irving often refers, Addison generalizes the elements of Italian scenery, "Her blooming mountains and her sunny shores": "For wheresoe'er I turn my ravish'd eyes, / Gay gilded scenes and shining prospects rise."[35] The picturesque asks its practitioners to assume a lower point of view and to linger on each "scene" before they "turn" their eyes to the next. Eighteenth-century commentators agree that it is difficult to make a prospect from an elevation satisfying as a picture, in part because there are no internal structures ("side scenes") to focus the roving eye. William Mason, landscape gardener and author of *The English Garden* (1772–81), indicates the aesthetic and social ramifications of this distinction between the prospect and the picturesque: "The *Picturesque* point is always thus low in all prospects, a truth which though the landscape painter know, he cannot always observe, since the patron who employs him to take a view of the place usually carries him up to some elevation for that purpose."[36] The middle-class painter is a step ahead of his landowning patron; like the period's landscape gardeners, he knows that to immerse oneself in a scene's details and to "assist" nature in composing itself creates harmony more effectively than the top-down dominance of the prospect, which, as John Dixon Hunt notes, resists the "particular" and does not engage in "dialogue with the scenery" (116). The painter's art is a modern form of representation. While his patron clings to an aristocratic point of view, the artist reveals an emerging middle-class perspective. This adaptability of the picturesque accounts for its longevity in bourgeois culture; as a method to harmonize an acknowledged heterogeneity, the picturesque pervaded nineteenth-century culture and was especially persistent in tourism.[37]

The journal's sketches combine these perspectives; Irving depicts "picturesque objects in [an] extensive prospect" (62). His compositions reveal his dutiful acquisition of these cultural tools. On his way to Italy, he reworks an extensive landscape from brief notes – a few hints on the scene's structure, contents and lighting (472–3) – into a fully elaborated view. The scene combines the commanding position of the prospect viewer, whose gaze grasps the total picture, with the picturesque's harmonizing of contrasting elements. Irving uses the passive voice to insist that what he sees does not originate with himself and his acquired conventions but with "nature"; most of the active verbs go to natural agencies, such as the Rhône and the sun:

> Towards Sun set we came to where the road descended from the heights, and the view that here broke upon us surpassed every landscape I had seen in france. At the foot of the hill lay the town of *Villeneuve* thrown in shade by the hill excepting an antient convent of Chartreuse. . . . This stood on an eminence high above the rest of

the town, and the rich gleams of the setting sun, cast upon its towers & battlements of yellowish Stone, rendered it a prominent and
interesting object. At a small distance were seen the antient towers
& castle of Avignon half buried in trees. . . . [N]ature seems to have
exerted herself . . . to harmonize the scene. . . . The valley is highly
cultivated. the Rhone wanders irregularly thro it and is seen to a vast
distance. . . . The view is bounded by ridges of mountains. . . . the
sun . . . threw partial gleams of the mildest radience on the landscape
in one place lighting up the walls of an old tower, in another resting
in rich refulgence on a distant mountain, while the others were envel-
oped in the shades of evening. After descending from the heights we
entered the town. . . . [In Avignon] we passed under a high cliff. . . .
[O]n an old tower or rampart on the brow of the cliff were seated
two soldiers, enjoying the setting sun and playing on a french horn &
clarinet. Their situation, appearance and music . . . seemed to accord
with the romantic scenery around. (73–4)

Irving's prospect is geographically and historically "vast." Nature
heightens the scene's complexity (with the rich *chiaroscuro* of the
sun's "partial gleams"), gives it direction (the river leads the eye into
the distance), and frames the view with "ridges of mountains." By
emphasizing the effect of the setting sun, Irving conflates human with
natural agency in composing landscapes; the tourist's selective gaze
is duplicated by the sun, nature's brush. Acting on behalf of the tourist's eye, the sun highlights a few architectural and natural objects
– the convent, an "old tower," a "distant mountain" – and, by its
"harmoniz[ing]" tone, unites these historical and natural objects in
an idealized landscape of the past.

One addition to the notes is that Irving begins on the heights and
then descends into the picture; he moves from a prospect to a picturesque point of view. As he does so, he gets a closer look at its picturesque objects. The two soldiers – the final picturesque detail – appeal
to his taste as entirely appropriate; like the field laborers he sometimes incorporates into his sketches, but unlike the mobile tourist,
they are anchored within the scene and expressive of its meanings.
Like the historical buildings, their appearance "accord[s] with the
romantic scenery." U.S. and northern European tourists, in creating
these southern European views, preside over the landscape of the
past without being contained or defined by it, as are its lower-class
inhabitants.

Critics note that the picturesque, with its predilection for ruins,
irregularity, and anachronism, calls for human figures which share
these traits; Uvedale Price finds an "analogy" between decaying

mills and cottages and the rural poor: "gypsies and beggars," old women, and "the wild forester."[38] Andrews and Bermingham, who discuss this passage, link the picturesque to a conservative response to late eighteenth-century social and economic change. This aesthetic "entailed a suppression of the spectator's moral response."[39] Bermingham argues that even as the picturesque represented nostalgia for a pre-industrial, "preenclosed," "paternalistic" landscape, its "distancing of the spectator from the picturesque object" indicates a tacit support for the emerging bourgeois order; the picturesque "mystified the agency of social change" (74–5). Therefore, aesthetics worked as a bridge, easing even as it partially concealed the transition of power from a rural aristocracy to a mercantile class. Bermingham's characterization of the picturesque points to its adroitness in incorporating the prospect's sense of distance from the human and nonhuman objects in the landscape even as it purports to move down among them.[40] Irving sidesteps the ethical dimensions of encounters with the human picturesque by internalizing the prospect. Once tourists have grasped the total view, they can descend into picturesque particulars with impunity. The soldiers on the cliff are not prospect viewers in his sense of the word; instead, Irving carries his social and cultural authority with him, as he looks up at them.

In a series of sketches in Naples, he continues to blend the lessons of the prospect with the picturesque. He uses the view from his hotel window to focus both natural and human landscapes; looking from a high vantage point, he has a commanding view of the city, the bay, and the surrounding mountains: a "prospect truly sublime & beautiful" and "picturesque" (232). The window is a framing device for natural sights ("Vessuvius") and for the human theater without. In an elaborate passage on the square his window "commands" (225), he comments on "the infinite variety of objects . . . before my eyes." He adds, apparently to a prospective reader, "you may fill up the picture to suit your own fancy with groups of Lazaroni . . . Equipages of the nobility . . . Greek sailors – priests – charlatans" (251). In this view, it is the tourist's eye that creates order; the window is the sign of this distancing and aestheticizing eye that converts the diverse population in the square into a pictorial harmony.

This principle of picturesque distance from the spectacle also informs Irving's historical reveries. On the way to Rome, he pictorializes history in one such reverie – a conventional gesture of the tourist – and creates a triptych of the classical, medieval, and present eras:

There is no country where the prospects ... awaken such a variety
of ideas as in Italy. Every mountain ... every plain tells some striking history. On casting my eyes around some majestic ruin carries
my fancy back to the ages of Roman splendor ... [A]n old castle
frowning on the brow of an eminence transports my imagination to
the later days of chivalry & romance. I picture to myself issuing from
the gateway the gallant knight. ... From these pleasing reveries my
mind is recalled to ... present ... objects. I behold misery indigence
& ignorance on every side. ... The works of former ages – magnificent in their ruins – reproaching the nation with its degeneracy. (257)

Irving ends this sequence with lines from Addison's "Letter from
Italy" that associate "smiling plenty" with "O liberty thou goddess
heavenly bright" (258); he thus reasserts the eighteenth-century tourist's habitual contrast between English prosperity and modern Italian
"degeneracy."[41] His management of the historical prospect echoes
his approach to natural landscapes; he highlights the internal variety
of the scene in a pleasing *chiaroscuro* while casting over it the unifying tone (here the note of reverie) that Gilpin recommends and containing it within the authorized framework of Addison's equations
of bourgeois (English) freedom and material "plenty." In this version
of the sketch, informed by the association of ideas, Irving appropriates history just as, according to Andrews, "the Picturesque artist
'appropriates' natural scenery and processes it into a commodity. ...
[H]e converts Nature's unmanageable bounty into a frameable possession."[42] Irving's sketches become such possessions and signal his
arrival as an American gentleman, someone who oversees landscape
or history. His attempts to "fix" historical and natural scenes are
attempts to fix his class identity. This context makes his sketches
repetitive; he produces a similar set of "reflections," complete with
lines from an eighteenth-century English poet, on the "contrast"
between the past and the present in Rome (278).

The formulaic nature of Irving's exercises in constructing aesthetic and social perspectives indicates an underlying anxiety – what
Hedges calls an "uneasiness" (36) – that qualifies much of the surface
charm and even exuberance of the journal. Irving's self-conscious
provincialism, his sense of cultural distance from the origin of these
conventions, makes him doubt the compatibility of European artistic
forms with U.S. identity. As Albert von Frank argues, Irving worries
that "the pursuit of art is ... related to the pursuit of older, traditional values ... associated with Europe" and that his literary pose
may estrange him from "home," from his American self (62–3). But
this provincialism also leads him toward a critical appraisal of the

conventions themselves; Hedges notes that "For all his fondness for picturesque views, Irving sensed distortions in them."[43]

This awareness appears in an entry where he reflects on the conventions through which he sees. While sailing from Genoa to Messina, he sketches a sunrise: "the sun emergd in full splendor from the ocean – his beams diffused a blaze of refulgence thro the clouds . . . – and the snowy summits of Corsica . . . brightned with reflection of his rays." This leads to a digression on the source of poetic inspiration, which seems to come from Italian nature itself: "So enchanting a scene was sufficient to inspire the poet – nor do I wonder that this climate should have been particularly productive of poetry & romance" (144). But his train of thought continues:

> Had those happy days continued when the Deities made themselves visible to man . . . we might have been entertaind by the *raree show* of Neptune and . . . [his] train. . . . But those days of romance are over. . . . In these dull *matter of fact* days our only consolation is to wander about their once frequented haunts and endeavor to make up by imagination the want of the reality.[44]

Irving is of course making fun of the *staffage* of the neoclassical landscape – gods, nymphs, and so on. More importantly, he shifts the origin of the aesthetic response from the object to the subject, which is now construed as supplying a lack in the object – a "want of the reality";[45] he proceeds to focus on the action of the tourist's "eye":

> There is a poetic charm . . . that difuses itself over our ideas in considering this part of the globe. We regard everything . . . thro a romantic medium that gives an illusive tinge to every object. Tis like beholding a delightful landscape from an eminence, on a beautiful sunset. A delicious mistiness is spread over the scene that softens the harshness of particular objects – prevents our examining their forms too closely – a glow is thrown over the whole that by blending & softning . . . – gives the landscape . . . a loveliness of coloring not absolutely its own, but derived . . . from the illusive veil with which it is oerspread.

Looking at Italy is "like" looking at a landscape "from an eminence"; that is, the tourist's view of Italy is inherently a prospect view. Irving acknowledges the naiveté of externalizing "romance" in the landscape and discusses the "romantic medium" of the traveler's vision. The "charm" depends on a willed illusion provided by the paired habits of the prospect and the picturesque; the harmonizing tone of a sketch derives from the tourist's "illusive veil," which unifies "particular objects" by "softning" the "harshness" of their particularity. As he works through this logic, he moves from the "full splendor" of the rising sun, whose "blaze" dominates the scene (appropriate to the aristocratic confidence of a prospect view), to the "mistiness" or "partial gleams" of a sunset, which flags the more tentative, self-conscious aesthetic of the picturesque.

His glimpse into the complexities of aesthetic response on this early trip is somewhat vague; he adds, "I do not know whether I express myself intelligibly." And he does not pursue these insights. Instead he seeks out picturesque prospects, especially at twilight, and works on his command of the necessary conventions. When his ship is quarantined at Messina, he amuses himself by sketching its harbor and neighboring coast, "a charming subject for the pencil" (157). From the detached position of the ship, he exults in "the luxury of the prospect":

> The sun ... declining behind the sicilian mountains amid a rich assemblage of clouds that render his exit more splendid – Their colors gradually deepening into a glowing crimson . . . and at last sinking into a modest gray. By this time the moon begins to show her paler glories. . . . By degrees she attains a commanding height, pours a full stream of radiance oer, the . . . tranquil waters of this delightful harbor. Her "silver beams" brighten up the surrounding forts and . . . the white buildings of Messina. (167–8)

The "radiance" of sunset and moonlight blends the scene's natural and man-made components – sky, water, forts – into a tranquil unity. The tenuous atmospheric moment in which the picturesque vision works best, marked here by the passing of perspectival "command" from the masculine sun to the feminine moon, seems easily available and aesthetically satisfying in such sketches. But in later works Irving problematizes the conventions of the landscape sketch.

After the tour, Irving did not publish the sketches but plunged into the parody of *Salmagundi* and of his *History of New York*. He returned to the landscape sketch in the 1820s, when he drew on the apprenticeship of the journal; as Wright says, "the typical Irving landscape, with its softened outlines . . . and meditative atmosphere, which did not appear in print until *The Sketch Book . . .*, emerges repeatedly in his first European journal" (xxxi). In the Italian section of *Tales of a Traveller*, however, Irving deconstructs the conventions of the prospect and the picturesque. His sketches, embedded in a framework of fiction, imply that an aesthetic appropriation of landscape is after all an unstable form of property.

In the poetic coda to his *Three Essays*, Gilpin indicates what is at stake in the picturesque sketch through an analogy between civic and aesthetic peace. At the end of his lesson on drawing landscapes, he asks the aspiring sketcher:

> Are now thy lights and shades adjusted all?
> Yet pause: . . . *harmony*
> May still be wanting. That which forms a whole
> From colour, shade, gradation, is not yet
> Obtained. Avails it ought, in civil life,
> If here and there a family unite
> In bonds of peace, while discord rends the land,
> And pale-eyed Faction, with her garments dipped
> In blood, excites her guilty sons to war?
>
>   To aid thine eye, . . . wait for the twilight hour . . .
> Then in some corner place thy finished piece,
> Free from each garish ray: Thine eye will there
> Be undisturbed by *parts*; there will the *whole*
> Be viewed collectively . . .
>   [I]f shade or light be out of place,
> Thou seest the error, and mayest yet amend. (116–17)

In such a passage, the transatlantic habit of conflating aesthetic and political language surfaces strikingly and, as Edward Cahill has argued, indicates not only why aesthetic theory is "a paradigmatic discourse of the eighteenth-century public sphere" but also why in the period of the early Republic its "dialectic of liberty" and "constraint" "offered American writers a rich . . . vocabulary for articulating the imperatives and challenges of political liberty and, thus, for confronting the social contradictions of Revolutionary and early national culture."[46] In the picturesque view, the work of integration is more difficult than the simpler domination of the prospect or the self-assured parodic survey of the social scene. Irving explores the anxiety associated with the picturesque as an aspect of and a metaphor for bourgeois hegemony and national harmony in *Tales of a Traveller*. In these tales and sketches, the harmonious coloring of aesthetic response cracks as it is applied over an intrinsically divided and fractious landscape.

Insupportable Contrasts: "The Italian Banditti"

Critics agree that *Tales of a Traveller* (1824) represents a crisis of authorship and identity. After the success of *The Sketch Book* (1820) and *Bracebridge Hall* (1822), Irving's controlled, if often ironic, handling of his period's conventions breaks down in a number of places in this collection of fiction and especially in Part III, "The Italian Banditti." The *Tales* vacillate uneasily between a playful manipulation of these conventions and an assault on them. As Hedges notes, the tales of rape and murder in Part III take "vengeance on the sentimental heroine," an interpretation which Jeffrey Rubin-Dorsky extends into "an outright attack on the ideal [of womanhood] itself." Michael Davitt Bell finds that these stories are "Radcliffean parodies" that "burlesque . . . the gothic tradition."[47] I would add that Irving also undermines the picturesque here, even as he relies on it to define his narrator's vision. As with the sentimental and the Gothic, his treatment of the picturesque is variously inflected by attitudes of acceptance, amusement, and hostility. "The Italian Banditti" depicts aesthetic habits whose ostensible programs of closure and harmony prove to be hoaxes, conventions whose shortcomings may be amusing but whose failure leaves the observer who has depended on them in an untenable position.

Critics reading through Irving's entrance into professional authorship in 1819 to 1824 also note the crisis in gender identity that accompanied this decision. David Anthony analyzes *The Sketch Book* in terms of the "increasingly . . . anxious form of masculinity emerging in the period" of the financial Panic of 1819, which helped to bankrupt the Irving brothers' business. This "anxious" manhood was linked to a new and vulnerable economy based on "apparitional" paper money, credit, and speculation that cut elite male identity loose from a dignified "Federalist manhood rooted in property" and created the "paper money man of the new economy" – a "gothic male subject" "haunted" and "hystericized" by the specter of an "alienable form of manhood." Andrew Kopec builds on this analysis to argue that Irving saw professional authorship as a speculative "capital investment" and decided, in spite of his worries, to embark on a "capitalist identity" in "an unstable literary marketplace."[48] Irving's new sense of the precariousness of class and gender identities informs his treatment of the aesthetic perspectives that are the "property" of tourists and that constitute the "capital investment" of authors and artists working in the unstable post-1819 economy.

Tales of a Traveller includes an international group of stories and settings; the Italian setting features a heightened possibility for painterly contrasts. If the tourist's perspective on Italy is that of a prospect view, then the landscape on which the tourist gazes is inherently picturesque; Italy promises the pleasure of seeing the most startling contrasts blended into the most "delicious" harmony. But as the tales and sketches unfold, the reverse happens. Instead of moving from observed contrasts – mountains and plains, wild and tame, sublime and beautiful – toward a vision of aesthetic unities, the reader finds that these contrasts resist reconciliation. In Gilpin's terms, *"parts"* do not coalesce into a *"whole"* and "Faction," literally bloody here, overcomes *"harmony."*

In his second view of Italy, Irving explicitly studies the picturesque as a tool of social management. Given his own experience of initiation into aesthetic response twenty years before, Italy seems the natural site on which to analyze the compositional impulses of the middle-class tourist. He associates Italy with painters and includes far more landscape descriptions in this section than in the others. But in this work of fiction he brings tourists into his scenes and stages middle-class confrontations with the picturesque landscape and its characters. The tourists embody a series of bourgeois pursuits: merchants, an antiquarian, a minor government official, an artist. As mobile travelers, they assume they can preside over the Italian scene financially, intellectually, and aesthetically. The tales document threats against these managerial positions. The banditti – the scene's picturesque inhabitants – collapse the distance between viewers and viewed, invade middle-class and elite spaces, and threaten to drag their spectators into an unmanageable landscape of danger, loss, and death. They steal property, undermine professional expertise, attack women, and flout the law.

Irving makes the artist's experience central and, so, highlights aesthetic response in its relation to other forms of bourgeois order. He asks, what role can aesthetic perspectives and products play: first, as a form of property in a society no longer defined by a landed gentry or perhaps even by a secure mercantile elite but by the vicissitudes of the new economy; and, second, as a strategy to integrate disruptive elements into a harmonious social scene? The two characters who deal the most adroitly with the robbers – and whose masculinity is the least "anxious" – are the artist and a wealthy member of the British bourgeoisie. Their juxtaposition connects the aesthetic enterprise with a major concern of New York Federalist ideology: the relationship between a mercantile or (more precariously) a cultural elite and the revolutionary "mob" of democracy. In setting the artist's efforts next to the wealthy traveler's, Irving asks what function aesthetic response has not only as a sign of class membership but also as part of this class's attempt to manage the possibly violent energies of an insurgent lower class.[49]

The conclusion of these stories shows little faith in either function. Aesthetic insight turns out to be an unsound basis for identity or property. And, unlike Allston, Irving doubts that aesthetics are an effective method of social control. *Tales of a Traveller* confirms what the journal implies: that the picturesque will not take the ideological weight assigned to it. What "The Italian Banditti" reveals is that aesthetic order must be backed up with force. The artist's initially promising efforts to "fix" a disorienting landscape ultimately fail; the task of restoring order to a disturbed Italian picture belongs finally to the wealthy property owner – the emblem of a pre-1819 bourgeois stability – who relies not on aesthetics but on hired soldiers. The following three sections examine the conjunction of aesthetic conventions and bourgeois ideology in "The Italian Banditti," discuss Allston's alternate artistic theory and practice, and consider the conclusion of "The Italian Banditti" in the light of this alternative.

Tourists, Painters, and Bandits

"The Story of the Young Italian," in an earlier section (Part I, "Strange Stories by a Nervous Gentleman"), previews the ways in which setting determines character in Part III. The landscape, which changes over short distances from one exaggerated type to another, creates similar contrasts in the protagonist's character; his life alternates between monastic imprisonment in a "gloomy gorge," lit at night by the "baleful light" of Vesuvius, and exhilarating freedom in "the voluptuous landscape" around the Bay of Naples.[50] After such descriptions it comes as no surprise that the young Italian is both an impetuous murderer and a sensitive artist and lover.

Irving explores these correspondences more thoroughly in "The Italian Banditti." He sketches a similarly divided landscape and transfers the young Italian's internal polarity to an equally irreconcilable opposition between two types of characters: the civilized, hierarchical society living on the plains and the anarchic, predatory bandits in the mountains. By opting for bandits, Irving invokes a romantic convention with conflicting ideological implications.[51] As Hugh Honour explains, the romantic vogue for bandits in art and literature is associated with liberal movements for personal and political freedom.[52]

On the other hand, the Gothic tradition on which Irving draws defines the energies of brigands as destructive. In her study of the English Gothic novel, Kate Ferguson Ellis argues that the heroine's "endangered position" was "ideologically useful" for its middle-class readership in that this position could "stand for the class itself, beset on all sides by aristocratic license and lower-class violence" (xi). Irving's version of the Gothic dispenses with the aristocratic villain, unnecessary to his U.S. concerns with class, and focuses on confrontations between middle-class travelers and "lower-class violence."[53] His banditti are an uneasy conflation of freedom fighters, with whose desire for political liberty middle-class readers can identify, and brutish thugs who disrupt a series of analogous forms of order important to middle-class identity.

Irving's double-sided depiction of these figures already appears in the journal; in Genoa he witnesses the execution of the "notorious robber" Giuseppe Musso, whose "genius," "courage," and struggles against the French had ennobled him in the popular imagination. On the other hand, he recounts being robbed by pirates on the way to Messina; he is in the midst of writing an entry on these "*Banditti of the Ocean*" when real pirates board his ship. Irving resumes the entry after their departure and sketches a collective prose portrait of these "assassin like figures,"[54] a strategy of attempted understanding and containment that anticipates the French painter's observations in the central episodes of "The Italian Banditti." By drawing on Gothic conventions of outlaws in the *Tales*, Irving shifts the function of his Italy from a school for aesthetic response (its role in the journal) to a site where social disruption can be most fully imagined because it is the furthest from home.

The opening scene introduces the travelers who hear the tales and are part of the final action; a beautiful Venetian woman and a brusque John Bull are the most fully characterized. The Venetian, leaning on her husband's arm, is "young and tender and timid," with a "musical" voice and "the soft witchery of a Venetian eye." The English traveler, like his well-constructed, fully stocked carriage, is "tall, stout, and well made; dressed with neatness and precision." He is also incredulous, rude, and eager to make traveling a business – "to get on." Although his wealth makes the local Italians assume he is a "Milor," he is clearly a bourgeois tourist following in the path of the aristocratic Grand Tour and determined to rationalize the process of touring.[55] The Venetian embodies the domesticated Italian landscape against which the banditti and their scenery will define themselves. The English tourist, on the other hand, is set apart from his surroundings at the outset; his carriage and his servant conspire with him to carry "England about the world with him" (151–4). He functions as a reluctant auditor of tales and finally as the spell-breaker, the man of decisive action who disengages the reader from the picture of Italy.

Irving also includes the backdrop; the inn at Terracina, the site of the story-telling, stands between a castle-capped mountain and a languid sea. The juxtaposition is the most pointed in the first edition: "A vast, rocky height rises . . . above it, with the ruins of the castle of Theodoric the Goth, crowning its summit; before it spreads the wide bosom of the Mediterranean, that sea without flux or reflux."[56] Here Irving invokes the opposing poles of eighteenth-century aesthetics: the masculine, violent sublime and the feminine, passively agreeable beautiful. These extremes together create his Italian version of the picturesque. The inn's borderline position is clear; it stands between Gothic ruins and the "bosom" of a calm sea, as well as between two political units: "on the frontiers of the Roman territory" (150).

This intermediate spot represents the tourist's point of access to "Italy"; it offers a privileged look at the extremes of a bifurcated natural and social landscape. As a good picturesque tourist, Irving uses these standard aesthetic categories to define this landscape; Edmund Burke supplies the vocabulary of the sublime and the beautiful that defines the central opposition, while Gilpin's version of the picturesque provides the integrating technique which allows the spectator to "see" the larger harmony that contains and defuses the tension. Irving had, by this time, read Burke and Gilpin and thoroughly exploits their premises.[57] The rocky height is a textbook example of what evokes the sublime and could be drawn almost verbatim from Burke's section on "Vastness" in his *Philosophical Enquiry into the Origin of Our Ideas of the Sublime and Beautiful* (72). Theodoric's castle suggests the barbaric invaders who ended the classical era; its "crowning" the vast height signals the triumph of lawless power. On the other hand, the calm Mediterranean represents a docile nature, feminine, static, and, true to Gilpin's assessment of the beautiful (6–8), pictorially somewhat boring. The following tales and landscapes reinforce this initial opposition.

Both in individual scenes and in the structure of "The Italian Banditti," Irving uses the compositional tactics of the picturesque. Like Gilpin, he looks for landscapes that match preconceived standards,[58] derived from two seventeenth-century painters of Italian landscapes; he divides his scenes between the "picturesquely beautiful," based on Claude Lorrain's works, and the "picturesquely sublime," based on Salvator Rosa's.[59] As he did in the journal, he tries to "fix" both landscapes and their inhabitants. Just as the picturesque artist uses foreground elements as an internal frame, Irving distances his pictures from the reader through multiple narrative frames. As he focuses increasingly on the bandits in action, he presents the plots at increasing removes. The first indirectly narrated story, "The Adventure of the Little Antiquary," which describes a harmless meeting between bandits and an aged hunter of ruins, is told by a friend of the antiquary. The next, "The Adventure of the Popkins Family," which describes, more seriously, the robbing of an English family, is pieced together from hearsay. The most violent tales, told by the banditti themselves, are narrated at two removes: tales within a tale within a tale. Although Irving includes Gothic trappings in these robber tales, the approach he asks readers to take is the opposite of the Gothic reader's willing abandonment of critical faculties.[60] Instead of being thrust into the action, readers look at events through a series of filters: the detachment of second- or third-hand reports, the comedy of the immediate action, and, in the longest tale, "The Painter's Adventure," an artist's eyes.

As Gilpin says, a picture's foreground defines the spectator's point of view; it "give[s] a value" to the rest of the composition (69). The opening and closing scenes of "The Italian Banditti" frame the narrative and establish its tone as that of a farce. Irving starts with something like a dirty joke; a government courier arrives at the inn without his pants, which the bandits have stolen. This crime – "so wanton an outrage" – flags the connections among the theft of property, uncontrolled sexuality, and the attack on social order that shape these tales. As he rides off in a new pair of breeches, the courier articulates the implications of his exposure by the outlaws: "'*Corpo di Bacco*! they stiletto all the men, and as to the women – ' Crack! crack! crack! . . . – the last words were drowned in the smacking of the whip, and away galloped the estafette" (149–50). The crack of the whip both obscures and punctuates the brutality of rape, but it is also a piece of slapstick.

The early episodes encourage both comic detachment and skepticism; how does a middle-class tourist read art and landscape and robbers correctly? The first two tales are full of false connoisseurship and misreadings. The "Little Antiquary" is on a wild goose chase, combing the mountains for lost cities that Irving hints never existed. He wears what he thinks is "a veritable antique intaglio" (159) but what the bandits tell him is a counterfeit. The Popkins family misreads the danger of their situation – Mr. Popkins mistakes the chief

of the banditti for a goatherd – and parodies the nouveau picturesque traveler; the daughters, their heads full of Byron, Moore, and
Scott,[61] label the landscape without understanding it: "The Misses
Popkins, who were very romantic, and had learnt to draw in water
colours, were enchanted with the savage scenery . . .; it was so like
what they had read in Mrs. Radcliffe's romances, they should like of
all things to make sketches" (176). Even after their narrow escape
from violence, they persist in their pursuit of vision-blocking conventions; they write their adventures up in their journals (much as
Irving himself once did) and decide that the bandits were "'quite
picturesque!'" (178).

Irving's lesson applies both to the tourists within the tales and
to his readers. Neither should be swept away by these scenes but
should respond with the connoisseur's cooler appreciation. Irving's
hopes for this approach are clear in the Frenchman's paradigmatic
response in "The Painter's Adventure," as I argue below, but also
in a letter he wrote defending the *Tales* after they were published.
In this often-discussed letter, usually seen as his major statement on
his literary art,[62] he says he writes "sketches and short tales" rather
than novels because he is interested less in plot than in constructing
a picturesque artifact:

> I consider a story merely as a frame on which to stretch my materials.
> It is the play of thought, and sentiment and language; the weaving in of
> characters, lightly yet expressively delineated; the . . . exhubition [*sic*]
> of scenes in common life; and the half-concealed vein of humor . . .
> playing through the whole – these are among what I aim at . . .
>
> There is a constant activity of thought and a nicety of execution
> in writings of the kind. While the novelist can throw in chunks of
> dull filler as long as the plot is moving toward an exciting end, in
> a short piece every page must have its merit – The author must be
> continually piquant – woe to him if he . . . writes a stupid page: the
> critics are sure to pounce upon it. Yet if he succeed: the very variety
> and piquancy of his writings; nay, their very brevity; makes them
> frequently recurred to – and when the mere interest of the Story is
> exhausted, he begins to get credit for his touches of pathos or humor;
> his points of wit or turns of language.[63]

Irving's depiction of the writer as painter and the reader as connoisseur reveals the difficulty of the picturesque project. His plea that he
is creating an art form for an elite audience rests on his privileging
the work of picturesque integration over that of novelistic proliferation, but the letter also conveys his sense of the tenuous grasp he

and his readers have on an elite sensibility. The audience must be educated well enough to give "credit" for aesthetic "touches"; the author's "artist like touch" is "not a thing to be appreciated by the many." The writer is always in danger of slipping; the critics who validate his efforts may also devalue them.

The letter's sense of vulnerability stems in part from the critical and popular failure of the *Tales*.[64] Both the elite and the "many" rejected the book. Rubin-Dorsky finds a severe disjunction between the illusion of artistic control in the letter and Irving's professional and personal panic during and after the writing of the *Tales*, as expressed in his journal (179–80). But this vulnerability is also inherent in the picturesque itself. The aesthetic ideal of the letter is anti-narrative; it removes the plot from the center and relegates it to the "frame." The "story" is an occasion for the "variety" of detail and complexity of arrangement – the "points" and "turns" – at the heart of the scene. The picturesque artifact evokes a measured response rather than the confused, powerful response associated with the sublime, in which the reader feels "annihilated" (Burke, 68), and asks viewers to subordinate extremes to the balanced form of this aesthetic middle road. Irving tries to enact this ideal in "The Italian Banditti" by eschewing narrative movement for compositional stasis and by offering a "play of thought" that promises to render the bandits' violence picturesque through its repetitive, typical quality – a strategy which collapses as the tales unfold.

The opening scene and first two tales enact this repetitive quality with compulsive but comic invasions of the orderly by the violent. The antiquary is submerged in his possibly fallacious notions of the past – "his wits" are "wool gathering among the Goths and Romans" – when the dangerous, unclassifiable present breaks in on his historical speculations; the bandits are instantly recognizable because of their "saucy demeanour" and their socially anomalous clothing, "half peasant, half huntsman." Their assault on the antiquary is an assault on his rational faculties. When they take him drinking, he gets "fuddled with their talk and their wine," and his carefully written treatise on the Pelasgian cities winds up "warming under him," forgotten as he sits on it, listens to their stories, and feels "half tempted himself to turn bandit" (159–61). The Popkinses' carriage sets up another orderly but vulnerable world, like that of the scholarly treatise; it "is an epitome of England; a little morsel of the old island rolling about the world – every thing about it compact, snug, finished and fitting" – a succinct image of the middle-class domesticity made possible by the father's bourgeois activities as a merchant and alderman in London. The Popkinses' inability to imagine its disruption is punctuated by Irving's emphatic alliteration, which seals off the sentence. The "ransacking" the bandits predictably give the carriage is the reversal of the tourist's orderly process of gathering foreign commodities into this domestic space; their trunks are "turned inside out" and result in "a chaos of Venice beads . . . and Paris bonnets" (176–7).[65] The extent of this reversal of power is lost on the family, whose faith in English superiority and aesthetic pleasure remains largely unshaken.

The narrative tone changes in the culminating story, "The Painter's Adventure." After ridiculing middle-class faith in such feeble props against "chaos" as governmental authority, historical research, and domesticity, Irving now tests seriously the use of aesthetics to provide conceptual stability in an unstable landscape. In *The Sketch Book* and elsewhere in the *Tales*, his unreliable narrators expose the fallacies of a variety of assumptions. But here he presents a set of landscapes through the eyes of an authoritative narrator. In contrast to the amateurish ignorance of the Misses Popkins, the French painter represents a masculine professionalism. His "air" of "frankness" (179) inspires even the anonymous Englishman's trust. He has been "schooled to hardship during the late revolutions" (182); the possibly feminized nature of his artistic pursuits has not insulated him from action and knowledge. As in the journal, Irving temporarily drops a parodic mode to take up the question of aesthetic response.

The painter tells his story to the Venetian woman, her husband, and the wealthy English traveler in a landscape implicitly linked with the beautiful Venetian; they amble along the Mediterranean beach under the illuminator of ideal landscapes, the "rising moon." In this calm end of the natural spectrum, the bandits appear only in the form of "galley slaves" taking supervised recreation on the sand. To the "fair Venetian" they seem "like so many serpents writhing together" (178–9). The following story, in which the painter moves from a pastoral setting into the bandits' mountainous territory, justifies the Venetian's sexual anxiety and underscores the irreconcilability of these extremes. Because he is not bound to either – like Irving, he is a foreign artist with a privileged perspective and an affinity for the picturesque – the painter becomes Irving's vehicle for aestheticizing the two poles of the Italian landscape.

The painter first describes the social and aesthetic geography of an idealized norm against which the forced excursion into aberrant territory is set. He lives in surroundings that would make the Venetian comfortable: "in the bosom of a soft and luxurious repose," in "the midst of delightful bowers." This landscape is "full of poetical and historical associations" (180) of classical antiquity. Following eighteenth-century travelers, Irving invokes this period of Roman history as a model of an ordered life.[66] The painter's sojourn in this idyllic "refuge . . . from . . . toils" echoes a classical pattern; he lives in the villa of his princely patron in an area once frequented by Roman poets (Horace) and patrons (Maecenas) within sight of a now quietly fallen Rome, which he describes in terms borrowed from Pope.[67] And he follows Burke in associating beauty with the instinct for social cohesion.[68] Inhabiting the landscape of the beautiful is the smoothly running household of the Frenchman's prince. A class hierarchy of nobility and servants is firmly in place; the prince's paternal authority makes the landscape and household of the beautiful possible. The Frenchman invokes another category of ordered priorities when he tells his audience, "I am an historical painter by profession." The Reynoldsian hierarchy of genres, which ranked history painting higher in national and cultural significance than landscape painting, lingered long in the nineteenth century[69] and gives Irving an additional hierarchy for the bandits to disrupt. The artist's other work for his patron also privileges a reverential approach to the past; a more sophisticated version of the old antiquary, he supervises the excavation of ancient "fragments" of sculpture (179–80).

But Irving is not merely reproducing eighteenth-century concepts of the beautiful, or of history painting, or of a purposeful Roman order from which Italy has fallen; Irving's vision of order is frail, only pseudo-classical, and immediately preliminary to disorder. His vague sketch of Italian serenity functions as a nostalgic backdrop of the lost cultural stability he associates with a landed aristocracy and contrasts with the vulnerable forms of middle-class property, such as the portable goods of the Popkinses' coach, and of middle-class perceptions, embodied in the painter's compositions. There is a genealogy of aesthetic response buried in "The Italian Banditti"; the tales model the perils of such responses cut loose not only from aristocratic patronage (and its grounding in land-based wealth) but also from their function as consolidators of that world. The prince remains a shadowy background figure, the aristocratic father of bourgeois aesthetic response who stands off-stage, in the past, while middle-class characters try to adapt this aesthetic inheritance to the instability of their immediate experience.

Into this prelapsarian garden "serpents" are bound to enter; bandits steal into the villa, assault and rob the painter, and carry him away for ransom on the assumption that he is the prince. Repeating the pattern of their meeting with the antiquary, they assault his rational powers; a blow to the head echoes the ascent of wine to the antiquary's head. But the painter's response to his abductors departs from the pattern of the previous narratives. The antiquary becomes "fuddled," but the painter, after being initially "stunned" (181), resists the bandits with strength and method: "with my right hand I seized [the ruffian's throat], with my left hand I grasped the arm which held the carbine." A better reader of character and environment than Alderman Popkins, he knows when physical resistance is no longer possible and is able to manipulate the bandits to further his ransom and release.

At once artist and connoisseur, the painter applies his picturesque vision to wild landscapes and characters, which contrast at every point with those of the villa. The undomesticated terrain is difficult to negotiate (the "rugged heights" are covered with "thick forest," "rocks and brambles") and confusing: "Our march was long and painful, with many . . . windings" (182–4). The bandits, whose chief is a "vigorous mountaineer," are at home in this undisciplined region. Refusing to be bound by social castes, as the antiquary observed by their clothes, they are peasants who have become lordly. These anomalous social types contain a "singular mixture" of "ferocity" and "kindness"; they are "both lofty and ludicrous" (183, 185, 187). And by mistaking, however briefly, the painter for the prince, they intrude social confusion into the lives of others. The two stories they tell the Frenchman – the murder of a chief of police and the rape and murder of a middle-class virgin – describe crimes against two shapers of the landscape of the beautiful: disciplinary authority and a feminized domesticity. Their efforts at organization parody without reproducing social norms; they have "almost formed themselves into an order of society" and mimic a "military" appearance through a "kind of uniform" (150).

An apparent similarity between the bandits and the obedient laborers of the villa actually places each group more firmly in its setting. The thieves communicate by animal sounds: "the cries of hawks" or "the bleating of . . . flocks" (184). The artist also associates the laborers with animals; he uses the animal warmth of one of these fellow captives to keep him warm at night: "Whenever one of my limbs became chilled I approached it to the robust limb of my neighbour, and borrowed some of his warmth" (183). But something like Burke's distinction between a tame, "serviceable" ox and a wild, "dangerous" bull underpins Irving's associations: "Whenever strength is only useful . . . then it is never sublime; for nothing can act agreeably to us that does not act in conformity to our will; but to act agreeably to our will it must be subject to us; and therefore can never be the cause of a grand and commanding conception" (64–5). At the villa strength is subject to an authority that keeps the machine of the beautiful running smoothly. In the mountains force triumphs over control; belying their imitations of sheep, the bandits represent physical impulse, here identified with the "lower-class violence" that besets the Gothic heroine, run amuck.

The painter's connoisseurship is more flexible than that of the antiquary, who comes to the mountains looking for ruins and is surprised to find savagery. The artist sees the aesthetic possibilities of his new environment at once. The mountain men reveal pictur-esque attributes as they shield a fire with their cloaks: "Anxious as was my situation, I could not look around this screen of dusky drapery, relieved by the bright colours of the robbers' underdresses, the gleaming of their weapons, and the variety of strong marked countenances, lit up by the flambeau, without admiring the pictur-esque effect of the scene. It was quite theatrical" (182–3). However the bandits may shatter social and political norms, the artist finds another organizing principle – the aesthetic – which enfolds villa and mountain life as versions of the beautiful and the sublime. By seeing them in painterly terms (here they seem almost pedantically to dem-onstrate *chiaroscuro*), he discovers that he can enclose them within the conventions of the picturesque.

This discovery permits him to sketch a series of mountain scenes both literally (he has somehow managed to bring along "a quire of drawing paper," 184) and figuratively, in his tale. His captivity temporarily reorders his generic priorities; instead of pursuing his high vocation of history painting, he depicts landscapes and local characters. His stepping out of this artistic hierarchy has economic and social parallels; instead of being sponsored by a patron, he suits himself. Instead of unearthing art objects from the past or produc-ing studio paintings of historic events, he is an impulsive *plein-air* sketcher of the present and of dangerously alive subjects. In one sense, the bandits do go to his head; he embraces his new meth-ods and subject with a repeated "enthusiasm" (184, 189, 193). The informal sketches not only draw on socially anarchic energies but are also accessible to socially liminal figures; they evoke "a gleam of good feeling" (185) in the bandit chief. As Charles Rosen and Henri Zerner argue, "The attack on the system of genres challenged a tra-dition that made intelligibility dependent on connoisseurship";[70] the painter's work offers participation in aesthetic knowledge to those who ordinarily serve only as figures in a landscape perceived and structured by an elite. In other words, the Frenchman becomes a modern painter in a democratic, unstable marketplace.

Nevertheless, the artist's excursion into immediacy also works to bring bandit life and landscape back under control through the forms of the picturesque. His aesthetic subjugation of the brigands is clearest in his portrait of their leader. Finding precedent in Salvator Rosa's bandit sketches, the Frenchman turns socially wild Burkean bulls into aesthetically tame Burkean oxen:

> I recollected that Salvator Rosa . . . had voluntarily sojourned for a time among the banditti of Calabria, and had filled his mind with . . . savage scenery and savage associates. . . . I seized my pencil with enthusiasm at the thought. I found the captain the most docile of subjects, and . . . placed him in an attitude to my mind.
>
> Picture to yourself a stern, muscular figure, in fanciful bandit costume, with pistols and poniards in belt, his brawny neck bare, [his] handkerchief . . . strung with rings of all kinds, the spoils of travellers. . . . Fancy him on a mountain height, among wild rocks and rugged oaks, leaning on his carbine as if meditating some exploit, while far below are beheld villages and villas, the scenes of his maraudings, with the wide Campagna dimly extending in the distance. (189)

Just as the painter fits savagery into the control of alliterative language ("savage scenery and savage associates"), so does he recuperate the captain's predatory usurpation of the prospect view within his own aesthetic gaze. As the captain surveys the pastoral landscape in anticipation of exercising power over it, so the artist surveys the captain and even poses him in accord with conventions of genre paintings of bandits. His detailed description of the chief's "costume" and the neat contrast he draws between the bandit (and his "wild" environment) and the placid backdrop of pastoral Italy freezes the figure's chaotic energy into a conventional tableau. The "portrait" echoes the bandit paintings being sold and exhibited in Paris, where Irving wrote "The Italian Banditti" in 1824. Léopold Robert, one of the most popular painters of Italian bandits, similarly juxtaposes costumed banditti and calm Campagna in such works as *The Brigand on the Watch* (1825, Fig. 1.1).[71] When the picturesque tourist fits new visual experience into pre-existing forms, the "dangerous" subject matter of the Burkean sublime becomes "serviceable."

Unlike the painter, the banditti do not recognize their habitual prospect view as an aesthetic experience; they are "astonished" (184) at his enthusiasm and momentarily accept his ability to recognize

Figure 1.1 Léopold Robert, *The Brigand on the Watch*, 1825. Oil on canvas. © The Wallace Collection, London.

compositional forms as a sign of authority. The painter interprets the captain's "physiognomy" for him in an effort to reintegrate his entrepreneurial energies into a disciplinary society: "[I] told him . . . that he had but to change his course of life, and . . . the same courage and endowments which now made him an object of terror, would assure him the applause . . . of society" (185). This revisionary portrait, both visual and verbal, elicits the captain's confessions of his own bourgeois and domestic fantasies, in which he dreams of legitimizing his relationship to his "spoils": "He . . . told me he was weary of his hazardous profession; that he had acquired sufficient property, and was anxious to return to the world and lead a peaceful life in the bosom of his family. He wished to know whether it was not in my power to procure him a passport for the United States" (201). The painter's aesthetic insight has apparently revealed that inside of every bandit is a bourgeois – an Alderman Popkins – waiting to get out. That his art has not only a liberating but also a coercive effect becomes apparent when the artist inadvertently writes his ransom note on the back of the portrait; the captain's vanity prompts him to send both the note and the sketch and to forget "what use might be made of this portrait in his . . . capture" (190). Social control certainly makes aesthetic composition possible; Léopold Robert used bandits imprisoned in Rome as models for his paintings.[72] Here Irving exposes the tourist's hope that composition makes control possible, that catching the captain's likeness may help to catch the captain.

As the Frenchman works to squeeze new experiences into familiar aesthetic molds, he begins to associate the bandits with figures of classical antiquity, an association earlier reserved for civilized Italians. The connection is first suggested by the head bandit, who compares his murder of a chief of police with Brutus's patriotic assassination of Caesar. The painter reacts ambivalently; he is amused but also feels a latent nobility in the assassin. By the end of the story the artist himself has come to associate the bandits not with the literate Romans of the late Republic and early Empire (Cicero, Horace, Maecenas) but with Homer's "grim warriors of Greece" (201). The assimilation of these aberrants into literary and aesthetic forms now seems complete. And so the painter's "enthusiasm" is prompted more by recognizing old forms than by confronting the new. He busily sketches morning, noon, evening, and night scenes; he pencils individual portraits and group pictures of bandits eating a "rude repast" or taking an afternoon nap. Nevertheless, in spite of the sense of power these exercises give him, the way in which Irving structures the painter's landscapes implies the illusory nature of aesthetic insight and control and anticipates both the painter's final mood of depression and the need for military action in the last scene of "The Italian Banditti."

The Frenchman's major landscape combines the power of the prospect view with the integrating techniques of the picturesque. This view from a mountaintop is a climactic moment of triumphant synthesis:

> Here it was that I felt all the enthusiasm of my art suddenly awakened; and I forgot . . . all my perils . . . at this magnificent view of the sunrise in the midst of the mountains of the Abruzzi. It was on these heights that Hannibal . . . pointed out Rome to his followers. The eye embraces a vast extent of country. . . . Tusculum, with its villas, and its sacred ruins, lie below; the Sabine hills and the Albanian mountains stretch on either hand, and beyond . . . spreads out the immense Campagna, with its line of tombs, and here and there a broken aqueduct stretching across it, and the towers and domes of the eternal city in the midst.

> Fancy this scene lit up by the glories of a rising sun, and bursting upon my sight, as I looked forth from among the majestic forests of the Abruzzi. Fancy, too, the savage foreground, made still more savage by groups of banditti armed and dressed in their wild, picturesque manner, and you will not wonder that the enthusiasm of a painter for a moment overpowered all his other feelings. (184)

Like the historical reverie in Irving's journal, this prospect of past and present is available only to the artist and his educated auditors, the "you" of the passage, who share an elite sensibility with the ideal readers of Irving's letter. To such a sensibility the composition is naturalized: the "scene . . . burst upon my sight." But the view does not appear to those who live within it; the robbers do not see the picture but are contained by it.

The prospect is ambitiously comprehensive; it contains the full spectrum of Italian possibilities for tourists of this era. The eye ranges from the "wild" mountains to the domesticated countryside and the ancient city below, from the chaotic energy of the present to the declining forms of the past – "sacred ruins" and "broken aqueduct" – and finally to a timeless image of civilization: "the eternal city." As the eye moves from mountains to "domes," the mind moves from associations of violence and military heroism (Hannibal) to the pastoral life (for "Sabine hills" read "Horace") and then to the urban life, represented by Rome but not depicted in "The Italian Banditti." This picture embodies romantic theories of the stages of historical change, modeled on Roman history and later visualized by Thomas Cole in his series of paintings *The Course of Empire* (1836).[73] It includes savage potential, the pastoral and the ruinous stages intertwined in the middle distance, the culminating city, and even a hint, provided by the bandits, of that romantic necessity in the history of civilization: the sacking.

The second paragraph of the passage notes the picturesque strategies the painter uses to achieve Gilpin's aesthetic "bonds of peace." The various scene is harmonized by the sun's light and framed by the trees of the foreground. The painter's treatment of this foreground indicates both his picturesque hopes and the limitations of his method. As later U.S. painters were to do,[74] he blends a structure derived from Claude with details taken from Salvator. Irving would have been familiar with this structure and its pastoral harmonies not only from the popularity of Claude's Italian landscape paintings in Anglo-American elite culture but also from his 1805 visit to the Galleria Doria Pamphilj in Rome, where he probably saw *Landscape with Dancing Figures (the Marriage of Isaac*

Figure 1.2 Claude Lorrain (Gellée), *Landscape with the Marriage of Isaac and Rebecca*, 1648. Oil on canvas. 152.3 x 200.6 cm. Bought, 1824 (NG12). © National Gallery, London/Art Resource, New York.

and Rebecca) (1647; see Fig. 1.2 for another version of this painting), and where several antebellum U.S. travelers responded to the Claudes on view.[75]

Christopher Hussey sums up Gilpin's advice to sketchers, advice based on the Claudean formula: "the most fitting kinds of foregrounds . . . consisted in broken ground, trees, rocks, cascades, and valleys. Whereas the ruling character of the distance was tenderness, in the foreground this must give way 'to what the painter calls force and richness, [and] variety of parts'" (116). By turning Claude's and Gilpin's compositional device of the contrasting foreground into Salvator Rosa's "savage" territory, the picturesque artist tries to employ its disruptive energy in the service of a unified composition. The idea of power separated from any hegemonic strategies is frightening; like "vultures" the robbers "command" this "uninterrupted prospect" (184) without the ameliorating understanding of aesthetics. In discussing Burke's *Reflections on the French Revolution*, Terry Eagleton argues that the "danger of revolutionaries is that as fanatical anti-aestheticians they offer to reduce hegemony to naked power" (58). The painter's excitement in sketching the prospect and incorporating the bandits and their foreground into his composition stems from the picturesque's reintegration of "naked power" into a social and aesthetic picture which seems ruled by consensus and which implies that the "tenderness" of the pastoral distance or the more cloaked power of Rome is the eye's ultimate destination. Just as Irving's letter moves the narrative impulse from the focus to the "frame" of his work, so the painter's sketch pushes the narrative motor of these tales – the robbers – from the center to the frame in an effort to assert the power of the middle-class gaze over these semi-revolutionaries.

Nevertheless, compared to other options in composing landscapes, this exercise undermines its own efforts. Although the rough foreground is supposed to serve as a threshold to the harmonious distance, Irving's description reverses the direction of the reader's eye and ends with the problematic foreground, a reversal that he repeats in a subsequent landscape.[76] The artist is not sure of the implications of his aesthetic response for his understanding of historical order. The fact that the description proceeds at first forward, into the distance, and then backwards, ending with the undisciplined foreground, suggests that there are no sequential connections between savagery and civilization and no necessary progressive movement from predatory to hegemonic forms of power; they simply coexist inexplicably.

In speaking of the mountain villages which produce the bandits, the Frenchman says, "It is wonderful that such rude abodes . . . [are] embosomed in the midst of one of the most . . . civilized countries of Europe" (190). In attempting the union of the sublime and the beautiful in Italy, Irving's character can get no further than a tenuous harmony, a composition based neither on a vision of unity sanctioned by nature nor on a progressive view of the trajectory of history but on a "wonderful" coincidence. Read in terms of the kinds of faith that produced Allston's paintings, the skepticism that informed Irving's aesthetics becomes clear.

Allston's Italian Landscapes and Transcendental Aesthetics

During his friendship with Allston in Rome in 1805, Irving says that he almost threw over "the dry study of the law" in order to "turn painter" and to join Allston in "the constant study of the sublime and the beautiful."[77] However, even as Irving was developing the earthbound habits of the picturesque, Allston pursued an aesthetic with transcendent, mystical meanings. David Bjelajac has read Allston's similarly transatlantic career – early years in Paris, Rome, and Britain, and then a return to the U.S. – in the context of the Masonic language of his circles, a language of illumination that carried "the alchemical ... mythology of the arts" into the early nineteenth century. Reacting against the "Lockean demystification of light," romantic artists and clergy connected the chemical "compounds of pigments" and the optical "compounds of light" in a theology and an aesthetic that saw the painter as a "chemist" or alchemist who "released the vitalist light within material pigments" to access heavenly wisdom: "The triune chemical connection of primary colors – blue, yellow, red – to light maintained an animated, enchanted universe where one could still find, as Saint Augustine had phrased it, 'footprints of the Trinity.'" This alchemical understanding of light and color led English painters – and Allston – to search for the "secret" of Renaissance Venetian painters, whose technique of creating luminous colors through layers of paint represented an animated nature, suffused with spirit. For Allston, the "Venetian glazing technique ... symboliz[ed] spiritual sublimation to a state of higher consciousness." In his paintings of figures, his "glowing surfaces" indicated the "soul" within the "earthly body."[78] This orientation to his art explains his synesthetic response to the Venetians:

> Titian, Tintoret, and Paul Veronese ... enchanted me, for they took away all sense of subject. When I stood before the *Peter Martyr* ... and *The Marriage of Cana*, I thought of nothing but the gorgeous concert of colors ... procreative in its nature, giving birth to a thousand things which the eye cannot see.... I understand why so many great colorists ... gave so little heed to the ostensible *stories* of their compositions. ... They addressed themselves, not to the senses merely, ... but rather through them to that region ... of the imagination which is supposed to be under the exclusive dominion of music.[79]

In his minimizing of narrative, Allston echoes Irving's letter, which slights "the mere interest of the Story" for "a nicety of execution"; the achievement of Veronese's *Marriage at Cana* is not its "ostensible stor[y]" but the "concert of colors." But Allston's sense of narrative arrest arises from the "procreative" transmutation of pigment into a "poetry of color" that "giv[es] birth to ... things which the eye cannot see," an aspect of the "imagination" that transcends "the senses."

Like Irving's *Tales*, Allston's works imply a polarized vision of Italy; in the first half of his career, Italy is a landscape which, with a dreamlike tendency toward extremes, can reveal either Claudean or Salvatorean views.[80] In his Gothic tale *Monaldi* (finished by 1822),[81] Allston's only extended landscape description uses the same clichéd contrast of a "terrible" Vesuvius with the "harmony" of the Bay of Naples ("Glorious . . .!," 209–10) that Irving features in "The Story of the Young Italian."[82] But Allston develops a different approach from this common body of ideas; after a youthful period of "bandittimania," as William H. Gerdts notes,[83] he links both the sublime and the Italian scene less with danger than with "harmony," less with Salvator than with Claude. He begins his career with such titles as *Landscape with Banditti* (1798) and as late as 1815 paints a scene, from *Gil Blas*, of Spanish bandits and their genteel female captive: *Donna Mencia in the Robbers' Cavern* (Fig. 1.3). But in his continuing series of Italian landscapes,

Figure 1.3 Washington Allston, *Donna Mencia in the Robbers' Cavern*, 1815. Oil on canvas. 55⅞ x 43¾ ins (41.92 x 111.12 cm). Gift of Martha C. Karolik for the M. and M. Karolik Collection of American Paintings, 1815–1865, 47.1239. Museum of Fine Arts, Boston. Photograph © 2018 Museum of Fine Arts, Boston.

from *Landscape with a Lake* (1804) and *Coast Scene on the Mediter-ranean* (1811) to *Italian Landscape* (1828–30), Allston transfers the wonder associated with the sublime from the banditti's rugged terrain to scenes that exude a supernal calm.

Gerdts and Bjelajac have discussed Allston's association with German expatriates and artists in Rome, especially with the circle of Wilhelm von Humboldt, whose aesthetics were shaped by Immanuel Kant as well as by Prussian Rosicrucians and Freemasons. Irving introduced Allston to this circle, where Allston also befriended Sam-uel Taylor Coleridge.[84] However, unlike Irving's, Allston's landscapes embody a romantic shift in the concept of the sublime from Burke's empirical sense to Kant's transcendental aesthetics. As Samuel H. Monk has argued, Kant's connection between the sublime and reli-gious experience sums up the tendency of eighteenth-century English thought as well.[85] In the *Critique of Judgment* Kant maps out the sublime experience in such a way so as to incorporate Burke's empiri-cal response as a first step. Being overwhelmed by external appear-ances, whether in art or in nature, prompts a spiritual "resistance" out of all proportion to the spectator's physical strength; the newly discovered spiritual capacity, which dwarfs the object that stimulated it, indicates "our supersensible destination," that is, the observer's spiritual immortality.[86]

Not merely an elaboration of the Burkean, domesticated beauti-ful, Allston's landscapes evoke supernal harmonies, an order beyond human control. Placing his works within the Kantian structure helps to interpret them. To adapt Thomas Weiskel's discussion of the romantic sublime's stages, the perceiver is jolted from ordinary con-sciousness by a sudden "disequilibrium" between mind and object, an "intuition of a disconcerting disproportion between inner and outer. . . . We are reading along and suddenly occurs a text which exceeds comprehension. . . . Or a natural phenomenon catches us unprepared and unable to grasp its scale." In the final stage, the mind rises above its confusion and strikes a new balance with the object; this new sense of meaning is based on "the very indeterminacy" which first disrupted habitual perception and which is now "taken as symbolizing the mind's relation to a transcendent order." The com-pleted pattern includes a release from anxiety and an empowering imaginative assimilation of the threatening or incomprehensible: "a burden . . . is lifted and there is an influx of power" (23–4, 11).

The Frenchman's major landscape anticipates the visual equivalent to this psychological experience in Hudson River School landscape paintings. To indicate the spiritual assimilation of the stupendous, these paintings contain both the anxiety-provoking force (the Burkean sublime) in the foreground and its assimilation in the background, a process Bryan Jay Wolf identifies in Thomas Cole's *Sunny Morning on the Hudson* (1827), where a dark, "threatening" mountain in the foreground serves as a "blocking agent" which the eye must circumvent to reach "a world of mist and light" in the distance.[87] The nationalist uses of this serial version of the sublime are clear in a later example – Asher B. Durand's *Progress (The Advance of Civilization)* (1853) – where, as Angela Miller argues, "visual mastery" is a "metaphor" for the U.S. control of nature.[88] Although the threat of the foreground is less than in Irving's scene, the sequence is the same. The progress of the eye – from the foreground's dark, Indian-populated, broken-treed heights to the shining, mildly industrial background – matches the literal "progress" of the U.S. landscape. In the sublime national prospect, the stages of aesthetic experience match those of U.S. history.

In his landscapes of transcendence, Allston represents only the final stage of the sublime moment; rather than depict the disruption that initiates the sequence of aesthetic response, he represents the observer's state of mind after the assimilation of the initial "excess":[89] the "spiritual sublimation to a state of higher consciousness" or the intuition of "the mind's relation to a transcendent order." To do so, he draws on his study of the "Venetian secret" and on Claude's technique of a unified tone, often gold, diffused throughout the painting as light is diffused through a hazy atmosphere.[90] In his *Lectures on Art* (1850) Allston says that the sublime has a "supernal source" and that its "awful harmony" moves the observer toward this source, "the Infinite Creator"; both the beautiful and the sublime are based on "Harmony" perceived: the beautiful on the correspondence between finite objects and the observer's spiritual self and the sublime on the accord between the human spirit and the infinite.[91] To evoke this harmony, as E. P. Richardson explains, Allston paints in layers so that colors are "floating in suspension," "seen through one another, so that, while here and there the tone is brought up to certain color accents, the general effect is a harmony in which all colors are united" (117–18). According to Bjelajac, these "alchemic glazes" obscure his paintings' basis in material particularity and construct a unified vision that seems to transcend "normal sense experience." Rejecting Burke's sensational derivation of the sublime, he opts for Coleridge's Christian "moral . . . sublime," which offers glimpses of the supersensual "harmony of God's universe."[92] Allston remarked that Italian art, including the tradition of idealized landscape paintings, gave him the greatest access to this "'Ideal world'": "'It is only there that you will find the existence of invisible Truth proved palpable.'"[93]

Figure 1.4 Washington Allston, *Moonlight*, 1819. Oil on canvas. 25⅛ x 35¾ ins (63.82 x 90.8 cm). William Sturgis Bigelow Collection, 21.1429. Museum of Fine Arts, Boston. Photograph © 2018 Museum of Fine Arts, Boston.

Unlike Irving's sketches, Allston's landscapes indicate "things which the eye cannot see"; his *Moonlight* (1819, Fig. 1.4) is just such a transfigured vision of an Italian scene.[94] As Gerdts observes, the dim light, in which "forms are indistinctly glimpsed," leads to "a mood of harmony."[95] Allston creates this mood through a continuity of shape and color. The dark shapes of the buildings blend into and are at points indistinguishable from the natural formations – riverbanks and hills. And the landscape is composed primarily of only two colors, blue and brown, which define the upper and lower halves of the canvas but which mingle freely, especially in the central mountain in the distance. The viewer's sense that this landscape is extra-ordinary, that its meaning lies beyond the surface information of sense perceptions, derives from this high degree of structural and chromatic union.

The human figures also participate in this harmony. Like the buildings, they have generic forms; the dim light reveals no period props or costumes. Instead of being set aside from their surroundings by the color of their clothes, these archetypal figures (a solitary figure, a family group, and a man on horseback) are simply indicated by darker versions of the brownish hues that dominate the painting's lower half. Other man-made objects – a bridge and two boats – are also generic in their shapes and colored by the same dark hues. As Richardson might put it, the tones of the figures and objects are the same as those pervading the rest of the landscape; they are merely more concentrated instances, merely "brought up" a bit. This immersion of the figures into the scene entails "a process of arrested narrativity,"[96] a subordination of action to vision. The moon's harmonizing light may, Bjelajac implies, have further implications in Allston's Christian and Masonic symbology. The landscape's "silvery lunar glow" may indicate the passive alchemical (female) catalyst for spiritual vision; just as believers could "spiritually see" grace reflected in the "visible . . . symbols of the church," so the moon's reflection of the sun's (masculine) rays made this light accessible through a "sensible, material medium."[97]

As do other aesthetic strategies, this version of the sublime can function as an analogy for social strategies of managing two associated categories: the world of the senses and the energies of American democracy. As Bjelajac points out, Allston belonged to those New England Federalists who, deprived of political power by Jefferson's party and diluted in influence by "the elimination of property restrictions for voting and officeholding," tried to shape and unify the republic by "mold[ing] the national character through the control of culture and education."[98] Exemplifying the quality he admired in Venetian paintings, Allston's landscape transcends "all sense of subject"; just as the subject matter is subsumed into an ideal vision, so the details that bind the viewer to the material and the immediate disappear. This aesthetic asks the viewer to become subsumed into the timeless world presented on the canvas, to blend into that which is larger than the individual self. Imagining such harmony beyond the surface distractions of the senses and the disorder of the social world provides the release from anxiety and the "influx of power" Weiskel mentions; the painting offers this transforming vision to its spectator even as it asks for the spectator's allegiance to a shared cultural ideal of unity.

Picturesque Order, Property, and Violence

In applying his pictorial eye to Italy, Irving chooses neither Cole and Durand's serial mode nor Allston's harmonic one. Because his medium is prose, he can control more precisely the movement of his reader's "eye." The structure of the Frenchman's major landscape is like Durand's, but Irving ensures that our eye lingers last on the foreground, not on the distance. This choice accords with the aesthetics of his letter defending the *Tales*. Instead of a narrative movement from intimidating foreground to welcoming background, we have a controlled "play of thought" moving among the picture's elements. The references to association-starting places support the picturesque effect. Like the detailed portrait of the captain, the landscape achieves the "variety & piquancy" Irving mentions; within the frameworks of the sketch – literal (the trees) and figurative (the painter's story) – the eye wanders among tokens of security and danger, present and past, each emblem rendered more "piquant" by the presence of the other. These juxtapositions of opposing elements provide neither direction nor union but a momentary *chiaroscuro*. His aesthetic prevents Irving from emphasizing, as Allston may have done, the coloring lent to the scene by the "rising sun." The picturesque invites the eye's repeated movement between contrasts; Allston's landscapes, on the other hand, represent that moment when the eye is stilled by a vision of unity behind surface contradictions.

The handling of the human figures in *Moonlight* and in the artist's scene clarifies the distinction. While Allston binds his figures to the landscape only through the extra-ordinary connection of color, Irving ties his characters to their backdrop by a plethora of attributes. He has only to remind his audience of the mountain wilderness and of the bandits' appearance, "dressed in their wild, picturesque manner," to evoke their close association; the "savage foreground" is "made still more savage by . . . the banditti." As the captain's portrait demonstrates, Irving adds more and more characteristics to both figures and landscape to convince the reader of their appropriate conjunction, whereas Allston, in search of a visionary unity, strips his figures and scenery of distinctive traits. His harmonious "concert" directs the viewer past "the senses" toward the "Harmony" of "the Infinite Creator." Irving instead uses an artistic language of discrete elements, of "touches," "points," and "turns." The "variety" of the picturesque keeps our attention on the immediate world of the senses.

Gilpin warns "the admirer of nature" against expecting to find "a higher purpose" in aesthetic experience, such as "religious awe" (47), even as his own language sometimes encourages it. Irving's sketches imply a desire for "a higher purpose," less religious than social, at the same time that they critique this desire. Kim Ian Michasiw has usefully divided eighteenth-century British proponents of the picturesque into two classes: Gilpin's "disempowered traveler[s]," whose sketches do not alter the scene but who "leave the landscape as they found it," and "improving landowner[s]" who see their land as "subject" to their will and whose aesthetics carry over to the colonial management of "other peoples' lands." Michasiw argues that "Gilpin's project stands in opposition to the colonialist, or imperial, eye of . . . the picturesque's second phase." Even as other tourists are finding a middle way – social empowerment via the displaced arena of foreign sites and sights – between these positions, Irving stumbles into Gilpin's awareness of the "contingency and fragility of the picturesque order."[99] The parallels between his aesthetic and social visions create the final tableau of "The Italian Banditti."

As the painter awaits his ransom, his compositional energy becomes overtaxed. The first tale he hears – the captain's account of his revolutionary assassination of a repressive police chief – is easy to integrate into middle-class values; this "Brutus" represents the liberal aspect of the romantic outlaw convention. But near the end of his captivity another tale represents the other side of this literary construct: the destructive impulses of "lower-class violence," as Ellis puts it. The narrator is a member of the lower middle class whose inability to discipline his desires plunges him into the anarchy of bandit life. His passion for a surveyor's daughter, an emblem of middle-class domesticity whose white dress and skin mark her as "different from the sunburnt females" of the village, leads him to murder a sexual rival, to join the banditti, and finally to betray the object of his desire into the hands of the band, where she is repeatedly raped. The tale recapitulates the invasion of the pastoral space of the beautiful (the girl is captured in her father's vineyard), the equation between rape and theft (the father refuses to ransom his damaged property), and the inability of the two extremes of the landscape to coexist; the robber can only help his love-object by "tenderly" stabbing her after her ordeal (194–9).

This tale exhausts the artist's ability to integrate the landscape of the bandits into the framework of the picturesque. "[H]arrassed and fatigued," he sits "horror-struck, covering my face with my hands; seeking . . . to hide from myself the frightful images he had presented to my mind"; losing visionary control, he finds that "the sight of the banditti began to grow insupportable to me" (199–200). The tale links the two aspects of outlaws; the fact that the captain is the first to assault the virgin implies that the revolutionary impulse toward freedom and the violent threat to the middle class are nauseatingly related.[100] This point in the *Tales* marked a disjunction in the experience not only of the artist but also of many of Irving's reviewers. While readers were disappointed in other aspects of the stories, the U.S. critic John Neal summarized much opinion when he charged Irving with "smuggl[ing] impurity" into the reader's experience.[101] In a reaction similar to the painter's, readers felt that the conventions under which the author operated had betrayed them; the picturesque point of view promised to retrieve the bandits for middle-class use but instead it subjected the readers to uncontrollable "images."

Having arrived at this impasse, Irving concludes the painter's story with his release and ends "The Italian Banditti" with a distracting sleight of hand designed not to resolve the contrast in the Italian scene but to release the reader, as well, from its contemplation. Irving abandons aesthetic perception for action and gives the final episode – the first directly narrated action since the galloping departure of the government messenger – to the wealthy Englishman. The conclusion turns middle-class anxiety over property from a comic vulnerability (as portrayed by Alderman Popkins) into a bulwark of social order. And it does so by a dissociation of action from aesthetics; the Englishman respects the French artist but is himself impervious to the aesthetic and verges on the philistine.

The morning after their stroll on the beach, the Frenchman's audience – the Venetian couple and the English traveler – set out in their respective carriages for Naples. The fact that the Englishman has "much property about him" leads him to the rational decision to hire a military escort, but his anxiety about his possessions also makes a fool out of him. Having mislaid his purse in his own carriage, he calls a halt and projects banditry onto the face of all Italy in his accusations – "'The waiter had pocketed it. . . . The inn a den of thieves – it was a d – -d country'" – and threatens the innkeeper with the police. Embarrassed by his mistake, he throws money at the "cringing waiter" and drives off after the Venetians (202–4). Meanwhile the couple has moved into the bandits' landscape, complete with "rugged, precipitous heights" and the "entanglements of . . . bushes." The robbers, of course, begin their mechanically murderous assault, and the reader has the opportunity to see at first hand the confrontation between the representatives of the Italian extremes – the bandits and the "beautiful Venetian lady" (the husband, not of paramount importance in Irving's scheme, remains helpless). Things are proceeding as usual – their carriage is being plundered and the beautiful Venetian is being carried "shrieking up the mountains" – when the Englishman arrives with his soldiers and drives the robbers back into their half of the picture. After surviving the usual assault to the head (the bullet only takes off a bit of hair), and assisted by his English servant, he rescues the lady and returns her to her ineffectually raving husband (205–6).

While his preoccupation with property can generate false crises, it also makes the property owner effective in a real crisis. Like the artist, he categorizes other characters, draws a line between the domestic and the violent, and works to freeze the narrative movement of the bandits and restore order to the scene. But he does it better. Where the artist crosses the line between wild and tame, the mob and the middle class, the id and the ego, in an attempt to integrate these two landscapes, the Englishman polices the line and enforces their separation. The painter's efforts result in depression. The Englishman's strategy of disciplined violence invigoratingly succeeds. If the undisguised power of the outlaws is frightening, then the Englishman's rescue of the Venetian woman restores the proper, protective relationship between power and beauty, where the beautiful is the mark of a disciplined and productive society. And so the final contrast between feminine repose and masculine action appears between two safe, socially bound types; the Englishman performs with athletic valor, and "the fair Venetian" is rendered into that state which is the logical epitome of beauty: "senseless on the ground" (206). She still echoes her end of the scale: the tideless Mediterranean, "that sea without flux or reflux." But the opposite end – the barbaric castle on the cliff – is blocked from sight by the interposition of the Englishman and the rational, bourgeois values he represents.

This ending throws the painter's enterprise further into doubt. Although more qualified for his job than the Misses Popkins, he does, after all, operate from the same habit of matching what he sees to imported forms, as Bell points out.[102] Once he recognizes that he is in Salvator Rosa territory, he responds just as they do when they recognize Ann Radcliffe in the landscape; he "should like of all things to make sketches." The distinction between the virile artist and the female tourists and victims always threatens to collapse and is further imperiled by the artist's exclusion from the final action. While aesthetic insight offers some success, it is a shaky foundation for the work of social control and for middle-class identity. Rubin-Dorsky documents a surge of gender anxiety in Irving during the period in which he wrote the *Tales*; having a marriage proposal rejected at the age of forty seemed to deny him "heterosexual legitimacy" and "patriarchal standing in the community" and exacerbated his doubts in the value of his "literary property," the remaining foundation of his identity (195, 166, 200). His attempt to create an authoritative artist may have been an effort to compensate for these doubts. If so, then the subterranean parallel between the artist and the young women is inadvertently parodic.

In any case, the final action remains a facile sealing off of unsettling territory; the Englishman's tactic of containment is less satisfying than the artist's attempt at insight. Hedges points out Irving's propensity to conclude the stories in *Tales of a Traveller* with an anticlimactic ending, a "joke on the reader" (161). While the reader does get a climactic ending here, the tale's last words also imply a joke. The representative of domestic beauty embraces the representative of disciplinary power in an emblem of middle-class order and right relations: "'My deliverer! – my angel!' exclaimed she . . . sobbing on his bosom. 'Pooh!' said the Englishman, looking somewhat foolish, 'this is all nonsense'" (207). Irving's last gesture in these tales dismisses as "nonsense" the entire set of questions about the relationships among property, aesthetics, membership in a social elite, and middle-class power. Release from this quandary lies either in the dispersive impulse of humor or in a withdrawal from the contested grounds. His final return to the southern European landscape in *The Alhambra* blends these two responses.

Coda: The View from the Alhambra

Between the *Tales* and his last European sketch book, *The Alhambra* (1832), Irving invested his energies in a different kind of literary property. His *Life and Voyages of Christopher Columbus* (1828), researched and written in Spain, returned him to critical and popular success and marked a transition in his career from sketches and fiction to biography and history (the prose versions of the French artist's history paintings), a transition underscored by his political appointment as a member of the American legation to England (1829–32) and then as Minister to Spain (1842–6).[103] With his social identity no longer dependent on his sketches, Irving is free to experience the picturesque impulse as purely an exercise in wish fulfillment, disconnected from the world of trade and politics, and, by relegating it to vacations from this world, to indulge once more in the "luxury" of the aesthetic gaze. *The Alhambra* constructs the picturesque as a withdrawal from desire, from interaction with the landscape. His Spanish sojourn confirms his suspicion that the painter's effort to compose and integrate the Italian banditti is merely an irrelevant analogy to the workings of a disciplinary society. But the view from the Alhambra also transmutes the anxiety of this alienation into the pleasure of a regressive fantasy.

The elite view from the steeple enacted in the eighteenth-century Grand Tour modulates in two directions in middle-class U.S. culture. In an essay on Cole's painting *The Oxbow* (1836), Alan Wallach describes how the dominance of the prospect gaze became adapted to the needs of the middle class in the 1820s and 1830s; this panoramic painting of the view from a mountaintop represents power both through its scope of vision and through its detailed access to the objects within this field of vision. The tourist's pursuit of such views is a "metaphor" for middle-class "social aspiration" and "dominance." The combination of range and "telescopic" precision is Cole's solution to the picturesque artist's problem of representing hilltop views and conveys a specific kind of supervisory power to the spectator, a mode of aesthetic response Wallach (drawing on Foucault) calls "the panoptic sublime." An intensification of the hegemonic project behind the conflation of the prospect and the picturesque, the panoptic sublime connects domination and integration with the disciplines and institutions which based middle-class power in professions of knowledge and "supervision" (38, 41–2).

On the other hand, Hedges defines the literary sketch as developed by Irving in terms of the anxiety produced by the spectator's awareness of the unbridgeable distance between himself and the objects of his gaze. The "classic example," Hedges argues, is Hawthorne's sketch "Sights from a Steeple" (1830), which describes "an alienated observer's effort to see life"; such an observer aspires to the knowing and controlling vision represented by the panoptic gaze but is "unable to break out of the limitations of a personal point of view" (147–8)[104] and, therefore, to participate in the ritual of vision that binds tourists to their class's perspective. Removed from any class solidarity, experiencing the view from above as a symptom of alienation rather than as a metaphor for control, this solitary sketcher remains paralyzed in a web of uncertainty.

Irving's views from the Alhambra of the geographical, social, and historical landscape of Granada are both panoramic and alienated. At the same time that American tourist culture is developing a confident aesthetic for its particular view from above, Irving's sketches dissolve managerial certainty into dreamlike solipsism. Yet the tone of this "Spanish Sketch Book," as he called it,[105] is not the anxious voice of epistemological doubt but the relaxed voice of a confidant sharing a private pleasure. As critics have noticed, Irving drops such intermediary figures as Geoffrey Crayon, most explicitly in later editions, or the French painter and engages the reader – the "you" of the text – more directly; the object of his amused commentary on tourist subjectivity is a persona closely associated with the author.[106] Irving recognizes the architecture and situation of the palace of the Alhambra as embodiments of the aesthetic conventions that position the tourist with respect to the landscape. He invites the middle-class reader to explore this structure of pleasure and imaginary power with him – "Come, worthy reader and comrade, follow my steps into this vestibule . . ." – and to "Behold . . . a day-dream realized" (63, 39).[107]

From his privileged position in the Alhambra, high above the city of Granada, Irving surveys both the expanse of landscape and the details of human interaction within it. Just as his hotel window in Naples in 1805 was a sign of the framing and ordering principle of the picturesque, so do such architectural details as windows, towers, and balconies become signs of his perspective here. Two early chapters, "Panorama from the Tower of Comares" and "The Balcony," establish this perspective and immediately undermine its accuracy. They present, respectively, the heady scope and the totalizing access to detail of the panoptic sublime. The "bird's-eye view" from the tower includes not only the geographical "panorama" of the plain, its castles, "blooming groves" (63), and surrounding mountains but also glimpses into the historical panorama of battles between Christians and Moors that Irving will evoke in later chapters. The balcony, on the other hand, functions as an "observatory" from which, with the aid of a "telescope," the "aerial spectator" and "invisible observer" gains intimate access both to the "drama" of the streets and to the private courts and "domestic life" of Granada's inhabitants (71). Nevertheless, as Hedges points out by comparing "The Balcony" with Hawthorne's "Sights from a Steeple" (149), Irving emphasizes the fictional quality of the genre scenes he constructs from these voyeuristic glimpses. Although his vision brings him "so close" to the actors below that he thinks "I could divine their conversations by the . . . expression of their features" (71), the actual "conversations" escape his surveillance. Irving "weave[s] . . . tissue[s] of schemes, intrigues, and occupations" (72) to provide the spectacle with narrative threads, but these tissues are invariably exposed as false by his lower-class informant and guide, Mateo Ximenes, who turns Irving's romances into prosaic encounters.

But even as he severs the illusion of knowledge from the panoramic gaze, Irving converts this severance into an occasion for pleasure. The

varieties of physical, psychological, and historical distance from a spectacle and the distortions they create make pictorial order possible. In
The Alhambra the tourist exchanges the quest for visionary certainty,
a quest vulnerable to new information from without, for an acknowledged fantasy of achieved aesthetic order, what Irving calls, during one
of his historical reveries, a "phantasmagoria of the mind" (79). This
is a sketch book in which the integrating impulse of the picturesque
runs unchecked and leads, in spite of Irving's actually well-researched
stock of knowledge about the region, to repeated visions of resolved
antinomies. Every set of opposites raised in the *Tales* is reconciled here
– male and female, wild and pastoral, sublime and beautiful, rich and
poor – as well as a new polarity of ethnic and religious antagonisms
between European and Arab.

Irving distinguishes at first between Italian and Spanish landscapes; Italy is "voluptuous," while Spain is "stern" and "noble in
its severity" (3–4). But it is quickly apparent that their real difference
lies in his changed approach to the problem of picturesque integration. Where Italy becomes an uncomfortable view of incompatible
extremes, Spain is a fairy-tale scene where opposites are no longer at
war but in balance. Irving's pictorial habits in *The Alhambra* resem-
ble Allston's methods of evoking transcendent harmonies.[108] In his
own moonlit landscape, Irving uses the unifying lunar light to blend
the details of the scene into a continuous whole and, so, to escape
the demands of their specificity; he sees "the swelling mountains . . .
softened into a fairy land, with their snowy summits gleaming like
silver clouds against the deep blue sky" and "the vapory Vega fad-
ing away like a dream-land in the distance" (61). But unlike Allston,
Irving believes that atmospheric unity is a sign not of access to transcendent meaning but of the tourist's withdrawal from the embattled
world of competing meanings.

The central image of the Spanish landscape, a touchstone throughout the text, is a similar contrast between barbaric and domesticated
terrain to the one that shaped "The Italian Banditti":

> The ancient kingdom of Granada . . . is one of the most mountain-
> ous regions in Spain. Vast sierras, . . . destitute of shrub or tree, . . .
> elevate their sunburnt summits against a deep-blue sky; yet in their
> rugged bosoms lie ingulfed verdant and fertile valleys, where the des-
> ert and the garden strive for mastery and the very rock is . . . com-
> pelled to yield the fig, the orange, . . . and to bloom with the myrtle
> and the rose (6).[109]

But while in Irving's Italy these poles are antagonistic, in Spain (in spite of such language as "strive for mastery") the snow of the undomesticated mountain range feeds the plains of the pastoral landscape. This range is the "delight of Granada; the source of her cooling breezes and perpetual verdure; of her gushing fountains and perennial streams." The magical cooperation between natural extremes needs barely a human nudge – the slipshod maintenance of some "ancient Moorish channels" (65) – to work. Modern agricultural technology and the rationalization of the landscape are unnecessary. And although these mountains are as infested with "banditti" (6) as the Abruzzi, they are no longer destabilizing forces in Irving's revised vision of the picturesque scene. No wealthy Englishman and hired soldiers are needed to protect agricultural productivity, domestic peace, middle-class goods, or social hierarchy. If the disciplinary basis of social and aesthetic order surfaces in "The Italian Banditti," this foundation subsides again in *The Alhambra*. Mechanisms of control are wholly displaced into the landscape, where fertility and social peace occur naturally.

The historical legends and folk tales Irving includes corroborate the reconciliations enacted in the landscape. Chivalric tales of warfare between Muslim and Christian knights eventuate in mutual admiration, a shared ethic, and periods of peaceful cooperation. Buried treasure turns poor men into substantial citizens. And love stories almost always follow the pattern of bridging enormous differences; a commoner marries a nobleman, Muslims marry Christians, and prisoners elope with their captor's daughters. Irving insists that sightings of such enchanted unions of opposing principles depend on a gaze that is not panoptically precise but partially averted or historically distanced. As in Allston's late *Italian Landscape* (1828–30; Fig. 1.5), Irving blends natural harmony with a social calm based on the suppression of conflict into the past. Framing devices – the tree in the painting and the Alhambra's windows and balconies in the book – together with the harmonizing glow of light or reverie serve as the instruments of nostalgia, delivering to the viewer a distanced but visually accessible image.

The aesthetic perspective embodied by the Alhambra puts divisiveness to sleep and thrusts its memory below ground. The tale "The Legend of the Arabian Astrologer" ascribes the Alhambra's "charm" to a state of suspended animation. After a three-way power struggle among an astrologer, a king, and a "Gothic" princess, the astrologer and the princess – both magicians – keep each other in

Figure 1.5 Washington Allston, *Italian Landscape*, 1828–30. Oil on canvas. Minneapolis Institute of Arts. Founders Society Purchase, Dexter M. Ferry, Jr. Fund. Bridgeman Images.

eternal captivity in a mythical cave below the palace: "[T]he old astrologer remains in his subterranean hall, nodding on his divan, lulled by the silver lyre of the princess. The old invalid sentinels who mount guard at the gate hear the strains . . . and, yielding to their soporific power, doze quietly at their posts . . . so that . . . it is the drowsiest military post in all Christendom" (119–20). The tourist also gives in to this slumber: "Every thing invites to that indolent repose, the bliss of southern climes; . . . the half-shut eye looks out from shaded balconies upon the glittering landscape" (33). This perspective heals contested territories of their conflict; property is not stolen but found, sex is not forced but consensual, and a once-armed fortress is, like Allston's castle in *Italian Landscape*, crumbling into ruin. Just as the moonlight heals "Every rent and chasm" and restores the Alhambra's "pristine glories" (61), so the tourist's gaze stills the scene's narrative movement and permits its harmony.

But Irving's view from the Alhambra is not Allston's transcendent vision, however much his pictorial techniques echo the painter's;

instead he represents the tourist's aesthetic trance as an identity-depleting somnambulism in which he is "'feeding my fancy with sugared suppositions,' and enjoying that mixture of reverie and sensation which steal away existence in a southern climate" (62). In calling travelers' visions "dreams" (276), he is like his contemporaries, but, in cutting the connection between these dreams and the tourist's desire for managerial control, he implicitly questions tourism's capacity for developing an upper-class self.

The following chapter examines the sketches of other Americans in southern Europe in the late 1820s and 1830s; Cooper, Cole, and most of the writers and artists who made the Italian pilgrimage embraced the option that Irving avoids in *The Alhambra*: the faith in aesthetic response as transcendent insight and as a basis for elite identity and cultural oversight. The period's largely masculine tourist culture endorsed the view from above and the integrating techniques of the picturesque as modes of visualizing and, sometimes, reimagining the power relations they left behind them in the U.S. The rescued Venetian lady at the end of "The Italian Banditti" points to the image of Italy that dominated their perceptions: not the Gothic image of outlaws and violence but its opposite – the image of a feminized and idealized landscape which acted as a repository of the values which the commercial and pragmatic U.S. society believed itself to have marginalized. In travel writings and paintings, the errant masculine energies represented by the banditti and their mountainous landscape were thrust into the background and, in a reversal of the Frenchman's scene, framed and tamed by the pastoral and feminine scene of the foreground. Italy, as an ideal feminized image, was not represented as imperiled, as is Allston's *Donna Mencia*, but enshrined.[110] Although the later Irving is a minority voice in the confident project of tourism, *The Alhambra* was nonetheless a more popular and durable text than most; as Rubin-Dorsky notes, Irving voiced widely shared, even if uncommonly stated, anxieties in his American readership.[111] His ability to transmute uneasiness into pleasure may actually have smoothed the way for the large production of tourist sketches to come.

Chapter 2

The Protected Witness: Cooper, Cole, and the Male Tourist's Gaze

> I thought of the singular position of the American traveller in Italy. It is like that of a being of another planet who invisibly visits the earth. He is a protected witness.
>
> Ralph Waldo Emerson[1]

The beginning of the sustained influx of American tourists into Italy – in the 1820s and 1830s[2] – coincided with the peak of what C. P. Brand calls the "Italianate fashion" in England. As travel became possible again after the Napoleonic Wars, this English vogue resulted in a wave of visual and literary representations of Italy and things Italian.[3] The widely diffused nature of the fashion, which spread through elite and popular culture, suggests that the encounter with Italy was a vehicle for the ongoing construction of a national subjectivity. "Italy" represented aspects of experience defined in opposition to "English traits";[4] it therefore helped to define the traits themselves. For middle- and upper-class Americans, at work on situating a national identity with respect to the English model,[5] tourism became a way of furthering a similar cultural project. U.S. tourists entered into the English complex of assumptions behind the Italian journey and replicated the English sense of the tourist as a privileged observer who could comprehend non-English traits without being determined by them. In the journal of his 1833 tour, Ralph Waldo Emerson defined the American perspective on Italy in terms of this model of privileged spectatorship; while surveying the Italian landscape, the alien tourist – the "being of another planet" – remained invulnerable or "invisibl[e]" to its counter gaze.[6] In establishing their "singular position" with respect to Italy, these "protected witness[es]" were conscious of engaging English habits of perception and of their own mixed feelings about identifying with these habits. But while they often resisted British assumptions that England was normative,

American travelers easily adopted the view of Italy as a foil and set up a similar opposition between Italy and the U.S.

In this period Anglo-American tourists approached the difference that Italy represented quite consistently through the terms and ideology of gender; they constructed a feminine Italy as a counterpoint to the normative and masculine world identified with Britain or the U.S. Their depictions of this encounter drew on an analogous cultural opposition of the period: that between word and image, linguistic and visual forms of expression. Associating the visual with the feminine, many U.S. travelers, including James Fenimore Cooper, concentrated their search for the meanings of "Italy" on an aesthetic scrutiny of its landscape. This scrutiny enabled male tourists to displace debates about the formation of an elite American self onto their interaction with the Italian scene. A trip to Italy offered the chance to reconsider and visualize power relations between an elite self and the cluster of attributes assigned to the landscape of the feminine other. Tourists enacted the debate over national identity through their aesthetic responses and by examining aesthetic categories. By reworking the concept of the sublime to include feminine traits, Cooper and the painter Thomas Cole, as Irving tried to do in his handling of the picturesque, formulated a concept of power that was culturally hegemonic rather than politically coercive. Through their responses to Italy, Americans valorized a model of cultural authority based on the ability to create social harmony by enlisting the energies of those traits associated with the feminine and visible in "Italy."

As critics have emphasized, Cooper and Cole are conspicuously active in the work of defining an American identity.[7] Although they are best known for depictions of the U.S. landscape, both spent crucial years in mid-career in Europe and produced works that reflect their special engagement with the Italian landscape. Cooper lived in Italy for eighteen months of his seven-year European sojourn (1826–33), while Cole's three-year stay in Europe (1829–32) culminated with a sixteen-month Italian visit, a visit whose lessons were confirmed by a subsequent trip in 1841–2.[8] The amount of their work on the Italian landscape – Cole's frequent Italian paintings, which he produced steadily for the rest of his life, and Cooper's treatment of Italy in his fiction and especially in his travel book *Gleanings in Europe: Italy* (1838) – makes their efforts a good focal point for analyzing the implications of American representations of Italy. This chapter will first explore the English patterns of reading, depicting, and consuming Italy that most affected American perceptions, then study the works of U.S. writers and painters – predominantly male in the 1820s and 1830s – who worked within this tradition, and finally discuss Cole's and Cooper's participation in the gendered aesthetics of the Italian journey.

"Oh Italia!": The European Paradigm

In 1853 George Hillard, a tourist from Boston, comments on the qualities which different foreign landscapes bring out in their visitors. The Alps are

> stern, sublime, and appalling. . . . The traveller's satisfactions are associated with toil and endurance. He must earn all he gets: he must pant up the sides of the mountain, . . . cross the slippery glacier, . . . brave the cold of icy summits and sleep in lonely chalets. But a day's journey [into Italy] throws him at once upon the lap of the warm south, where he becomes a mere passive recipient of agreeable sensations. . . . [S]tretched listlessly upon the grass . . . an enchanting picture is ever before him. Such scenes, such influences, are not nurses of the manly virtues.[9]

In spite of this warning against enervating "influences," Hillard seems quite comfortable in putting his "manly virtues" at risk; the book that follows this passage is titled *Six Months in Italy*. In describing Italy as a feminized landscape with feminizing effects on its inhabitants and visitors, Hillard is evoking what, by 1853, has become a cultural cliché. Sandra Gilbert argues that by mid-century the "trope of Italy" as a "woman" in Anglo-American culture goes far beyond the convention of representing nationhood in terms of female figures (such as "Columbia") and takes on a more "palpable" and "intensely felt" life; Italy becomes a "seductive" or "maternal" country set against the English "fatherland" (196). This trope becomes firmly established during the renewed British tourism after 1814.

Implicitly defining the Italian landscape as other – apolitical, female, noncommercial, even paradoxically ahistorical – British culture (and northern European culture generally) presents the ritual of "the" Italian journey as an exposure to displaced or repressed categories of experience. This exposure sometimes appears as a risky enterprise in romantic literature and its antecedents, as it does in Goethe's autobiographical *Italienische Reise* (*Italian Journey*,1816–17) or in Radcliffe's Gothic novels of the 1790s.[10] But writers and painters generally cooperate with tourists in controlling their contact with the Italian scene through the aesthetics of the ideal. The early nineteenth-century construct of Italy becomes an easier and more pleasurable "other" to confront than those defined by the oppositions of gender and class at home, oppositions that the tour at once escapes and embodies. The recourse to aesthetics is a complex way of encountering difference; by idealizing the region of the other, by labelling the Italian experience "transcendent," the tourist is able both to contemplate the antithetical and to keep it separate from the mundane.

The dichotomy of England and Italy mirrors the opposing sets of gendered definitions associated with literature and the visual arts in the eighteenth and early nineteenth centuries. To adapt W. J. T. Mitchell's formulation of these definitions, England is the masculine sphere of language, history, intellect, and artifice, while Italy becomes conventionalized as the locus of the feminine and "silent" properties of space, painting, nature, and the body – a place outside of history where temporal motion has ceased.[11] Tourist culture in the early nineteenth century seems governed by a pair of equations between these two landscapes and different aspects of a bifurcated subjectivity: between the rational – and rationalized – self and England, on the one hand, and on the other between an "aesthetic" self, which becomes the repository of marginalized values, and the Italian landscape. England is associated with a rational ideal of language, that is, language understood as an ordering, determining, controlling force. Italy stands for visual experience, often a liberating force whose implications can be suggested but not contained by language. These sets of oppositions are present in the works of both male and female travelers, although they may position themselves differently with respect to this tradition, as I will argue in Chapter 3. But for both the European tour is implicitly an exploration of the meanings assigned to the two poles of experience that England and Italy represent.

The dynamics between these poles are clearly mapped out in two of the texts which most influenced tourist perceptions of Italy: the fourth canto of Byron's narrative poem *Childe Harold's Pilgrimage* (1818) and Germaine de Staël's novel *Corinne, ou l'Italie* (*Corinne, or Italy*, 1807). As critics have noted, these texts informed the consciousness of two generations of English and American travelers and shaped their patterns of response.[12] Cole's paintings, according to Alan Wallach, show an extensive engagement with Byron.[13] He and Cooper used lines from Byron as epigraphs for some of their subsequent, Italy-inspired works.[14] Cooper's remarks on both writers reveal an ambivalent reaction to this predominance; he seems at once to participate in and to resist the cultural program suggested by Staël and Byron.[15]

In both works the male protagonist's exile from England is the sign of an alienation from the normative self that leaves him open to an intimate contact with Italy. In some of the most frequently quoted apostrophes in the history of nineteenth-century tourism, Byron defines Italy in two complementary ways. Italy appears as a woman whose beauty has repeatedly invited military and political rape:

> Italia! oh Italia! thou who hast
> The fatal gift of beauty. . . .
> Oh, God! that thou wert in thy nakedness
> Less lovely or more powerful. . . .

But he also sees Italy as a bereft "mother" of the arts, of religion, and of lost "nations":

> Oh Rome! my country! city of the soul!
> The orphans of the heart must turn to thee,
> Lone mother of dead empires. . . .
> The Niobe of nations! there she stands,
> Childless and crownless, in her voiceless woe. . . .[16]

The "other" that Italy represents is simultaneously the object of desire and the point of origin for, or the "mother" of, the speaker's "soul," the aspects of his identity that seem to have no place at home. The transgressive behavior of Byron's persona in England, implied earlier in the poem, ejects him from the flow of history – "all was over on this side the tomb" (211) – and allows this recognition of kinship with a post-historical, mute, but visually expressive Italian land-scape. Giving a voice to "her voiceless woe" thus offers the speaker a momentary release; he is able to define an alternate "country" or validating context for his non-English self. On the other hand, he perpetuates the image of a passive and silent Italy lying open to the victor's conquest or the traveler's eye, whether hostile or friendly.

Italy gets a voice more directly in Staël's title character, the Italian improvisatrice Corinne, whose Platonic love affair with a Scottish nobleman unfolds in terms of a prolonged debate between British and Italian values as the couple tours the sights of Rome. Their encounter opens with an explicit inversion of British norms as Oswald wit-nesses a ceremony honoring Corinne's artistic accomplishments. Oswald is surprised at this adulation of the arts in place of the cus-tomary adulation of "power and wealth" ("la puissance" and "la fortune") and at the public elevation of "a woman" instead of the "statesmen" ("des hommes d'état") honored in "his own country"; Corinne's apotheosis occurs at the traditional site for the acclama-tion of poets, the Capitol, where she in effect displaces the spirit of politics and history that, along with the arts, is also associated with the spot.[17] Oswald temporarily gives up British habits of perception: "In England he would have judged such a woman severely, but he did not apply any social conventions to Italy" ("Il aurait jugé très sévèrement une telle femme en Angleterre, mais il n'appliquait à l'Italie aucune des convenances sociales").[18]

Unlike Byron's Italia, Corinne does not begin the book as mute or victimized; as Gilbert points out (197–8), Staël is already attempting to reconceive the icon of a feminine Italy as articulate, that is, as incorporating the masculine attribute of expression. But Corinne ends as the picture of "voiceless woe." When Oswald returns to England, he resumes British values, values that Staël presents as admirable: political freedom and order, a strong sense of moral duty, with its concomitant internal repressions, and "the life appropriate to men: action directed toward a goal. Reverie is the portion of women" ("l'existence qui convient aux hommes, l'action avec un but. La rêverie est plutôt le partage des femmes"). He disassociates his Italian experience from his normal life; "The year spent in Italy had no connection to any other period in his life. It was like a dazzling apparition" ("l'année qu'il venait de passer en Italie n'était en relation avec aucune autre époque de sa vie. C'était comme une apparition brilliante"). And when he is "himself again" (the original is stronger: "Il se retrouvait lui-même"), Oswald obeys the wishes of his dead father and marries an English wife.[19] Corinne proves mortally vulnerable to abandonment, is silenced, and dies. Kenneth Churchill notes that the "pattern" of English interaction with Italy as imagined in the literature of northern Europe is one of "repeatedly" failed attempts to establish "fruitful contact with the South";[20] as Oswald returns to what Avriel Goldberger calls "the unredeemably masculine world from which he comes" (xliv), Staël seems reluctantly to confirm that the masculine sphere of "action" in the service of reason and history and the feminine sphere of "reverie" and the arts must remain separate.

In discussing the concept of the aesthetic at the turn of the nineteenth century, Terry Eagleton emphasizes its ambiguous ideological functions within the emerging bourgeois societies of northern Europe. As power moves from "centralized institutions" to the newly defined "independent subject," this subject must be reconstituted so as to internalize "the law" – to act spontaneously in the interests of the political order. To the extent that the aesthetic serves as a consensual tool, it works as an "effective mode of political hegemony." Aestheticizing social relations, such as class and gender roles, naturalizes them. And so, in its ability to produce social harmony through taste and feeling instead of through force, the aesthetic, like a woman, is an enabling "co-partner" to reason, as long as she continues to "know her place." But in taking a "detour . . . through the feelings and senses," in "deconstructing the opposition between the proper and the pleasurable," the aesthetic also draws attention and grants power to the aspects of experience that middle-class rationalism wishes to colonize – the body, the passions, the "imagination" – and so provides the grounds for an equally effective critique of authority.[21]

The Italian journey becomes in Staël's hands just such a "detour" through the senses staged by the aesthetic faculty for the rational faculty – that is, by Corinne for Oswald. If aesthetic response in this period provides, as Eagleton argues, the connecting link between abstract reason and the sensual world, it may be either a vehicle through which the perceiving gaze can structure this world or, conversely, a conduit through which the external can invade or destabilize the premises of the rational spectator. Corinne teaches Oswald to see the Italian landscape, but this "dazzling" vision remains foreign to him, and, to save his identity, which is rooted in the literally patriarchal dictates of his conscience, he rejects the offer of aesthetic insight. The failure of the aesthetic and the rational to marry results in the atrophying of the aesthetic faculty (Corinne wastes away) and in the alienation of the rational from "nature and the arts"; Staël sets Oswald's second trip in the winter when all that is possible is "a kind of unsatisfying flirtation with Italy" ("une sorte de coquetterie qui n'était pas satisfaite").[22]

Staël's novel is at once an enactment of northern assumptions about the subordinate position of Italy to England, women to men, and the aesthetic to the rational, and a protest against this complex of assumptions. Together with Byron, she injects into the tourist's experience an ambivalent view of Italy. The Italian journey releases and idealizes marginalized categories of experience; the tourist enjoys this temporary reversal both in the external landscape and within, as values identified with the "soul" – that is, repressed to the point where the tourist experiences them as deep – undergo a momentary resurgence. The question then becomes what use to make of this kind of aesthetic response, perhaps an especially problematic issue for U.S. travelers, with their iconoclastic Protestant background. As Neil Harris has demonstrated, one American response to Italian art in this period is simply to warn against the "dangers" of its "appeals to the senses." But he also argues that many middle-class tourists instead grasp perhaps for the first time the efficacy of the aesthetic faculty as a "means of engineering consent" and of creating deference for hierarchy in the "unruly" crowds of American democracy; like the theorists Eagleton discusses, these tourists often learn "the uses of art as an instrument of social control" and, when they return home, participate in a "campaign of conservative culture."[23] By embracing and idealizing the visual object, they both acknowledge its power and resubordinate this power to the force of the transcendent idea it supposedly reveals.

Henry Wadsworth Longfellow grapples with this problem during his first extended tour of Europe in 1826–9, a tour taken to prepare himself for the position of professor of modern languages at Bowdoin College.[24] His ensuing sketch book, *Outre-Mer: A Pilgrimage Beyond the Sea* (1835), records both his delight in encountering the religious art and poetry of southern Europe and his careful subordination of their sensual and visual impact – their tendency to celebrate the "bodily presence" of divine figures – to "the contemplation of the sublime attributes of the Eternal Mind" (187). Although he does not want to denounce the "divine arts of painting and sculpture," he points out that "the handiwork cannot equal the archetype, which is visible only to the mental eye." He implies that the spectator best suited to the study of the visual arts is not the inhabitant of the country for whom this art was produced but the educated Protestant tourist; the "enlightened mind" will move beyond the imperfect representations of art toward the idea of "moral sublimity," whereas the "superstitious mind" will remain trapped by the "stained window" of religious art, unable to transcend the "prison" of the material (190–4).

Similarly, Samuel F. B. Morse, a friend of Cooper's and in Europe at the same time, found ways to navigate the conflict between his pursuit, as a painter, of the high art tradition represented by Renaissance religious works and, as Patricia Johnston notes, "the iconoclasm of his own strict Calvinist faith." Johnston explains that Morse's diary during an extensive sojourn in Italy reveals his grappling with the "'propriety of introducing pictures into churches in aid of devotion'"; while "'the effect'" on some worshippers may be "'rightly to raise the affections,'" such images would surely elicit "idolatry" (Johnston's term) in most and thus prove "'dangerous.'" Johnston concludes that "to resolve these . . . conflicts, Morse developed a highly aestheticized method of analyzing and appreciating paintings," promoted "a change in their cultural work from devotion to education," and, by "drain[ing] Catholic imagery of its religious power," helped to move their rightful place from churches to museums.[25]

Nevertheless, the pattern of the tourist's response is often more complex than venturing out of "England" into "Italy" and then incorporating the results of this "detour" back into the ideology of "England." The Italian sojourn offers the chance for a play of possibilities – even a surfeit of sensed meaning – that cannot always be integrated back into the premises that shape life at home, as Staël points out. Nor can the visual always be smoothly subordinated to the word. In his Italian tour, the English critic William Hazlitt uses the same idealist aesthetic as Longfellow does, an aesthetic in which art objects and landscapes function as a rhetoric of sensual signifiers indicating a transcendental signified, Longfellow's sublime "archetype."[26] This aesthetic, however (in spite of Morse's best hopes for the anti-sensual possibilities of aesthetic response), allows for a slide in focus from idea to object. Hazlitt's arrival in Italy (in 1825) creates a shift in the relative status of "words" and "things": "Things . . . are but a lower species of words, exhibiting the grossness and details of matter. Yet, if there be any country answering to the description or idea of it, it is Italy."[27] Italy (along with the stupendous natural phenomenon of the Alps, as Hazlitt quickly adds) is the exception, the place where visual experience fulfills and sometimes exceeds language, where images rank equally with words.

Indeed, Hazlitt's high expectations of the power of images in Italy lead, perhaps inevitably, to a series of disappointing first impressions; art works such as Michelangelo's *David* and *Bacchus* seem "awkward" and "pot-bellied" (220), while Rome's "modern-built houses" and such signs of business as "a stupid English china warehouse" momentarily block his vision of its transcendental meaning. In order to see "Italy," he irritably sweeps all signs of the commercial (i.e. English) "*commonplaces*" (232) of a city like Rome out of his consciousness; only then can he experience the "dream" state (282) in which objects trigger transcendence and art lifts "the soul half way to heaven" (232). His usual strategy in opening himself to the power of the visual is to reorient his consciousness through a reaction to landscape. Ridding a scene of its English attributes enables him to rid his mind of its critical habits. For Hazlitt, as for most tourists, the essential Italian scene is that in which the absence of purposeful activity implies the immanence of meanings antithetical to English traits. An evening stroll in Ferrara elicits this essential vision. Its silent and "peaceful decay" makes Ferrara

> the *ideal* of an Italian city, once great, now a shadow of itself. Whichever way you turn, you are struck with picturesque beauty and faded splendours. . . . You look down long avenues of buildings, or of garden walls, with . . . fruit-trees projecting over them . . . – you turn, and a chapel bounds your view one way, a broken arch another, at the end of the vacant, glimmering, fairy perspective. You are in a dream, in the heart of a romance; you enjoy the most perfect solitude, that of a city which was once filled with "the busy hum of men" . . . [N]o sordid object intercepts . . . the retrospect of the past – it is not . . . patched up like Rome, with upstart improvements. . . . (265–6)

The aesthetic intuition of meaning depends on the cessation of cultural narrative. Hazlitt's description of Ferrara is also a description of the workings of the romantic image – suggestive, motionless, at once open to the enchanted tourist's exploration and yet elusive, resistant to categorical definitions.

Like Hazlitt's prose sketch, visual representations of the Italian scene create a conceptual space of free play that cannot be integrated into the tourist's home world but that also does not impinge upon it. J. M. W. Turner's *Childe Harold's Pilgrimage – Italy* (1832, Fig. 2.1), painted after his second trip to Italy and at the time that Cole was making his acquaintance in London,[28] indicates the romantic sense of excess in the "ideal" Italian landscape. Cecilia Powell explains that the painting is a "composite depiction," in which several locations are merged to present what its nineteenth-century reviewers called an "epitome" of Italy.[29] The figure of Childe Harold is absent, nor does the painting illustrate any specific episode; instead, the viewer stands in Harold's place and receives the visual sum of canto IV (188). Turner exhibited his work with one of Byron's more general apostrophes to "fair Italy!" (16; stanza xxvi). Both the contents and the structure, derived from Claude Lorrain (168), are conventional for Italian scenes of the period.[30] The painting shows a post-historical scene, where past activity, represented by ruins, has given way to a timeless pastoral present; contemporary but generalized peasant figures, mostly women, sit quietly talking or dance sedately at

Figure 2.1 J. M. W. Turner, *Childe Harold's Pilgrimage – Italy*, 1832. Tate Gallery. © Tate, London 2017.

the center of a landscape shaped in part by the ruins and in part by natural formations. Lying on the ground are musical instruments and containers of food, but no signs of labor. The typically Claudean structure of the painting reinforces these hints of Arcadian harmony; a pine tree and the gently rising ground on either side frame the view, and a calm body of water in the middle distance reflects a serene sky whose light casts a unifying golden tone over the entire scene.

The idealizing Claudean structure becomes the preferred vehicle for at once displaying and containing those social and psychological categories perceived as analogous to each other and assigned to "Italy."[31] In his study of tourism, Dean MacCannell remarks on the double-edged character of the tourist's "nostalgia" for the past, for nature, and for societies that seem "outside of historical time." The modern world feels "vulnerable" to this nostalgia – to its own apparently regressive desires. But rather than promote capitulation, this yearning actually exercises "control over tradition and over nature" by recreating them as museums and "attractions."[32] In her popular *Diary of an Ennuyée* (1826), informed by both Byron and Staël, the British writer Anna Jameson identifies English agricultural rationalization with "Civilization" and Italian agricultural inefficiency with civilization's "sworn enem[y]," the "picturesque": "a tidy . . . hay-cart, with a team of fine horses, is a . . . civilized machine; but a grape-wagon reeling under its load of purple clusters, and drawn by a pair of oxen in their . . . ill-contrived harness . . . is . . . picturesque." She controls her nostalgia for the past by recasting it as aesthetic pleasure; Claude is her guide in pictorializing the Italian scene and in enabling her to respond to it by saying, "'How like a picture!'"[33] The Claudean view – with its distancing internal frame and its unifying, tension-resolving light – functions as the structure of nostalgia. Used over and over in paintings, illustrations, and prose sketches, this mode of composition and perception makes the contents of "Italy" available to English and American spectators even as it asserts the gap between them.

Tourists sometimes comment on the exquisitely redundant pleasure of seeing paintings by Claude in Italian galleries. Nathaniel Parker Willis, an equally popular U.S. writer who sketched sights both at home and abroad, says that viewing the Claudes in Rome legitimized his "Arcadia[n]" fantasies of Italy: "I can conceive no higher pleasure for the imagination than to see a Claude in travelling through Italy. It is finding a home for one's more visionary fancies." The traveler's "pastoral" reveries may feel "ridiculous and unreal" until the supporting evidence of a Claude gives him permission to "acknowledge" his "dreams."[34] The Claudean convention permits a safe, temporary reversal of the direction of influence; the aggressively rationalizing mind of the northern observer becomes the passively receptive dreamer open to the power of a feminine, nonutilitarian, and instinctual landscape. Tourists insist on this "willingness to be acted upon, and not to act"[35] as essential to a true experience of Italy. But they also insist on a more cheerful version of Oswald's inability to absorb permanently the lessons of this "dazzling apparition"; their own posture of nostalgia assures them that this territory, with its antithetical but attractive values, is unreachable – in other words, that it does not demand to be integrated into their familiar world. What Hazlitt says in general about travel is especially descriptive of the Italian tour; "travelling into foreign parts [is] . . . like a dream or another state of existence [and] does not piece into our daily mode of life. It is . . . a momentary hallucination."[36]

Strategies of evoking and containing the pleasurable estrangement of travel in the Italian dreamscape moved easily across the porous boundaries of popular and elite culture. Annual giftbooks published engravings of drawings and paintings by both well known and lesser known artists, including Allston and Turner,[37] and thus made possible a broadly shared middle-class set of assumptions about the meanings and uses of Italy. Samuel Rogers, an English writer whose influence was almost as widely diffused through American tourist culture as Byron's and Staël's, was especially effective in presenting literary and visual approaches to Italy together in the same publication and in connecting them implicitly as parallel and complementary products of the same posture of nostalgia. His 1830 edition of *Italy*, a literary product of his tour written largely in blank verse, derived much of its popularity from the illustrations he commissioned; Thomas Stothard contributed vignettes of figures – often women and children – based loosely on the sentimental stories Rogers included, while Turner provided a number of Claudean landscapes which Rogers juxtaposed with his own landscape descriptions and with trains of association prompted by historically significant sites. His marketing strategies targeted both elite and popular audiences with a range of expensive and inexpensive editions.[38] Reissued for decades, *Italy* solidified the conventional response to the south for at least the next two generations;[39] Rogers' lines on Venice (as well as Turner's views) stirred John Ruskin and were still quoted without irony by Mark Twain in *The Innocents Abroad*.[40]

Particularly important for my argument is that Rogers took an active interest in befriending American artists and writers, including Cole and Cooper, and in introducing them to members of the London social, artistic, and literary circles. Cooper commissioned an American landscape from Cole as a gift to Rogers, while Cole mentioned Rogers as one of the bright spots in a depressing English residence.[41] Ellwood C. Parry finds it probable that Cole owned a copy of *Italy* (211). Cooper certainly did; he writes to Rogers that in composing his Italian novel *The Bravo*, "I frequently stimulated the imagination by reading your own images and tales of that part of Europe."[42]

Rogers uses a familiar technique of the picturesque tourist; he splits his experience of Italy into two parts. He establishes the conventionally pastoral character of the landscape, as well as his own posture of passive "ravishment," with his first Italian chapter, "Como"; the theatrical and pictorial scene, where "purple mists / Rise like a curtain" and towns appear "just as Gaspar [Poussin] drew," offers the spectator the "delight" of watching "the peasant at his work" (grape harvest, of course) and, later, of watching women at an aristocratic party: "a fairy queen . . . Led in the dance, disporting as she pleased / Under a starry sky – while I looked on, / . . . Reclining."[43] This type of landscape, with its compositional harmony and its sentimentalized and eroticized class and gender contents, functions in subsequent chapters as a calm place to stand while Rogers experiences the second aspect of travel in Italy: fantasies of past scenes of turbulence – of Roman battles and political intrigue, or of Renaissance episodes of passion. Turner's quiet landscapes operate as part of the text, corroborating the pastoral foreground and so providing a controlling framework as Rogers' imagination travels toward the distanced movement and emotional *chiaroscuro* of historical or sentimental associations. This pull away from the visual toward the play of association, typical of the sentimental tourist, prompts Rogers to add, "In Italy the memory sees more than the eye" (257).

In this polished sketch book the visual and the literary work to mediate each other's impact; the tourist's textually derived "memory" moderates the power of Italy-as-picture, and the illustrations, along with Rogers' own descriptions, emphasize the quiet figures and pastoral scenery that permit the traveler's innocent "surrender" (178) to violent historical associations or to tales of love and revenge. The end of his book brings even the visual aspects of the tour into the orbit of "memory"; Rogers says that his experiences will be transformed into memories that will function as nostalgic works of art. He will "recall to mind . . . scenes" and "Many a note / Of wildest melody" to fend off the anxious northern weather, to provide a refuge "While the wind blusters and the drenching rain / Clatters without" (243). In doing so he suggests that *Italy* will function for the reader as the memory of

"Italy" functions for the author – as a contained and private vision of the enabling antithesis to "England," an opposite whose sight allows the observer to bear up under the pressures of life as one of the pillars of a rationalized, masculine, history-making culture.

"Like Another Wife": The American Response

In the half-articulated iconographical economy of the American tourist, these opposites, once defined, continue to depend on each other for their meaning; "England" and "Italy" become symbiotic, mutually reinforcing concepts, reified by their distance from the U.S. As Nathalia Wright says of a later tourist, "England and Italy composed for Hawthorne twin centers of the civilized world."[44] Cooper and Cole arrive in Europe as part of a generation of Americans engaged in constructing an elite subjectivity in terms of this polarized vision of cultural identity. Central to their theory and practice is a concern with the relationship between viewer and viewed, that is, a concern with genre. The reliance in both media on forms that emphasize spectatorship rather than narrative, landscape instead of history, and calm landscapes instead of active ones, in conveying the significance of Italy derives from the different kinds of authority tourists grant verbal and visual experience – "England" and "Italy."

The American "England" functions as a sort of cultural superego: the locus of a regulative power and authority, at once admirable and oppressive.[45] Cole's often-cited depiction of his "melancholy" in England, where his contact with the English art world and its institutions proved intimidating and isolating, indicates one reaction to this perceived atmosphere of judgmental authority.[46] Catharine Maria Sedgwick comments on the impressive "Order" of English society, an order apparently achieved without overt repression but which nonetheless depends on a "*caste*" system that is "unhealthy."[47] Cooper and Emerson consistently emphasize England's imperial "machinery,"[48] its "artificial construction" that has utterly transformed the landscape, so that even the "geography" is "factitious."[49] Emerson connects this imperial control explicitly with the abstraction of language, which, together with military power, extends English definition into other territories: the *London Times* "by its immense correspondence and reporting seems to have machinized the rest of the world" (21). For Margaret Fuller, writing in revolutionary Rome, English interpretations of events, epitomized in the *Times*, are not only antithetical but hostile to Italy, both culturally and politically.[50]

As Americans move from England, from the logocentric seat of patriarchal authority, toward Italy, they go from "the head of civilization . . . – a country that all respect, but few love," as Cooper puts it (*England*, 308), toward an often mute but visually powerful territory associated with the heart or the unconscious. After he returns to Paris, Cooper writes to the sculptor Horatio Greenough, whom he had known in Florence,[51] of a fellow New Yorker traveling in Italy:

> What has become of the Willis? Is the Eternal City blushing at the honor of his presence. Well, let him wander among her ruins, I am a man of too liberal a temper to envy him, though Italy, Master Horace[,] haunts my dreams and clings to my ribs like another wife. *The fact is*, I do often wish myself on your side, not of the Alps, for that would not satisfy me, but of the Appenines, the naked, down-like, shadowy Appenines – [52]

Both in his joking reference to N. P. Willis's rival travels and in his own indulgence in the expression of romantic desire for the Italian landscape, Cooper enters easily into the discourse of tourism in which this landscape figures as a female body.[53] The experience of this body has its greatest lingering impact on the tourist's emotional or unconscious self – it "haunts" his "dreams." And Cooper finds that this encounter is best described in aesthetic terms.

In the 1820s and 1830s the male traveler feels called upon to identify, however anxiously, with "England" and to understand an Italian tour as a temporary visit to a desirable and complementary other. His relationship with Italy is at once intimate – a "wife" – and distanced, as the necessarily fictional concept of "another" wife indicates. Lifted out of his social, political, and economic environment, he is set down in what Louis B. Noble, Cole's friend and biographer, calls "a painter's paradise . . . remote from the spirit of politics and money-making."[54] "Remote" from the primary demands of his own culture, from what Cooper calls the "terrible *energies* of trade,"[55] the tourist shifts from one language to another, from a language of aggressive analysis to one of aesthetic reception. Looking at Italy is like looking through one-way glass; the "protected witness" does not enter the landscape or participate in its temporal life but passively receives revelations of its "eternal" significance through the medium of artistic insight.

The stance of the invisible, protected witness informs works in both media. Paintings of this period exclude tourists from the landscape and offer the viewer the illusion of being the solitary and privileged observer of the scene. The only exception is the occasional insertion of the figure of an artist, sketching the same scene. In Cole's *The Temple of Segesta with the Artist Sketching* (ca. 1842), his inclusion of himself in the foreground works less to familiarize the Sicilian landscape than to assert its difference, to remind us that he is mediating our glimpse into a "painter's paradise." Only in the 1850s do artists begin to insert tourists into the painted landscape, and then rarely.[56]

Although less uniform in this exclusion, writers pause to compose set pieces of descriptive prose in which foreign presences melt away and leave the real (i.e. ideal) Italy apparent. These pieces often focus on ritual objects of the tour. By the 1820s a moonlight visit to the Coliseum was already a hackneyed tradition;[57] Jameson remarks how difficult it could be to manufacture the solitude of the privileged gaze at such sites. Although the visual impact is "sublime," she says, her experience is substantially marred by the linguistic intrusions, the "misplaced flippancy," of fellow tourists (130–1). Longfellow's pose as the isolated witness of the approach to the Coliseum is both conventional and obligatory:

> The moon is full and bright, and the shadows lie so dark and massive in the street that they seem a part of the walls that cast them. . . . Before me rose the Phocian Column, an isolated shaft, like a thin vapor hanging in the air . . . the ruins of the Temple of Antonio and Faustina, and the three colossal arches of the Temple of Peace, – dim, shadowy, indistinct, – seemed to melt away and mingle with the sky. . . . I saw below me the gigantic outline of the Coliseum, like a cloud resting upon the earth. (251–2)

What the lone "I" hopes for and sees is a disruption of his customary orientation to the physical world; shadows become "massive" and wall-like, while stone structures turn into "vapor," and the most solid and enduring object of all – the Coliseum – is a fragile "cloud" whose visitation to the earth seems as magical and fleeting as the state of mind Longfellow enacts.

This liminal state, when daytime perceptions of boundaries recede and opposites "mingle," is for the romantic "pilgrim" (20) a moment of transcendent vision. The painter Rembrandt Peale, in Rome at almost the same time, gives a more prosaic analysis of the effect of the Coliseum in moonlight:

> The dim light of the moon, which only exhibits the great architectural masses without the minute details that during broad daylight disturb the attention, produces its effect, by merely permitting the spectator to be fully impressed with the simple perceptions of bulk

and proportion. A similar effect is produced by a fog or mist; and
. . . by the device employed by artists of looking with one eye nearly
closed.[58]

Longfellow uses the artist's squint not to study a structure's architectural principles but to induce the sensation of witnessing a numi-
nous presence. His brief detour through the senses (Cooper often
lingers longer on a visual impression) tells him that what ordinarily
seems solid or important are actually the "minute details that during
broad daylight disturb the attention"; at this moment of reversal the
phenomenal "daylight" values of "England" become superficial and
those intuited via the catalyst of "Italy" essential.

The implications of "Italy" raise questions of genre in both media.
When Cole leaves England for Italy he is leaving behind the judgmental hierarchy of the Royal Academy for the informal but more
productive company of other American artists in Florence.[59] But he
is also showing his uneasiness with the English generic hierarchy that
privileges historical painting, whose source and authority is textual,
over landscape painting. Working in Italy reinforces Cole's predilection for landscape; he undermines the language of "rank" to argue
for the equality of these two genres and their practitioners:

> Claude, to me, is the greatest of all landscape painters: and, indeed,
> I should rank him with Raphael and Michael Angelo. . . . Will you
> allow me to say a word or two on landscape? It is usual to rank it
> as a lower branch of the art, below the historical. Why so? Is there a
> better reason than that the vanity of man makes him delight most in
> his own image?[60]

In this formulation, art derived from the silence of nature, from the
other's "image," takes on an authority usually associated with art
derived from written sources, an art which for Cole is potentially
narcissistic. Cole experiences the academic discourse on genre as
an ideological one, preoccupied with power relations. As Mitchell
points out, "the relation of genres [is] . . . like a social relationship
– thus political and psychological, or . . . ideological. Genres are . . .
acts of exclusion and appropriation which tend to reify some 'significant other.'"[61] The dichotomy of England and Italy draws on and
reinforces the separation and mutual reification of literary and visual
arts, but it also highlights the divisions and relations between the
genres within each medium: between historical and landscape painting or between critical and descriptive writing.

This sense of difference also prompts attempts on the part of writers to bridge the gap, to escape the "English" uses of language and to approximate the visual. A. William Salomone comments on the "pristine ahistorical response" of nineteenth-century Americans to modern Italy; in a period in which Americans produced a range of historical writings on other cultures, he notes that "not a single original and influential work was produced in the United States dealing with contemporary Italy." Instead, Americans constructed "an Italy . . . beyond historical time."[62] Daniel Huntington embodies the pictorial version of this construct in his painting *Italy* (1843, Fig. 2.2) as a dark-haired woman in Renaissance dress who is gazing off to our left and is in the act of sketching what she sees. In the landscape behind her, as Otto Wittmann notes, are "classic ruins and a Tuscan bell tower,"[63] twin symbols of the pastness of history and the presence of art. "Italy" is both an object of the spectator's gaze and a model for the tourist's behavior, which, in its openness to visual impressions and its eschewing of the linguistic aggression of historical analysis, should imitate "Italy's." It may be no coincidence that

Figure 2.2 Daniel Huntington, *Italy*, 1843. Oil on canvas. Accession number: 1973.41. Smithsonian American Art Museum. Museum purchase.

the first attempt to write what Salomone calls "a full-fledged . . . piece of contemporary history" (1377) belongs to a woman. For Fuller the Italian journey is a chance to reconceive the feminine and the visual as historically dynamic; the Roman revolution of 1848–9 prompts her to reimagine Italy as an active and self-determining part of an ongoing historical narrative.[64]

Like Fuller a handful of English writers, especially Shelley, saw the antithetical values represented by Italy as the basis for a radical politics.[65] But the predominant approach to reading the Italian scene remained ahistorical and apolitical. Sedgwick indicates the prevalence of this approach and its difference from one's orientation at home when she advises Americans to assume the tourist's posture, whether in Italy or elsewhere in Europe, only if they have "strong domestic affections" or "some . . . worthy pursuit at home." Otherwise they might feel on their return to the U.S. "as one does who attempts to read a treatise on political economy after being lost in the interest of a captivating romance" (*Letters*, II, 193). By reading a feminine text – a "romance" – the tourist can be seduced not only by a feminine presence but into the feminine activity of "reverie," a seduction that is only temporarily desirable.

The habitual disjunction between aesthetics and politics informs the tourist's favorite genre: the sketch book.[66] Like Rogers' *Italy*, such texts as Longfellow's *Outre-Mer*, Henry Tuckerman's *Italian Sketch Book* (1835), and Willis's *Pencillings by the Way* (1835) interweave landscape descriptions with sentimental tales and generalized historical associations that transform the particularities of historical periods into moral or emotional universals. In Longfellow's sketch of the Coliseum, its present silence makes him think of its noise and violence in its days as the "imperial slaughter-house"; he launches into an *ubi sunt* train of reflections, punctuated by Byron's famous line on the statue then known as the Dying Gladiator ("butchered to make a Roman holiday") and ending in a universalizing meditation on mortality: "Where were the senators of Rome? . . . Where were the Christian martyrs? . . . The dust below me answered, 'They are mine!'" (253). Like Longfellow, Willis finds that his "imagination is too disturbed and hindered in daylight" but that a moonlit view of the Forum produces similarly undifferentiated visions of "emperors, senators, conspirators" (64–5). This practice of turning history into reverie reinforces the use of visual response to erase historical sequence.

In his avoidance of such sight-dimming associations, Cooper's travel books are different from those of many of his contemporaries;

as his editors say, "he never allows his recollections to obscure his response to ruins as visible objects in a landscape."[67] But his five-volume series *Gleanings in Europe* (1836–8) also shows a segregation of aesthetic and political approaches. Cooper engages in political and economic debates in Paris, his central home in Europe; Robert E. Spiller has documented Cooper's association with Lafayette during the early days of the July monarchy and his resulting writings in defense of republican values.[68] And these concerns are reflected in his books on France and especially England; as John P. McWilliams points out, they are critiques of "political structure[s]," while his *Italy* "is a work of personal nostalgia."[69] *England* anticipates Emerson's *English Traits* (1856) in its focus on social and political institutions and its analytical language. Cooper turns the "English" tools of analysis on England, and he does so to make U.S. readers more culturally independent of this "father" land; J. Gerald Kennedy argues that Cooper's critique of its "invidious" and anti-republican "conservatism" works to "exorciz[e] England as a possessive presence" from the U.S. national psyche.[70] But he frankly puts political questions on the back burner in *Italy*. He supports, for example, Italian unification, but he confines some of his most considered political comments to the last few pages, after he has recounted his physical departure from the Italian landscape (295–9).

He even continues to separate aesthetic and political functions in his literary uses of Italy. The travel book relates his visual experience of the landscape in pictorial descriptions that value the eye as the vehicle of truth; indeed, he presses the experiment of relying on the aesthetically educated eye further than most British or American writers of this period do. On the other hand, his historical novel *The Bravo* (1831), set in eighteenth-century Venice, has little to do with his visual experience of Italy but is, as Donald Ringe notes, a political parable for the benefit of his U.S. readers – a parable that warns, among other things, against British forms of aristocracy.[71] Unlike *Italy* the novel features abrupt discrepancies between appearance and reality – between what the eye sees and what the mind comes to know – and thus echoes Cooper's exasperation with the "mystification" of such English institutions as Parliament.[72] Cooper assumes that while Italian sites and historical moments may be useful as a stage for the investigation of American and English political issues, the genre with which to confront the essential, timeless Italy is not the historical novel but the sketch book. If northern Europe and the U.S. are now the province of time, of history-in-the-making, then southern Europe is the province of space.

This dichotomy, expressed in thematic and generic terms, informs the painterly gaze as well, which conceives of Italy as a world of delightfully inverted values. After a visit to Italy, Robert Weir composes two representative paintings of American and Italian subjects in 1828 and 1829. His famous portrait of the Seneca chief Red Jacket is at once a heroic image of a marginalized figure and an example of the U.S. appropriation of native figures into its own ideology of energetic individualism; the background of sublime natural forces (Niagara Falls and a lightning bolt), as Elizabeth McKinsey explains, corroborates Red Jacket's identity as a political leader and orator whose resistance to white expansion made him an active agent in the shaping of history.[73] In his *Fountain of Cicero* (Fig. 2.3), on the other hand, Weir depicts a feminized landscape; two women quietly talk as they linger at an inscribed fountain that marks the place of Cicero's assassination.[74] They and the area around the fountain – with its regular flagstones, a dozing dog, and their polished water vessels – suggest a domesticized space within the surrounding ruins of classical architecture. The masculine activity of "statesmen," empire, and oratory is past, and, as in Turner's *Childe Harold's Pilgrimage – Italy*, the women's anonymity replaces the heightened individual identity (of Red Jacket or

Figure 2.3 Robert Walter Weir, *Fountain of Cicero*, 1829. Oil on canvas. Courtesy Berry-Hill Galleries, New York.

Cicero) Americans associate with historically active cultures. Instead of confronting them head on, as one does Red Jacket, the spectator overhears them; they are oblivious both to the classical past and to the present tourist and seem to exist "out of time."[75]

"A Sublimity of a Different Kind": Cooper's and Cole's Representations of Italy

Taken together, Cole's and Cooper's work represents perhaps the most thorough visual exploration of the Italian landscape in the U.S. tourist culture of the 1820s and 1830s. They pay attention to a spectrum of Italian scenes: from those which focus on "Italia" itself to those which, like Weir's *Fountain of Cicero*, contrast the present, feminized Italy with ruins – emblems of a past, masculine history. Central to their efforts is the belief that this landscape is intrinsically ideal, that its composition and atmosphere combine to reveal a transfigured reality. Cooper's comment on a view of Naples serves as a general epigraph to his and Cole's approach to Italy: "That bewitching and almost indescribable softness . . ., a blending of all the parts in one harmonious whole, a mellowing of every tint and trait, . . . threw around the picture a seductive ideal, that blended with the known reality in a way I have never before witnessed, nor ever expect to witness again" (111–12). Italy is the site on which natural ("real") formations seem obviously to validate cultural ("ideal") constructions. Here the contents of "Italy" undergo their most complete transformation and appear to the tourist's gaze in a form that invites intimate contact even as it assures him of his ultimate control over the nature of this contact. The visual approach to "Italy" offers the male traveler access to insights from which he believes his prevailing rational and verbal identity tends to bar him and, through the aesthetics of the ideal, permits him both to surrender to and to preside over what he finds.

Thresholds of Reverie in Florence

Cole's and Cooper's engagement with the essential (nonruinous) Italian scene emerges clearly in their similar views of Florence. Cole's painting *View of Florence from San Miniato* (1837, Fig. 2.4) is both a representation of this "Italy" and a study of the tourist's posture toward the Italian landscape and toward the silence of visual insight.

Figure 2.4 Thomas Cole, *View of Florence from San Miniato*,
1837. Oil on canvas. Framed: 49⁵⁄₁₆ x 73½ x 3⅝ ins (125.3 x
186.6 x 9.2 cm); unframed: 39⅛ x 63⅛ ins (99.5 x 160.4 cm).
The Cleveland Museum of Art, Mr. and Mrs. William H. Marlatt
Fund 1961.39.

This panoramic view is a picture of resolved tensions, of a reconciliation of nature and "humanity"; as Noble explains on Cole's behalf,
Italy, unlike the U.S., offers a vision of nature "after long centuries
of marriage with man" (110–12).[76] The sunset throws a golden tone
across the landscape, natural and artificial, "blending . . . all the
parts in one harmonious whole." The river leads the eye back toward
the setting sun, as though its harmonizing function were the subject
of the painting.

The way in which Cole adapts Claude's structure of nostalgia
indicates his faith in the exceptionalism of the Italian landscape, in
which "the known reality" does not oppose but rather reveals the
"seductive ideal." In composing the painting, Cole stays close to the
detailed sketch he made on the spot (Fig. 2.5). As Elizabeth Ourusoff points out, he does not resort to the convention of the *coulisses*,
"traditional framing devices . . . such as large trees which . . . gave a
distinct focus to the ideal landscape." Instead he uses another "cliché";[77] the most striking addition to the sketch is the wall that runs
across the foreground. Cole jots down the presence of a "wall" on
the sheet of the sketch but does not yet consider it important enough
to draw. In the painting, the wall becomes the visible sign of the

Figure 2.5 Thomas Cole, *Panorama of Florence*, c. 1831 (pencil sketch, right panel). Detroit Institute of Arts. Founders Society Purchase, William H. Murphy Fund. Bridgeman Images.

invisible barrier protecting and privileging the American "witness." Like Rogers' "curtain" of mist, it emphasizes that this transfigured landscape is a spectacle for the spectator's benefit, even as it underscores its inaccessibility.

Unlike Allston, whose Italian landscapes are all "compositions" (that is, inventions), Cole exhibits a faith in the intrinsically "ideal" nature of Italy's physical "reality." The painting's structure and its foreground figures imply this faith in immediate visual access to meaning and mark the dreamlike threshold of this other "planet," which is accessible only to the aesthetic gaze. Parry suggests that Cole may have seen one of Turner's versions of this frequently painted scene (192); Turner's view, engraved by E. Goodall for the 1831 edition of the giftbook *The Amulet* (Fig. 2.6), turns the foreground, with its seated groups and religious procession, into a large part of the scene.[78] Cole, instead, brings us up to the verge of immersion into the landscape beyond. His foreground figures function differently from Turner's; in the *Amulet* engraving, the figures appear in three planes: the seated groups closest to the viewer, the procession, and the two small figures kneeling at the cross on the left. Although

Figure 2.6 J. M. W. Turner, *Florence*, engraved by E. Goodall, in the giftbook *The Amulet*, ed. S. C. Hall (London: Westley and Davis, 1831). Harvard College Library, President and Fellows of Harvard College.

they are all on this side of Turner's wall, their successive distances from the viewer, as well as the communication with the landscape beyond that the open gate implies, make them not only symbolic of the scene's life but a part of it; their diminishing sizes lead our eye into the picture.

Cole's figures are primarily symbolic in their function; there is an abrupt disjunction between them and the "real" people inhabiting Florence, who are merely specks of color in the city's streets. As Ourusoff says, the figures arranged along the wall serve as "an explanatory caption" (18) and mediate between the observer and the transfigured landscape. A monk, a musician playing to two young women and a young man, and a boy herding goats, their presence suggests that the way into this dreamlike visual encounter lies through a meditation shaped by religious belief, art, and pastoral values. They are figurative – representations of the spectator's suggested point of view. Together, the wall and the figures help to define the relationship between the "protected witness" and the contents of Italy. This aesthetic relationship offers the landscape to the tourist but also asks that he momentarily submit to its requirements and permit it to define his subject position. This "detour . . . through the feelings and senses," to return to Eagleton's words, places on him demands similar to those of Huntington's *Italy*. To see Italy, he has to be for a moment like Italy; the male figures on Cole's wall represent feminized pursuits and define the frame of mind through which the observer must pass in order to see "Florence." Such barriers or frames or distancing devices suggest the gap between the male spectator (or the female spectator in a masculine culture)[79] and the cluster of attributes assigned to the feminine other; they also define the spectator's sense of the threshold between rationalism and the aesthetic as habits of perception.

If this painting is Cole's memory of a "painter's paradise," then Cooper's reverie on Florence in "Letter IX" of *Italy* (67–71) is his memory of the aesthetic approach to Italy. He sets his chapter in early summer, when the heat has cleared most foreigners and members of the upper classes, who live in historical time, out of the landscape; their absence permits the timeless Italy to compose itself for the lingering tourist. The Coopers' suburban villa places them in a privileged spectator position: "it has two covered belvederes, where one can sit in the breeze and overlook . . . all the crowded objects of an Italian landscape." Cooper describes a "panorama" of Florence and its environs from a nearby elevation. His "view" includes many of the same elements as Cole's and presents a similar "admixture" of nature and artifice, a harmony made possible by the "sleepy haziness of the atmosphere": "Indeed, everything . . . invite[s] to contemplation and repose. . . . There is an admixture of the savage and the refined in the ragged ravines of the hills, the villas, the polished town, the cultivated plain, . . . the costumes, the songs of the peasants, the Oriental olive, the monasteries and churches, that keeps the mind constantly attuned to poetry." The rest of the chapter explores this landscape from the perspective of a "mind . . . attuned to poetry," or, as Sedgwick puts it, "lost" in the "romance" of the Italian scene.

Other chapters are more characteristic of the sharper Cooper, who follows his enthusiastic exploration of Florence's cathedral with the sentence, "This night I first learned to respect a musquito" (17), and who checks his submission to this conventionally exotic scene by occasional, deflating comparisons between Italy and the U.S. But after one such leveling remark ("The town is as hot as Philadelphia"), "Letter IX" unfolds by the logic of reverie, through strings of sensual responses to sights, sounds, even tastes. For once the language of reverie applies to Cooper as easily as it does to Irving or Allston. As Gaston Bachelard puts it, "The dreamer's being is a diffuse being. . . . The world no longer poses any opposition to him. The I no longer opposes itself to the world. In reveries there is no more non-I."[80] Recourse to the feminine, open-ended pattern of the reverie blurs the boundaries between subject and object.

Like Cole, Cooper is preoccupied with walls, with structures that mimic these sorts of conceptual boundaries or thresholds. His recreation of the frame of mind appropriate to Italy – "attuned to poetry" – arranges itself in a series of glimpses across walls. His villa's balconies overlook a walled lane that communicates with a church; this vantage point offers "rare touches of the picturesque. . . . The *contadini* assemble in their costumes beneath my belvedere." He foregrounds the same kinds of figures that Cole seats on his barrier: figures that represent religious faith, music, and the conventionally pleasant labor of a pastoral landscape. He mentions encounters with "the lower classes," whose songs and dialect he discusses, with religious figures (he has conversations with the local priest), and with a woman – all of whom exist, as MacCannell puts it, "outside of historical time" (77) and in a landscape magically drained of narrative content.

Cooper's acts of "overlooking" and "overhearing" across boundaries play with the dialectic between the dominant eye, which presides over the open Italian landscape, and Rogers' posture of "ravishment," the fantasy of surrender to this landscape. In an episode exemplifying the first stance, he hears a woman singing in a vineyard: "getting on a stone that overlooked the wall, I found it came from a beautiful young *contadina*, who was singing of love as she trimmed her vines: disturbed by my motions, she turned, blushed, laughed, hid her face, and ran among the leaves." In this moment of cultural voyeurism, the tourist's gaze signifies power; the singer does not return his look but covers her eyes and runs. On the other hand, he recounts the experience of watching a nocturnal funeral procession whose "beauty" and music invade and overwhelm him. The Coopers observe the procession from their balcony, in a receptive posture which allows a provisional reversal of power between subject and object: "Lounging in the clerical belvedere . . . we saw torches gleaming in a distant lane. Presently the sounds of the funeral song reached us; and these gradually deepened, until we had the imposing and solemn chant for the dead, echoing between our own walls, as if in the nave of a church." In this version of the tourist's relationship with Italy, the aesthetic experience is momentarily transforming; the music surrounds the spectators and recreates the Coopers' rooms – their vantage point – as a church.

Cooper ends the chapter by moving out into the space he describes in his opening panorama; one of his "dreamy walks" takes him through scenery that reminds him of the backgrounds of Renaissance religious paintings. He and an Italian acquaintance find themselves "beneath the walls" of a hilltop monastery; the gates are open, "yet no one was visible," and they explore this "image of silence and solitude" without meeting any of its inhabitants, much as Hazlitt explored the silent "dream" of Ferrara. Only after they leave do they see, from the road, one of the monks "dressed in his white robe . . . mending a pen at a window." The chapter concludes with this visual focus on the monastery and without any analysis of its significance, which remains suggestively embedded in the scene itself – and in the sequence of "Letter IX" as a whole. The movement of the reverie is from sound to silence, from rural groups toward monastic solitude, from partial contact with the singing *contadina* or the priest to the evocative glimpse of the monk. The essential "Italy" remains that which seems painted, which is primarily glimpsed across barriers or through windows, and which requires the temporary and pleasant alienation of reverie. Wandering across the frame and into the painting is, by definition, not something the art museum spectator can sustain for very long.

Repose, Transport, and Italy's "Beloved Countenance"

In their concern for according the sort of aesthetic experience they receive in Italy the highest status, both Cole and Cooper re-examine their period's aesthetic terms. They give the Burkean sublime, whose energy and violence appear in the U.S. landscapes of *The Last of the Mohicans* (1826) and in Cole's *Falls of the Kaaterskill* (1826), a secondary importance and elevate a definition closer to Allston's, where the sublime is a glimpse into the "supernal source" of all "Harmony."[81] In a late journal entry, Cole puts the case for the "highest sublime": "Not in action, but in deep *repose*, is the loftiest element of the sublime. With action waste and ultimate exhaustion are associated. In the pure blue sky is the highest sublime. . . . [W]e look . . . into the eternal . . . – toward the throne of the Almighty."[82] Unlike the divided skies of many of his American paintings, where moving clouds imply the passing of a storm, Cole's Italian skies are usually clear and calm. In his *View of Florence*, the serene sky remains above the reach of trees and buildings, which neither intrude into it nor frame it, and acts as a benediction on the landscape. While Weir's *Red Jacket* links the "action" of history with that of natural history in its iconography, the "repose" of Cole's and Cooper's views of Italy point to another concept of power.

Cooper interprets his shift in allegiance from one definition of the sublime to the other as evidence of maturation. He contrasts the Italian landscape with that of Switzerland. In returning to the Alps for a second (enthusiastic) visit, Cooper jokingly insists that "the vulgar astonishment was gone": "We have seen too much to be any longer taken in, by your natural clap-traps; a step in advance, that I attribute to a long residence in Italy, a country in which the sublime is so exquisitely blended with the soft, as to create a taste which tells us they ought to be inseparable."[83] Rather than equate Italy with Burke's category of the feminine beautiful,[84] Cooper defines the Italian landscape as an adult version of the sublime.

He explores this fusion of aesthetic categories through an extended visual encounter with the Bay of Naples. His "Letters" from Naples and Sorrento present "pictures" (126) from a number of perspectives – from the water, from mountaintops, from buildings – of this "*'pezzo di cielo caduto in terra'*" ("'A little bit of heaven fallen upon the earth,'" 108). But he also attempts to define "the vast superiority of the Italian landscapes over all others," to distinguish "the commoner feelings of wonder that are excited by vastness," feelings he associates with Salvator Rosa's paintings, from the "ideas awakened" in the elite traveler by the Italian scene, which he compares to a "landscape by Claude":

> I can only liken the perfection of the scene we gazed upon this evening to a feeling almost allied to transport; to the manner in which we dwell upon the serene expression of a beloved and lovely countenance. . . . In sublimity of a certain sort . . . Switzerland probably has no equal on earth . . . but these Italian scenes rise to a sublimity of a different kind, which, though it does not awe, leaves behind it a tender sensation allied to that of love. I can conceive of even an ardent admirer of Nature wearying in time of the grandeur of the Alps, but I can scarce imagine one who could ever tire of the witchery of Italy. (132)

A sublimity which "does not awe" but inspires "love" replaces the coercive force of the sublime with a feminized power whose authority is based on the transformation and completion of nature's body by culture. Cooper compares the coast at Leghorn – a "scene of magnificent nature, relieved by a bewitching softness" – to "an extremely fine woman, whose stateliness and beauty are relieved by the eloquent . . . expression of feminine sentiment" (84). The tourist's "transport" occurs at scenes which suggest that this transformation of nature by "sentiment" is itself natural; nature is the author of its own cultivation.

By insisting on the word "sublimity," Cooper insists not only on the beauty but also on the power of "Italy," an image which "pour[s] a flood of sensations on the mind" (132) and so reconstructs the relationship between the gazing subject and its object. The range of gendered "expression[s]" Cooper finds in the "beloved . . . countenance" reveals this relationship's fluidity: the bay on a stormy day is "a beauty covered with frowns" (139), a sunset sky looks like "the cheek of a young girl" or has "a blush as soft . . . as that of youth" (173–4), while the *refinement* of Italian nature" is similar to that of "the man of sentiment and intellect" (132). Cooper continues to define the "soul" (132) of the Italian other via the erotics of tourism, but in the potentially open-ended play of the tourist's frame of mind Italy sometimes moves from erotic spectacle to a mirror of the self; it has the characteristics not only of a "Venus" (143) but of a "wife" and of the cultivated man. In observing these blendings within the landscape, he seems on the verge of reimagining his relationship to the categories of experience which "Italy" signifies.

To return to the structural opposition that informs romantic tourism, Emerson defines the contrast between Italy and England in terms borrowed from an Italian poet: "Alfieri thought Italy and England the only countries worth living in; the former because there Nature vindicates her rights and triumphs over the evils inflicted by the governments; the latter because art conquers nature and transforms a rude, ungenial land into a paradise of comfort and plenty."[85] These extremes present two models for male American attitudes toward nature and such related categories as the feminine: the English promise of "paradise" through conquest and the Italian promise of paradise in spite of conquest and through submission to a nature that is not inherently "rude" but civilizing. The dichotomy also implies two models for an elite U.S. self: an energetic individualism that exercises power through the direct "action" represented by the natural or historical sublime and a refined cultivation whose power is based on an openness to and an ability to use aesthetic or emotional experience. Cooper's ambivalence toward this question in his American fiction, and in such characters as Judge Temple in *The Pioneers* (1823), turns momentarily into a relieved embracing of the Italian model abroad.

This sense of release pervades his descriptions of southern Italy. As opposed to his Tuscan sketches, Cooper's views of the Bay of Naples often include ruined or superannuated structures, such as medieval castles or Roman "remains" (130), within the serene ascendancy of nature and of the "teeming" (93) lower-class life on and around the bay. The following "fairy picture" mingles the "superb" beauty of nature with the relics of past authority – "old castles" – and with the present "movement of life":

> [S]ailing through an element so limpid that we saw every rush and stone on the bottom . . . we bore up for the town of Ischia. . . . Here a scene presented itself which more resembled a fairy picture than one of the realities of this everyday world of ours. I think it was the most ravishing thing . . . eye of mine ever looked upon. We had the black volcanic peaks of the island for a background, with the ravine-like valleys and mountain-faces, covered with country-houses and groves, in front. The town . . . lies along the shore . . . but [the island] terminated in two or three lofty, fantastic, broken fragment-like crags. . . . On these rocks were perched some old castles, so beautifully wild and picturesque, that they seemed placed there for no other purpose than to adorn the landscape. . . . The whole population seemed to be out enjoying themselves . . . and a scene in which a movement of life was so mingled with a superb but lovely nature, it is indeed rare to witness. (131–2)[86]

The scene fulfills the tourist's dream of harmonized contrast; the clarity of the water heightens Cooper's sense of the clarity of his own vision, in which geological and social differences blend into a composed painting, complete with foreground and background. This is a self-regulating picture, in which "old" military structures have become aesthetic accessories and no longer impose order on their surroundings.

Although he describes ruins in more detail on visits to specific sites, in his larger landscapes Cooper invariably submerges a brief reference to them in a flood of descriptive material drawn from the natural setting and the activity of contemporary life. This compositional habit enacts his desire to see emblems of historical action superseded by and blended into the picture of a naturalized, timeless culture. A view from Naples, in which the eye runs from the "foreground" of the town to the sea in the "distance," includes "objects of historical interest" which give the scene "the semblance of a physical representation of things past, adorned . . . [by] much that is exquisite in the usages of the present" and harmonized by the "drowsy repose" of the natural surroundings. But rather than focus on those objects of the past, Cooper describes the present setting: the color of the water, the "hundreds" of "fishing-boats," and the quality of the atmosphere (111). The submersion of historical structures into the landscape intensifies the "softened sublimity which reigns all through this region" (109) and testifies to its superior, "muted power,"[87] which has absorbed and supplanted the direct force of historical action. In these landscapes tokens of past modes of power are subsumed into the province of the aesthetic; castles "seem placed . . . for no other purpose than to adorn the landscape."

Cole's landscapes with ruins also focus on the immersion of history into art and on the combined triumph of nature and the feminine. He paints a number of views and compositions – that is, both actual and invented scenes – which, as Matthew Baigell notes, juxtapose the crumbling ruins of the ancient empire with the immutable forms of distant mountains; they include *A View Near Tivoli (Morning)* (1832), *The Roman Campagna* (1843), and *Italian Scene, Composition* (1833).[88] In some of these scenes, such as *A View Near Tivoli* (Fig. 2.7), Cole augments the commentary provided by the background mountains with a foreground of female figures and male figures engaged in pastoral activity. In this view Cole punctuates the ruined arch of an aqueduct and a still-usable bridge with two male figures and frames them with two women, dressed in the same red and white peasant costume. These women represent the "eternal" values of maternity and pastoralism; they accompany a child and a herd of goats. They have just passed through this architectural site and, with their backs to it, are moving toward the edges of the pic-

Figure 2.7 Thomas Cole, *A View Near Tivoli (Morning)*, 1832. Oil on canvas. 14¾ x 23⅛ ins (37.5 x 58.7 cm). Rogers Fund, 1903 (03.27). The Metropolitan Museum of Art. Image copyright © The Metropolitan Museum of Art. Image source: Art Resource, New York.

ture; their upraised arms point off the sides of the canvas. None of the figures is engaged by the ruins; the man on the bridge is looking at the mountains, while a couple on the far left is walking away into the distance. The ruins are the monumental focus of the painting, but Cole emphasizes the impermanence of structures that order natural forces, as the aqueduct once did, or that survey the landscape, the erstwhile function of the watchtower on its top.[89]

He also paints a series of compositions which contrast the masculine past and the feminine present in settings that are more intimate in scope. These works, as Bruce Chambers argues, include medieval ruins as emblems of a past military and temporal "authority" which no longer controls the lives of the "shepherds, wayfarers, washerwomen" who appear in the landscape. Cole's frequent insertion of shrines in these paintings indicates his faith in the presence of a divine, "higher authority."[90] The figures customarily kneeling at shrines in American images are peasant women; this convention includes both such paintings as Morse's *Chapel of the Virgin at Subiaco* (1830, Fig. 2.8) and such illustrations as *The Shrine* (1841, Fig. 2.9), the

Figure 2.8 Samuel F. B. Morse, *Chapel of the Virgin at Subiaco*, 1830. Oil on canvas. Worcester Art Museum, Massachusetts. Bridgeman Images.

Figure 2.9 P. Williams, *The Shrine*, engraved by G. B. Ellis, frontispiece to the annual *Friendship's Offering* (Philadelphia: Marshall, Williams, and Butler, 1841). Harvard College Library, President and Fellows of Harvard College.

frontispiece of the annual *Friendship's Offering*.[91] In these works male figures are sometimes behind the figures of the women – slightly removed from the focus of the picture. Morse revised his initial oil study by inserting the praying *contadina* and by using Allston's glazing techniques, as William Kloss notes, to cast an idealizing light over the scene.[92] Cole also combined a transfiguring atmosphere with a praying female figure in paintings such as *Italian Landscape (The Vesper Hymn)* (1838–9), which at once depicts the iconophilia of a feminized religion and recreates the scene itself as an icon for the American art worshipper.[93]

In *An Italian Autumn* (1844, Fig. 2.10), however, Cole puts a goatherd in the position of the worshipper at the shrine (a painting of the Madonna and Child), and places a woman and child, who echo the subject matter of the shrine, on a bridge in the middle distance. The painting's structures are signs of the disintegration of centralized power; the three towers are fragments of a fortified complex of buildings whose center is now a luminous void. Goats ignore the heraldic

Figure 2.10 Thomas Cole, *An Italian Autumn*, 1844. Oil on canvas.
32⅛ x 48½ ins (81.6 x 123.19 cm). Gift of Martha C. Karolik for the
M. and M. Karolik Collection of American Paintings, 1815–1865,
and bequest of Helen Wood Bauman, by exchange, 1989.229.
Museum of Fine Arts, Boston. Photograph © 2018 Museum of
Fine Arts, Boston.

emblem over the main entrance, and the fallen arches of the stone
bridge have given way to improvised wooden spans that can bear
only the light pastoral traffic of the present rather than the armed
retinues of the medieval past. The light of the setting sun pierces the
ruined towers, to which most of the figures have their backs, as it
streams toward the image on the shrine. The painting shows the full
absorption of the masculine presence into the feminine landscape
and into the feminine posture of spontaneous religious devotion, just
as it shows nature's absorption of the ruins of "the terrible *energies*"
of the past, to use Cooper's language.

"The fairest panoramas of earth": Vision and Mastery

But even as the contents of their scenes celebrate this absorption, their
mode of seeing, of establishing their position with respect to these contents, increasingly moves toward the opposite: the dominant stance
of a totalizing comprehension. In their depictions of Italy Cole and

Cooper draw on the supervisory mode of seeing that Irving questions in *The Alhambra*. Unlike Irving they sense no gap between vision and knowledge; their later works, especially, represent the unproblematic visual access to the scene that results in the empowering moment of the "panoptic sublime," to return to Alan Wallach's term.[94] Rather than Irving's "doze" of pleasurable alienation, the "drowsy repose" of their landscapes signals a trance of clarity, a fulfilled dream of unmediated insight. Two panoramic scenes of the 1840s codify this panoptic command of Italian geography and embody sustained reflections on the relationship between the U.S. spectator and this geography: Cole's painting *Mount Etna* and a lengthy landscape description in Cooper's *The Wing-and-Wing*, which has this piece of tourist writing at its center.

Cole's monumental (6½ by 10 feet) *Mount Etna from Taormina, Sicily* (1843, Fig. 2.11), painted after his second trip, uses the ruins in the foreground much as he used the wall in his *View of Florence*: as a contemplative threshold between the spectator and the domesticated landscape of the middle distance, which gives way to the transcendent mountain in the background. But this view, which

Figure 2.11 Thomas Cole, *Mount Etna from Taormina*, 1843. Oil on canvas. 78⅝ x 120⅝ ins (199.70 x 306.39 cm). Purchased by Daniel Wadsworth, 1844.6. The Wadsworth Atheneum Museum of Art. Photograph: Allen Phillips/Wadsworth Atheneum.

Cole painted six times,[95] awards the viewer a fuller scope of power over "Italy" than do his earlier paintings. As Parry explains, Cole intended it for public exhibition in New York and accompanied it with a geographical and historical description – "the kind of thing one might find in a pamphlet purchased at the door of a Panorama" (294). Nineteenth-century panoramas were forms of public entertainment, either enormous circular paintings (viewed from a central platform) or moving sequences of large-scale scenes (unrolled before an audience): cityscapes (e.g. London), spectacular landscapes (the length of the Mississippi), or significant events (the Battle of Waterloo). Combining edification with pleasure, they offered an apparently unlimited scope of visual access to urban, natural, and imperial worlds for a broad popular audience.[96] A "signature" form of nineteenth-century culture, as Bernard Comment says,[97] the panorama democratized previously privileged ways of looking and opened up the gaze of knowledge and conceptual ownership to a wide cross section of middle- and working-class spectators.[98]

Art historians have explored the impact of panoramic ways of seeing on U.S. landscape paintings, especially the conjunction of scope of vision with detailed access.[99] As Wallach notes, the "panoramic convention expanded upon the prospect" in mid-century paintings that took "visual possession of vast stretches of terrain," a celebration of Manifest Destiny, he argues, about which Cole was "ambivalent."[100] *Mount Etna from Taormina* draws on these conventions even as what is possessed is not territory but subjectivity. Unlike the wall in *View of Florence*, the foreground ruins of a Greek amphitheater signify the historical depth of the vista, an analogy to its visual depth; perhaps like the railing that separated the circular panorama viewer from the scene, the ruins also stabilize the viewer's gaze into its otherwise vertiginous geographical depths. The lower-class male figure in the foreground, unlike the earlier threshold figures, signifies not reverie but merely the fallen Italian present, a contrast to the classical ruins. The tourist's exhilaratingly penetrating grasp of the scene includes the village seen above the ruins on the right, the road snaking along the coast below, the agricultural area it approaches, and even individual sails on the bay. Such a work combines the haze of ideality with panoptic precision and incorporates the tourist's reverie into a larger pattern of response. This pattern returns the power of the scene – of its dizzying geographical and historical scope – to the spectator and locates this power within the tourist's comprehending gaze. The ability to lose oneself in reverie in this landscape (or in contemplation of this painting) results in the finding and possession of a capacious cultivated interiority – as much the subject of the painting as Mount Etna is – a subjectivity that authorizes viewers to represent and shape their national culture at home.

In both the composition and its accompanying description, Cole emphasizes a tripartite division of the scene; the foreground ruins represent the past, the pastoral middle distance is the present, and the mountain represents the eternal. By disentangling the tokens of past and present often blended in images of Italy, Cole shapes these elements into a narrative whose meaning he articulates in a two-part essay, "Sicilian Scenery and Antiquities," published in the *Knicker-bocker* in early 1844, while *Etna* was on public display. Looking from another site of antiquities, Cole composes a similar scene:

> From this deserted citadel, . . . the eye embraces the whole site of the once populous Syracuse; and what does it behold? . . . [A] desert of rocky hills, a goat-herd, and a few straggling goats. Turning away from the melancholy scene, we behold afar off the snow-clad Aetna. What a contrast is this . . .! *That* is the work of God! Since its huge pyramid arose, nation after nation has possessed its fertile slopes. . . . [B]ut the roar of the battle is past; the chariot and the charioteer are mingled in the dust.

Cole structures his scene as a narrative of human mutability, a contrast between ruins indicating the rise and fall of human empires and the natural sign of a transcendent God. And, as he does in his series of the 1830s, *The Course of Empire*, he applies the "deep lessons" of the scene to the U.S. He argues for the building of permanent cultural monuments and the pursuit of "virtue," religion, and the arts in place of the pursuit of gain and the lapse into "pride" and "vice" that imperil empires.[101] As cultural historians have pointed out, Cole's "politics became strongly anti-Jacksonian, in line with the views of most of New York's gentlemen of property and standing," that is, with the class of many of his patrons.[102] In *Etna* the ruins in the foreground provide a palimpsest of history; as Cole says in his pamphlet, this was a Greek theater, modified by the Romans, later a "Saracenic Palace and Fortress, and more recently the Villa of a Sicilian Noble" (Parry 294). This compressed survey of history becomes a contemplative threshold over which the spectator views the "smiling" pastoral world of the Italian present. The view constructs the viewer as the conceptual master of history and nature; unlike the scene's peasant figures, the central figure and the goatherd (on the right, near the ruins), who represent the region's historical decline and present stasis, the American spectator is capable of interpreting the landscape. The "lessons" Cole draws from such scenes imply that historical agency has passed from the inhabitants of Italy to those of the U.S.; the viewer is in a position to see, to know, and to act – to shape the course of the American empire so that it might avoid the fate of previous nations. The only thing that escapes the U.S. citizen's vision is the divine, of which the mountain is a Protestant marker.

In a similar synthesis of Italy's lessons, Cooper published his most comprehensive picture of the Italian scene four years after *Italy*, in his nautical novel *The Wing-and-Wing* (1842). A panorama of the Bay of Naples at the novel's center enacts a ritual of seeing that reaffirms the class-inflected vision of the author and extends this vision to a wider range of readers. Panoramic views of the Bay of Naples, as Parry points out, whether they appeared as large public exhibits or as privately owned prints, were common by the 1820s; Cole included a panoramic view of the Bay in one of his sketch books (124–5). The exemplary status of the Bay of Naples for picturesque travelers as "the parent of all Ideal Landscape" derived, according to Christopher Hussey, from its amphitheatrical shape.[103] John Conron and Constance Ayers Denne, his editors, explain that Cooper uses this shape as a touchstone in his descriptions in *Italy*; the background of mountains "isolates" the landscape from "the rest of the world" and provides a clearly demarcated stage for the display of the "Arcadian ideal" (xxxvii–xxxviii). In his earlier travel book Cooper revels in his sojourn in the heart of this culturally designated epitome of the picturesque aesthetic, both plunging into the picture and pulling back to see its totality. The panorama in the novel represents a final distancing from the scene and a consolidation of its elements. And, like Cole's *Mount Etna*, it returns power unambiguously to the viewer. Moving beyond the settled gaze of the prospect, this textual panorama enacts the moving eye that recognizes picturesque detail and picturesque local compositions within a broad sweep of geography and, therefore, that represents a more modern form of power.

Cooper sets his historical romance in the 1790s at the time of British and French conflict in the Mediterranean and of the joint emergence of modern aesthetics and modern politics. The action of the novel centers on a French privateer, at the time of Napoleon's invasion of northern Italy, whose fictional activities intersect with a historical episode: Admiral Horatio Nelson's hanging of the Italian Admiral Francesco Caraccioli, a sometime British ally who then fought for the anti-monarchical republican movement in Naples. The novel thus brings revolutionary-era action together with the impulse toward legal and procedural order and with the integrative aesthetic of the picturesque. By placing his panoramic view in the middle of a book about European power struggles at the moment of the emergence of nineteenth-century habits of vision, Cooper positions the American reader as the overseer of the meanings generated by this historical moment and offers aesthetic composition as a strategy for organizing both the social landscape and the viewer's subjectivity.

Readers have noted that the rise of theories about aesthetic response and the elaboration of new technologies of seeing coincided with the rise of the modern nation-state in the later eighteenth century. To return to Chapter 1's definitions of the picturesque, Sidney Robinson argues that the British debate in the 1790s over the nature of the picturesque as a middle ground of aesthetic experience between the wild and the tame was related to Whig debates over the proper definition of "liberty" as a middle ground between "license" and "tyranny." The French Revolution and its attendant questions of liberty, license, and tyranny – of class relations, centralized authority, property rights, and individual rights – served as the context of both debates. Hence the testy nature of the debate over the picturesque, during which one critic accused Richard Payne Knight, a Whig M.P. and a proponent of picturesque landscape design, of promulgating "the Jacobinism of taste." Just as these Whigs helped to lay the groundwork for nineteenth-century liberalism, so they also developed the visual orientation of the newly dominant class. The picturesque emerged, as Robinson notes, congruently with a liberal politics that conceived of national unity as a composition of "contending forces"; by attempting "to arrange the parts of a composition" neither "by tyrannical imposition" nor "by giving up" on "stable composition," the picturesque sought to "reconcile" a "passing world based on . . . static classification" with a new world of "transformation" – the world of the landed gentry with that of a "mobil[e]" bourgeoisie.[104] Landscape tourism and other forms of aesthetic experience became ritualized internalizations of this ideology. The decade of the 1790s also saw the first exhibit of a panorama and the beginning of its popularity.[105] Cooper's description of the Bay of Naples maps out the social and political implications of the transitional aesthetic of the picturesque and of the encompassing vision of the panorama.

Cooper sets *The Wing-and-Wing* in 1798–9, precisely in the late eighteenth-century period of British and American reaction against the French Revolution and of the debate over the picturesque – indeed, of the elaboration of strategies of seeing, generally, on behalf of the citizen. For Cooper this is an important moment in the formation of the U.S. republic, and he uses this moment in 1842 to assist in the ongoing formation of the U.S. citizen. The novel wards off attractive "French" democratic/radical/rationalist/anti-property impulses and, in spite of Cooper's antagonism to the English political system, solidifies "English" picturesque theories of social order. In a sense, the novel enacts a debate between French and English contributions to nineteenth-century liberalism.

The plot of *The Wing-and-Wing* is a subplot of the French and English war at the end of the French Revolution. Raoul Yvard, a patriotic French corsair, and his almost mythical ship, the Feu-Follet (will-o'-the-wisp) or the Wing-and-Wing, harrass English and Italian shipping in the Mediterranean until his love for the pious Italian Ghita Caraccioli leads first to his capture by the British and then to his death in a battle. As he often does, Cooper asks his readers to romanticize and then to abandon what he considers a historical deadend, in this case French revolutionary values. Yvard is an atheist; his rationalism precludes his belief in a Christian God and thus precludes his marriage to Ghita, who will not marry an unbeliever. However, Cooper also suggests the possible recuperation of Yvard's gallantry, individualism, and patriotism within an orderly social landscape in two related ways: through domesticity and through the law. Ghita's presence draws Yvard into Italian territory and eventually onto a British war ship. As in other Cooper novels, there is a trial scene; Yvard is court-martialed by the British for being a spy. But legal mechanisms for bringing the French citizen, here defined as the renegade individual and a threat to property,[106] within British disciplinary order do not work on their own; he escapes. Yvard is eventually defeated by the British. But it remains for Ghita, at his deathbed, to put him, perhaps, on the road to belief (whether he has a deathbed conversion remains ambiguous); women bind men more effectively to the state or to heaven than does the law. As an aspect of Italy, Ghita offers to bind the self-ruling subject to the nation not through external force but through his affective and aesthetic life.

As do Longfellow and Morse, Cooper constructs religious experience as Protestant, as directed to an invisible Godhead; his preface highlights the religious arguments between Ghita and Yvard, who sees a rational order pervading the universe but no personal God. Cooper echoes the language he gives Ghita when he posits a hierarchy of vision with God at the top, an all-seeing being who cannot himself be seen: "the impenetrable veil that is cast around the Godhead is an indispensable condition of our faith, reverence, and submission. A being that can be comprehended is not a being to be worshipped" (vi). Defining Yvard's revolutionary rationalism as a mark of immaturity, he implies a narrative – at once historical and individual – that moves from reason to faith. The French Revolution let "the audacious" loose on a "sea of speculation" (Yvard's element); such prideful reliance on one's own powers of reasoning defines youth:

> few young men attain their majority without imbibing more or less of the taint of unbelief, and passing through the mists of a vapid moral atmosphere, before they come to the clear, manly, and yet humble perceptions that teach most of us . . . our own insignificance, the great benevolence . . . of the scheme of redemption, and the philosophy of the Christian religion. (v)

As Yvard lies dying, a wind clears "all perceptible vapor from the atmosphere" (454) and the sight of the stars, together with Ghita's angelic ministrations, leads him for the first time toward the clarity of seeing what he cannot see: an ultimate authority over him. That is, as the "mists of a vapid moral atmosphere" disperse, the ensuing clarity permits him a view of the limits of human vision; the stars function as Etna does in Cole's painting.

The Wing-and-Wing is almost obsessive in its preoccupation with interpretation, vision, and surveillance. It begins with the inhabitants of Elba trying to read Yvard's ship (is it an English ally or a French enemy?) and with Yvard's masquerade as an English officer. Yvard is tried for spying, that is, unauthorized gazing. Issues of defining national identity through appearance and manner pervade the narrative. These national identities are not fully clear to all participants until the final battle, which includes a microcosm of British imperial forces, including English, Scottish, and Irish officers and representatives of different classes. Yvard's chief collaborator, the New Hampshire Yankee Ithuel Bolt, who seeks vengeance on the British for their earlier impressment of him, fights alongside Yvard's French men. Cooper defines all of them as acting out of their national, ethnic, and regional characters.

These conjoined issues of nation and vision come to a crisis in the historical episode at the romance's center: the execution of Caraccioli, who turned against the king of Naples and colluded with the French, for treason, an execution supervised in this novel by Nelson.[107] In revolutionary times, treason is hard to define, as the English captain Cuffe points out: "as to treason, it is not easy to say who is and who is not a traitor in times like these, in such a nation as this" (224). In late eighteenth-century national and ideological realignments, political acts become hard to interpret. Cooper's panorama prefaces the chapters surrounding Caraccioli's execution and the troubling questions it raises about national identity and interpretation and stabilizes the reader in a position distanced from this episode. This strategy parallels the structure of the book; the year it spans marks the end of the French Revolution and Napoleon's ascent to power, but its opening site – Elba – already anticipates Napoleon's fall, to which the opening chapter refers. Thus both the visual strategy and the historical and geographical positioning of the narrative bracket the French Revolution and its effects. *The Wing-and-Wing* asks its readers to see the emergence of the modern nation-state – including the U.S. – out of the instability of this period and invites these readers to become American democrats who supervise the liberality of a diverse but orderly national landscape.

In presenting "one of the fairest panoramas of earth" in *The Wing-and-Wing*, Cooper positions "the reader" on the water ("at the mouth of a large bay") and conducts the reader's gaze from right to left in a slow panning motion along the entire coastline. In this extended passage, he withholds the names of the places he surveys in order to recover for the reader the sense of a first, unmediated encounter with what has become a hackneyed scene.[108] The description touches on the highly differentiated (and unnamed) geographical formations and human structures of the scene: Capri ("a high, rocky island . . . rendered gay, amid all its magnificent formations, by smiling vineyards and teeming villages, and interesting by ruins [from the time of] the Caesars"), the town of Sorrento, Vesuvius and its surrounding landscape ("The human eye never beheld a more affluent scene of houses, cities, villages, vineyards, and country residences than was presented by the broad breast of this isolated mountain"), the "wall" of the Apennines that "bounded" the plain behind, the city of Naples, the northern coastal region of Baiae ("rich with relics of the past"), and finally the island of Ischia ("a glorious combination of pointed mountains, thronged towns, fertile valleys, castles, country houses, and the wrecks of long-dormant volcanoes, thrown together in a grand yet winning confusion"). Only in the last line does Cooper name the location; this description is "an outline of all that strikes the eye as the stranger approaches Naples from the sea."[109]

This survey of the tourist's estate reveals the essential "Italy": a dreamscape whose overflowing natural vitality is inherently harmonious and thus makes overt patriarchal and rationalist order unnecessary. As opposed to Cole's sequenced historical stages in *Etna*,

Cooper submerges signs of past power and present authority into the "smiling" and "teeming" landscape. His descriptive lists de-emphasize hierarchy and jumble tokens of past and present, upper and lower classes, and sublime and beautiful together into a fantasy of picturesque integration without oppressive regimentation. This theater of vision reveals mountains that are "now wild with precipices . . ., now picturesque with shooting-towers, hamlets, monasteries"; heights that "teem with cottages and the signs of human labor"; and a shore that is "a confused mass of villages, villas, ruins, palaces, and vines." These images of unrepressed vitality, of a "grand, yet winning confusion," are all harmonized and framed by the "distant" "walls" of the Apennines and by the shape of the bay, which allows the "eye" comfortably to grasp the totality of the scene. Order is naturalized and "strikes the eye" of a viewer whose posture of passivity indicates the success of his or her culturally determined projections onto the landscape.[110]

Cooper's "Letter XIV" in *Italy* flags the associations between aesthetic perceptions and class identity that clarify this scene's meaning. As they did in Florence, the Coopers rented a villa in Sorrento from which they could survey the "panorama" of the bay.[111] Cooper describes the view and a series of "excursions" into "the noble amphitheatre of this bay"; the "picture[s]" he sees along the coast are made "perfect" by the picturesque details of boats, buildings, fishermen, and "domestic groups" of children and women. His description of their "costumes" leads him to connect the tourist's aesthetic delight with the static nature of the social picture:

> The pleasure of a residence in such a spot is enhanced by the circumstance that . . . the inhabitants of these country towns . . . seldom affect the airs of a capital, but are mere assemblages of rustics, and not children in wigs and hoops, like those of our small places. Here, the distinctions between a capital . . . and a hamlet are all freely acknowledged and maintained; but the aspiring qualities of our population will not submit to this. (119–23)

Unlike the shifting class identities and tensions of the U.S., the coexistence of Italian classes is easy (apparently) because class identity is thoroughly internalized – as naturalized as the harmonious composition of the panorama's "winning confusion." And the social centrality of an elite – its position in the capital – is unchallenged. Unlike the U.S., Italy features a merging of social and political roles for which Cooper seems nostalgic, however much he argues against an elite's explicit political domination in the U.S. In sharing such views with an American middle class, Cooper relieves the tension between inviting community and retaining ownership of the national gaze through describing this European peasantry, a class beneath both the American gentleman and the middle-class reader and so a class exposed to their shared gaze.

The panorama in *The Wing-and-Wing* not only offers class and ethnic others at which Americans of different classes can join in looking but also indicates, even shapes, the internal composition of the viewer. The liberality of the visual landscape is commensurate with the social liberality of the implied reader. In its liberality, the scene transcends both the law of the English, which needs to suppress lower-class individuals to serve the state (the book is also concerned with the impressment of Americans into the British navy), and the maverick individualism of the French, represented by Yvard, whose lack of faith in a transcendent "being" and predatory occupation threaten this integrated order. In his capacity to see the scene, the reader, guided by Cooper, shares in the perspectives and liberal character of the social elite – capable of seeing a social and aesthetic order that, visually at least, integrates an extraordinary diversity into a composition marked by neither "tyranny" nor "license." Cooper claims this picturesque perspective for Americans.

"Italy" provides the freedom to have dreams of submission to an unregulated, "glorious combination" (*The Wing-and-Wing*, 197) within the assurance that the dreamer retains a final measure of control. During his excursions into the "picture" in *Italy*, Cooper visits the hilltop ruins of convents and from these vantage points studies the "holy calm" of this "Sabbath of nature" and "of man," in which the "sublime" and the "beautiful" are "blended": "I felt as if I could almost become a monk, in order to remain there for life" (142–3). As in Cole's *View of Florence*, the reference to the monk implies the posture of reverie that enables the spectator to enter the scene visually but that also ensures a permanent distance from its contents. These views from above provide the distance necessary to envision the ideal form – "what things might be" – rising out of the compromised reality – "what things are." Cooper equates this visionary ability with the perspective of a cultural elite, a perspective he aligns once more with maturity. Looking down on the landscape from another set of mountaintop conventual ruins, he documents the stages of aesthetic development: "In boyhood my feelings on such places was ever . . . to cull the beauties by . . . approaching them; but, as life glides away, I find the desire to recede increase, as if I would reduce the whole earth to a picture in a camera obscura, in which the . . . general beauties are embraced, while the disgusting details are diminished to atoms" (141). Italy's value lies in its remaining an ideal picture of possibilities for the cultivated spectator.

His remark on leaving the country underscores both his love of this vision and his compartmentalization of it: "I felt that reluctance to separate, that one is apt to experience on quitting his own house" (295). The visual power of this spectacle and its meanings are available primarily to the gentleman and his family – Italy is "his own house." In submitting to this icon he is submitting to the influence of an "other" that is already domesticated on his own property. Indeed, Cooper and his family, on their return home, enacted that domestication of Italy by mounting engravings of the places they had visited, especially the area around Sorrento, on panels of a room divider and, as Hugh C. MacDougall has explained, setting this screen in "the central hall of Otsego Hall, where it could be admired by visitors."[112] In leaving Italy, Cooper is "quitting" the private scene of the "triumph" of nature and the feminine and returning to the public sphere of history and language. But he is also bringing this scene with him as part of the furniture of his subjectivity.

If Irving was concerned with adapting an aristocratic aesthetic to the needs of an American bourgeoisie, Cooper is more concerned with sustaining the connection between landscape aesthetics and the perspective of a landed gentry, albeit a republican one. He returned from Europe in 1833 to his estate at Cooperstown to find that his class and its perspective were losing ground. As McWilliams explains, Cooper's works in the next few years increasingly defend the Jeffersonian ideal of an agrarian aristocracy, whose power and sense of public responsibility is based on landownership and whose social superiority is a natural product of the openness of democratic institutions. His accurate sense that this "American gentleman" and the values he represented – "individual liberty," private property, and the rule of law over the influence of public opinion – were losing power to commercial interests and to a newer version of democracy intolerant of social distinctions informed both his travel sketches and other books he wrote at the time.[113] Blake Nevius has connected Cooper's interest in landscape aesthetics and landscape gardening with his status as "the landed proprietor" whose "connoisseurship" indicates his social authority.[114] Like many of the original proponents of the picturesque, Cooper was an elite landowner trying to imagine the landscape of representative democracy and to shape an aesthetic – a gaze – that could be shared by a broader citizenry. Like other elite writers, such as Sedgwick, who moved away from their parents' Federalism toward a genuine if somewhat uncomfortable allegiance to the more egalitarian politics of Jacksonian democracy, Cooper reconceived of the role of a U.S. elite as social and cultural rather than as explicitly political.[115] In *The American Democrat* (1838), he attempts to differentiate between the "political" and the "social duties of a gentleman"; politically the gentleman has no more rights than his fellow citizens but his rank, leisure, and cultural training allow him a larger, more "liberal" view of the social and historical landscape: "The class to which he belongs is the natural repository of the manners, tastes, . . . and, to a certain extent, of the principals [*sic*] of a country." Thus the American gentleman is the "head of society . . ., necessary to direct the body of society." His direction of the body politic is not political but cultural and is based in the "Liberality" of his vision; he is capable of offering his nation "a high and far sighted policy, and lofty views in general," "views" which ensure that he is "a guardian of the liberties of his fellow citizens."[116]

This far-sighted vision depends not only on its bearer's elevation over the social scene but also on his immunity from being watched himself. In its angry rejection of the invasion of privacy, *The American Democrat* reflects Cooper's embattled position as a member of an older, landed elite in the 1830s and the intrusive quality of the democratic mode of social regulation: public opinion. As Cooper says, "public opinion constitut[es], virtually, the power of the state." The submission of public life to the public gaze is crucial, he continues; the citizen must subject elected officials to "a steady, reasoning, but vigilant superintendence." However, the public gaze should not invade private life; if it does, its leveling effect will destroy the liberal, individual character of the elite: "The habit of seeing the publick rule, is gradually accustoming the American mind to an interference with private rights that is slowly undermining the individuality of national character" (*American Democrat*, 80, 101, 231). Ross Pudaloff has noted Cooper's critique of the invasive scrutiny of the public gaze in his novels beginning in the 1830s; he says (quoting Foucault), "The disappearance of private character is . . . [the] result of the belief of eighteenth-century revolutionaries that 'opinion would be inherently just, . . . that it would be a sort of democratic surveillance.'"[117] Of course, in his insistence that the public and private functions of the elite were separate Cooper was protesting too much; his own language shows the entanglement of cultural and political power at the nexus of vision or "opinion." In his public career as a novelist, he is offering not only to direct but also to share his cultural vision with a broadly middle-class public.[118] There is a tension between his "social duty" of educating the eye of the citizen and his reservation of "lofty views" for his own class.

In a novel published the same year as *Italy* and *The American Democrat*, *Home as Found* (1838), Cooper's characters voice his opinions; newly returned from Europe, they critically survey the natural and social landscapes of New York State, discuss landscape gardening, and encounter a fictionalized replaying of the legal battle over property rights into which Cooper had plunged.[119] Instead of the naturalized order of the Italian scene, the shores of the Hudson reveal an artificiality, a disjunction between human structures and nature that is born out of the twin evils of greed and social ambition; the river is lined with Greek revival houses, the "offspring of Mammon," whose beautiful temple-like forms are subverted by their inappropriate domestic function and awkward placement in the scene. One of Cooper's well-traveled characters finds these discrepancies in "the wors[t] taste" but also believes that the energy the architectural proliferation reveals "shows what might be done with so ready a people under a suitable direction."[120]

Cooper's call for a cultural rather than a political elite to give "direction" to the promising but disturbing energy of the American scene reflects a desire shared by men without property, such as Cole. But his literary return to the Arcadian landscape in *Italy* derives some of its warmth and pleasure in the exercise of the aesthetic gaze from his position as an embattled American gentleman rather than as a social aspirant. He punctuates his sketches with frequent contrasts between Naples and New York City, which are "as unlike as their scenery. . . . One is all commerce, . . . the other all picturesque" (96). As McWilliams notes,[121] the characters in *Home as Found* act out his nostalgia at the novel's end; they plan to re-embark for Europe, especially Italy, and to leave both New York and the fictional version of Cooperstown behind them for the social and aesthetic harmonies of the Italian scene, harmonies which seem attainable only in the private vision of the educated tourist.

Like Cooper, Cole sees Italy as the idealized counter possibility to English and American traits. His sense of the ultimate inaccessibility of this alternative vision may influence his decision to separate pastoral and ruinous motifs and to reinsert them, as *The Pastoral State* and *Desolation*, into historical time in his series *The Course of Empire* (1833–6). As William Vance says, it goes against its nature for an Arcadian scene to be "forced into a narrative."[122] In her influential remarks on "visual pleasure" and film, Laura Mulvey addresses a similar tension between "spectacle" and "narrative"; she argues that the presence of the feminine other as spectacle tends "to freeze the flow of action in moments of erotic contemplation," but that "[t]his alien presence then has to be integrated into cohesion with the narrative."[123]

In the 1820s and 1830s Italy is the place where the male tourist may suspend his impulse to integrate spectacle into the agenda of narrative, where he may succumb to "erotic contemplation."

But the conventions of tourism also provided ways of managing this contemplation without a coercive recourse to narrative. Drawing on the idealizing modes of nostalgia, tourists composed the cluster of attributes associated with Italy into a canonized museum piece which transcended historical contingency. These conventions of spectatorship educated the viewing subject in strategies of responding to the viewed object; aestheticized experience became privatized experience. Contact with the other, however rich and imaginatively varied, was naturalized as private, outside the scope of public life. Once canonized, icons of the feminine other in turn became tools by which "the man of sentiment and intellect" tried to manage the "flow of action" at home, in part by reinforcing distinctions in class threatened by "the anarchic forces of democracy and materialism."[124]

However, this cultural elite also disseminated these ways of looking and being through print culture – through travel books, giftbooks and annuals, children's books, literary magazines and other periodicals, poetry, fiction, and the engravings of landscape paintings.[125] As Cooper says at the beginning of his panorama of the Bay of Naples, "Let the reader fancy himself standing at the mouth of a large bay"; in doing so, he is inserting a broadly middle-class reader into the scene and into the subjectivity it allegedly elicits. As did the visual forms of the panorama, such descriptions offer participation in elite perspectives (thereby both perpetuating and adapting them) to a more broadly defined citizenry. This project informs such group publications as *The Home Book of the Picturesque, or, American Scenery, Art, and Literature* (1852), to which Cole and Cooper – together with other writers (Irving, Bryant, Willis, Taylor, Tuckerman, Susan Fenimore Cooper), painters (such as Weir, Durand, and Frederic Church), and clergymen – contributed landscape views and descriptions.[126] Touring the Italian scene, together with the textual and visual products of the tour, offered a pedagogy of identity in which middle- and upper-class citizens learned to use vision both to encounter and to control difference and, therefore, to confirm their function as bearers and shapers of the American social vision.

Chapter 3

Gazing Women, Unstable Prospects: Sedgwick and Kirkland in the 1840s

But really this prospect-seeing is the most trying experience of the traveler. You ascend innumerable steps, . . . at the top you find a breeze that half blows you away, or a sun that quite bakes you, . . . Then your guide insists upon your seeing certain things which he declares all travelers do see, and he evidently suffers so much if he cannot make you see them too, that out of common humanity you put yourself to great inconvenience in staring, not at, but for, something which he assures you is a town, or perhaps an ocean, but which to you might as well be called a parcel of clothes drying in a meadow.

Caroline Kirkland[1]

In concluding the previous chapter, I argued that James Fenimore Cooper's later depiction of the Italian landscape in his novel *The Wing-and-Wing* (1842) worked to compose a normative subjectivity for the male citizen – the "American democrat" – by making generally available an elite gaze developed on the displaced grounds of Italy and through the mechanism of aesthetic response. Acquired abroad, this gaze would harmonize and preside over the heterogeneous social landscape of Jacksonian democracy at home, that is, it would create an imagined unity in a diverse, often unruly scene. By setting his novel in the 1790s, Cooper revisited the period in which the related nineteenth-century formations of liberalism and the picturesque emerged and re-naturalized these formations. By choosing Italy, so strongly coded as feminine in U.S. culture, as one of the sites on which this normative gaze was trained, he confirmed the association of "Woman, the aesthetic[,] and political hegemony" which, as Terry Eagleton noted, characterized this period.[2] The aesthetic training made possible by the conjunction of the tourist gaze and the Italian site bound the self-ruling subject to the nation through his affective life and, in its further development, certified its owner as a "liberal" gentleman, the cultural guide of the middle class and the particular keeper of his nation's gaze.

If tourism and its expressions were part of the project of forming a national subjectivity through "culture," a project steered by a northeastern elite, then they invited participation by women. As Mary Kelley has said of Catharine Maria Sedgwick, the conjunction of class and gender ideologies in the Jacksonian period engaged elite women in the "construction of culture"[3] and, therefore, in the concomitant construction of what one might call the female American democrat. In the 1840s a number of U.S. women writers traveled to Europe, published accounts of their tours, and thus participated in the first wave of an increasing volume of women's travel writing.[4] To a great extent men and women shared the nationalist and class-based project of tourist perception; women writers laid claim to the authorized gazing the European tour provided, to the membership in the cultural elite which the position of the tourist implied, and to a role in developing a U.S. subjectivity. As Nancy Armstrong has argued, the middle-class woman became the normative bourgeois subject by virtue of her ability to produce her own identity within the province of domestic culture.[5] In addition, as Doris Sommer explains, the emerging ideologies of democratic nations in the Americas required women to be represented as desiring, gazing subjects, whose participation in mutually desiring heterosexual relationships modeled the internal coherence of the new nations.[6]

But the ambiguous place they occupied between being, like the sites they visited, objects of the male gaze and being themselves gazers at aestheticized objects inflected their touristic performances and prompted an awareness of the constructed nature (and the labor) of "prospect-seeing," as Caroline Kirkland puts it in this chapter's epigraph. The white middle- and upper-class woman's own availability as an icon "employed symbolically," as Lauren Berlant says, "to regulate or represent the field of national fantasy"[7] allowed them to reexamine the conventions of seeing and the power relations between spectator and object. Christina Zwarg describes the possibilities Margaret Fuller sensed in the "unstable" position of the construct "Woman": "situated at once inside and outside its ideological formations, Woman occupied a unique site from which to offer a critique of culture, even though the terms of that critique would always be viewed as provisional."[8] Although Fuller's theoretical understanding of "Woman's" position was the most clearly articulated, the two writers discussed here also used the instability of their performance as gazing women tourists to engage in such provisional critiques.[9]

Before turning to Sedgwick and Kirkland, I want to consider them together with Fuller, whose dispatches I will discuss in Chapter 4, in terms of their gendered interactions with tourism's project of creating a national gaze. My purpose here is not to imply a kind of separate spheres of tourist experiences but to insist, as I did in the chapters on Irving and Cooper, on the centrality of gender in the aesthetics of nationhood.

Sedgwick, Kirkland, and Fuller published their travel accounts in another decade, like the 1790s, of emerging national formations: the 1840s, which culminated in Europe in the nationalist revolutions of 1848 and in the U.S. in the Mexican War of 1846–8, an expansionist development of the American national identity which Fuller decried and set in contrast to the republican spirit of European revolutionaries. All three treat the confluence of politics and aesthetics in the tourist's experience. At the time they traveled, they were well-known writers whose works had addressed questions of national identity and gender and who could assume broad audiences for their writings. Her contemporaries saw Sedgwick, especially in such historical romances as *Hope Leslie; or, Early Times in the Massachusetts* (1827), as one of the "founder[s] of American literature," part of a triumvirate of fiction writers, together with Irving and Cooper, who had first given American writing a distinctly national cast and brought it international acclaim.[10] Kirkland was a satirical sketcher of life on the Michigan frontier in *A New Home, Who'll Follow? or, Glimpses of Western Life* (1839) and a magazine editor. Fuller was widely known for her feminist critique *Woman in the Nineteenth Century* (1845), but more widely read through her columns in Horace Greeley's reformist newspaper, the *New-York Tribune* (1844–6).

In addition, all three were deeply engaged in new kinds of periodicals in the 1840s that explicitly sought – and sought to shape – a national audience. Sedgwick was one of the featured "'Lady Contributors'" of *Graham's Magazine*.[11] As Susan Belasco says, the principal "legacy" of its publisher, George R. Graham, was "the national magazine," a magazine that addressed a nationwide, rather than regional or sectarian, readership and that featured U.S. writers: according to Belasco, Graham defined *Graham's* as "'a magazine thoroughly *American*.'"[12] Kirkland contributed to and edited a similar magazine, *Sartain's Union Magazine*, which followed *Graham's* (and others in the decade) in publishing nationally known U.S. writers; I will return to her editorship below.[13] And Fuller's work for the *Tribune* immersed her in what Charles Capper calls the "first national newspaper,"[14] as Greeley in 1841 conceived of his paper's audience as not only based in New York but also distributed around the U.S., and, indeed, the *Tribune* attained a wide national circulation.[15] Their similarly visible status in U.S. print culture and their participation in the new, national periodical culture led them to understand travel writing as part of a nation-forming public discourse. Sedgwick's *Letters from Abroad to Kindred at Home* (1841), Kirkland's *Holidays Abroad; or, Europe from the West* (1849), and Fuller's European dispatches to the *New-York Tribune* (1846–50) simultaneously enact and critique conventions of looking, the dual subjectivity of women as tourists, and the workings of the national imaginary in the displaced arena of European tourism.

Reading these three texts in sequence illustrates an accelerating sense, from Sedgwick's generation to Fuller's, of the ways in which inhabiting the gap between being an "aesthetic subject" and an "aesthetic object" could become intellectually productive.[16] Sedgwick's travel book enacts and examines elite and gendered sensibilities as sites of national subjectivities and, in doing so, makes a spectacle of male aesthetic response. Kirkland's disjunctive text alternates between aestheticism and iconoclasm, even as it moves between canonical tourism and viewing the "sights" of the republican upheavals of 1848 in Italy and France. Fuller's dispatches contain overt critiques of the tourist gaze, analyses of the connections between visual and political forms of representation, and the clearest attempt of any U.S. writer of her generation to intervene directly in the creation of nations in 1848; she tries to hail an Italian nation into being in part by inscribing it into the American, in other words, an international, political imaginary.

For each writer the highlight of her European experience and the most beloved visual object is Italy; Fuller spent the last three years of her life there, while Sedgwick and Kirkland gave their Italian tours a disproportionately large share of their European travel books. Sandra Gilbert once pointed out that the "trope of Italy" as a "woman" in Anglo-American culture in this period led women writers, such as Elizabeth Barrett Browning, to experience a trip to Italy as a recovery of lost aspects of the self.[17] And Annamaria Formichella Elsden has more recently explored American women's Italian writings as an "escape" from national and "domestic boundaries."[18] My interest is rather in the implications that gazing on the simultaneously foreign and familiar body of "Italia" had for women's understanding of the construction of vision itself, and especially of the workings of the tourist gaze. In looking at the feminized scene of Italy, these women reveal an emerging awareness of the socially determined structures of gazing: of, to quote E. Ann Kaplan, the role "looking relations" play in the "formation of subjectivities" and of "the way in which the construct 'nation' implies a looking relation."[19]

Elite women's seeing practices in the mid nineteenth century were both formalized along restricted trajectories of vision and diversified by such emerging fields of endeavor as reform movements and periodical publishing. Art and women's historians have traced what Deborah Cherry calls the "proper targets and suitable situations for a woman's gaze," that is, its regulation and its opportunities.[20] Elite women's gazes increasingly moved beyond a look shaped by and exercised within domestic space to include a series of related gazes – the consumer's, the philanthropic, the aesthetic, the tourist, and what I can only call the editorial – perspectives which extended the legitimate visual field for female spectators and which were shared with male elites.[21] However, sharing gazes with male contemporaries also stimulated their analysis. Joy S. Kasson's study of class- and gender-inflected patterns of viewing statues of women connects aesthetic spectatorship with masculine authority, as "the gaze directed at art is but a variant of the gaze to which women are . . . submitted," but Kasson also documents how participation in this gaze, especially by women, revealed instabilities in the constructions of power and gender themselves.[22] Cherry emphasizes that the "contradictions central to the social . . . construction of female spectatorship" fractured any unitary gaze and triggered multiple "viewing positions."[23] Tourism elicited these socially determined viewing positions but also provided an opportunity for becoming conscious of their contradictions. And it offered women the chance not only to be national icons but also to become carriers of the national gaze.

Like the act of writing itself, tourism simultaneously depended on and eroded cultural boundaries between public and private; it was a privatized sphere of perception and expression that moved in a public orbit and served national ends.[24] Women travel writers were alert to their position in public or private space and to the ways in which touring moved them across the lines between. As Mary P. Ryan has pointed out in her study of nineteenth-century American women and urban space, women "entered a field of sexual objectification" when they stepped into public, a field of vision which identified them as either "endangered or dangerous," "emblems of propriety . . . or object lessons in social differences."[25] And, as Elsden points out, travelers such as Sedgwick also experienced this objectification abroad.[26] But even as they experienced themselves as signs in a visual code whose meaning reinforced the class- and gender-based structures of male citizenship, women also used spectatorship to navigate public space. As Ryan notes, Lydia Maria Child moved freely across class lines in her explorations of New York in the 1840s (she walked both along Broadway and through the Bowery) and published her observations as *Letters from New-York* (1843).[27] Women tourists especially found that using the aesthetic gaze associated with tourism transformed them provisionally from objects of the gaze to authorized subjects.

Art authorized gazing, and seeing others as art authorized gazing at a broad social landscape. These writers followed the travel-writing convention of describing the art objects they saw, often in considerable detail. Sedgwick's response to the "painter's divine art" in a number of Italian galleries is so strong that she places her love of art second only to her love of "home."[28] Kirkland tells the reader that "Art . . . interested me above all else."[29] And they extend their aesthetic gaze to Europe's social scene. Italy is the culmination of this aestheticizing project; as Sedgwick says, "what is *not* picturesque in Italy?" (*Letters*, II, 138). Her first act on arriving in Italy is to sketch, textually, the social view from her hotel window in Turin; her description is similar to those of such male contemporaries as Irving in its detail and its insistence on Italy's essential difference from modern nations, its status as aesthetic spectacle rather than historical narrative. The piazza below is "a stage" filled with picturesque types, stock figures on the tourist's Italian stage: musicians, friars, royalty, soldiers, "*priests* and peasants, plenty of priests." These figures, almost none of whom are working at the time she sees them, seem to be "actors of some poetic dream of my youth," a dream defined in opposition to "life in our working-day world" (*Letters*, II, 21–3). Fuller's dispatches often avoid the plural self, the "we" that is so characteristic of Sedgwick's book and that marks female gazing as a socially sanctioned and circumscribed activity: "I have seen all the pomps and shows of Holy Week in the Church of St. Peter. . . . I have ascended the dome and seen thence Rome and its Campagna."[30] Her phrasing here implies a deliberate assumption of the sovereign gaze of the elite male spectator and is connected to her effort to see and interpret Italian history as well as its art.

Just as it did in male-authored texts, art's transcendent status, in these accounts, often configured aesthetic response as a displacement of social concerns into an idealized vocabulary of perception where they could be at once avoided and managed. And Sedgwick's, Kirkland's, and Fuller's viewing positions, as well as the structure and content of their representations, also drew on the modes of painting and graphic representation which were most popular in the antebellum U.S. and which particularly informed the tourist's gaze: landscape and genre images. However, their texts both invoke and resist these supervisory genres; at times each writer finds ways to distance herself and her reader from such perspectives and, so, to make them available for analysis. In much of her travel book and especially in its most obvious set piece – an elaborate genre and landscape scene constructed out of an experience near Naples – Sedgwick writes from within these generic imperatives and from within the role male writers such as Cooper assigned women, operating almost as part of the aesthetic process itself in the creation of the elite male subject. On the other hand, she also satirizes this same process of making the liberal gentleman in a tale about tourism. Kirkland's text, which embodies a dialectic of engagement with and resistance to the tourist gaze, is striking in its periodic refusal to deliver the conventional, visually encompassing landscape view; in addition, in describing her tour in France and Italy during the revolutionary year of 1848, she pays attention to the struggle, both within the tourist and without, between the lure of icons and the power of iconoclastic impulses as agents in the production of nations. And, as I will argue in the next chapter, Fuller invokes a third characteristic antebellum visual genre – history painting – as she tries to bring Italy into a world marked by agency and by a progressive historical narrative, the world of the nation-state.

Tourism and Visual Subjection in Sedgwick's *Letters from Abroad* and "An Incident at Rome"

In 1845, five years after her European tour, Sedgwick published a tale about touring Italy in *Graham's Lady's and Gentleman's Magazine.* "An Incident at Rome" recapitulates a myth in nineteenth-century culture about the interaction of north and south, one that reverses the northern tourist's visual and economic domination of southern Europe: the myth of Italy's seduction and emasculation of the northern male traveler.[31] The female American narrator hears the story from an English aristocrat, "Lady C – ," as they make a day trip outside Rome. A middle-class English widow encourages her son, Murray Bathurst, in "the study of antiquities" until his obsession turns him away from wholesome present interests, such as sex and money; his utilitarian, mercantile uncle wants him to marry his daughter, inherit his money, and take up a "manly career," but Bathurst wants six months in Italy instead.[32] During the trip Italy comes to feel like his "lover," Bathurst loses his sanity in a fever, disappears into the Italian landscape, and wanders as a beggar. His mother finds him "groping" among the ruins; the shock of recognition restores him to rationality. The tale ends with his return to England, his marriage to his cousin, "a more fitting mistress than Italy," and his restoration to healthful striving in the world of the present: the world of the British bourgeoisie.[33]

This tale illustrates the ways in which tourism produced the modern national subject and, so, serves as a commentary on the tradition of masculine tourist writing mapped out in Chapter 2. Successful tourism entailed an excavation of and libidinal engagement with nationally suppressed traits in the self that were experienced as inhering in foreign scenes; this engagement ideally functioned as a pleasurable disciplining of the self, a subordinating of "othered" aspects of human experience through their aesthetic embrace.[34] Northern European and American male tourists, who defined themselves and their nations through language, through "*logos*,"[35] located these "othered" aspects in the visual image and in destinations, such as Italy, which represented the visual. As language's "unspeakable other,"[36] the image evoked attempts to incorporate it in language and resisted such incorporation.[37] "An Incident at Rome" associates Bathurst's antiquarian impulses with the excavation of un-English characteristics in himself; his succumbing to these characteristics, rather than completing the ritual of subordination and integration, signals the touristic enterprise gone awry and the risk (usually treated comically in travel books) of a reversal in power relations, of the subordinated icon and its associated traits overwhelming and silencing the spectator. Here, the term "Rome" conflates a pagan classicism with Catholicism and associates both with the anachronistic power of the visual, which must be superseded yet contained by the self-determining rationalism of the Protestant, republican subject.

The tale is a useful gloss on the Italian half of Sedgwick's travel book. *Letters from Abroad to Kindred at Home* (1841) participates in the nationalizing project of tourism even as it projects a distinctly gendered tourist consciousness. In her reading of British women travel writers, Elizabeth A. Bohls argues that the double position of these women, participants in the tourist gaze by virtue of class but its objects by virtue of gender, creates "the intimate distance that fractures the female subject."[38] As I will argue below, Sedgwick creates a scene in her travel book that enacts this fracture, that positions her as the observer of aesthetic response in a male alter ego. This scene has the effect, on the one hand, of displacing her subjectivity from center stage and, on the other, of giving her the ultimate supervisory positon: the spectator of elite male consciousness. But this and other scenes also shed light on the role of women in binding the republican nation – and a republican brotherhood – together through acts of witnessing and representation and through the articulation of an ideal masculine aesthetic response. Read together, Sedgwick's book and her tale both comment on the process of elite male cultivation and illuminate the function of elite women in the construction of a normative national subjectivity.

Receptive Men, Sympathetic Women

Like many such accounts, *Letters from Abroad* is informed by the tension between the pleasurable visual submission to the foreign scene and the need to put the "spectacle" of otherness into the service of U.S. ideology.[39] Sedgwick says that what she will miss most when she goes home is the explicitly aesthetic experience of Europe, and especially Italy, and that this experience constitutes the chief risk to Americans. To return, more fully, to her point cited in Chapter 2: "I would advise no American to come to Italy who has not strong domestic affections and close domestic ties, or some absorbing and worthy pursuit at home." Such unprotected exposure may result, on returning home, in feeling "as one does who attempts to read a treatise on political economy after being lost in the interest of a captivating romance" (*Letters*, II, 193). For both women and men the visual and feminine scene of Italy can thwart the formation of republican subjects by drawing tourists away from the symbiotic and nation-constructing activities of "domestic" pursuits and "political economy" back into a pre-modern, pre-linguistic past in which the image dominates and, therefore, renders a rational citizenry impossible.[40] Sedgwick describes her "attachment" to the objects of Rome as "the fond feeling of [a] lover" (*Letters*, II, 221) but criticizes British expatriates in Naples for staying away too long from home: "Life is rather too short . . . to be consumed in mere passive enjoyment!" (*Letters*, II, 272).

Her language, with its opposition of domesticity, commerce, and politics, on the one hand, to "romance," on the other, and its half-humorous warnings of being "lost" in a captivity of the senses, has connections with the oppositions that structure her historical romance of the Massachusetts frontier, *Hope Leslie* (1827). As Jenny Franchot argues, Euro-Americans of her era were engaged with two problematic sites of national identity: the American frontier, with its possibly "contaminat[ing]" native cultures, and an aesthetically imagined but "tainted" European – and especially Catholic – past.[41] As did many of her contemporaries, including Kirkland, Fuller, Irving, Cooper, Hawthorne, and Grace Greenwood, Sedgwick wrote both about the incipiently national community on the frontier and about Europe.[42] Through its doubled captivity narratives, where both whites and American Indians are held prisoner by the other culture, *Hope Leslie* imagines various approaches to intimacy across racial and cultural lines, but the novel finally reinforces racialized national boundaries between English settlers and Native American tribes. This segregation is secured apparently in spite of but also, I would argue, by means of its development of elective affinities between white and Native protagonists.[43] As does the novel, her travel book instates a national subjectivity by means of a temporary affective engagement with the representatives or the scene of an "other" nation, or rather, as with the Pequots in the novel, with what Anglo-Americans would have designated a proto- or non-nation.

Bathurst's captivation by the Italian icon of pre-bourgeois values signals Sedgwick's sense of the greater vulnerability of men and of the rising middle class to the image. On the other hand, Sedgwick's status as upper-class woman enables her to pursue the cultivation that a visual exposure to "Italy" offers through a more sophisticated encounter with the positions of submission and dominance that tourists assumed. Her framing of the story is a strategy that, in effect, shapes the travel book as well. The American narrator and the English teller of the story form a compact of elite women who, themselves apparently immune to Italy's dangers, discuss the extreme version of tourism Bathurst represents. By implication, they extend this compact to the middle-to-upper-class readers of *Graham's Magazine*, one of the leading monthly magazines in the 1840s.[44] This interpretive community is asked to consider the problem of tourism as simultaneously a formative influence on a governing, managing elite and a threat to the self-possession of the members of this elite. By displacing the dialectic between the rational and the affective self onto English characters and Italian landscapes, where it is performed for the benefit of her American readers of both sexes, Sedgwick gives her tale a pedagogical function; U.S. readers are asked to see the English characters as near-equivalents to themselves, as displaced case studies of the promise and pitfalls of tourism in the creation of a national identity.

The promise and threat of Italy involve the whole complex of Anglo-American middle-class identity. While Italy threatens manliness, defined as the ability to act decisively in the public sphere, it also threatens femininity and domesticity; it warps Mrs. Bathurst's mothering and almost denies Murray the chance to start his own family and thus ensure the continuity of the middle-class home. By the same token, Italy is able to enrich the private, interior life of the tourist by showing how one brings marginalized values into the service of dominant ones, the spectacle of the senses, of antiquity, and of Catholicism into the sphere of the rational, Protestant, and domestic self. Bathurst's philistine uncle embodies the expansionist, entrepreneurial qualities Sedgwick would have seen as defining the rising wealthy classes in Jacksonian America; his wealth is founded in imperialist activities in India but remains unaccompanied by the cultural knowledge and sensibilities of the older elite. He represents the new male elite's liability of a "thoroughly *mercantilized*" mind, convinced of the "unproductiveness of all learning" (105). But his nephew is able to achieve the potentially higher, more influential status of the cultured man through his temporary submission to Italy and his return to England, one of the sites of political and economic agency. Having recognized the power of Italian scenes, he has learned to manage his response to them through the distancing conventions of poetry and the picturesque; Sedgwick ends the tale with a quotation that re-encloses Italy within English verse: mother and son can now "look back with tranquil minds, to that 'beautiful region' where 'A spirit hangs o'er towns and farms, / Statues and temples, and memorial tombs'" (108).[45]

In her tale, Sedgwick examines the uses masculine texts found for the Italian tour in addressing a central problem of the modern nation. If the nation-state (to recapitulate the logic of this body of texts), especially the U.S., defined itself as historical, linguistic, and characterized by manly agency, it nevertheless depended on what its culture defined as oppositional traits, especially aesthetic response and affective bonds, to keep its self-regulating and individualized subjects together. As I argued in Chapter 2, the Italian tour particularly was an engagement with the American dreamscape of the feminine, visual, silent, post-historical, noncommercial, and pre-national. The tour offered resources to bind a widening middle class to the nation at home via "culture," that is, literature and art, disseminated by an elite. Opening oneself to "Italy's" influence, cultivating "feminine," aesthetic, and affective aspects of the self, prepared an elite to guide the nation culturally. Sedgwick's two texts create a distance between the reader and this training process, the tale through its ironic treatment of male cultivation and the travel book, paradoxically, through its sympathetic viewing of the cultured man's gaze. *Letters from Abroad* posits the elite woman both as a participant with male elites in aesthetic tourism and as the especially insightful spectator of this practice in male elites. This sympathy, which assumes both identification and difference, together with what critics have argued is the "relational self" often evident in nineteenth-century women's writings,[46] leads Sedgwick toward an understanding of the tourist gaze as a social product, an effect of multiple social relations.

Sedgwick represents her tourist experience and gaze as emanating out of and sustained by a web of tightly interrelated interpretive communities; she traveled with one brother, Robert Sedgwick, and his family and cast her travel book in the form of a journal addressed to another brother, Charles. Like the tale, *Letters from Abroad* contemplates Italy and tourism through the medium of an implied conversation between intimates who share a class identity and who participate in "culture":

> My Dear C., . . .
>   Would that I could surround you with the . . . balmy atmosphere of this most delicious place and transport you to its orange bowers! but since that cannot be, pray, the next time you pass by my bookcase, take down a certain yellow-covered book, "Kenyon's Poems," and read the few last lines of "moonlight," and you will find the poet doing for you what I cannot. (*Letters*, II, 228)

The sensual and visual experience of Naples is multiply mediated here: through her relationship with her brother, through the literary reworking of such scenes, and, at this stage of the trip, through the literal presence of the English poet John Kenyon, whose work Sedgwick cites and who accompanies the Sedgwicks.

Such passages reveal the complex relationship between gender and class in the role of the elite woman tourist, a role Sedgwick consciously occupied. To reiterate Mary Kelley's point, in her generation Sedgwick's class sought to recuperate the political power they lost in the more egalitarian Jacksonian period by transferring their guardianship of the nation from the political to the cultural field. This shift permitted elite women – excluded from the overt political arena – to join their brothers in "ruling" the nation culturally.[47] But her "letters" to Charles also illuminate the function of women *as* the aesthetic principle itself, to refer to Eagleton's equation between "Woman" and the aesthetic – as ceaselessly constituting the national brotherhood by modeling and evoking and witnessing aesthetic and affective engagement.[48] This "letter" brings together the (male) poet, who can best incorporate the Italian image and the emotions it evokes into language, and the brother at home; her own aesthetic response, which she codes as less articulate, is the medium of exchange.[49] Kelley has described Sedgwick's intimate and mutually sustaining relationships with her four brothers;[50] Sedgwick's *Letters* are addressed, I would suggest, to a national fraternity as well, whom she engages in a cultural conversation and whose subjectivity her discourse molds.[51] Her "relational self" is, then, also an ideologically functional self, necessary to the union of the nation.

However, Sedgwick extends this openness to emotion beyond the aesthetic to the social. Even as she supports the aesthetic project of evoking and managing feeling on behalf of the nation, she nevertheless undermines some of the national distinctions on which the tourist gaze depends. Her travel book models scenes of sympathy which clearly locate national identity in affective attachments but which also ask her American readers to identify with elite Italian subjects; she describes social contacts with a series of Italian elites and especially women.[52] The Sedgwicks were connected with upper-class circles of resistance to the Austrian occupation of northern Italy through Italian exiles in the U.S. (*Letters*, II, 31).[53] The letters of introduction they carried from Italian political refugees gave them entrée into Italian society in a number of places; Sedgwick's descriptions of what she sees are often linked with an account of the person showing them the sights and her comments on their host's sensibility and political views.[54] Her conflation of aesthetic touring and political discussions is unusual in travel books on Italy in this period and results in an equally unusual sense of a shared class perspective across national lines; Sedgwick presents a transnational vision of stewardship among the elite with respect to their nations or "the people." She assigns different functions to upper- and lower-class Italians; the philanthropic, aesthetic, and supervisory gaze is shared across national lines by a mobile elite that trains this benevolent gaze on a fixed, picturesque lower class.

One effect of this shared elite perspective is Sedgwick's emphasis on cross-national sympathetic alliances – sympathetic "looking relations" – between elite women.[55] In two scenes especially she shows herself in intimate contact with Italian women who pour out their grief at the loss of exiled, imprisoned, or deceased family members in Sedgwick's sympathetic presence. Here she counters standard tourist definitions of Italy by extending domestic space into Italy as the basis for patriotic and revolutionary activity. Like Fuller, who wrote about Italy during a more active phase of the Risorgimento in 1848–9, Sedgwick asks her readers to visualize Italy as a potential nation-state.[56] She at once re-masculinizes Italian elite men by comparing them to U.S. revolutionaries and evokes the republican connection between domesticity and national agency.[57] These domestic moments modify her aesthetic response to Italian sights and emphasize the connections between political oppression and domestic distress. After touring the exquisite estate of a Milanese woman, Sedgwick remarks to her "hostess":

> "What a happy woman you must be!" said I . . ., "to be mistress of this most lovely place!" . . .; her face changed, her eyes filled with tears, and after alluding to repeated afflictions from the severance of domestic ties by death, and to the sufferings of her friends for their political opinions, she concluded, "you know something of the human heart – judge for me, can I be happy?" (*Letters*, II, 63)

She describes another "*scene*" by quoting from her niece Kate's journal a description of herself listening to the sister of an Italian political exile in New York: "'I came into the drawing room to find . . . Aunt K. [Sedgwick] holding the hand of a lady in black, who . . . was pouring out a rapid succession of broken sentences.'" Sedgwick emphasizes the intersection of politics and domesticity by describing the pain that one sphere can inflict on the other: here the ability of Austrian repression to turn "the sweet streams of domestic love into such bitter, bitter waters" (*Letters*, II, 121–2). And through the evocation of the sentimental, she also seeks to forge affective ties between her American readers and these Italian citizens and citizens' wives, sisters, and mothers.[58]

"The floodgates of poetry and sympathy": Witnessing Aesthetic Response

Nevertheless, such anti-tourist sections coexist with conventional responses to Italy as a non-national, aesthetic space. In Sedgwick's *Letters*, as in travel writings from Addison to Goethe to James, the destiny of "Italy" is to evoke an aesthetic response in the cultivated man.[59] The class and gender structures of the tourist gaze surface most fully in a combined genre and landscape scene she composes near Naples. She sets a genre scene of dancing peasant girls within a large backdrop that is meaningful to the tourist (but not to the girls); its "materials" are an epitome of the romantic Italian landscape and, therefore, part of the American cultural unconscious (signaled by the "dream[iness]" of the scene): ruined temples and villas, Vesuvius, the wide expanse of the Bay of Naples, and the island of Capri "far off in the bay, so soft and dreamy that it seemed melting away while we were gazing at it." A group of children and

"Moorish-looking" teenage girls surround the tourists, trying to sell them souvenirs; their lower-class status, gender, and racialized identity make them available for the tourists' aesthetic gaze. Sedgwick locates the episode's significance not only in the scene itself but also in the response of the man of sensibility, in this case the poet, Kenyon.[60] Her description of his response becomes a case study of the role of cross-racial and cross-gender gazes in the formation of subjectivities:

> Our merry followers were joined by an old woman, . . . the living picture of Raphael's Cumean Sibyl . . . holding . . . a tamborine, on which she was playing [a] wild air . . . and accompanying it with her cracked voice. To this music [a] gleeful bare-legged girl . . . was dancing a tarantella around K – n, who, though far enough from a Bacchus or Faun, has in his fine English face much of the joyousness of these genial . . . worthies. [The] girl danced and shouted like a Bacchante . . .; there were children with tangled locks of motley brown and gold, and eyes like precious stones, leaping and clapping their hands. . . . [A]nd we pilgrims from the cold North were looking on.
>
> K – n . . . [gave] himself up to the spirit of the scene. The floodgates of poetry, and of sympathy with these wild children of the South, were opened; and over his soul-lit face there was an indescribable shade of melancholy, as if by magic he were beholding the elder . . . time, and that were an actual perception which before had been transmitted by poetry, painting and sculpture. He threw a shower of silver among the happy creatures, and we drove off. (*Letters*, II, 267–9)

This scene echoes standard antebellum representations of Italy. Elizabeth Johns has argued that American genre paintings of U.S. subjects, such as George Caleb Bingham's *Jolly Flatboatmen* (1846), focused on the lower-class male figures with whom the middle- or upper-class viewer was increasingly asked to share power in Jacksonian America.[61] Italian genre scenes, on the other hand, often placed lower-class women and children, tokens of the lack of political or economic agency, in the foreground and displaced the ruined traces of an active, masculine history – of empire, technological transformations of the environment, or cities – into the background. As I argued in Chapter 2, engravings in English and American giftbooks, annuals, and other publications of the 1830s and 1840s present a timeless, feminized world without modern forms of labor and without access to the transformations of contemporary history; ruins here come to signal not only the history that originally produced them but more fully the pastoral world – the "elder time" – which supposedly preceded and followed this history. The engraving *Tivoli*, published in *The Landscape Annual* (1832, Fig. 3.1), positions, typically, a *contadina* with two children in the foreground, as a conceptual threshold that defines the tourist's perspective on the Roman ruins behind them; the figures in the middle distance are upper-class tourists, the current possessors of the scene(s) of history and pre- and post-history through their presumed knowledge and connoisseurship, a knowledge which does not draw them into the scene and, so, make them abject subjects of its power, like Bathurst, but which affirms their self-possession. Thomas Stothard's *The Fountain* (Fig. 3.2), published in a book known to Sedgwick, who had, as so many touring U.S. writers did, breakfast with its author in London (Sedgwick, *Letters*, I, 78), Samuel Rogers' *Italy, A Poem* (1830), rehearses the tourist's sense that this feminine, "elder" world has superseded the masculine one of military activity and repeats the trope of the hero's

Figure 3.1 J. D. Harding, *Tivoli, The Landscape Annual* (London: Jennings and Chaplin, 1832): title page. Harvard College Library, President and Fellows of Harvard College.

Figure 3.2 Thomas Stothard, *The Fountain*, engraved by W. Findon, in Samuel Rogers, *Italy, A Poem* (London: T. Cadell and E. Moxon, 1830). Harvard College Library, President and Fellows of Harvard College.

tomb transformed into a fountain; a sister, the poem tells us, is giving her brother a drink.

On the other hand, an image from *Godey's Lady's Book*, the most widely circulated family magazine in antebellum culture, represents the Italian "present" – as epitomized by the area around Naples, as it is in Sedgwick's scene and, indeed, in much tourist writing. *Neapolitan Peasants* (1841, Fig. 3.3) accompanies a poem on a festival in honor of the Virgin which enumerates a number of types – the artisan, the "Good Mother," the sailor, the fisherman, and the "maid" – and includes a typical explanatory note: "Nothing can be more picturesque than the groups of peasants. . . . Indeed the whole scene is one of the highest interest as well to the eye of the painter, as to the mind of the moralist who delights in the contemplation of the innocent enjoyments of a happy people." The illustration, again typically, reduces the number of male figures in the scene and places them behind figures of women and children who, together with the tokens of natural bounty they bear (grapes, fruit, a corn stalk, the bowl of

Figure 3.3 T. Uwins, *Neapolitan Peasants*, engraved by A. L.
Dicks, *Godey's Lady's Book*, January 1841: frontispiece. Milne
Special Collections and Archives Department, University of New
Hampshire Library, Durham, NH.

fish in the left foreground), are appropriate objects of the tourist gaze.
This is the world of the visual, a passive, eternally feminized, pre-
industrial and ahistorical world; the crucifix in the background serves
as a token of the distance between the mobile and historically viable
Protestant tourist, who consumes this "picturesque" world as an aesthetic object, and the Catholic inhabitants of this world, peasants who
are contained and determined by it.[62] By showing the losses incurred
by the emergence of the rational self and by at once inviting recontact
with the "lost" characteristics of the visual and controlling this contact
through the distancing conventions of the tourist gaze, images such as
the one in *Godey's* replicated the process by which tourism ordered
affect in order to create the modern national subject.

Landscape paintings of the period subsumed such genre themes
into vistas that are visual analogies of the structure of the tourist's
gaze. To return to the example of the major landscape painter of
Cooper and Sedgwick's generation, Thomas Cole's *Italian Scene*,

Figure 3.4 Thomas Cole, *Italian Scene, Composition*, 1833. Oil on canvas. Framed: 51⅛ x 68 x 5½ ins (129.9 x 172.7 x 14 cm); unframed: 37½ x 54½ ins (95.3 x 138.4 cm). Object number: 1858.19. New-York Historical Society.

Composition (1833, Fig. 3.4) rehearses the motif of nonproductive activity, here figured as dancing, in an ideal landscape composed of different elements of Italian scenes. The genre scenes of the foreground, the dancing peasants and the contemplative youth, whose reflection, as William L. Vance notes, in the pool next to him puns on his reflective state,[63] act as the threshold to a landscape of psychological depth that belongs to the tourist. This is a space of imagined memory. As commentators have pointed out, Cole's paintings often embodied anxieties about the commercial and industrial expansion of the Jacksonian period, as well as the increasing claims on political power by a broadly defined electorate.[64] His *Italian Scene*, with its stable, framed structure (the tree on the left and the horizontal line of the pool in the foreground), its peasants engaged in aesthetic and meditative activities, its decaying, rather than burgeoning, technologies (the aqueduct), and its pointed lack of current political and military activity (the ruined fortress), represents the elite cultural memory of a pre-modern world.[65] The nostalgic depiction of these receding planes of the landscape derives from the elite desire to manage its opposite – the Jacksonian world of instability, commerce, and political struggle – and, together with this assumed conceptual grasp of the modern world, constitute part of the implied consciousness of this elite; the double view of the "past" and the present make up a national gaze, a gaze that also becomes available to middle-class spectators through the training which tourism and aesthetic experience provide.[66]

At the same time that they were creating such images of Italy, painters in the northeast U.S., especially those following Cole, constructed what Angela Miller has called a "national" landscape based on conventions that "sublimated economic ownership . . . into aesthetic proprietorship"; American landscapes presented a "displaced language of visual mastery – a metaphor for other types of control – in which the eye . . . enact[ed] the rituals of power, property, and custodianship by which Americans defined their relationship to the natural world."[67] Tourist paintings of Italy offered a national ownership not of land or economic resources but of interiority, that is, of the scene of the imagined costs of modern identity and, by the same token, the site on which this identity was stabilized and affectively organized. Less concerned with the masterful visual grasp of historical sequence than his *Mount Etna from Taormina* (1843),[68] Cole's *Italian Scene* brackets the contingencies of contemporary history and republican nation-building by conflating a gaze into the "past" with one into a far-off (at least for the U.S.) future, after the fall of empire. The painting conflates pre- and post-national images, an Arcadian scene with the end of history. In doing so, Cole offers a vista into an elite U.S. subjectivity which can comprehend the American present in the broader context of images of pre- and post-national identity, in other words, which is not overwhelmed by the transformations of history.[69] The tourist gaze consolidates an American national subjectivity by at once validating the "feminine" contents of this non-national landscape and relegating them to the realm of the aesthetic, that is, subordinated to the present identity of the U.S.

In her own "scene" (*Letters*, II, 267), Sedgwick is the sympathetic spectator of the elite male tourist's sensibility at work. If "Italy" stimulates an engagement with those nationally suppressed traits in the self labelled as archaic, childlike, or primitive, then the cultivated male tourist is the site on which these "Faun"-like traits are "remembered" and reintegrated into the self-governing modern citizen, whose pleasurable "melancholy" marks the distance in his own internal landscape between the childlike past and the mature present. The paid performance of archaic identities, safely distanced via the mechanisms of nostalgia and aesthetics, is one of the means by which the tourist purchases a modern subjectivity. Sedgwick constructs an epitome not only of "Italy" here but also of the erotics of tourism. The desire of the tourist is less for the teenaged dancing girl, whose tarantella affords him the opportunity to integrate the primitive intoxication of a Bacchus and the lasciviousness of a Faun into "his fine English face," than for the entire panorama of the "elder . . . time," a scene which simultaneously evokes a sense of loss and offers the occasion for aesthetically experiencing and managing the emotions bound up with this imagined loss.

The slippage between identification and difference in the spectator's relationship with Kenyon, who is English yet also part of the "we" of the passage, signals his function as an exemplary male subject from whom the U.S. middle-class reader can learn, but it also matches the slippage in Sedgwick's simultaneous identification with and sense of difference from this male other self. The difference submerged in the travel account is accentuated in the tale, which separates male and female travelers and which creates a mirror image, at once comic and bathetic, of the poet's aesthetic response.

Gender, Identification, and Difference

"An Incident at Rome" supplies a more detached reading of the spectacle of the cultivated English man submitting himself to the influences of "Italy." Bathurst possesses in an exaggerated sense the latent capacities to which "Italy" speaks in all northern tourists. He is actually already Catholic, Italian in appearance, and fluent in the language; he has "large dark melancholy eyes, . . . and tangled long dark hair" (105). This feminized self – indicated by his "un-English person" – is the nonproductive self that needs at once to be acknowledged and disciplined. His "love" for Italy is figured as a narcissistic passion that prohibits the development of his heterosexual, reproductive, commercial self – the self-regulating, self-reproducing, and future-oriented citizen necessary to the vigor of the modern nation. When he loses his reason in Italy, he moves from being a subject (a tourist) to being an object, from independent traveler to dependent beggar, from the surveyor of the scene to a figure in the landscape. He disappears from police and consular records, from a form of surveillance that authenticates middle-class status, and appears in tourist observations, a form of surveillance that denies it. His immersion into his own delusional world of wandering and ruin-hunting parodies the tourist's proper cultivation of interiority. In this respect the tale is a parable of a national "brother" becoming an "other," a warning, displaced onto an English character, to American republicans about the necessity of maintaining the boundaries of identity.[70]

However, through the American and English frame narrators of her tale, Sedgwick also opens up a gap between the spectatorship of elite women and that of men. These female narrators contemplate the emerging ruling class via the acculturating mechanism of tourism; caught between his mother's "enthusiasm" for things Italian and his commercially successful but boorish uncle, the protagonist has to forge a properly elite identity composed both of "learning" and of money. Sedgwick prevents this fusion from becoming entirely naturalized by a disjunction between the languages associated with these two identities in the tale. Mrs. Bathurst speaks in a heightened sentimental discourse that indicates her own passionate engagement with classical antiquities as well as her remorse at having impelled her son on this less than "natural" path: "'I developed prematurely, and most unwisely, his taste. . . . Thus I fed the flame that was to consume my poor boy'" (105). Sedgwick treats the uncle as a comic figure, and so the tone of the tale itself becomes comic as Bathurst moves into the uncle's sphere of influence at the end. The uncle comments that the immersion in Italy has turned out to be the antidote for Murray's love of Italy: "saying, somewhat coarsely, that to be sure the hair of the same dog would cure the bite, if you ate hide and all" (108). The mother's "enthusiasm" for Italian ruins makes her a pathetic figure of feminine middle-class susceptibility to Italian values and contributes to her son's feminization, insanity, and temporary plunge out of the bourgeoisie, whereas the uncle would block the acculturating process of the Italian tour altogether. Sedgwick's use of two separate linguistic registers prevents the reader from identifying with their point of intersection, their common heir, as Sedgwick does with Kenyon in her Neapolitan scene, and creates an ironic distance between her narrators (with whom the reader *is* asked to identify) and the subject matter of the story: the education through tourism of male elite sensibility.

In her study of British women travel writers, Sara Mills emphasizes the tension between "feminine and colonial discourses," a tension which results in "heterogeneous" narratives that reinforce the dominance of the imperial gaze even as they subvert it.[71] By reading these two tourist texts together, I have argued that Sedgwick similarly reinforces the project of shaping a masculine republican subject and creates the conditions for a critique of this project. The tension between difference and identification that characterizes Sedgwick's studies of masculine subjects also informs her responses to Italian women. As such analysts of women's travel writing as Mills and Schriber have pointed out, the relationships between the female tourist from an economically and politically dominant culture and the women inhabiting the toured country remain defined by the power relations of their respective nations.

I want to end this section by returning to the question of Sedgwick's relations with Italian women, this time by discussing two moments of contact with lower-class women, moments that highlight her half-articulated concerns about the structures of power that support the tourist gaze. In Viterbo the Sedgwicks' carriage runs over and kills a woman; Sedgwick spends two pages on the episode, detailing it and trying to piece together the responsibility for the death from the intersecting roles of the postillions, who had urged the horses to a reckless speed, and themselves, whom Sedgwick finally depicts as trapped in the juggernaut of the tourist's vehicle. She and her niece vainly shout to the postillions, try to protect her invalid brother from the "shock" of the knowledge of the event, and feel carried away helplessly from the "scene of the tragedy" in the "apparent barbarity of galloping away, unheeding the misery we had inflicted" (*Letters*, II, 145).

This difficulty of conceiving of choices in the tourist's relationships with the lower-class inhabitants of the picturesque scene recurs in a later, more benign episode when Sedgwick engages a young woman working at an inn near Perugia in conversation.[72] The girl, whose name she gives (Clotilde Poggione) and with whom she feels an "elective affinity," confides to Sedgwick that she has a middle-class suitor but no dowry and so will probably enter a convent, a fate to which she seems resigned. She shows Sedgwick a love letter from the man and accepts some unnamed advice from Sedgwick. Sedgwick adds in a note that she was tempted to develop this "incident" into a tale for a giftbook annual but finally "preferred preserving the unadorned fact to ingrafting upon it apocryphal additions for the sated appetites of souvenir readers" (*Letters*, II, 278–80). In spite of Sedgwick's doubts about turning the life stories of the powerless into objects of consumption and her attempts to use speech and an intimate, reciprocal look between women to break down the structure of the tourist gaze, Clotilde Poggione remains a sentimental genre figure, associated with the rural "lassie[s]" of Robert Burns's poetry, in a text sold in the marketplace.

By noting the limits of Sedgwick's sympathy, I wish to point out that the conventions of the tourist gaze both made certain objects visible and virtually dictated the terms of their visibility. Kirkland investigates women's gazes and the figures of European women more explicitly; her narrative strategy of disjunction at times disrupts these conventions, a strategy allied with her understanding of the possibilities of a republican press. If Sedgwick explores the confluence of tourism, class, and gender in her travel writings, Kirkland begins to articulate the impact a perspective derived from the popular press might have on these elements of the national gaze.

Gender, Nation, and the Tourist Gaze in the European "Year of Revolutions": Kirkland's *Holidays Abroad*

The scene of the nationalist and republican revolutions of 1848, especially in France and Italy, provoked a double vision in American spectators. Supportive of these movements for national self-determination, especially to the extent that they seemed to follow a U.S. model of iconoclastic republicanism, elite Americans also wanted to preserve Europe as a source of icons and as a site of instruction of consolidating social and national identities through images.[73] This double demand on Europe accorded with antebellum nation construction in the U.S., where elites were moving from the universalizing political discourse in the public sphere that had characterized the early Republic toward more cultural, visual, and privatized forms of expression as a means of nation-building. As Michael Warner claims, "although the nation-state was a product of the eighteenth century, the national imaginary was a product of the nineteenth."[74] Even as writers, artists, and politicians were engaged in creating this national imaginary through developing American cultural icons, a persistent Protestant iconoclasm made them wish to subjugate image to text and, as Larry J. Reynolds points out, stimulated the "secularization of art," the appropriation of icons for national rather than religious uses.[75] Touring Europe in 1848 brought the diverging iconoclastic and iconophilic tendencies in U.S. elites into high relief; it did so with special urgency in women tourists, whose own already double status as icons and spectators highlighted this ambivalence and whose texts enacted the contradictions within antebellum modes of visualizing and gazing on behalf of the nation.

Kirkland's travel book *Holidays Abroad; or, Europe from the West* (1849) embodies a dialectic of engagement with and resistance to the normative tourist gaze and its gender and national implications, a dialectic shaped by the conflicted relationship of elite Americans to images. The book's enactment of multiple, even contradictory "viewing positions," to return to Deborah Cherry's terms, becomes clear in the context of three other arenas of the cultural production of the nation: the antebellum periodical press; the continuing representation in paintings and prints of a feminized and aestheticized Italy; and American responses to the revolution in France, the revolution which seemed the most text-based and iconoclastic. Because she traveled in 1848, the politics of nation construction intersect with the tourist's aesthetic project in her narrative, even as revolution-ary activity rendered the image of Europe itself unstable and less available for appropriation. Kirkland's text illuminates the multiply determined nature of the tourist gaze and its function in the shaping of national subjectivity.

Magazine Work, Tourism, and Women's Gazes

In the late 1840s, Kirkland edited *Sartain's Union Magazine*, then called the *Union Magazine of Literature and Art*, which, as a monthly devoted to supplying the middle-class household with fiction, poetry, engravings, and features on religion, music, and travel, participated in the antebellum projects of nation- and citizen-building by offer-ing a process of enculturation similar to that of tourism.[76] Just as tourism exposed citizens to a series of ideologically charged images, positions, and locations, so magazines similarly offered their readers visual and textual aids toward their self-fashioning as middle-class Americans.[77]

In her editorial statement for the *Union*'s inaugural issue, Kirk-land associated the nation-building project of the popular press with the masculine "defen[se of] our country" but defined its means of "exhibiting patriotism" in the feminized terms characteristic of ante-bellum descriptions of aesthetic production:[78]

> To elevate the intellectual and moral character of the people, is a work no less necessary and commendable . . .[;] this is the aim of the author and the artist. Magazines . . . constitute in a country like ours, a powerful element of civilization. . . . [P]eriodical literature . . . [is] the best possible means of disseminating information, and diffusing the principles of a correct taste.[79]

Here, the work of the editor, writer, or artist is to shape readers' national subjectivities through shaping their sensibilities. Kirkland saw this work as congruent with the persona of middle-class Ameri-can womanhood (she always insisted that her work be published under the name of "Mrs." Kirkland).[80] Magazine work and tourism both tapped the association of elite and middle-class women with aesthetic labor and cultural influence, and they reconciled women's productive labor with their iconographical status as "emblems of antebellum America."[81]

Her preface to *Holidays Abroad* invokes the national and class-based project of enculturation even as it addresses itself specifically to women; "These sketches are written for Americans" (vii), particularly those of the middle class: those, "women especially," who are likely to go to Europe only once if at all (v). Positioned at the intersection between the feminized power of a cultural elite in a modern democracy and the status of women as cultural icons themselves, Kirkland uses the occasion of her European tour to consider the following related topics: women as subjects and objects within a public visual field, the modes of vision tourism brought to the task of forming a national subjectivity, and possible forms of public expression and iconography in a republic.

Her role as a representative of the popular press, together with her previous experience as a satirist of frontier culture in *A New Home, Who'll Follow? or, Glimpses of Western Life* (1839), accentuated the tourist's double vision. Steven Fink observes that Kirkland's "split identity" as a "'lady editor'" resulted in a "bifurcated discourse": a "language of . . . genteel femininity for public consumption" in print, and a "language of commerce" and of the "marketplace" to conduct editorial business (210, 212). And Jeffrey Steele has argued that in *A New Home* Kirkland employed the "tactic" of "constant shifting between genres [and] voices" to "confront her readers with multiple viewpoints that momentarily place them into the subject position constructed by each narrative mode."[82] Her gendered immersion in periodical publishing and her multi-voiced critical assessment of the Michigan frontier prompted both a civilizing, philanthropic gaze, whose transmission to "the people" via "periodical literature" ensured a type of cultural iconophilia, and an iconoclastic gaze, whose critiques of Old World visual experience defined the cultural boundaries of the U.S.

Even strongly positive responses to the icons of the European tour were infused, in Kirkland and others, with the desire to spiritualize them, that is, to de-materialize them. As Franchot observes, antebellum liberal Protestants continued to understand their culture, as opposed to image-saturated European and Catholic cultures, as text-based and to "perform . . . [the] anti-incarnational function of extracting spirit from flesh, text from image" in their theology and in their viewing practices, even as they were increasingly drawn to "an iconic Catholic 'past,' sealed off from the present and available for aesthetic and psychological rumination."[83] Thus Kirkland elevates St. Peter's Basilica in Rome, with its "glorious beauty" and its "lofty and noble vault," to a transcendent, nondenominational aesthetic and spiritual status, while she drains the "sumptuous" and visually striking religious service within it of meaning by separating its "actual beauty . . . presented to the eye" from its spiritual significance: "Soul it had none to me" (I, 286–7). Such divided tourist responses appropriated European and Catholic icons and visual forms for a universalizing Protestant and republican discourse by disengaging them from their specific historical or religious uses and by treating their physical presences primarily as signs of spiritual truths (or, as in Kirkland's viewing of the mass, as empty of such truths).[84]

Her reactions to icons become more complex when these objects of the tourist gaze are representations of women or, as the next section will argue, women themselves, transformed into representations by this gaze. In Florence, Kirkland's viewing of the *Venus de' Medici* prompts her to join in a nineteenth-century debate in which the statue's proponents extracted "spirit from flesh" by deflecting attention from her naked body and finding the spiritual and intellectual traits in her face which defined her as the ideal "of Womanhood itself"; the statue's critics, however, argued that its face was, as the American sculptor Hiram Powers said, "that of an idiot."[85] Kirkland also de-spiritualizes the statue by commenting on the "imbecility" of its head, but her recorporealization of it does not merely devalue the statue; instead, her attack on this icon both becomes an argument for allowing women a fuller embodiment, a more powerful physical presence, and suggests that the spectator's gaze elicits a performance in its object. Kirkland disputes the *Venus*'s "diminutiveness" as an ideal of womanhood and argues that the "universal judgment as to living women" emphasizes "power, and . . . flowing, luxuriant grace" as defining "perfect development" (I, 204). She also criticizes the "affected," or performed, "modesty" of the *Venus*, who, violating the canon of feminine sincerity of the late 1830s and 1840s,[86] is like a "danseuse" who "throws herself into an attitude, and looks with an express killingness at the audience" (I, 204). Kirkland at once argues for a more substantial image of the embodied woman and hints at the ways in which the "audience['s]" gaze shapes the "posture" of its object.[87] Her response to the statue reveals both her investment in representative images, such as a properly conceived image of womanhood, and her half-articulated critique of the gendered structures of the normative gaze. Kirkland's text uses the multiple viewing positions available to women at once to consolidate and to unsettle a national tourist gaze. Just as her response to the *Venus* validates a male-generated discourse of connoisseurship yet questions it by observing that acts of looking create their objects, so

Holidays Abroad's repeated shifts of perspective point to the contradictions within republican "looking relations."

After a nine-year career as a writer, a career that became fully professional, because of financial need, with the death of her husband in 1846,[88] Kirkland funded a trip abroad in part by sending sections of what would become her travel book to the *Union Magazine*.[89] In her book, Kirkland addresses her audience with the semi-intimate, egalitarian, and informal voice of the trusted public "friend" that Patricia Okker argues characterized the print-personae of antebellum women editors (23); Kirkland promises to "tak[e] the reader with me through the medium of sympathy" (v). And, as did nearly all antebellum women travelers,[90] she traveled not alone but with companions, her friends Eliza and Henry Bellows.[91]

Even as it articulates an audience defined by nation, class, and gender, Kirkland's preface anticipates the double focus of her book and of the interests of this audience. "Art" and politics will both "naturally" engage a republican audience building a national culture, but the "love of Beauty" (together with its "high office") coexists in an unresolved tension with progressive liberalism. While she pursues the standard tour of European sights (England, France, Italy, Switzerland, Germany, and the Netherlands) and emphasizes her aesthetic responses to these sights, Kirkland also witnesses republics struggling to be born: the Second Republic in France (1848–51) and the phase of the Risorgimento that would result briefly in the Roman Republic (1849). She shares most Americans' support of the revolutions of 1848. But like most U.S. elites she is uncertain of the relationship between the two desiderata – liberal revolutionary movements and aesthetic culture. The latter consolidates national identity by "elevat[ing] the . . . character of the people," as she said in the *Union*, while the former destabilize such consolidations: "No future traveler will perhaps see France and Italy just as we saw them. . . . Much as I should rejoice to see the liberties of Italy confirmed, I am disposed to congratulate those who saw Rome as it was in 1848. Republicanism is good, but it has not yet learned to be beautiful" (vi). This dialectical tension of the "good" and the "beautiful" often emerges as Kirkland considers women in their double role as iconic representations of their national cultures and as among those who control the means of cultural and national representation. The figure of the double woman – the icon and the producer of a national culture – becomes the site on which the tension between beauty's "high office" as the transmitter of transcendent national values and republicanism's definition of nationhood as progressive and transformative can be provisionally resolved.

Women as National Signs and Subjects

Holidays Abroad repeatedly comments on women: as signs or icons, as spectators, and as subjects who are specifically located (socially, geographically, physically). As part of public iconography, the bodies of women could be read as both official signs of a nation and expressions of individual subjectivities.[92] Kirkland marshals a series of national types to shape, implicitly, the American women reading her book; she warns that representative visibility often comes at the expense of any status as a full subject and, therefore, access to the power to shape a national culture. She observes that women's lives in Holland are determined by a culture of visible domestic sanitation; Dutch women are "sacrificed to [a] . . . routine of useless cleansing," "a species of labor inimical to improvement . . . in mind or manners" and, Kirkland suspects, designed to "keep women out of mischief" – engaged in the work of representing national order rather than participating in it (II, 262–3). Kirkland's Italian "ladies," on the other hand, in a formulation of Italian women unusual in tourist writings, are liberated by having fewer prescribed "petty cares" about the household. By not living in the consumer society that prompts U.S. women to "mean little emulations" and "display," they are less fixed by the public surveillance of their domestic lives, a freedom which gives them "more time for self-cultivation" (I, 238).[93] Lower-class Italian women, however, are more available for the tourist gaze both because they live in the public eye and because they fall out of middle-class norms of cleanliness and, so, into pure spectacle: "If these picturesque creatures could only be washed up a little! In their natural state they are fit for nothing but to be painted" (I, 169). While elite Italian women can create the basis for participation in a national culture – "self-cultivation" – working-class women seem merely representational and do not shape public life.[94]

In Paris Kirkland sees a compelling combination of the roles of representing and producing the nation. She describes a performance of the revolutionary anthem, the Marseillaise, by the famous tragic actress Rachel Felix, already a "sight" for mid-century tourists as well as a national icon; Kirkland exhaustively reads both her body and performance and presents Rachel (known by her first name) as at once personifying the new republic and expressing her own republican sympathies and aspirations: "she grasps the tri-color; she kneels before it; she clasps it to her bosom" (I, 131).[95] Like the hundred-foot-high plaster statue of a female "Republic" Kirkland sees at a celebration of the revolution in Paris, a "*Fête de Fraternité*" (I, 127), Rachel embodies the republic and, as an icon, enables incipient citizens to join in a national imaginary. But like Kirkland she is also an "artist" (I, 132) who produces the republic by molding the subjectivities of her audience; at once symbol and agent, she bridges immutable and historically transformative, republican values.

Kirkland responds strongly to Rachel as a figure who holds opposing cultural categories in suspension. Echoing her contemporaries' appraisals of Rachel,[96] Kirkland at once compares her to a classical "statue" and views her declamation as spoken "naturally" (I, 131–2). Such conjunctions of art and nature, canonical drama and popular expression, as well as monarchical and republican France (both of which she represented in different phases of her career), were made possible by her sex, by "Woman's" construction as a sliding signifier, according to Rachel Brownstein. This transcendent duality also emerges out of cultural perceptions of Rachel's Jewishness: at once inside and outside of French culture, at once "Citizen Rachel" and, because of her lack of a racially defined French identity, able "to represent . . . anything."[97] As the figure of an "other" in a central position of cultural authority, Rachel is both a spectacular object who "fascinates the eye" and a subject whose own "eye" is "passionate" and authoritative and whose performance joins cultural and political agency (I, 131). Kirkland classes her performances "among the grand things of Europe" (I, 132).

Kirkland is also concerned with other women's gazes in public. Her stay in Paris elicits an awareness of the ways in which gender, class, and sexuality structure mid-century looking relations.[98] Lower-class women "look one full in the eyes, as if quite accustomed to taking their own part." Here Kirkland explicitly, if somewhat uneasily, connects the direct gaze with agency; while such women lack "meekness" and would not make good models for Madonnas, they have, she is told, a large "share of power" in day-to-day life and would make effective models for Judith, the biblical figure who killed an oppressor of her nation in her bed (I, 140–1).

In Kirkland's class, using the aesthetic gaze associated with tourism transformed women travelers provisionally from sexualized objects of the gaze to authorized subjects. Kirkland discusses this transition as she describes the novel spectacle of elite women eating in public, a "considerable feat" at home. She says that "Dining at a restaurant is one of the novelties of the lady-traveler in Paris" and that this exposure of herself to the public eye takes some "boldness": "to sit down in a public room, to a regular dinner of an hour's length or more, . . . requires some practice before one can refrain from casting sly glances around during the process, to see whether anyone is looking." What helps her to get used to this exposure – to move from feelings of "transgression" to a sense that this is a "natural event" – is the restaurant's solicitation of her eye through its decor of "immense mirrors, statuary, flowers"; the restaurant, like many tourist spots, positions its consumers as spectators rather than as objects. Kirkland adds, "though there may be twenty other parties dining . . . nobody looks at you." It is not clear whether she is aware that this act also takes "boldness" in Paris; Griselda Pollock mentions that it was "scandalous" for a bourgeois wife to eat in a restaurant with her husband, while it was accepted for a man to eat out with his mistress.[99] It seems that tourists were granted special status in public dining practices in Paris. In any case, Kirkland is generally aware of the semiotic risks she is running but treats them comically, by describing the experience of dining out as "a feeling of agreeable *abandon*, unalloyed by any sense of naughtiness" (I, 133–4). In a café in Florence she sees, approvingly, a "lady breakfasting quite alone, with as much nonchalance as if her feet were on her own fender, . . . with twenty men in sight" (I, 227). The shift from being in the sight of others to having others "in sight" is the shift in viewing positions that aesthetic tourism authorized.

Her interest in women and vision is especially pronounced when she encounters institutional attempts to regulate the female gaze. In London she ridicules the "exclusion of women from the House of Commons" ("very funny and very provoking") and having to view its proceedings from "a sort of dust-hole, from which we could peep down through blinds" (I, 66–7). This confinement of women's gazes recurs in a cathedral in Genoa, in a chapel forbidden to women through a "law enacted by some wiseacre of a pope"; Kirkland goes in anyway and casts her experience as a drama of the iconoclastic freedom of the modern gaze overcoming the superstitious prejudices of archaic cultures, figured by the "petrified astonishment" of a priest. She achieves one of the more satisfying aims of this gaze, the exposure of the emptiness of another culture's fetishized object: "there was nothing remarkable in the chapel after all. The relics of [St. John the Baptist] are *said* to be . . . under the high altar, but I could espy nothing, although I peeped through the carved open work most sedulously" (I, 179–80). By participating in her nation's demystifying look at other cultures, Kirkland resists being cast as a representative figure of womanhood and assumes, momentarily, the power of the national gaze.

Iconophilia and Iconoclasm in Italy

As the part of the European tour which elicited the connections among gender, nation, and visual experience most insistently for Americans, Italy presented images to tourists which were icons in a double sense: both revered objects and places (art, architecture, cities) within Italian religious and aesthetic traditions and objects whose function it was to trigger aesthetic responses which confirmed elite status in the U.S. This book has drawn on the work of art historians such as Alan Wallach and Jonathan Crary to describe a reorganization of vision in industrialized nations in these decades; the formation of newly normative modes of vision at once created "an observer fitted for the tasks of 'spectacular' consumption" and developed visual practices of managerial "oversight" and "supervision."[100] But I want to add here W. J. T. Mitchell's examination of the historically situated language(s) of aesthetics; his consideration of iconoclasm as a discursive project explains tourists' tendencies to ward off the same visual images they embarked to find. Kirkland's responses to Italian sights shed light on tourism as one of the normalizing visual techniques of the period and reveal how the discourse of iconoclasm at once reinforced the impulse toward surveillance in these visual practices, as in the cathedral at Genoa, and provided a strategy of resistance to them, both possibilities inflected by her cultural position as a woman.

In reading such episodes as Kirkland's "peep[ing]" at the relics in Genoa, I draw on Mitchell's discussion of the "rhetoric of iconoclasm" as an aesthetic and social mode of verbal response to others' valued objects. Mitchell argues that nineteenth-century forms of iconoclasm often operated in the service of imperialist nations as they placed cultures on an evolutionary scale, from "primitive" to "advanced." For the religious iconoclast, the idolator is someone "who has 'forgotten' something – his own act of projection" of value into the fetishized object, while the iconoclast "sees himself at a historical distance from the idolator, working at a more 'advanced' . . . stage in human evolution, therefore in a position to provide a . . . historicizing interpretation of myths taken literally by the idolator." Aware that contemporary critical practices, such as his own, are an offshoot of this rhetorical tradition, Mitchell wants to save iconoclasm as "an instrument of cultural criticism" by setting it in dialectical opposition with an imaginatively "sympathetic" understanding of icons.[101] I would suggest that this dialectical relation sometimes characterizes tourist writings and particularly women's tourist writings;

what Mitchell does not explore is the impact of gendered viewing practices on rhetorics of iconoclasm.

Kirkland's text performs the instability of the simultaneously iconophilic and iconophobic tourist gaze and provides an incipient analysis of such national looking practices.[102] *Holidays Abroad* contains a sporadic dialectic between what Kirkland, using the religious vocabulary appropriated by tourism, as William W. Stowe points out,[103] calls "faith" and a "prying and sceptical spirit" (I, 302–3) with respect to the icons the tourist gaze finds. She vacillates between the response of "One of our American friends," that there is "no soul in anything but literal and available facts" and that while the aesthetic pilgrimage to Europe "must" be made there is "a good deal of humbug" in it, and her investment in the tour, her "surrender" of her "imagination" to it. After "perversely" refusing to "invest" in the stories told by her guide to the Roman catacombs, Kirkland cautions, "There is nothing against which the traveler for pleasure should more sedulously guard than this prying and sceptical spirit. There is a faith which suffices for the imagination without weakening the judgment; without this we cannot get at the soul of things in Italy" (I, 302–3). At once aware that the tourist's pleasure depends on participation in tourism's "rite[s]" of projection and "illusion" (I, 301–2) and alert to other ways of looking – the heterogeneous visual field formed by the graffiti, iconography, and resistances of a noncanonical, "news" culture, as I will argue below – Kirkland alternates between these ways of seeing. This shifting among viewing positions and her ambivalence toward the male-authored models of looking she, as a tourist, inhabits prompt a critique of the tourist gaze.

In Italy Kirkland at once is most fully the sightseer and turns what Mitchell calls the "rhetoric of iconoclasm" onto the tourist gaze itself. Some of her scenes do mirror the oil paintings and magazine and giftbook illustrations of Italy, images which corroborated such allegorical paintings in the 1840s as Daniel Huntington's *Italy* (1843, see Chapter 2), which depicted Italy as a woman associated with aesthetic implements. Like most tourists, Kirkland understands Italy's primary function as offering such aesthetic visions: "I had always cared far more about Italian pictures than Italian politics" (I, 182). And the Italian chapters are obviously the most enthusiastically written portion of her book (they take up, disproportionately so, nearly half of the text). However, the Italian section of *Holidays Abroad* moves back and forth between the rapt visions which signal the successful displacement of national issues onto aesthetic harmonies and comic moments which collapse their structures.

Rome is the most concentrated scene of her visual engagement and pleasure; in these chapters iconoclastic impulses are almost absent. She sees the city and its "eternal" sights – churches, galleries, ruins – in part through the textual guides of Byron's *Childe Harold's Pilgrimage* (1812–18), one of the most frequent touchstones for tourists,[104] and Fanny Kemble's *A Year of Consolation* (1847), which she recommends (II, 31). Both are texts in the tradition of connecting sightseeing to an experience of exile, personal anguish, and a search for healing – elements absent in Kirkland's account but elements which tied touring to affective management. Her description of the approach to Rome is like Cole's *Italian Scene* in its extent, structure, and detail. She sees an illuminated "panorama," framed by "the Alban hills" and shot through with "brilliant" color; the wide "plain of the Tiber" combines pastoral elements with the familiar emblems of superseded power whose current stillness makes them "picturesque": "fields of waving grain," an "old tower," Roman tombs, and "melancholy cypresses." Rome itself is "grey as if literally covered with ashes, perhaps from some mistiness in the air. . . . Sadness befits the 'Niobe of Nations'" (I, 281–2). This scene, with its virtually automatic quotation from Byron,[105] organizes the visual elements of the Campagna toward a dreamlike revelation of the "soul" of Italy, here defined by its loss of nationhood, fused with its transcendent aesthetic status. As do the receding planes in Cole's painting, these details lead the eye into a deep vista of elite national fantasy; as Mitchell says elsewhere, landscape images represent the "dreamwork of ideology."[106]

Elsewhere in Italy, however, Kirkland often writes an unstable prose that at once invokes and undermines such conventions. Near Naples, she begins to sketch a similarly typical Italian landscape, one that focuses not on the loss of a historical nationhood signaled by Rome but on the landscape of Arcadian pleasure, but then turns the passage away from any claims of seeing eternal truths through the veil of the landscape's physical presence and draws attention to the material and social basis of the tourist's pleasure: "The sea was of a dazzling blue; . . . the shore was all alive with people and children; the far islands were hung with silver gauze, through which we could see their beautiful outlines . . .; the road of the most perfect smoothness, and F. [their courier] silent – it was too delicious!" (II, 103). This move intrudes the tourist as an embodied and socially located self into a description whose aesthetics depend on the configuration of the tourist as a disembodied eye, an unimplicated surveyor of landscapes and their meanings.

Kirkland's most sustained deployment of a rhetoric of iconoclasm against tourist-generated landscapes occurs in an account of the "prospect from the top" of the Leaning Tower of Pisa. The passage is worth quoting at length because, as a comic anatomy of the tourist gaze, it reinserts the suppressed element of the national landscape – what Crary calls the "fully embodied viewer"[107] – into the scene of viewing and, by emphasizing the exertions and labor of this body, reveals the constructed nature of the tourist's visual experience:

> We were told that we saw Leghorn, and the Mediterranean, and several other very interesting things, and we tried hard to make it true. But really this prospect-seeing is the most trying experience of the traveler. You ascend innumerable steps, . . . at the top you find a breeze that half blows you away, or a sun that quite bakes you, . . . Then your guide insists upon your seeing certain things which he declares all travelers do see, and he evidently suffers so much if he cannot make you see them too, that out of common humanity you put yourself to great inconvenience in staring, not at, but for, something which he assures you is a town, or perhaps an ocean, but which to you might as well be called a parcel of clothes drying in a meadow. . . . Then he tries a long spy-glass, which, after much engineering, he is sure he has adjusted for a point-blank gaze; you place your aching eye as directed, and find . . . a chimney-pot, or catch an undulating glimpse of something blue, which you declare to be the sea, in spite of conscience. . . . [T]ravellers who have not very long sight, and who have tender consciences, are put to sad straits in towers and belfries. (I, 195–6)

In viewing such prospects, tourists were supposed to experience (the guide personifies this cultural imperative) the thrilling release from bodily limitations through the eye and the empowering moment of the "panoptic sublime" (to return to Wallach's useful formulation): an experience of the "sudden access of power" offered by landscape views that were at once totalizing ("the spectator . . . preside[s] over all visibility") and "telescopic," that "aspired to control every element within the visual field." Such views trained elite and would-be elite tourists in their roles as the professional and cultural supervisors of the nation.[108] Kirkland's "bake[d]" body and "aching eye" prevent the consumption of this spectacle of power from taking place. In his study of the transformation of "the observing subject" in the 1820s and 1830s, Crary shows that the discovery of the physiological and contingent nature of vision both disrupted older modes of perception and led to the recuperation of the newly embodied observer in "new technologies for imposing a normative vision."[109] Kirkland features here a comically over-embodied viewer, whose physiology bars incorporation into new visual regimes.

Kirkland's view from within the machinery of the tourist/national gaze recounts a resistance to the tourist's production of icons that is also linked to her gendered viewing position. She resists the panoptic sublime by using a domestic detail to balk at its promises of extent and precision; the potentially sublime vista of the Mediterranean may be just a glimpse of drying laundry. If Italy-as-woman and the receding landscape view are both figures for the displacement and organization of ideology into aesthetics, then Kirkland's resistance to seeing the deep prospect view is a resistance to the gendered structure of such displacement. Looking on Italy's body, on the incarnations of art, and on women's bodies are culturally equivalent acts. Kirkland's response as gazer is to become conscious of her own positioning and of the technology – the spy-glass – of gazing. The totalizing gaze becomes an overt construct, and Kirkland is not, in Lauren Berlant's words, "reconstituted as a *collective* subject"[110] in the presence of a nationally meaningful icon. The limits of her ability or desire to participate in elite acts of supervision and in the generation of new modes of perception, efforts Crary implicitly defines as male, seem marked by gender in such passages.

Indeed, the Italian sections of *Holidays Abroad* are punctuated with comic or unsatisfactory views from high places, unrealized views on which Kirkland expends as much prose as she does on her fully achieved tourist visions. The vaunted view from the top of the cathedral in Milan is suddenly shut out by a driving rain storm, an event which Kirkland puts in terms of political gatherings: "the clouds, which had been having mass-meetings among themselves for some time, made an overwhelming demonstration" (II, 122). She forgoes a "birds-eye view" from the Capitol in Rome in order to watch the immediate "Roman panorama" of genre types ("friars," "beggars") (II, 34). And, being too sick to climb Vesuvius with her party, she recounts a friend's disgruntled appraisal: "'an excursion more thoroughly disagreeable can hardly be imagined, while the sight at the top does not pay.'" Her friend's account also emphasizes a cultural discomfort with physically ambitious sightseeing in women; the "'only tolerable views'" of the top itself "'are caricatures, showing the various distresses of ladies who heroically make the ascent'" (II, 96–7). The one Italian prospect she recounts as wholly unproblematic ("enchanting") is a view from the top of St. Peter's in Rome (II, 40). Just as the visual mastery of the

landscape seen from Milan's cathedral is disrupted by the revolutionary and discursive "mass-meetings" of the clouds, so, too, do revolutionary expressions at times fragment national scenes and disrupt the
tourist's gaze.

Texts and Graffiti in Revolutionary Rome and Paris: Breaking Up the Visual Field

Kirkland finds an antithesis to the vistas and icons of the canonical
pilgrimage in the temporary tourist "sights" of 1848, what she calls
the "flying picture" (I, vi) of revolutionary Paris and Italy. She is
especially interested in the ubiquitous republican images and inscriptions, whose ephemeral and political nature indicates that they are
one of the modern forms of cultural expression, connected to such
forms as the periodical press. As a journalist engaged in producing
a republican citizenry, she is drawn to the public texts and popular
images of these incipient republics as alternative sites of vision and,
therefore, of an emerging national subjectivity; however, she is also
worried that these transitive expressions will finally not provide the
affective bond necessary to hold a nation together.

Kirkland vacillates between seeing popular expressions of republican sentiment as continuous with older forms of piety and interpreting
them as revolutionary, as a break with such forms. Italy exhibits the
greater continuity, as it seems to mix "patriotism" with the "picturesque" (I, 249). In Rome Kirkland comments on the ubiquity of proto-
revolutionary images of Pope Pius IX, images circulated in the spring
of 1848 during his period of pro-liberal declarations.[111] In these days
of the Pope's lingering popularity, "Pictures, busts, medals, cameos of
him are everywhere. . . . Every poor woman in the street has his image
hanging with the cross on her rosary. . . . His name occurs on every
corner; 'Viva Pio Nono' graces every old wall and broken arch" (II,
52). The significance of hanging an image of the pope next to a cross
on one's rosary slides easily from religious belief to republican support. Kirkland interprets this popular iconography and the accompanying inscriptions as a republican citizen would, that Pius's "temporal
sovereignty" depends on his continuing "to exhibit the liberal spirit
which has made him so popular" (II, 53). Catholic rituals themselves
blend seamlessly into republican demonstrations. On traversing the
Apennines, where the "scenery becomes in all respects more Italian,"
Kirkland describes a classic genre scene, a religious procession, complete with costumed peasants; on hearing news of a military victory

in the revolt against Austria, the crowd becomes celebratory: "the joy of victory superadded to the festa feeling, brightened every eye and animated every voice" (I, 170–1). In such scenes, as opposed to her preface, Kirkland momentarily imagines the sentiment of liberal revolution as merely an intensification of the "festa feeling."

On the other hand, in Paris, which she visits in a lull between the euphoric days of the relatively bloodless February revolution and the violent repression of a workers' revolt in June, Kirkland notes that revolutionary iconoclasts literally rewrite the city's appearance by inscribing the "magic words" of "Liberté, Egalité, Fraternité" onto the visual "traces" of king, church, and empire (I, 130) and so replace one system of meaning with another.[112] Her attention to the eruption of modern, republican forms of cultural expression in Paris becomes clearer when read against similar depictions by her American contemporaries in Rome and Paris in 1848–9. Fuller, who covered the revolution in Rome for the *New-York Tribune*, also notes continuities between religious and political processions but emphasizes the rupture between iconographical and textual bases for national identity, between "Priestcraft" and "Reform." While such traditional religious ceremonies as the feast of the Bambino included the carrying of a figure – here the infant Jesus – in an "idolatrous" ritual, processions in support of republican reform replace such an "idol" with a text; Romans demonstrating their appreciation of a liberalizing edict, Fuller observes, carry "a banner on which the edict was printed" (204–5, 136).

A similar replacement of image with text occurs in an unusual genre painting of Rome by Kirkland's contemporary Martin Johnson Heade, who depicted public iconography from a later stage in the revolution, when Pius had fled the city and Rome had briefly become a republic. Unlike the usual genre scenes of Italy, Heade's *Roman Newsboys* (1848, Fig. 3.5) uses its childish figures to draw a parallel between Italian and American popular and political culture.[113] American newsboys were associated with an aggressively entrepreneurial masculine identity and also at times with an insurgent lower urban class,[114] the opposite of the noncommercial and pastoral meanings Americans assigned to Italy. In Heade's image, Italian boys sell the news of the rapidly shifting events of a modern and nationalist moment.[115] William L. Vance, Theodore E. Stebbins, and Paul A. Manoguerra have deciphered the graffiti, posters, and other details of the painting, which document an increasingly radical rhetoric: the news sheet one boy is selling is the antipapist *Il Don Pirlone*, what Manoguerra calls the "satirical voice of Rome's revolutionary

Figure 3.5 Martin Johnson Heade, *Roman Newsboys*, 1848. Oil on canvas. 28½ x 24 ⁵⁄₁₆ ins (72.5 x 61.7 cm). Toledo Museum of Art, purchased with funds from the Florence Scott Libbey bequest in memory of her father, Maurice A. Scott, 1953.68. Photo credit: Photography, Incorporated (Ray Sess and Carl Schultz), Toledo.

culture"; a caricature of Pius IX is on the wall; and the same boy wears a Greek cap, "symbol of the liberal cause."[116]

Missing from their meticulous reading of the painting is its denial of prospect or of the vista. Unlike Cole's landscape or even most genre scenes, the wall behind the boys flattens our attention into the immediate visual plane; like the news itself, this wall of posters and caricatures denies the viewer's desire for the opening vista into an imagined landscape which mirrors the tourist's cultivated interiority. Unlike other images of Italy in the 1840s, Heade's painting avoids the visual coherence of woman-as-nation or of the landscape view and articulates an iconoclastic aesthetic in which the American viewer is forced to pay attention to surfaces and to the fleeting nature of political history. Heade places the spectator in the street, in a position similar to that of a possible buyer of the news sheet.[117] We have no overview, no possibility for supervision, in this work but are instead placed in the position of the consumer of news; both political history and the marketplace define this view of Italy. This painting resists even as it comments on the tourist gaze; like Kirkland, Heade seems temporarily to reject the totalizing vista for a visual structure that replicates modern, republican ways of looking.

Nevertheless, while painted in support of the Risorgimento,[118] *Roman Newsboys* presents an ambiguous image of the function of the press in a republic; the news in this scene is, as Vance says, "ephemeral"[119] and infinitely replaceable, perhaps not as sure a foundation for a nation-state as canonical, "eternally" significant icons. This latent anxiety about the stability of a textual, press-based republic appears most strongly in Kirkland's accounts of Paris. In spite of her stated editorial faith in the power of the periodical press to "elevate the . . . character of the people," to be a force for "civilization," to "disseminat[e] information" and "diffus[e] . . . taste," revolutionary Paris makes Kirkland aware of public forms of discourse as a contested field, not secured to the interests of any one class (including the benevolent cultural elite) but open to conflicting voices and characterized by the entanglement of elite, governmental, and popular expressions. She notes the interplay between ephemeral political texts and street conversations that will shape the future course of the republic: "At the present time, the men . . . have an anxious look, and gather into knots, talking earnestly, or surrounding the bulletins and placards, of which there are plenty" (I, 139). As a journalist engaged both in producing a citizenry and in gratifying the demands and desires of her readers, she is interested in the ambiguity of the words and images she sees in the "Year of Revolutions" (I, vi), in the tenuous distinction between their roles as shaping agents and spontaneous expressions of the popular will, and in the uncertain outcome of revolutionary discourse.

Furthermore, in viewing revolutionary Paris, Kirkland finds the distinctions between text and icon blurring in disturbing ways that result in spectacularized words. Priscilla Parkhurst Ferguson explains that each of the century's revolutions, including that of 1848, brought with it a "rewriting" or renaming of Paris – of its buildings, streets, squares. These "battles over nomination and representation" accompanied the literal destruction of some "emblems of the past" but focused on the transformation of iconic objects through texts, on the "inscription of the revolution on the cityscape."[120] In her passage on republican inscriptions, Kirkland comments that the words themselves begin to seem iconic; even as revolutionaries write the iconoclastic rhetoric of republicanism onto the visual structures of church and monarchy, their words become "things," a new order of icons and, for Kirkland, who is generally sympathetic to the 1848 revolutions, possibly a new form of idolatry:

> The French are a nation of sentiments. Words are things to them. The number of inscriptions of "Liberté, Egalité, Fraternité," in the city, already, when the old king's traces are hardly cold, is truly wonderful. These magic words appear not only on every public building, churches included, but on every gateway; on the Arc Triomphale, . . . on the statue of Louis Quinze – in short, wherever the government or the people have any power. . . . They are set up, as if to give direction rather than expression to the feelings and sentiments of the people. (I, 130)

Kirkland signals the ambiguity between engineering consent in a republic (giving "direction") and offering a platform for a grass-roots "expression" of consent by shifting from the near equation of "the government" with "the people" to the suggestion that the "magic words" she sees are the revolutionary government's "direction" of the popular will. This ambiguity in the function of French republican pronouncements implicates them in the "magic" of pre-republican – that is, monarchical and Catholic – icons, from a U.S. Protestant point of view, which interpellate subjects through their feelings.

The confusion of word and image seems paradoxically related to the excessive textual iconoclasm of the French Republic, to the need to replace the organizing meanings of all pre-existing imagery with new meanings, as well as to secularize religious iconography. These inscriptions threaten to sever republicanism from any transcendent realm of meaning. One of Kirkland's favorite moments in Paris is a visit to the Church of the Sorbonne, where she engages in the unrepublican act of buying a silver cross from "old women with little trays of images, . . . beads, and reliquaries . . . for sale": "The quiet of this Church, its solemn light, the poor *marchandes* with their holy wares, the tomb of the saint – all seemed consecrated." By contrast, republican Paris is a city of "unsound principles . . . and not even Catholic religion. It was a city without homes – without a Sabbath, and yet aiming to be republican" (I, 124–5). Faced with France, Kirkland connects U.S. republicanism by contrast with religious faith and a body of unchanging values that transcend news culture. "The idea of a republic" is progressive; nations, therefore, must leave behind "brute force" for the "immutable principles" of Christianity. By abandoning not only monarchy and Catholicism but also a more generalized Christianity for an "accursed military spirit," the French invest overly in ephemeral political language and so lose the access to the "immutable" that religious belief and its iconography provide (I, 128–9). Kirkland echoes the usual American anxiety that the revolution of 1848 will repeat the "horrid scenes" (I, 139) of the first French Revolution.[121] Such a response marks the limits of U.S. iconoclasm in the 1840s and reveals the desire of elites to balance the social possibilities of word and image in the service of a gradual and contained "progress" that avoids revolutionary rupture.

In looking at Italy and France in 1848, Kirkland looks at the functions of icons and iconoclasm in the shaping of citizens and republics. Projecting the ambivalence of the managers of American culture toward images onto these two European sites, she complicates the problem of constructing a U.S. subjectivity further by her sporadic resistances to the gendered structures of the aesthetic gaze. Written during the U.S. turn to visual culture in its nation-building, *Holidays Abroad* enacts a split subjectivity. On the one hand, its humor gestures toward the dismantling of the national, often masculine gaze of supervisory power, while Kirkland is drawn toward those habits of vision that emphasize incongruity and disjunction. On the other, her emphasis on art, "homes," and the "Sabbath" as foundational to republics reinforces the conventional vehicles of aesthetics, domesticity, and piety for women's cultural agency, vehicles which usually required women to represent transcendent ideals, that is, to act as icons themselves. At the same time that Kirkland records this dual response, Fuller is formulating more explicit analyses of women, images, and revolution – and a more explicit critique of the tourist gaze.

Chapter 4

Fuller and Revolutionary Rome: Republican and Urban Imaginaries

I ... went forth to seek the Republic. Over the Quirinal I went, through the Forum to the Capitol. There was nothing to be seen except the ... [statue of the] emperor ..., a few dirty bold women, ... Murillo boys in the sun ... [and] all the horrible beggars ... as usual. ... At last the procession mounts the Campidoglio. ... One of [the Deputies] reads ... the following words ...

The form of Government of the Roman State shall be a pure Democracy, and will take the glorious name of Roman Republic.

... The crowd shouted, *viva la Republica! viva Italia!*

The ... grandeur of the spectacle to me gave new force to the thought that already swelled my heart ... and I longed to see in some answering glance a spark of Rienzi, a little of that soul which made my country what she is. The American at my side remained impassive.

Margaret Fuller[1]

Margaret Fuller was unusual among American travelers in the late 1840s in her decision to remain in Rome throughout the revolutionary period of 1847–9, in the depth of her personal and political immersion in Rome, and in her ability, honed in her U.S. writings, to function as a transnational public intellectual, as Charles Capper has argued, whose dialectical and cosmopolitan approach to culture and politics shaped her dispatches to the *New-York Tribune*.[2] Her equally dialectical work as a gender theorist in *Woman in the Nineteenth Century* (1845), to return to Christina Zwarg's point,[3] led Fuller to understand the power of cultural binaries and to develop strategies for deconstructing such mutually constitutive ideological categories as male/female or United States/Italy.[4] In his reading of Fuller's intellectual and psychological development, Jeffrey Steele connects her gender analysis with her ability to theorize the reclaiming of political power. Noting Fuller's use of the language of idolatry in her discussion of the ways in which "indoctrination within an ideology of white male supremacy" led women to inhabit "idolatrous relationships" with fathers, husbands, and other male figures, Steele defines this idolatry as the incorporation of images of patriarchal power ("male idols") within female psyches, an incorporation which leads to passivity, abjection, and melancholy. Recovery from abjection entailed, Fuller discovered, the work of mourning, of developing counter narratives and myths of "feminist agency," of naming the cause of one's loss, and so of turning grief into "grievance" – the beginning of political agency.[5] Fuller's theorizing of a process to work through and out of women's melancholic imprisonment in postures of idolatry prepared her to diagnose and address Italy's construction in American culture as abject, feminized, and idolatrous.

As a public intellectual constituted in such ways and as the influential foreign correspondent of an urban newspaper rapidly becoming "America's first national newspaper,"[6] Fuller was in a position to use the press both to train her readers in the deconstructive, even iconoclastic methods of reading that cleared a space for seeing Italy as a republic and to invoke, paradoxically enough, just those normative habits of seeing – those often patriarchal conventions of visual representation – that circulated widely in antebellum culture, but to do so in the service not only of U.S. nationalism but also of Italian nationalism. Her juxtapositions of tourist, social, aesthetic, and critical writings in her columns – what Andrew Taylor calls "the rhetorical and generic diversity of her political journalism" – sometimes operate similarly to Martin Johnson Heade's *Roman Newsboys* (see Chapter 3) in denying the U.S. observer the single, valorized point of view that grasps the essential, static "Italy." As Taylor notes, the "bricolage of discourses and textual registers" that characterized the front page of antebellum newspapers matched "Fuller's vision of a pluralized intellectual space of competing and circulating ideas."[7] Charlene Avallone argues that it was just this sense of the multi-generic, hybrid, experimental possibilities of travel writing and journalism that drew Fuller to George Sand's works, including her *Lettres d'un Voyageur*.[8] Fuller uses the "pluralized . . . space" of the *Tribune*'s front page and the hybrid forms of her dispatches both to disrupt conventional, genre views of Italy and to link its political scenes with other visual conventions, this time explicitly nationalist ones. Aware of the contradictions within American demands on Italy that Caroline Kirkland explored in her contemporaneous treatment of revolutions and republics, visual experience, and the press,

Fuller sent her *Tribune* readers a sustained case study of a tourist site as a re-emergent capital city and thus formulated an argument for re-seeing Rome.

This chapter is organized around two features usually absent from the American picture of Italy: contemporary history and the city. Its two sections are, therefore, organized around two methodologies, both of which continue to be focused on the ideological implications of visual modes of apprehension: the comparative reading of Fuller's *Tribune* correspondence with a third visual arts genre evoked in this book, history painting, and a comparison of the representations of Roman space as urban space in Fuller's dispatches and in her friend Nathaniel Hawthorne's novel *The Marble Faun, or, The Romance of Monte Beni* (1860). Bringing Fuller's journalism and Hawthorne's fiction together juxtaposes descriptive strategies in these genres – that is, their incorporation of travel writing – and contrasts U.S. representations of a revolutionary phase of the Risorgimento with those of a period of political reaction. But these works are also bound, more closely than these contrasts imply, by Hawthorne's retrospectic imagination; as Thomas Mitchell has argued, Hawthorne's transnational and feminist character Miriam represents in large part his ambivalent response to Fuller's public, political, and sexual life in Rome and thus his own work of mourning for the possibilities that Fuller represented.[9]

Both Fuller and Hawthorne were in Europe in highly visible public capacities. Fuller traveled and lived in Europe in 1846–50 as a foreign correspondent for the *Tribune*. During her travels in England and France, she met a number of republican activists and exiles, including the Polish poet Adam Mickiewicz and Giuseppe Mazzini, the leader of the revolutionary republican movement Young Italy. She arrived in Rome in 1847, in time to witness and report on the attempt by northern Italian states to throw off Austrian rule, on revolutionary activity throughout Italy, and on the brief exile of Pope Pius IX from Rome and the equally brief existence of a Roman Republic in 1849. Like Mazzini and others, Fuller understood the Roman Republic as a movement toward a unified Italy. And she understood herself as its historian; she was working on a manuscript of the history of the Roman Republic at her death in 1850.[10] Her political activism as a correspondent writing in support of the Roman Republic and as director of one of the field hospitals during the siege of Rome in 1849 was matched by her personal investment in Rome: her affair and possible marriage with a Roman revolutionary and the birth of their son in 1848.[11] On the other hand, Hawthorne arrived in Europe after the revolutions of 1848–9 had failed and Fuller had died. Appointed U.S. Consul to the important post at Liverpool, he served as a representative of the U.S. government in England for four years, 1853–7, and followed his term in office with a sixteen-month sojourn in Rome and Florence in 1858–9.[12] Associating primarily with American and British expatriates and tourists, especially artists and writers, Hawthorne focused his ensuing novel, which I discuss more fully in the next chapter, on American artists and on the importance of visual perception in composing both national identity and the nation's other. Their Italian texts were widely read; while Fuller's dispatches shaped feminist and abolitionist political theory and practice, moving, for example, abolitionists towards warfare as a means of liberty,[13] Hawthorne's novel became in future years a popular guidebook for American tourists in Rome.[14]

Representing Italy: Fuller, History Painting, and the Popular Press

In one of her dispatches to the *New-York Tribune* during the euphoric early days of the Roman Revolution (1848–9), Fuller recounts a pivotal historical moment: the founding of the short-lived Roman Republic. On 9 February 1849 she walked through the center of Rome to hear one of the deputies of the new Constitutional Assembly proclaim the Republic from the steps of the Capitol. As she puts it, "I . . . went forth to seek the Republic" (256). Fuller chooses to present this moment, to which I will return below, through three different modes of viewer response: her own and those of what she depicts as two conventional types of spectator – the English tourist and the American artist. By shifting the focus from the event itself to the different forms of its visual reception, she highlights, as she does throughout the dispatches, the connection between visual and political forms of representation. The passage implicitly asks a series of questions about visualizing nationhood: how does one see a republic or, more specifically, see the invention of a modern nation? In addition, how does one recognize the republican citizen who inhabits the republican scene? And finally, how do the various modes of visibility granted to nation-states and their citizens by aesthetic conventions shape the political representation of their interests?

By implicitly asking such questions, Fuller critiques the U.S. cultural task in which she is also deeply engaged: the antebellum consolidation of national and civic identities through such cultural expressions as journalism, histories, historical romances, and land-scape paintings.[15] As correspondent to the *Tribune* and self-conscious historian of the revolution in Italy, Fuller is aware of the constitutive nature of writing history; she is trying not only to shape Italy in the eyes of her U.S. readers but also, much like one of her heroes of the Risorgimento, Giuseppe Mazzini, to call the ideal "Italy" into being, that is, to use representation as a means of constructing a political reality. As critics have recognized, these efforts on behalf of Italy are intimately linked with her attempts to create an "America" through her repeated direct address to "my country" in the years she wrote for the *Tribune* (1844–50).[16] Fuller's descriptions of pivotal moments in the Roman Revolution, a revolution which attempted to create a modern nation-state, draw on but also critique American habits of visualizing such nations and their populations, habits embod-ied in two major forms of visual expression in the 1840s: the genre painting discussed in previous chapters but also the prestigious and nationalist form of history painting. That Fuller is aware not only of the pervasive conventions of genre scenes but also of the academic conventions and high cultural status of history painting, as well as its subject matters – national and historical events, biblical episodes, and moral allegories – is clear from her reviews of Washington Allston's and Rembrandt Peale's paintings in Boston and New York.[17] In pub-lishing such scenes in Horace Greeley's reformist newspaper, Fuller employs the press – perhaps the primary medium of national imag-inings[18] – for her own attempts to shape two nations: a republican, unified Italy and a revived U.S. But she also uses the popular press as a site of critical inquiry into the process of visualizing nationhood.

American Periodical Representations of Italy in the 1840s

Fuller's critical inquiry is prompted by a disjunction in U.S. represen-tations of Italy during this phase of the Risorgimento. Most Ameri-can newspapers and periodicals that published pieces on the Roman Revolution were sympathetic to Italian efforts to unite the coun-try under a republican government. As Dennis Berthold has docu-mented, the presence of Italian political refugees and the influence of British writers supporting Italian unification caused "Risorgimento sympathies" to spread "rapidly in New York's literary circles" in the 1840s – during and after Fuller's time in New York.[19] Many of the journals that reported on the political ferment also included tourist sketches; the *Tribune* serialized Bayard Taylor's picturesque *Views*

A-Foot in the mid 1840s, just before it began running Fuller's dispatches.[20] However, the period of the revolution did not alter tourist representations significantly but merely added the familiar icon of the republican patriot to older habits of depiction.

The art critic Henry Tuckerman's 1835 *Italian Sketch Book*, for example, celebrated the Italian scene as a timeless counterpoint to the rapidly changing American landscape; in his expanded 1848 edition Italy's dependable status as a place outside of or beyond history continued to serve as a foil by which returning U.S. tourists could measure changes in themselves. Tuckerman notes that the Italian "scene is the same; but what revolutions may not [the tourist's] own feelings have undergone, since he last beheld it!"[21] In the revolutionary year of 1848 Tuckerman extended his sympathetic descriptions of the political situation of "modern" Italy; he supported Italian unification, and therefore Italy's re-entrance into history, but in all editions he appended his political observations onto his picturesque sketches of the changeless types of the eternal Italian scene: peasants, beggars, and priests. He seems unaware of the disparity between his political ideals for Italy and his aesthetic demands on it, the possible conflict between his desire to sense a "revolution" within his own consciousness (which depends on the stability of "Italy") and any revolution in the scene itself.

Such periodicals as the *American Whig Review* and the *United States Magazine and Democratic Review*, whose writers Fuller knew in New York,[22] sustained this bifurcated image of Italy and the Italians throughout the 1840s. And these two magazines did so in spite of serving opposing political parties in the U.S.[23] In 1846–7, the *Whig Review* published a series of sentimental and picturesque tourist sketches by Ik Marvel (Donald Grant Mitchell), such as "A Glimpse of the Appenines," that blend vistas into "dream"-like landscapes with genre images of women, children, and goatherds; it also published an article by an Italian exile in New York, Francesco Secchi de Casali, "Italy in 1846," which reprises the movements for Italian "liberty" from the 1790s to the present and argues that "*Men*, in Italy, have not ceased to be men; nor is the country itself to be forever a butt for esthetic sentimentalism."[24] Throughout this period (1845–50) the *Whig Review*'s column synthesizing news abroad, its "Foreign Miscellany," strongly supported liberal movements in Italy. On the other hand, the magazine reiterated unchanged the polarity of U.S. activity and Italian passivity that had characterized Cooper and Sedgwick's generation. An anonymous book reviewer notes that the American "absorption in business" and the "excessive anxiety" of "its feverish life" can only be assuaged by a trip to Italy or contact with the fine arts, forms of revitalization the author equates; from the perspective of Italy, an American sees the U.S. as "'some vast battle-field in the dim distance'" and can revive the neglected faculties of his "'soul'" through Italy's aesthetic repose – or, as Casali puts it, by making Italy "a butt for esthetic sentimentalism."[25]

Similarly, while consistently supporting the revolutionary efforts of Mazzini's republican organization Young Italy, and figuring the participants as "gallant . . . patriots," the *Democratic Review* also included such tourist sketches as "A Day in Pisa," by William Gillespie, whose delight in the "picturesque" and eminently sketchable landscape is matched only by his delight in the "picturesque figures . . . of the peasantry" which populate it: "lounging men with their jackets thrown over their shoulders with a coquettish carelessness, and the embrowned but beautiful women with the graceful white drapery folded on their heads."[26] Images of Italians as middle-class revolutionaries impelled by bourgeois liberalism coexisted in the 1840s, rather illogically, with images of Italians and their landscape as racialized, apolitical "others" that helped white, middle- and upper-class Americans define their own national and class identities by contrast. As Paola Gemme explains, this representational disjunction in the American press and especially in the *Democratic Review* emerged from twinned but uneasily coexisting ideological perspectives – "American political evangelism and exceptionalism" – which led U.S. writers to view (inaccurately) Italian revolutionaries as "disciples" of an exportable American republicanism but to view the Italian people as "not ready for freedom" and, unlike Americans, "unfit for republicanism."[27]

Fuller inserted into her dispatches prose sketches of public events and urban spaces that revised the traditionally timeless and often pastoral Italian scene of Anglo-American depictions, she found aesthetic conventions to represent Italians as fit republicans, and, in doing so, she intervened in American public perceptions of Italy. Christina Zwarg has argued that Fuller saw the popular press as a powerful vehicle to effect social change, in part by making readers conscious of their structures of perception; in Fuller's book reviews for the *Tribune* in New York, says Zwarg, she drew her readers into the "unsettling" work of reading, which disrupted "stable subject position[s]," brought subaltern perspectives into dialogic relation with dominant ones, and exposed "the way we are all framed by a bewildering grid of ideological formations."[28] I would argue that Fuller's descriptions for the *Tribune* also address the specifically visual structures of perception which were at their peak in U.S. culture in the 1840s and which were associated with genre painting and history painting: that is, the ways in which scenes both of daily life and of nationally significant events were quite literally "framed" by the ideological perspectives of a white, northeastern elite. To return to Elizabeth Johns' analysis of Jacksonian-era genre painting, this art form, with its focus on scenes of "everyday life," tried at once to place recently enfranchised lower-class males safely within the U.S. body politic and to type them as distinct from the elite consumers of those images; as I argued in Chapter 3, American depictions of Italian everyday life used genre strategies for typing Italian figures as non-citizens and included no visual devices for incorporating these figures into a progressive polity.[29]

Art historians have also explored the functions of the other mid-nineteenth-century visual form that incorporated multiple figures into a culturally emblematic composition: history painting. Throughout the antebellum period painters were preoccupied with consolidating the national status and the union of the U.S. by painting what Wendy Greenhouse calls "original moment[s]" or "significant individual birth-events" in the discovery, exploration, and founding of "America."[30] By 1840, these originating scenes usually focused on a central heroic individual who embodied the spirit of the moment and of the future American republic and thus corresponded with American romantic biographies and histories of exploration, colonization, and the founding of the U.S. by Washington Irving, George Bancroft, and others, who localized political agency in a pantheon of patriarchal figures.[31] Examples of such history paintings, often monumental in size, include a number of scenes from the life and explorations of Columbus, such as John Vanderlyn's mural for the U.S. Capitol Building, *The Landing of Columbus* (1837–47), and paintings of events from the Revolutionary War, such as Emanuel Leutze's *Washington Crossing the Delaware* (1851).[32]

These two forms of painting corresponded with the two forms of political perception Americans exercised upon Italy. Nevertheless, it is significant that the visual depictions of Italians by Americans continued to occur overwhelmingly within genre scenes, even during active phases of the Risorgimento.[33] Political writings about Italy from a distance, such as the *Democratic Review*'s articles praising Mazzini, employ the rhetoric associated with descriptions of the U.S. Founding Fathers; such essays on republican patriots may be accompanied by engraved portraits of Mazzini or the military hero Giuseppe Garibaldi, just as the *Democratic Review* featured portraits of contemporary American statesmen (primarily belonging to the Democratic party). Although not history paintings, the portraits do emphasize the possibility of historical transformation through individual agency.[34] But there were few prints of contemporary Italian *events* in the periodical press,[35] and the writings of Americans actually in Italy predominantly drew on the visual habits associated with genre scenes, as did numerous paintings and magazine illustrations. Unlike genre paintings of American people and scenes, these pictures were not about imagining lower-class men with whom the middle-class spectator was being asked to share power but about permanently apolitical figures: women, children, and "peasants," a term that solidified the concept of "citizen" by contrast. "Italy" continued to be constructed by U.S. tourists as a post-historical, feminized, and aesthetic realm – outside and opposed to the modern world of rational, masculine agency and progressive history. Embodying Amy Kaplan's concept of "manifest domesticity," in which the antebellum domestic sphere intimately supported an expansionist nationalism by "generat[ing] notions of the foreign against which the nation can be imagined as home,"[36] both political periodicals and women's magazines printed visual and textual depictions of this imagined world with a ritualized repetitiveness that worked to stabilize U.S. national identity.[37]

Two images from *Godey's Lady's Book* exemplify this body of representation. In June 1849, even as French troops were bombarding Rome and putting an end to the Roman Republic, *Godey's* published a short story about a male American tourist whose love rescues an Italian flower girl from destitution and transforms her into a middle-class wife; the accompanying illustration, *The Italian Flower Girl* (Fig. 4.1), shows an image of an Italian who is passive to the point of unconsciousness: an adolescent girl asleep after gathering flowers among the ruins of a past civilization.[38] Italy, when construed as feminine, can be reawakened to history and to a modern bourgeois identity, the story implies, by an American gaze and through a tutelary ideological intercourse with the bearer of this gaze, the middle-class male citizen.[39] This sentimental tale and image mirror precisely the *Democratic Review*'s premise, according to Gemme, that Italians depended on the model of U.S. republicanism in order to achieve national unity and modernity; further, the paternalism of the tale parallels the foreign policy the *Democratic Review* urged: support for the Risorgimento combined with an increased U.S. economic presence and influence in the Mediterranean. As Gemme puts it, such texts anticipate "the tie between political philanthropy and imperialism that has characterized American foreign policy in the twentieth century."[40]

THE ITALIAN FLOWER GIRL.

Figure 4.1 Edward Corbould, *The Italian Flower Girl*, engraved by Charles Heath, *Godey's Lady's Book*, June 1849. Milne Special Collections and Archives Department, University of New Hampshire Library, Durham, NH.

Leonardo Buonomo argues that antebellum tourist writing was characterized by what James Clifford has called "salvage, or redemptive ethnography," which includes the "paternalistic" assumption that the other needs to be represented by the tourist; Italians were, then, "unable to represent" themselves.[41] Transformations of male peasants into political figures able to represent themselves and their emerging nation were harder to visualize than that of the flower girl into the American wife. The closest *Godey's* came to violating its policy of abstaining from political commentary (as a lady's magazine) was in a poem accompanying another illustration (Fig. 4.2) in 1845:

"The Italian Peasant Boy"
Fair Italy, the land of love and song,
Still breathes in beauty on her lowly throng . . .
And to the unconscious child a charm imparts,
That, like a spell, can win and conquer hearts.

Figure 4.2 L. Pollack, *The Italian Peasant Boy*, engraved by J. C. Buttre, *Godey's Lady's Book*, December 1845: frontispiece. Milne Special Collections and Archives Department, University of New Hampshire Library, Durham, NH.

And who that gazes on our Peasant Boy,
Wrapp'd in a reverie more deep than joy,
But feels, in fancy, borne to Dante's land,
Where skies are soft and orange breezes bland;
And breathes a prayer that God will bless the child,
And make him strong in truth, in wisdom mild,
And guide him till, his country's freedom won,
He's hail'd the bless'd of heaven, Italia's Washington?

The poem and image highlight the unstable mixture of American modes of apprehension. The image of the boy is an essentialized one, firmly fixed in his pastoral setting and costume (goat skin breeches), linked, through his pipe, with a "natural" form of art, and given a backdrop of ruined aqueducts which just as firmly puts historical action in the distant past. How this "unconscious child" can become a Washington – that is, become a political and military "father" of the contemporary world – is difficult to imagine; the

anonymous poet assumes only God can effect the necessary transformation.[42]

This conventional approach to Italy does not change even after
the revolutionary years of 1848 and 1849. In 1852 *Sartain's Union
Magazine*, a periodical (edited earlier by Kirkland) which addressed a
mixed gender readership, published an image of "Modern Romans"
(Fig. 4.3) as part of an article on "Modern Rome." The illustration rehearses the conventional depoliticized figures of "Italy" with
two typically costumed women, who hold children and a container
of food, and a marginalized male figure who sits behind one of the
women. *Sartain's* also reveals the usual ambivalence about change
in the Italian scene in its texts. In a rhapsodic piece on "Southern
Italy" in 1848, George Curtis describes a highly eroticized landscape,
whose climate is characterized by a "careless indolence" and which
is populated by dancing women; he claims that Italy is antithetical to
the reform-minded and opposes aesthetic response to "conscience":
"Italy is a paradise ruined only to those whose minds and hopes, bent

Figure 4.3 Felter, *Modern Romans, Sartain's Union Magazine*,
1852. Harvard College Library. Digitized by Google. Courtesy of
HathiTrust.

strongly upon human welfare, are impatient of that repose which long depression and inactivity has created." Edward Pollock's poem "Italy" (1852), on the other hand, presents this feminized Italy as an endangered captive whose repose is really a troubled and "fettered slumber"; he looks back on the failed revolutions of the late 1840s as a prelude of the "fierce storm, and ruthless wind" that will some day free "her" from the vampire-like embrace of "priests, and kings."[43]

The tradition of seeing Italy as a feminized landscape whose inhabitants enact genre scenes continued not only in the periodicals but also in the "high" art of oil paintings. One standard genre scene of Italy – the image of female piety in a serene landscape – that appeared in the earlier works discussed in Chapter 2, such as Samuel F. B. Morse's painting *The Chapel of the Virgin at Subiaco* (1830–1) and the illustration *The Shrine* in the 1841 giftbook annual *Friendship's Offering*, recurred, for example, in John Kensett's painting *The Shrine – A Scene in Italy* (1847); these works depict women kneeling or sitting at roadside shrines, with male figures situated somewhat apart from the focal point of feminine prayer.[44] Another ritually repeated image, of women and children getting water at a fountain whose site, inscription, or iconography implied a grander historical past than the present, also persisted, as in William T. Carlton's *Italian Scene* (n.d.; probably 1840s–1850s). Such images, in which piety and domestic activity have replaced historical and public action, depict a feminized landscape whose purpose is to elicit a private, aesthetic reverie from the tourist.[45]

Fuller's History Painting: Revolution, Defeat, and National Birth

Fuller's dispatches invoke and address these habits of looking and representing; disturbed that American views of Italians are too often defined by the perspectives of genre painting, which turned its subjects into types, and conscious that she may be witnessing originating moments – "birth-events" – in the national narrative of a unified Italy, Fuller tries to train her readers to shift from genre perspectives to something like the perspective of history painting, to move from the timeless and static images of pastoral innocence to images which evoke the grand (masculine) narrative of history in the making. In this effort, she analyzes tourist ways of seeing, experiments both with genre perspectives themselves and with other ways of seeing "the people," and finally creates in prose a history painting of Garibaldi's departure from Rome after the defeat of Roman forces and the failure of the revolution. While her recourse to the rhetoric of history painting shifts her reader from one visual convention to another, her analysis of the tourist/genre gaze radically questions her culture's ability to see political change at all.

Her awareness of the ways in which the genre habit as it is practiced by tourists silences and renders invisible political change when it does appear becomes clear in her account of that important originating moment of the Italian national narrative – the proclamation of the Republic – with which this section began. Fuller does not construct a history painting of the event; instead she depicts its diffraction through the eyes of foreign spectators.[46] Her account begins in a flat, comic tone as she describes the area near the Capitol before the event; the political changes, she implies dryly, are not immediately visible in the scene:

> There was nothing to be seen except the . . . [statues of the] emperor, the tamers of horses, the fountain . . . as usual; among the marbles for living figures, a few dirty bold women, and Murillo boys in the sun . . . [and] all the horrible beggars . . . as usual. I met some English; all their comfort was, "It would not last a month." – "They hoped to see all those fellows shot yet." (256)

Fuller has already castigated English tourists several times in the dispatches; they become the type of tourists for her that use aesthetic conventions to reinforce class difference and to maintain the status quo. Her description of the pre-event scene is from their point of view. She references the classical statuary that attracted tourists, the abjection and poverty associated with Rome, and the translation of this powerlessness into the charm of genre scenes; the "Murillo boys" represent tourist perceptions modeled on the seventeenth-century genre paintings of children by the Spanish painter Bartolomé Esteban Murillo, paintings collected avidly by eighteenth-century English elites.[47] Her ventriloquized rendering of this English view makes plain both the contempt beneath this use of the genre perspective and the threat of force which backs up the order imposed by it.

When the procession arrives, an anonymous deputy reads the proclamation of the Republic "in a clear, friendly voice"; Fuller again steers away from creating a full-blown history painting with a heroic, particular individual at its center. And she again focuses on viewer responses; her understanding of the meaning of the moment and the cheers of the crowd enable her to see "the imposing grandeur of the spectacle." Her identification with the republican ideals she is seeing enacted make her look at her fellow witness, an American artist, in order to share this Italian/U.S. moment of commonality: "I longed to see in some answering glance a spark of Rienzi, a little of that soul which made my country what she is." The fourteenth-century Roman populist reformer Cola di Rienzi became a touch-stone for English and American observers sympathetic to the cause and seemed to them to prefigure democratic and Protestant values; also in 1849, the Pre-Raphaelite painter William Holman Hunt painted an image of Rienzi, who was catapulted into reform by the violent death of a brother.[48] But rather than acknowledge the spirit of liberty – the "spark of Rienzi" – common to Americans and Italians, the artist refuses to share his "birthright" of "Democracy" and differentiates between the two peoples (he has "no confidence in the People"); thus he sees neither "the artistic beauty of the scene" nor its political import. His reading of the participants as types prevents him from realizing that the "soldiers" in the scene (a genre category) *are* in this case "the people" – they are the Civic Guard, made up, says Fuller, of "all the decent men in Rome" (257–8).[49] The artist's inability to visualize an emerging nation, to read what genre conventions label as "only soldiers" as patriotic citizens, indicates Fuller's sense of the difficulty of transforming U.S. visual/political structures of perception.

Both visual responses – that of the violently oppressive tourist and that of the "impassive" and obtuse artist – base aesthetic pleasure on the stasis of the object of the gaze. Fuller uses them to frame a token of instability and change, the text of the proclamation, which she typically includes; she translates as many of the primary documents of the Revolution for her *Tribune* readers as she has space for.[50] Unlike Kirkland, who is uneasy about the possible representational instability of a text-based republic, Fuller embraces the fluidity of texts and, as critics have argued, of translation as a type of cultural mediation that entails an act of "un-settling," a "proliferation of meaning" and openness to "new values."[51] The text, which observes the end of temporal papal power in Rome and the advent of a democratic republic, is not understood by either set of tourists, who do not speak Italian. But Fuller's readership does "hear" the proclamation; for them Italy ceases being a silent aesthetic icon and achieves a historical voice. And the scene emphasizes Fuller's sense that representation does matter; the artist's ignoring the text threatens to silence this voice, just as the United States' lack of official recognition of the Roman Republic, according to Fuller, may have hastened its demise (282–4).

In a number of urban scenes Fuller tries to help her reader envision "the people" as the protagonist in the founding events of the Republic; as William L. Vance argues, in the dispatches the Roman people superseded even Mazzini, whom Fuller admired, as the main actor in her account of the revolution.[52] But here, too, Fuller realizes that to represent "the people" is also to construct them. Larry Reynolds points out that Fuller privately expressed considerable doubts about the Italian people (in private she sometimes sounded closer to the figure of the American artist) and that her "resolute" and committed "*Tribune* persona" is "an artful creation."[53] Fuller's descriptions of crowds, processions, and celebrations attempt to depict an agency diffused throughout the Romans and, therefore, to help her audience imagine these former genre subjects as citizens. Indeed, as Bell Chevigny notes, Fuller emphasizes republican revolutionary identity as inherently transformative, as "process": "she observed how the people gained autonomy through crises which exposed the limits of an ideology they had previously been unable even to discern."[54]

One crowd scene, in a strategy similar to Kirkland's description of a festival procession (discussed in Chapter 3), explicitly offers a transitional passage between one mode of apprehension and the other, as well as between modes of being for the "people" themselves. Fuller describes a revision in the final ritual of Carnival, the *moccoletti*, in honor of Milanese revolutionary victories over the Austrian army in March of 1848. Instead of the usual playful extinguishing of each other's candles, the crowd leaves them all lit; Fuller uses the occasion to create an image of a tightly packed city thoroughfare filled with light and with the dawn of democratic enlightenment:

> The fun usually consists in all the people blowing one another's lights out; we had not this; all the little tapers were left to blaze. . . . – Lights crept out over the surface of all the houses. . . . Up and down the Corso, they twinkled, they swarmed, they streamed, while a surge of gay triumphant sound ebbed and flowed beneath that glittering surface. Here and there danced men carrying aloft *moccoli*, and clanking chains, emblem of the tyrannic power now vanquished by the people. The people, sweet and noble, who, in the intoxication of their joy, were guilty of no rude or unkindly word or act, and who, no signal being given as usual for the termination of their diversion, closed, of their own accord and with one consent, . . . and retired peacefully to their homes, to dream of hopes they yet scarce understand. (211)

This infusion of picturesque spectacle with political will enables both the U.S. reader to see the "people" of Rome, mentioned in the first line, as "the people" by the end and the Roman crowd to move from social to political "consent" and self-governance. Fuller follows this passage with an exhortation to the corresponding "people" of the U.S. in the next paragraph; the agony of European revolutions should shore up American democratic principles: "To you, people of America, it may perhaps be given to look on and learn in time for a preventive wisdom."[55] For Fuller both revolution and newspaper reporting are creative acts that bring on nationhood – both in Europe and, she hopes, in the U.S.

Fuller explores and manipulates aesthetic conventions as she goes; she moves from her own early genre scenes toward a romantic vocabulary that naturalizes nationalist uprisings. Her letter of 17 December 1847 depicts a conventional, even essentialist scene of "the Trasteverini dancing the Saltarello in their most brilliant costume" and compares the "enchant[ing]" scene to art (176). Her next letter ruminates over the transition of public expression that will come with "the march of Reform," when expression will move from the politically silent spectacle favored by tourists to "speeches"; she shares with her reader an ambivalence over the possible loss of the "poetical" spectacle as it is superseded by the public life of citizens (180). Indeed, Julie Ellison draws attention to Fuller's "nervousness about the resemblance between her narratives and conventional tourism," about the fact that her own visual orientation to the "spectacle" of Italy is "very close" to the conventional tourism she castigates.[56] Nevertheless, she tries to move her reader toward romantic images of "the people" as embodying first a natural force, a "surge" or "wave" (211, 229) – metaphors of movement and emergent forms of national life too fluid "to be embodied by the pen" (239) – and then as expressing itself through its newly elected officials in the series of public documents she translates for the *Tribune*.

Her most explicit evocation of the conventions of history painting, however, comes out of the fall of the Republic and the deferment of its hopes.[57] Fuller's description of the exit of Garibaldi and his legion from Rome after its defeat by the French army is one of the most obvious set pieces of her letters and has received some critical comment.[58] As Dennis Berthold has noted, Fuller "first introduced" Garibaldi "to the American public"; the eventual unifier of Italy, this military figure was idealized as "'the Washington of Italy'" in the American press throughout the 1850s and 1860s.[59] Like Mazzini, with whom she was in frequent contact, Fuller was intent on forging a national narrative; as Charles Capper notes, Mazzini believed that an armed defense of Rome, even if doomed, was "essential for the creation of a national myth."[60] Therefore, she represents the scene of Garibaldi's retreat in the highest mode of history painting. By doing so she seems to have given up her analyses of modes of vision and instead, more simply, uses a broadly understood nationalist iconography in order to keep the myth of Italian nationhood alive in the moment of its apparent demise. Shifting away from the anonymous proclaimer of the Roman Republic, Fuller sets the heroic figure of Garibaldi in a fully articulated historical landscape. She invokes Sir Walter Scott, the writer of historical romances and part of the nineteenth-century nationalist imagination, as the writer most fit to "see" the scene.[61]

It is worth quoting the passage at length to notice its determined evocation of the rhetoric of history painting, with its central figure and representative crowd, its nationally significant setting, and its obsessive attention to details that are at once accurate and idealized:

> I went into the Corso with some friends; it was filled with citizens and military, . . . the lancers of Garibaldi galloped along in full career, I longed for Sir Walter Scott to be on earth again, and see them; all are light, athletic, resolute figures, many of the forms of the finest manly beauty of the South, . . . ready to dare, to do, to die. We followed them to the piazza of St. John Lateran. Never have I seen a sight so beautiful, so romantic and so sad. Whoever knows Rome knows the peculiar solemn grandeur of that piazza, scene of the first triumph of Rienzi, the magnificence of the "mother of all churches," the Baptistry . . ., the obelisk . . ., the view through the gates of the Campagna, on that side so richly strewn with ruins. The sun was setting, the crescent moon rising, the flower of Italian youth were marshaling in that solemn place. . . . They had all put on the beautiful dress of the Garibaldi legion, the tunic of bright red cloth, the Greek cap, . . . their long hair was blown back from resolute faces. . . . I saw the wounded, all that could go, laden upon their baggage cars, . . . the women were ready, their eyes too were resolved, if sad. . . . [Garibaldi's] look was entirely that of a hero of the middle ages, his face still young. . . . He went upon the parapet and looked upon the road with a spy-glass, and, no obstruction being in sight, he turned his face for a moment back upon Rome, then led the way through the gate. (304–5)

The setting's conflation of classical, Renaissance, and, in effect, Reformation (in the reference to Rienzi) markers signals Garibaldi's status as heir to Roman history, while the passage's emphasis on the "resolute" masculinity of both the "hero" and his followers parallels contemporary history painters' strategy of representing the U.S. "national past largely in terms of manly heroes" whose determination created national unity.[62] By saying that Garibaldi looks like "a hero of the middle ages," Fuller seems to refer to contemporary nationalist paintings, especially English and German, that interpreted medieval history – as did Scott's historical romances – as Ur-moments of modern nations. She toured expatriate artists' studios in Rome,[63] but her aesthetics in this scene seem closest to those of the German and German-trained American artists associated with Düsseldorf in the 1840s and whose history paintings were at the high point of their influence in the U.S. in the 1840s and 1850s. Indeed, as William Gerdts has documented, this American interest led to the opening of the Düsseldorf Gallery in New York in 1849 where such monumental paintings as Karl Friedrich Lessing's *Huss before the Stake* (1850) were shown and praised in the press. These paintings (though after Fuller's time in New York) depicted medieval and early modern episodes, such as the Czech priest Huss's proto-Protestant martyrdom, as events offering models of heroic action and the seeds of nationalism. And they sometimes commented specifically, as Lessing's does, on the demise of liberal revolutionary hopes in Europe.[64]

It is significant that Fuller appeals to the most clearly understood visual form of the nationalist narrative – the *"grande machine"* of history painting[65] – at the moment of the defeat of nationalist hopes. Like Lessing, Emanuel Leutze painted *Washington Crossing the Delaware* (Fig. 4.4) in Germany as a reaction to the failure of the 1848 revolutions there.[66] A German-American artist heavily involved in the Düsseldorf artists' organization the Malkasten, which agitated for democracy and for German unity, Leutze drew on American Revolutionary history in an attempt to revitalize the German nationalist movement, which in 1849, the year he began his painting, was faltering. He chose to depict what was to be a "psychological turning point" in the Revolution: Washington's leading his outnumbered and ill-equipped men out of defeat to a surprise victory at Trenton.[67]

In her depiction of Garibaldi, another military hero trying to "father" his country, Fuller uses an image of temporary defeat as an originating moment for a future national identity, or, rather, she seeks to make his exit from Rome visible to her readers as such a "birth-event." Like Leutze, she is trying to use the monumental representation of a nationalist revolution in jeopardy to call the future into being; as was the case with history paintings, these textual

Figure 4.4 Emanuel Gottlieb Leutze, *Washington Crossing the Delaware*, 1851 (post cleaning). Oil on canvas. 149 x 255 ins (378.5 x 647.7 cm). Gift of John Stewart Kennedy, 1897 (97.34). The Metropolitan Museum of Art. Image copyright © The Metropolitan Museum of Art. Image source: Art Resource, New York.

representations "attempt to be what [they] depict": agents of historical transformation.[68] In doing so she moves away from her previous analyses of modes of spectatorship and her critique of looking "merely with a pictorial eye" (169) to an act of faith that relies on one of those modes, from the multiple perspectives she highlights and dissects in her rendition of the announcing of the Roman Republic to the single, valorized perspective and the less experimental vocabulary of history painting. For Fuller visualizing nationhood remains a crucial means of achieving it; by using such visual perspectives, she lays claim not only to the masculine province of history painting but also to the "masculine" agency that leads to history making.[69] But perhaps just as crucially, she sees a connection between mythic nationalist representations and, to return to Jeffrey Steele's terms, the work of mourning. As she watches the defeated "men of Rome" that remained behind fall from the "energy" and "responsibility" of revolutionary republicanism back into the "effeminacy" of political repression and unemployment (308–9) – "they lounge along the streets . . ., [t]heir hands fall slack, their eyes rove aimless, the beggars begin to swarm again" – that is, back into the abjection of genre scenes, Fuller recognizes the affinity of history painting's triumphalist conventions with the representation of loss. As with Lessing and Leutze, whose most famous works she never saw, in Fuller's hands these conventions of visualizing nationhood become as well a means of articulating grief.

Fuller, Hawthorne, and Imagining Urban Spaces in Rome

It is worth emphasizing that for Fuller the Italian revolution was, in its final stages, a Roman revolution and that her revolutionary scenes – from the Carnival *moccoletti* in the Corso and the proclamation of the Republic at the Capitol to Garibaldi's retreat from the piazza of St. John Lateran – are urban scenes. As was true of her American and European contemporaries, Fuller understood revolutionary republicanism as an urban movement and the achievement of republics as contingent upon the re-vision of a capital city.[70] Her Roman dispatches attempt to construct a nation by visualizing what one might call a national city. In addition to the concerns of class, gender, and nation, U.S. concepts of the city were refracted through tourist responses to Italian sites. Critics have increasingly emphasized Fuller's identity as an urban writer; as Robert N. Hudspeth says, she almost always "wrote from a city and to a city audience."[71] Reading Fuller's *Tribune* articles together with Hawthorne's later fictional depictions of Rome in *The Marble Faun* – and reading them both for their representations of urban spaces – traces the emergence of a U.S. urban imaginary and its entanglement with tourist writings and republican formations.

Nineteenth-century urban space emerged as a category conceptualized through a web of contradictory discourses and visual practices. It was at once a cosmopolitan space and a national space, at once owned by a male gaze and traversed and looked at by women. And it was immediately covered and shaped by an expansive print culture already in place, a culture whose most widely disseminated forms – the newspaper and the novel – embodied and at times analyzed the contradictory perspectives that composed the urban imaginary. Following Benedict Anderson's influential work on the cultural construction of nationhood, scholars have examined the role of these characteristic nineteenth-century genres in developing and disseminating a national imaginary.[72] Similarly, the third popular bourgeois prose genre this book examines – travel writing – furthered the nationalist project by training the tourist gaze on other nations.

Examining Fuller's and Hawthorne's Roman texts as overlapping genres, as conflations of tourist writing with journalism, on the one hand, and with fiction writing, on the other, reveals their engagement with a national city and their concerns, displaced onto the foreign scene of Italian urban space, about the mutually constituting elements of gender, city, and nation in the U.S.

Fuller's dispatches during the Roman Revolution and Hawthorne's romance, derived from his Italian sojourn during the ensuing period of political repression in Rome, are linked through this nationalist function of their genres in constructing the imagined community of the modern nation-state. The novel carries out the tourist's familiar agenda of the surveillance of foreign scenes in order to consolidate U.S. national identity by contrast; Italy in *The Marble Faun* remains a post-historical, aesthetic space whose contrast helps to solidify the United States' identity as the province of language, political agency, and contemporary history. Fuller's newspaper account, of course, focuses on present, political, and nation-building activity in Italy, on Italy's possible emergence as a nation-state in its own right. But Hawthorne's romance complicates the standard tourist framing of Rome by casting its stasis as the result of political and gender repression and, as I will argue in Chapter 5, by examining the role of artists in mediating revolutionary impulses and ushering in modern and nationalist subjectivities. And finally both accounts are implicated in the related cultural effort of conceptualizing and representing the city, in developing an urban imaginary in antebellum U.S. culture.

City Gazing: Fuller, Hawthorne, and American Urban Space

The significance of Fuller's and Hawthorne's representations of Roman spaces as specifically urban spaces emerges in such descriptive moments as their contrasting treatments of the view from one of the traditional vantage points overlooking the city: from the Pincian Hill onto the Piazza del Popolo below.[73] Hawthorne gives us a panorama of Rome from the point of view of his American characters, Hilda and Kenyon:

> From the terrace where they now stood, there is an abrupt descent towards the Piazza del Popolo; and looking down into its broad space, they beheld the . . . palatial edifices . . . which grew . . . out of the thought of Michael Angelo. They saw, too, the red granite obelisk – eldest of things, even in Rome – which rises in the center of the piazza. . . . All Roman works . . . assume a transient . . . character,

when we think that this indestructible monument supplied one of the recollections, which Moses, and the Israelites, bore from Egypt into the desert . . .

Lifting their eyes, Hilda and her companion gazed westward, and saw . . . the Castle of Sant' Angelo; that immense tomb of a pagan Emperor. . . . Still farther off, appeared a mighty pile of building, surmounted by the vast Dome [of Saint Peter's]. . . . [A]t this distance, the entire outline of the world's Cathedral . . . is taken in at once.[74]

Their tourist gaze grasps the totality of the city and its major icons; their survey of the "varied prospect" (106) promises unlimited visual access to history (the Egyptian obelisk in the piazza prompts a cultural memory of Moses and the Israelites) and to architectural forms ("at this distance, the entire outline" of St. Peter's "is taken in at once"). As their gaze returns to the piazza below, they see the city's central avatar in the novel, the painter Miriam, kneeling ambiguously in the presence of her mysterious, monkishly clad "Model," and the difficulty of interpreting Rome returns; is she, as Hilda thinks, kneeling merely to get water from the fountain or is she, as Kenyon argues, and as the reader already knows, begging her persecutor for her freedom?

If Hawthorne emphasizes the promise and the limits of the tourist's gaze, especially as a function of the gazer's gender, Fuller, writing in December 1848 of revolutionary Rome, emphasizes the formation of contemporary history. She describes a gathering of troops, crowds, and government officials – all with republican sympathies – in the Piazza del Popolo and their movement to the Quirinal, the residence of the Pope, to demand political reforms:

I passed along, toward the *Piazza del Popolo*. . . . I heard the drums beating, and, entering the Piazza, I found the troops of the line already assembled, and the Civic Guard marching by in platoons; each *battaglione* saluted as it entered by trumpets and a fine strain from the hand of the Carbineers.

I climbed the Pincian to see better. There is no place so fine for anything of this kind as the Piazza del Popolo, it is so full of light, so fair and grand, the obelisk and fountain make so fine a center to all kinds of groups.

The object of the present meeting was for the Civic Guard and troops of the line to give pledges of sympathy preparatory to going to the Quirinal to demand a change of Ministry and of measures. The flag of the Union was placed in front of the obelisk; all present saluted it; some officials made addresses; the trumpets sounded, and all moved toward the Quirinal. (241)

The promise of access this passage makes is not to a totalizing panorama of history, arranged in fixed icons (the Egyptian obelisk, the classical tomb, and the baroque church), but to a theater of open-ended history in the making, a "fine," well-lit stage which serves as the backdrop to the ephemeral and fluid movements of flags, bodies, and trumpets.

Simon During offers a model for thinking about the urban imaginary in his account of an eighteenth-century English "civil Imaginary," a discursive formation which orders an emerging social world through the "production of narratives, moral cruxes, a linguistic decorum, and character types which cover the social field of the post-1688 world." The texts, especially novels and journalists' essays, produced by this eighteenth-century "civil Imaginary" "are a sympathetic attempt to circulate images of the forms of social existence available to the urban bourgeoisie of the time"; they also attempt to order this world by shaping the subjectivity of those who inhabit it.[75] Antebellum American cities offered a similar "new cultural space." Historians have documented the explosive rate of urbanization in the northeast U.S. in this period.[76] Accompanying this social change were discursive and visual strategies for seeing and ordering the city along middle- and upper-class lines. These strategies not only provided conceptual frameworks for seeing the city; they also normalized specific viewing positions, defined by gender and class, for the citizen of the city. And to the extent that they participated in the rhetoric of reform, they not only normalized but explicitly advocated ways of being in the city. Two approaches that define these positions and that I will draw on below are studies, derived from the work of Walter Benjamin, of the flaneur, the strolling male spectator of nineteenth-century city streets, and feminist histories of the place of women (physically and conceptually) in nineteenth-century cities.[77] The writings of this period participated in a broadly articulated urban imaginary, a bourgeois, gendered discourse whose function it was both to describe and to produce the city.

Fuller and Hawthorne participated in this discourse before they went abroad: Fuller through her writings covering New York social institutions during her two years there (1844–6) and Hawthorne primarily through his Boston novel *The Blithedale Romance* (1852). As a journalist, Fuller worked to render the city of New York visible to the reform-minded middle-class readers of the *Tribune*. Judith Bean and Joel Myerson note that the paper's editor, Horace Greeley, ran a "regular column on city life" and sought to represent the "multiple environments," social injustices, and emerging philanthropic movements of the new metropolis.[78] As Joan von Mehren says, Fuller "publicize[d] conditions in the city's charitable institutions": prisons, "almshouses, insane asylums, and homes for the blind and deaf."[79] Catherine C. Mitchell points out that Greeley's *Tribune* advocated a reformist agenda that included temperance, the abolition of slavery, labor unions, and Fourier's vision of socialism. Fuller edited and was the main contributor to the first-page "literary department," a department which blended literary criticism, travel accounts, social analysis, and political correspondence.[80] Fuller's columns on New York produced for her readers over time an aggregate presence of cultural events (book publications, a concert at Castle Garden, an exhibition of an important painting), of the ongoing operations of disciplinary and benevolent institutions, and of architectural structures (such as Grace Church).[81] Her attention to forms of urban life and space that existed outside the domestic sphere and yet simultaneously with it complicated the reader's subjective experience of the city.[82] Her frequent contributions (three articles a week) covered and ordered the emerging "social field," to use During's phrase, of the American city and sought to mold the consciousness of her audience.[83]

The Blithedale Romance is, on the other hand, Hawthorne's study of, as Dana Brand puts it, "an urban civilization on the point of becoming ubiquitous" and of "cosmopolitan modes of interacting with reality"; the novel is split between representations of Boston and representations of what Hawthorne emphasizes is an urban fantasy: the "return" to a communal, pastoral, unalienated mode of production and cultural expression at "Blithedale," modeled on the utopian agrarian community of Brook Farm, to which Hawthorne had briefly belonged.[84] Linking these two spaces is Hawthorne's narrator, Miles Coverdale, who appears as, according to Brand, the "representative subjectivity" of modernity – "that of the flaneur," the detached consumer of spectacle.[85] Unlike Fuller's persona of the reform writer, who seeks to intervene in the consciousness of her readers and to reorganize aspects of urban life, Hawthorne is interested in an urban subjectivity whose orientation to the city is primarily visual, a subjectivity which, as Griselda Pollock argues, is secured by gender and class hierarchies and located in middle- and upper-class male spectators; "The flaneur symbolizes the privilege or freedom to move about the public arenas of the city observing but never interacting, consuming the sights through a controlling but rarely acknowledged gaze."[86] The flaneur's impulse to type other urban characters – to know them through the eye – at once separates him from the crowd but also, in Benjamin's words, is an unsuccessful fantasy that viewing others can "break through" the isolation of urban inhabitants "by filling the hollow space created in him by such isolation, with the borrowed – and fictitious – isolations of strangers."[87] Hawthorne's exploration of Coverdale's modern position of visual privilege and social isolation, which dooms Coverdale's attempt to join a radical community, is connected with his interest in the tourist's visual consumption of foreign parts.

In addition to its function as post-historical aesthetic spectacle, Rome served as a historical model for the idea of the U.S. national capital as either the political center of a republic or an imperial capital; it also served, more specifically, as a source of architectural models for the Capitol Building in Washington.[88] Fuller's and Hawthorne's writings on Rome emphasize two possibilities for conceiving of American urban space: as political space or as consumable spectacle. While Fuller imagines a political city – a polis – and Hawthorne is primarily engaged by the tourist's or flaneur's vision of the city, aspects of these sometimes contradictory components of the antebellum urban imaginary are present in both texts. Both writers seem at times aware of and yet enact the dominating, totalizing view of foreign sites that William W. Stowe finds characterizes the period's guidebooks: "Tourists are sightseers: their subjugating gaze reduces individuals, institutions, art-works, and landscapes to bits of knowledge and elevates the tourists and their class, race, gender, and nation to the position of the authoritative knower."[89] As do philanthropic projects, tourism extends participation in a master gaze to women. Yet if Fuller wrestles with the contradictions between such a master gaze, with its visual sampling of other regions, and her project of releasing Italy and Italians from static types to dynamic historical presences, Hawthorne writes an analysis of what urban space looks like in which the political and historical have been repressed.

Fuller and the Republican Polis

In his study of U.S. urban literature, Sidney Bremer traces a variety of written responses to the nineteenth-century growth of the city from "polis" to "metropolis" to "megalopolis." He finds the dominant conceptual model in the pre-Civil War period is still the older one of the "polis," the "city-town." In this period, in which "fairly homogeneous, powerful mercantile elites dominated the economy and society of U.S. cities" and in which most published writers were members of this elite, the "city-town model in literature" is characterized by a voluntary sense of community, by a "strong sense of history," and by human agency; "the city-town's spaces form an environment that is shaped by human choices more than it shapes them."[90] Although in her previous descriptions of New York for the *Tribune* she began to sketch a more metropolitan city, characterized by the transformative flows of capital and immigration,[91] in her Roman dispatches Fuller draws on the city-town model to create an image of Rome as polis and as the emerging capital of the nation-state envisioned by the leaders of the Risorgimento. In doing so, she assumes the position of the elite republican writer or politician, whose voice guides the formation of the community, and thus follows her father's example; as her biographers point out, Timothy Fuller was a self-made member of the New England elite, a Jeffersonian Republican twice elected to the U.S. Congress from Massachusetts who did not survive politically the transition to Jacksonian democracy but who trained his daughter in Latin, classical Roman history, and literature.[92] Indeed, only in revolutionary Rome was Fuller, as a woman, able to become a "citizen" of the polis; as Leslie Eckel documents, during the Roman Republic, when "citizenship is the highest honour possible," a number of those writing letters to Fuller addressed them to "Cittadina Margherita Ossoli," her married name.[93] Like her evocation of the conventions of history painting, her invocation of the polis draws on a traditional and familiar model for framing an emergent political formation.

If she assumes a republican model of the city, one that her father would have understood, she fills its spaces with romantic, fluid images of political agency. Fuller's letters to the *Tribune* repeatedly describe a city defined by citizens in motion, by political processions, funerals, troop movements, and religious festivals whose meaning is increasingly political; she constructs a city increasingly "shaped by human choices" in the revolutionary days of self-determination. And she constructs a citizenry which, in spite of the lack of republican institutions and training, is already composed of self-regulating subjects. Her depictions of processions along the central thoroughfare of Rome, the Corso, de-emphasize the architectural structure of the street (that is, external forms of order) and emphasize instead a naturalized image of voluntary community in motion. In May 1847, during a period when Pius IX briefly allied himself with the proponents of liberal reform, Fuller sent this description of voluntary political association and benevolent patriarchal support of such association to the *Tribune*:

> A week or two ago the Cardinal Secretary published a circular inviting the departments to measures which would give the people a sort of representative council. Nothing could seem more limited than this improvement but it was a great measure for Rome. At night the

Corso . . . was illuminated, and many thousands passed through it in a torch-bearing procession. . . . [A]s a river of fire, they streamed slowly through the Corso, on their way to the Quirinal to thank the Pope, upbearing a banner on which the edict was printed. . . . Ascending the Quirinal they made it a mount of light. . . . The Pope appeared on his balcony: the crowd shouted three vivas; he extended his arms: the crowd fell on their knees and received his benediction; he retired, and the torches were extinguished, and the multitude dispersed in an instant. (136–7)

Here Fuller offers a way of conceptualizing the transition from paternal, papal authority (signaled by the crowd's kneeling for the benediction) to the internalized law of the self-disciplining subject of the republican state;[94] the "multitude" shapes itself into a political community and then disperses by its own will, a motif, as I noted in the previous section, which Fuller reiterates in her crowd descriptions. Such scenes combine the concept of the polis, the pre-metropolitan city-town shaped by the voluntary association of its inhabitants, with the romantic imagery of "the people" as a natural force ("a river of fire") to visualize the emergence of the agency of Rome's citizens.

Fuller is aware of the productive nature of the urban imaginary she is engaged in and helping to shape. She sees that the public sphere is discursively constructed; her reports repeatedly describe and often include translations of proclamations, accounts in the emerging liberal press of Italy, and the "news" orally transmitted from other regions of revolutionary Italy. The polis is invoked by language. The "circular" granting a limited representative body calls forth the procession, whose discursive origin is clear; the crowd carries the text of the edict printed on a banner. And citizens are also called into being through language; Fuller says that the first election in Rome (in early 1849 of the Constitutional Assembly for the Roman States) was a successful exercise of suffrage because of discussions held in the public sphere: "A few weeks' schooling at some popular meetings, the clubs, the conversations of the National Guards . . . was sufficient" (255).[95]

In *Paris as Revolution*, Priscilla Parkhurst Ferguson comments on Honoré de Balzac's and Victor Hugo's concept of the post-revolutionary writer's role in creating an urban imaginary. It is the task of the urban novelist to replace the gaze of the king, which had earlier given Paris unity, with that of the writer. The "urban imagination," she argues, is a "synecdochal imagination" that sees the apparent "fragments" of the city as parts of a whole: "Synecdoche thus bespeaks the aesthetic of integration. . . . Integration . . .

create[s] [a] unity that . . . does not exist. . . . [T]his creation is the vocation of the writer."[96] In this respect like Balzac and Hugo, but also like the political leader of the Roman Republic, Mazzini, whose speeches and writings she includes in her dispatches, Fuller tries to call forth Rome as polis, as republican capital, through language. The processions she describes become synecdoches, parts standing in for the whole, an image of the voluntary community she wants Rome to become and that she wants the U.S. to re-approximate.[97] Fuller attempts to revive American republicanism by means of an identification between her readers and Italian revolutionaries: "This cause is OURS" (160).[98] Both U.S. aid to the Italians and the American national revival from the sins of slavery and the Mexican War will happen through the agency of "individuals" and small groups, who stand in for the whole of the country and who represent the "Soul of our Nation" (161); "voluntary association for improvement . . . will be the grand means for my country to grow" (165). In such passages Fuller tries to call not only the modern Italian nation but also an American national subjectivity into being, a subjectivity characteristic of the polis. In doing so, she tries to connect the traditional, elite idea of the polis with the more revolutionary and egalitarian associationism of Charles Fourier and his American exponents, a connection that elides the differences between older American republicanism and current European socialism.[99]

Of course Fuller's Rome is also a spectacle, a theater of revolution which elicits aesthetic responses. Of the above torch-light procession, she describes the visual effect and notes, "I have never seen anything finer" (137). And as she overlooks the gathering in the Piazza del Popolo, she describes this urban space as one especially fit for civic performances; to repeat one sentence, "There is no place so fine for anything of this kind as the Piazza del Popolo, it is so full of light, so fair and grand, the obelisk and fountain make so fine a center to all kinds of groups" (241). Such passages suggest that, like urban novels and urban journalism, public performances of republican solidarity can invent the modern national capital. The unified city and its citizens can be performed into being. But these passages also invoke the language of tourism and perhaps of more "modern," metropolitan forms of visual consumption. Indeed, Fuller's text vacillates between two modes of presenting revolution to her *Tribune* readers: the spectacular, romantic movements of the body of the citizenry in such passages as the one on the torch-light procession, and deliberately sober, anti-spectacular accounts of the "tranquil[ity]" (260) and ordinariness of life in revolutionary Rome. During the siege of Rome, in order to counter rumors of violence and chaos within the city, she emphasizes the "order of Rome": "I go from one end to the other . . . alone and on foot. My friends send out their little children alone with their nurses" (284). Fuller's ambivalence about using a language of visual display to describe revolutionary activity may stem from her awareness that tourism operates in part by pictorializing characteristic events and people into types and, therefore, ultimately by depriving them of agency – exactly the opposite of what she is trying to do. As she says of British tourists, the "vulgarity" that "snatches '*bits*' for a '*sketch*'" makes them "the most unseeing of all possible animals" (132), a statement which associates the tourist gaze with reactionary politics.[100]

Hawthorne and the Gendered Geography of Rome

Hawthorne's Rome in *The Marble Faun*, as readers have pointed out, is primarily a series of tourist spaces – galleries, artists' studios, villa gardens, classical ruins, churches, catacombs – sites described in his journal and reworked in the romance.[101] As opposed to Fuller or Hugo, Hawthorne does not conceive of his writing as reinventing the city, and he visits Rome in 1858–9 at a time of the reassertion of papal temporal authority, after the failure of the 1849 Roman Republic and before the final unification of Italy. The book itself represents for many readers divided impulses; Richard H. Brodhead finds that the novel, in spite of its considerable ambivalence about the process of creation, winds up supporting the stratification of art into high and low and, in giving Hilda the last word, effectively supports the authoritative repressions associated with "high" art and with "subordination-demanding institutions."[102] Robert S. Levine, who reads the novel as a text concerned with political issues and revolutionary activity, finds that, in spite of Hawthorne's "partial sympathy" with Miriam's rebellion against "various reactionary forces depicted in the novel," he acquiesces with the recontainment of such rebellion at its end.[103] My argument is a similar one: that Hawthorne's urban imaginary is predicated on a gendered position, that *The Marble Faun* at once acknowledges and recontains women spectators' bid for public participation in cities and in the informing gaze onto cities, and that Hawthorne reflects the effort by his contemporary male journalists and flaneurs to order the emerging metropolitan city through a gendered geography. Rome becomes a space where both revolution and women's gazes are evoked and repressed, indeed where urbanity comes to imply their simultaneous presence and nullification.

Mary P. Ryan identifies 1840 as "a rough benchmark in the gender geography of public urban space" in the U.S. At this time, the separation of work from household space became increasingly standard for middle-class families and, as opposed to a greater "public mingling" that characterized earlier American urban life, public and private spheres became more fully separated and gendered. So just at the time that U.S. cities grew into unzoned, apparently chaotic metropolises, gender became especially available as a category to decipher the city. As Ryan says, a mid-century "army of flaneurs cum journalists . . . impose[d] cognitive patterns on the heterogeneous spaces of the city" through a "cartography of gender":

> Relations with women, clearly the "other" in this largely male construction of urban geography, provided male writers with metaphors that neatly encapsulated the central problem of urban social space: how to create order and hierarchy in an environment where social differences existed in close physical proximity. Sexuality was perhaps the most powerful metaphor for the interplay of diversity and proximity in the big city.[104]

In this version of the urban imaginary "dangerous" and "endangered" women became urban signs of class and ethnic difference.

As T. Walter Herbert argues, Hawthorne's visit to Rome coincided with a crisis in his faith in the coherence of the ideological and psychological structure of the middle-class family, and the romance is in part an attempt to recontain this crisis about authority and gender.[105] The Hawthornes followed, in their travels, "Fuller's path of exile" from Rome to Florence and "moved," according to Thomas Mitchell, in "essentially the same circle of friends."[106] Following Fuller's trail, Hawthorne both engaged and resisted her challenge to patriarchal and tourist habits of seeing, her support of violent revolution, and her reconfiguration of Rome as a capital city. His novel features two women who move freely about the streets of Rome – Hilda and Miriam – one endangered and one dangerous. Hawthorne both lauds this freedom of movement and worries about it; by the end of the novel Hilda's ability to move freely has been undermined by her witnessing the crime of murder and her subsequent captivity experience.[107] The novel wants virtuous middle-class and elite women to wander freely in urban spaces but the city's capacity to taint this virtue seems too strong and Hilda is best relegated to safe spaces for such women: the home. Miriam also wanders but always less freely; as an expression of the city – with her mixed ethnic and national heritage, her anti-patriarchal revolutionary impulses, as Levine points out, her masked identity, and her sexually ambiguous past – she is at once a victim of the city and linked to its subterranean power structures, even connected with someone in the papal government, as the narrator states in the Postscript (464).[108]

The novel finally separates these two women and keeps the possibilities for being in the city they each represent apart. Leonardo Buonomo argues that Hawthorne meticulously keeps Hilda and the Italian character, Donatello, separate as signs of two irreconcilable cultures;[109] it is also part of the cultural work of the novel to divide Hilda and Miriam, whom Hawthorne at first portrays as intimate. At the end Miriam is represented as being on the other side of an "abyss" (461) from Hilda, separated by categories of experience Hilda does not wish to acknowledge. Indeed, Hawthorne uses Hilda as an agent of repression for Miriam – Hilda's information leads to Miriam's loss of Donatello through his arrest and incarceration – and so cuts white middle-class women off from their ethnic and experiential others. By doing so he ignores the fact that a number of women writers, such as Fuller, Lydia Maria Child, also a journalist in New York in the 1840s, and Fanny Fern, famous columnist for the *New York Ledger* in the late 1850s, have already wandered through the emerging metropolitan space of modern cities and have assumed in their writings the gazing position generally held by men.[110] If, as Mitchell argues, Hawthorne's Miriam represents his attempt to come to terms with Fuller's Roman, revolutionary sojourn, then Miriam's fate forecloses on the possibility of a woman acting as a public intellectual shaping a national city.

But this trajectory of the novel, which moves from the intimate association of the New England "girl" and the cosmopolitan woman toward their separation, from their relative freedom of movement within urban space to this movement's curtailment, and from the assertion of women's artistic ambition to its demise, seems already archaic by 1860. Its references to Germaine de Staël's 1807 novel *Corinne* – which powerfully influenced many New England women, including Hawthorne's wife, Sophia – rehearse *Corinne*'s "feminist vision of thwarted potentiality"[111] and that novel's dooming of its heroine, pulled between the irreconcilable poles of art and domesticity, Italy and England. However, the late 1840s and 1850s presented a reversal of this plot. A number of often politically engaged women writers and artists – English, German, American, Italian – appeared in Rome and Florence and achieved considerable professional (and often personal) success; indeed, one of the most successful of these women and someone the Hawthornes knew,

Elizabeth Barrett Browning, published in 1856 her verse-novel *Aurora Leigh*, a revision of *Corinne* that awarded its poet-heroine a productive and sexually fulfilling life.[112] Women cultural figures – such as Barrett Browning, Anna Jameson, the German writers Fanny Lewald and Ottilie von Goethe, Fuller's fellow revolutionary, the Italian journalist and travel writer Cristina Trivulzio di Belgiojoso, and the American sculptor Harriet Hosmer and actress Charlotte Cushman – published, performed, and produced visual art in Italy in the years before and during Hawthorne's sojourn.[113] Melissa Dabakis has documented the generation of American women sculptors, including Hosmer, who settled in Rome in the 1850s and 1860s, in a community anchored by Cushman, and who became there "the first truly professional class of women artists" in U.S. history.[114] Hawthorne's insistence on silencing and isolating Miriam stems from the sexual and gender politics Herbert describes and from his uneasiness with the freedom of women artists in Rome. But it also, as Mitchell suggests, derives from his mourning of Fuller, whose feminist and political aspirations and subsequent death seemed to him to confirm the old tragic plot.

Kenyon and Hilda's contemplation of Miriam as part of their survey of Rome from the Pincian Hill anticipates the novel's conclusion in its movement away from the mutual look of intimate relations that characterizes their relationship with Miriam in the beginning of the romance toward a re-establishment of the hierarchical tourist gaze. It is like Fuller's scene from the same spot in that both passages are turning points in their respective accounts; Miriam's despairing supplication to the Model, the mysterious agent of her oppression, immediately anticipates his murder (and her supplicating kneeling to Donatello, who kills the Model and liberates her), while the movement of the republican procession to the Quirinal precipitates Pope Pius IX's flight from Rome and the beginning of the Roman Republic, a liberty as short-lived as Miriam's and Donatello's, after their overthrow of the Model. But here we have two interpretive gazers; while Hilda underinterprets the scene, Kenyon turns out to be a good reader of emblematic urban moments. His superior insight, even as it is presented as risky and in need of Hilda's domesticating discipline, permits him to continue to interact with Miriam, even to give her advice, that is, to shape the plot of her life. As Hilda breaks off her relationship with Miriam, Kenyon becomes the go-between, the mobile spectator and interpreter who can move between the two spheres they represent. In this scene Miriam – and other possibilities for women's cognitive grasp of the city – is returned to her status as a sign of the city; the possible woman gazer, as Fuller herself was for Hawthorne, moves from being a subject to being again an object of the gaze.

The city in *The Marble Faun* is the site of revolution repressed; Donatello, the pastoral, infantilized male Italian of much tourist writing, becomes in the city the violent revolutionary who destroys the Model, the figure of past modes of oppression, while Miriam's gaze, which triggers the murder, challenges patriarchal authority. But these possible historical agents – the Italian man and the urban woman – become pictorialized, part of the gallery of masked figures and allegorical images Italy offers to tourists, by the end of the novel, as they disappear first into the Carnival (costumed as a peasant and a *contadina*) and then, as Donatello does, into prison.[115] In a reversal of Fuller's project, the early identification between the American characters and these figures is weakened and made abstract, even psychologized, as the paradigm of the tourist's vision returns. In an association Fuller might have understood, Hawthorne connects his most thorough tourist's survey of Rome in the novel, in which he calls Rome "the City of all time, and of all the world!" (111), with Kenyon's vision of Miriam kneeling in the Piazza del Popolo, metaphorically "shackled" like the "captive queen" Zenobia (108), that is, determined by the capital city rather than shaping it through her gaze.

In the dreamwork of nation-building which tourist writings represent,[116] the tourist gaze is at once provisionally liberatory and disciplinary, releasing such figures as Miriam and Donatello and reincarcerating them. Similarly, the figure of Miriam/Zenobia speaks to the "dreamwork" of imagining the national, even imperial city. Hawthorne draws here on his viewing of Hosmer's statue of Zenobia (1859, Fig. 4.5), which he admired while in Rome and mentions in his preface to *The Marble Faun* (4).[117] In her biography of Hosmer, Kate Culkin (as does Dabakis) notes her development of *Zenobia in Chains* in conversation with Anna Jameson and Lydia Maria Child, who advised her to emphasize the physical strength and intellectual capacity of this historical figure, a Syrian queen defeated by a Roman emperor and paraded through Rome in chains. Unlike the other famous statue of a female captive by an antebellum American sculptor in Italy, Hiram Powers' *The Greek Slave* (1844), Hosmer's *Zenobia* exhibited self-possession and agency, in part through her forward stride and her powerful hands, which hold her chains rather than be weighed down by them.[118] Dabakis reads other marks of power Hosmer gave the figure, including the Medusa head on her belt, a "feminist emblem" of anti-patriarchal resistance for Hosmer.[119] As Joy S. Kasson says,

Figure 4.5 Harriet Hosmer, *Zenobia in Chains*, c. 1859. Marble. 44¼ x 14 x 18 ins. Saint Louis Art Museum, American Art Purchase Fund 19:2008.

Hosmer's statue evoked simultaneously female power and captivity.[120] And it did so explicitly, I would add, in the context of Rome, cast here as imperial metropolis.[121]

If the ambivalently rendered image of the shackled woman of power lies at the center of the spectacular metropolis for Hawthorne, just as similarly ambivalent images of women, according to Ryan, define the "gender geography" of the mid-century city for other male writers, Fuller, like Hosmer, at times participates in this trope and seeks to revise it. Larry J. Reynolds has argued that Fuller constructs a "public persona" in her dispatches, that she performs the "role of Liberty," the feminine embodiment of the spirit of revolution, an image available in European romantic culture.[122] If "Liberty" is defeated in the Roman Revolution, nevertheless, Fuller's adherence to this persona is an attempt to make a feminine sign speak, to merge image and discourse, representation and agency, and to do so in the context of political transformation played out in a national city.

As U.S. cities moved toward a metropolitan identity at mid-century, the task of constructing an urban imaginary became urgent, and Rome served, again, as a displaced arena for articulating American concerns. Both texts show the tensions within such a cultural project. If Hawthorne's engagement with the gendered gaze of the urban spectator is more attuned to the emerging visual strategies of the metropolis, and so more "modern," Fuller's attempt to revive the concepts of city and citizenship defined by the republican polis is more "progressive." Their works may indicate less any clear historical shift from polis to the city of spectacle than a dialectical relation between these models of urbanity that continued to shape nineteenth-century American urban representations. The next chapter will turn to the fictional incorporation of travel writing, even as it returns to the related questions of gender, nationhood, and visual response, in a more detailed reading of *The Marble Faun* and an examination of another romance written out of an experience of touring Italy: Harriet Beecher Stowe's *Agnes of Sorrento* (1862).

National Spaces, Catholic Icons, and Protestant Bodies: Instructing the Republican Subject in Hawthorne and Stowe

As the idea of a cathedral includes not only the central nave . . . [and] the massive buttress, but also the roses blooming in stone, . . . so in the idea of a state are comprehended, not only armies . . . and government . . . [but also] the arts.

George Stillman Hillard[1]

One could look down into the gloomy depths of the gorge, as into some mysterious underworld. Strange and weird it seemed, with its fathomless shadows and its wild grottoes, over which hung . . . long pendants of ivy, while dusky gray aloes uplifted their horned heads from great rock-rifts, like elfin spirits struggling upward out of the shade. Nor was wanting the usual gentle poetry of flowers; for white iris leaned its fairy pavilion over the black void like a pale-cheeked princess from the window of some dark enchanted castle. . . . A clear mountain-spring . . . fell with a lulling noise into a quaint moss-grown water-trough, which had been in former times the sarcophagus of some old Roman sepulchre . . .; a veil of ferns and maiden's hair, studded with tremulous silver drops, vibrated to its soothing murmur.

Harriet Beecher Stowe[2]

Perhaps more than any writer examined in this study, Harriet Beecher Stowe was an internationally known practitioner of a nation-producing genre by the time she traveled to Europe. Like Margaret Fuller, she grasped the possibilities of a popular print genre for reforming national subjectivities; her abolitionist novel *Uncle*

Tom's Cabin (1852) was the most politically important and widely translated American novel of the nineteenth century and prompted her first European tour, in 1853, during which she was lionized in England.[3] Like Nathaniel Hawthorne, she conflated travel writing with the novel; both wrote substantial descriptive passages based on their travels into the Italian romances they composed ten years after Fuller's coverage of the Roman Republic: Hawthorne's *The Marble Faun, or, The Romance of Monte Beni* (1860) and Stowe's *Agnes of Sorrento* (1862). And both also wrote travel accounts of their tours elsewhere in Europe: Stowe on northern Europe in *Sunny Memories of Foreign Lands* (1854) and Hawthorne on England in *Our Old Home* (1863). Seasoned tourists by the time they published their fictional compendia of the lessons of Italian sights, they were conscious participants in the U.S. print discourse on Italy and on tourism.[4] Although both authors frame their Italian novels as escapes from the social and political issues that animated their most important fiction – the sustained inquiry into national origins of Hawthorne's tales and of *The Scarlet Letter* (1850) and the indictment of a nationwide complicity in slavery in *Uncle Tom's Cabin* – they clearly engage questions of national identity and destiny.

This chapter returns to the relationship between tourist writing and fiction that opened this book. In both the 1820s and early 1860s writers used fiction to analyze American hopes for the social effects of the aesthetic Italian tour. While in 1824 Irving's "Italian Banditti" sought and failed to imagine aesthetic culture as a means of managing the predatory capitalist energies of a rising class of "self-made men," Hawthorne's and Stowe's novels concern themselves with the project of national consolidation through cultural iconography: a project whose success the impending Civil War has called into question. They conflate these characteristic genres of nation-building – travel writing and fiction – to consider the roles of national spaces and of a central body of images in ordering affect and belief in the life of a republic.

However, I want to foreground here Hawthorne's and Stowe's use of a variant of the novel, the romance, whose nineteenth-century status as an archetypal, "dreamlike narrative," concerned with the symbolic interpretation of visual experience,[5] matched the multiple, equally dreamlike displacements and visual encounters of tourism. In her study of the interplay between post-Renaissance, non-narrative forms of painting and the literary romance, Wendy Steiner argues that painting's status as "a symbol of the transcendent object" emphasizes the "transcendent self," the spectator separated from history. In a related fashion, the romance features moments of "frozen" aesthetic contemplation marked by the "enthrallment" of the viewer to a transcendent image. If art, like love, promises "perfect atemporal communication," then the romance, in its characteristic dialectic between stasis and flow, at first "aspires to the atemporal 'eternity' of the stopped-action painting" but then "subjects the image to the story" and returns its characters to the movement of history and to agency. Thus romance, often through plots in which love's "stopped-action" visual enthrallments give way to the reimmersion in time signaled by marriage, mediates among the image, the self, and history.[6]

The nineteenth-century romance was the perfect form through which to explore the visual work of tourism as it coincided with the visual education of republican subjects, both male and female. In discussing the managed, pleasurable submissions to Italian sights of James Fenimore Cooper and other male tourists in Chapter 2, I drew on Laura Mulvey's similar and well-known insight into filmic tensions between the erotic contemplation of the feminine spectacle and the masculine subject's desire to resubject the image to narrative. I argued that Italy was the province in which male tourists could suspend the impulse to integrate the image into the linguistic trajectory of political, historical, or social narrative and that this temporary enthrallment, paradoxically, made them more effective shapers of the national narrative when they returned home. But, as subsequent chapters have demonstrated, Italy was also a crucial site for female tourists negotiating the dialectic of aesthetic arrest and narrative movement and its role in shaping republican subjectivity. Hawthorne noted in his often-quoted preface that Italy "afford[ed] a sort of . . . fairy precinct" to the "romance-writer" – ground especially fit for the "Romance."[7] In addition to matching the cultural work of tourism, however, the romance also constituted, as Steiner says, a "theoretical mode,"[8] inherently analyzing its own contents. Hawthorne's and Stowe's romances simultaneously enact the conversion of aesthetic contemplation into republican narrative and comment on this process.

These generically characteristic dualities of arrest and movement, analysis and enactment, have particular relevance for republican fiction. If the novel generally is a product of modern bourgeois nations, the romance, its subgenre, has been frequently (although not exclusively) associated with the emergence of republics, especially in the Americas. The traditional critical pairing of the romance with the early American nation highlights the genre's axis of utopian/dystopian imaginings as its defining orientation.[9] Unlike what one might

call the later realist novel's Geertzian project of the "thick description" of an immediate social world,[10] the early nineteenth-century
romance's project is that of "national allegory," to adapt Shirley
Samuels' term.[11] As the sites of sometimes extravagant scenarios of
republican invention, whether of the self or of the family or of the
state, romances addressed the abstract, text-based nature of American republics both in their capacity to incarnate these "fictional"
polities and in their countervailing tendency to foreground the very
fictive quality of republics and, therefore, their inherent instability.

   In her study of the "foundational" romances of Latin America,
Doris Sommer uncovers an "erotics of politics" in which courtship and marriage plots figured the freely consenting association of
republican subjects and elicited readers' libidinal investments in their
nations; "tenuously constructed" republics found "a self-legitimating
discourse . . . in erotic desire," a discourse which naturalized "novel
national ideals." Rather than immobilize desiring subjects in asocial
postures of aesthetic contemplation, "sexual love" in these novels
became "*the* trope for associative behavior [and] unfettered market
relations."[12] Stowe fuses the erotic desire of the marriage plot with
the dynamic energies of both national union and spiritual aspiration in her own "manifesto" on the romance, published between her
1857 and 1859 tours of Italy; as Naomi Sofer argues, Stowe "defines
'romance' as the literary expression of the soul's divinity" and puts
the genre at the center of "a religiously based national aesthetic" that
would "preserve both Americans' religious faith and their political
system."[13] If romances could integrate the republican subject into
the state, they could also stabilize the new state within history. As
George Dekker has shown, the historical romance located nations
firmly within a universalized historical sequence marked by progressive "stages" of civilization; as practiced by Cooper, the historical
romance slid into "national epic" through its broad historical reach
and its claim to feature representative national characters and plots
– including, Sommer notes, marriage plots that secured the future of
the nation.[14]

   On the other hand, as Michael Davitt Bell states, the genre heightened an awareness of the contingent nature of the republican state
and, concomitantly, of the disjunction between any national originating impulse and its subsequent representation and institutional-
ization. Indeed, for such romancers as Hawthorne, the founding act
of the republic, the Revolution, itself severed connections between
traditional means of cultural expression – what Bell calls "the
'language' of imported culture" – and the nation, thereby making

national ideals potentially unrepresentable, either by fiction or by the state. Although such an awareness could be disabling to writers and states alike, anxiety about the fragility of republics could produce both romances and nations. For example, Robert S. Levine argues that, in his Farewell Address, George Washington invited his auditors to participate with him in the defensive creation of a romance of the Union, whose "existence would depend upon a consensual desire" to imagine it "into being." In spite of the difficulties inherent for Hawthorne in representing the nation, for him the nation and the romance remained linked, even in their dissolution. Bell quotes Hawthorne's preface to *Our Old Home*, where he comments at once on the Civil War and on his inability to finish another work of fiction; the war is a "'hurricane that is sweeping us all along with it, possibly, into a Limbo where our nation and its polity may be as literally the fragments of a shattered dream as my unwritten Romance.'"[15] What I will argue broadly below is that, as the last antebellum romances on Italy, Hawthorne's novel uneasily observes the process of national consolidation (displaced onto Italy) described by Sommer and Dekker, while Stowe's novel, a historical romance, enacts this process.[16] However, this somewhat reductive bifurcation will be complicated by their shared attention to the means of this consolidation: the sites, icons, and bodies offered as enabling aesthetic spectacles to prospective republican subjects.

In reading these romances I want to foreground two related aspects of American travel writing previous chapters have gestured toward but not adequately addressed: the attention to Roman space as national and imperial space and the tourist uses of Catholic spaces and iconography. In addition to treating Rome as urban space, as I argued in the last chapter, Hawthorne treats its tourist sites – and sites in other cities – as national spaces. This is a period deeply engaged with organizing American commercial and national space in ways that conjoin the ideology and the practical work of expansion in the U.S. The 1811 Commissioners' Plan of New York, for example, created the city's grid to embody new economic theories of a global and impersonally operating system of commodity exchange.[17] At the same time, the evolving plans of Washington, D.C., shaped the new national capital as an objective correlative to the abstract relations of state and federal governments articulated in the Constitution and provided room in its representational space for the future growth of U.S. territory.[18] This project of designing spatial analogies for a nation with increasingly imperial ambitions also produced nationally significant buildings. The ongoing construction of the U.S. Capitol Building and its decorative art, murals, and statues throughout this period defined the Union as a nation whose transcendence of geographical or European ethnic particularity permitted a national narrative which connected the colonial past with an imperial future.[19] In his brief editorship in 1836 of the illustrated *American Magazine*, Hawthorne featured such monumental projects for middle-class families and displayed a pantheon of Founding Fathers, such as John Adams, Alexander Hamilton, and Thomas Jefferson, both visually, in engravings, and textually.[20] While Stowe is also concerned with national space, Hawthorne is particularly so; at crucial moments in *The Marble Faun* he represents Italian and Catholic sites as national ones.

Similarly, Hawthorne and Stowe engage the visual experience of Catholicism – shrines, paintings, churches, and convents – as a means of considering American attempts to base a collective political belief, a national "religion," on a widely circulating iconography. Just as U.S. elites were organizing nationally meaningful urban, political, and architectural spaces, so were they completing the task, begun in the 1820s, of formulating through a now fully institutionalized practice of art an American secular iconography of historical heroes, typical citizens, and "national landscape[s]."[21] The advent of art associations, illustrated periodicals, public commissions of art, and American art colonies in Florence and Rome, and the explicit identification of artists in the 1850s with an expansionist U.S. ideology, worked to create and disseminate nationalizing images to a growing middle class.[22] Nevertheless, as I argued in Chapter 3, American tourists continued to be at once drawn to and wary of European and especially Catholic images. To return to Jenny Franchot's point, American Protestants found that the "overwhelming force of the visual encounter with . . . papal Rome" threatened to destabilize a nationally functional opposition between Protestant, language-centered, republican purity and Catholic, visually oriented, monarchical corruption; they responded to the pull of Catholic images by developing a "Protestant gaze on Rome . . . that . . . celebrated Catholicism as spectacle, and fantasized the consumption of this foreign substance rather than conversion to it."[23] In spite of this habitual polarization of a Catholic Italy and a putatively Protestant U.S., tourist writings suggest that, under the surface of this opposition, the example of "Romanism" – as an organization that shaped a community through powerfully consolidating aesthetic experiences – spoke to the evolving concept of the U.S. as a nation which was constructing itself not only as a governing entity but also as an affectively bound community, bound through a secular faith in the Union.

Stowe and Hawthorne follow American Protestant culture in revising even as they appropriate Catholic visual experience, especially by substituting sentimental icons for religious ones: American virgins for Madonnas. Furthermore, in introducing a sentimental heroine, Stowe implies that female subjectivity is a crucial site for the national imaginary; her novel is at once a narrative of the emergence of a universalized middle-class feminine subjectivity and a lesson in reading the visual. Agnes's childlike "Catholic" aesthetic response is salvaged for and integrated into a mature modern republican consciousness. In these romances, the bodies of the heroines, Agnes and Hilda, both of whom carry saints' names, replace religious images and become originating national Protestant icons, that is, icons which organize the emotional life of modern national subjects and yet "Protestant" bodies whose physical presences are dispersed, sublimated, into national life. These characters disappear increasingly from the narrative even as their function as domestic icons is assured. As Protestant icons, these figures lose their corporeal tangibility as they enter their most intimately efficacious roles as adult women who bind their male counterparts to the nation. At once symbols of the nation and representative national subjects, whose emotional openness to culturally hegemonic forces created the "imagined community" of the modern nation, women "were responsible for managing the relation between national embodiment and national bodies," as Shirley Samuels has put it; their double role as those most able to "feel right," to quote Stowe's famous phrase, and to act as icons drawing other citizens more fully into the nation enabled them to link "individual bodies to the national body."[24] This chapter examines the ways in which Hilda and Agnes as such double figures – both subject and icon – secure "Catholic" aesthetic response for U.S. national purposes.

Of course, in their dual role these women synthesize the two aspects of the national artist's job: the creation of images and the management of subjects. If the previous chapter treated Hawthorne's novel as an urban text, this chapter will foreground something more obvious – that it is emphatically "about" expatriate artists in Rome; Hilda herself is an American painter, her compatriot, Kenyon, is a sculptor, and Miriam, mysteriously cosmopolitan in origin, is a painter as well.[25] Stowe highlights the role of art in the transformations her characters undergo and creates a character whose role shadows Agnes's: her great-uncle, the painter Father Antonio. I will focus on national spaces and their associated iconography in *The Marble Faun* and on the transference of the subject's aesthetic response from Catholic to republican icons in *Agnes of Sorrento*. However, the romances are connected through their depictions of women and artists as reforming agents who themselves respond to ideologically charged sites and images and who try to cultivate proper responses in others. The narrative at stake in both novels is that of the journey of incipient citizens, through the mediations of women and artists, toward full republican subjectivity.

National Sites and Managed Reform in *The Marble Faun*

In a crucial scene in Hawthorne's novel, Hilda, a New England painter, decides to disburden herself of a crime she has witnessed by confessing to a Catholic priest. The narrative voice frames this decision sympathetically but also describes it as a seduction, a possible perversion of Hilda's identity as "daughter of the Puritans" (362).[26] In doing so, Hawthorne plays on a generation of nativist, virulently anti-Catholic writings in which the confessional served as a focus of "enormous political and sexual anxiety," the space in which souls were violated, women seduced, and voters manipulated in a papal conspiracy to dominate the U.S.[27] Hilda's more complexly rendered "seduction" occurs in St. Peter's Basilica, what seems to Hilda in her distraught state as the "material home" of religion, and Hawthorne makes it clear that the space of this cathedral orchestrates the confession and draws her, however momentarily, into a community of believers. As readers have noted, the Catholic Church generally serves in this Protestant romance as a representation of the power and potentially repressive authority of the state, especially the state seen as an archaic European institution, controlling its subjects through a mixture of coercion and idolatry.[28] In describing Hilda's response to its physical embodiment, St. Peter's, Hawthorne describes how the state incorporates its subjects' imaginings into its own structure. While the church at first seems disappointing compared to Hilda's anticipations of a Gothic, "misty," "illimitable interior," it gradually replaces her fantasies of ideal architectural space with its own (baroque) presence:

> The great church smiles calmly upon its critics, and . . . says, "Look at me!" – and if you still murmur for the loss of your shadowy perspective, there comes no reply, save, "Look at me!" – in endless repetition, as the one thing to be said. And, after looking many times, . . . you discover that the Cathedral has gradually extended itself

over the whole compass of your idea; it covers all the site of your visionary temple, and has room for its cloudy pinnacles beneath the Dome. One afternoon, as Hilda entered Saint Peter's, . . . [i]t seemed an embodiment of whatever the imagination could conceive, or the heart desire, as a magnificent, comprehensive, majestic symbol of religious faith. (350)

In this passage, Hawthorne conflates the language of the growth of aesthetic appreciation, as one architectural aesthetic gives way to another, with that of a spiritual awakening. But he is also tracing the process by which the state becomes adequate to the subject's desire and encompasses her utopian imaginings, a process in which the modern republican state uncannily mirrors the archaic European state.

Such influential figures as George Stillman Hillard – a Boston lawyer, orator, educational reformer, and Hawthorne's friend – characteristically used the image of a cathedral as a metaphor for the nation-state in which government, affect, and aesthetics were effectively conjoined: "As the idea of a cathedral includes not only the central nave . . . [and] the massive buttress, but also the roses blooming in stone, . . . so in the idea of a state are comprehended, not only armies . . . and government . . . [but also] the arts."[29] Like the U.S., as it was being ideologically constructed during Hawthorne's career, St. Peter's represents a capacious and "universal" union; it hails potential citizens through its many confessionals, which offer consolation in different European languages, and through its visual representations of sacred figures which offer mediation between the citizen/believer and the greater community. Hilda's interpellation into the state, if we want to put it this way, is intimate and affective. Drawn (however ambivalently) to images of the Virgin and seeing the inscription "PRO ANGLICA LINGUA" on a confessional, Hilda feels as though she had heard "her mother's voice from within the tabernacle, calling her," and she is brought to her knees before a priest, one of several (again, ambivalently rendered) benign patriarchal figures in the novel who absorb the conflicts supplicants bring to them and offer absolution and "benediction." This incorporation triggers a "transfiguration" in Hilda and brings her into a state of "peaceful beatitude" (357, 362, 364, 363).

Nevertheless, as her confessor points out, as a Protestant who has no intention of converting to Catholicism, Hilda is stealing the rite of confession, illegitimately appropriating elements of religious experience absent in her own faith. I would add that Hilda is also doing what Americans generally do in this period: appropriating elements of the visual repertoire of Catholicism for use in creating a national "faith." Hawthorne's depiction of Hilda in the cathedral reveals "the attractions of a faith, . . . marvelously adapt[ed] . . . to every human need," which "supplies a multitude of external forms, in which the Spiritual may be clothed and manifested" (344). Hilda watches a cross section of Italian society pray at various shrines within the churches in Rome – "peasants, citizens, soldiers, nobles, women with bare heads, ladies in their silks" (346) – and sees, in effect, scenes of voluntary union through the response to the aesthetic, "external forms" of Catholic iconography. As Franchot points out, Catholic rituals enact in antebellum texts a "simulation of the egalitarian democracy proclaimed by American republicanism,"[30] what one might call the Catholic shadow of the republican nation. Hilda's joining in this at once anti-national and national communion is triggered by a series of encounters with images within the sacred space of St. Peter's, encounters which show her sampling the visual images of the Church and choosing those which most suit her own needs. She has been, here and elsewhere, haunting shrines to the Virgin, which contain images of Mary that her Protestant aesthetic finds too "earthly" as represented by Italian painters but which she desperately needs as a transcendent replacement for the particular, "real" mother she has lost; indeed, the narrator suggests that the extraordinarily pure Hilda herself is a more fitting image of the Virgin than most Italian paintings, as, literally transcendent, she lives in a tower and, as part of her rental agreement, tends a shrine to the Madonna at its top. In the cathedral, Hilda sees the ancient statue of St. Peter but is repelled by the idolatry – the too-literal worship – with which it is treated. She then visits copies of two of the works which most appealed to Americans: Raphael's *Transfiguration*, which represented for Americans the "transformation of suffering flesh into spirit" (an engraving of which the Hawthornes hung in their home on their return to Massachusetts),[31] and Guido Reni's *St. Michael Archangel*, with its radical bifurcation of good and evil, its refusal to mingle earthly and spiritual characteristics, as the pictures of the Virgin do (347–8, 352). This last image, which one might call anti-incarnational in its separations, prompts her confession.

This training of the religious/national subject toward voluntary union through visual experience – through the configuration of space and through the creation of a unifying iconography – is the anxious subject matter of *The Marble Faun*. Just as St. Peter's serves as the displaced space of national piety, so do other tourist sites in the novel represent the spaces of the production and consumption of religious/national symbolisms. The conjunctions of art and space and the characters' responses to them display the process by which antebellum elites sought to consolidate national identities through icons, as they turned visual images from religious uses to national ones, thereby binding citizens to a transcendent Union. Furthermore, Hawthorne traces the elite conversion not only of religious but also of secular European images to republican uses through an idealizing aesthetic. The romance reveals a structural equivalence between the universalizing language of ideal art and the universalizing language of republican nationhood. But, by foregrounding the difficulty – even the exhaustion – of his own attempts (recorded in his journals) to respond properly to canonical art, Hawthorne's fiction revisits and denaturalizes the "labor of admiring" that the previous generation had attempted to render invisible. That is, Hawthorne makes their effort to naturalize this labor visible and, so, destabilizes the project of creating a nationalizing iconography.[32] His depictions of such important Roman spaces as St. Peter's, the Forum, and the Capitoline Hill, and of such extra-Roman sites as the central square of Perugia, posit different dreams of nationhood. I will argue that these often explicitly denominated "dreams" resist the usual tourist attempt to create order among them by organizing them chronologically, either in an Edward Gibbon-like narrative of republican virtue, imperial grandeur, decline and fall or in a Christian narrative of the triumph of the faithful over pagan precursors. Rather, they remain disconcertingly and simultaneously present in a phantasmagoria of national imaginings.

History and the National Artist

These sites and dreams are mediated through the central consciousness of the novel, the would-be national sculptor, Kenyon, who is in Italy to learn how to produce a secular version of the kind of official art Hilda consumes and, therefore, to learn how to use his aesthetic skills to train republican subjects. As Mark Kemp points out, Kenyon has ambitions to create public sculpture of the kind being commissioned for such sites as the Capitol Building.[33] An artist "of high promise" (21), he is setting out to become an influential expatriate sculptor, like Hiram Powers, Hawthorne's acquaintance in Florence, who sends his statues back to the U.S. Indeed, Hawthorne gives him the work-in-progress of exactly such an emerging American sculptor: the *Cleopatra* (1860) of William Wetmore Story, whom Hawthorne met and whose career he helped by advertising Story's statue in his novel. As did many mid-century marble representations of female figures, as Joy S. Kasson has documented, *Cleopatra* joins issues of women's sexuality, power, and defeat in a spectacle that, like the Italian scene itself, is at once an enthralling image and one controlled by the spectator's knowledge of the historical narrative of Cleopatra's subjugation.[34] And, as does Harriet Hosmer's *Zenobia* (1859), to which Hawthorne also refers, this statue requires its viewers to contemplate the subjection of the image to the expansionist narrative of classical Rome.[35] Navigating the tourist's and artist's double response of cultural dominance and aesthetic arrest – of the totalizing gaze and of the "feminine" susceptibility to the image or the scene – becomes a critical task for Kenyon in developing his capacity to create a unifying, republican art back home.

What's at stake for Kenyon in the proper management of aesthetic response becomes clear in the difficult conjunction of art and empire imagined in the travel book of Hawthorne's friend Hillard. As a man of letters concerned with "The Relation of the Poet to His Age" and "The Political Duties of the Educated Classes" (two of the titles of his orations), Hillard articulated for his class and generation the meanings of Italy most fully until Hawthorne's *Marble Faun* became the most popular "guide"; his *Six Months in Italy* (1853) went through twenty-one editions.[36] His book is characterized by a profound attraction to "Italy" and by the usual strategies for managing that attraction. Hillard's descriptions of contemporary Rome emphasize its post-national and "picturesque character" as "the great secret of that magic spell which it throws over every artist." Hillard's Rome is a city of political and aesthetic "repose" which is open to the tourist's gaze. He describes the favored tourist view from the Pincian Hill which Kenyon and Hilda share (see Chapter 4) and emphasizes its delivery of Rome as a picture, harmonized by the colors of the buildings, varied by the "irregularity" of the skyline, and framed by a "green ring of plain and mountain." This total view complements the "interior pictures," visible through open doors, and genre scenes of street life (II, 18–23). Like Fuller, Hillard discusses two characteristic foreign presences in Rome as models of response: artists and "Englishmen." While Rome is a powerfully aesthetic presence, its influence on American artists is ambiguous; by "bewitch[ing] the eye," it threatens the hard ego boundaries necessary for active life: "Excellence in art is to be attained by active effort and not by passive impressions, – by the manly overcoming of difficulties" (II, 253–7). The English, on the other hand, are impervious to aesthetic influence;

they are "not at home in the region of art." Their tendency to bring their culture and values with them renders them offensive, manly to a fault in their nakedly imperial dominance: "They stalk over the land as if it were their own." Nevertheless, Hillard warns Americans not to discount the English as models; their tread and gaze signal that they are the modern Romans, the "true Romans," and signify "national greatness" (II, 268–74). American men, he implies, must incorporate both responses to the Italian scene; they must construct a romance of aesthetic enthrallment brought into the service of the imperial, "English" values on which modern nationhood depends. This double imperative signaled the difficulty of creating the modern national subject, which, in the U.S., increasingly required a conflation of imperial ambition and an openness to the "states of feeling" underlying a sympathetic identification with the "imagined community" of the Union.[37]

But if Hawthorne gave Kenyon Story's statue, he put him into the studio of Louisa Lander, one of a growing group of women sculptors in Rome and for whom Hawthorne sat for his own bust.[38] While he sidesteps the presence of nationally ambitious women sculptors in Rome, such as Hosmer, whom he mentions, Hawthorne's two women painters offer alternative versions of the relationship between the artist and the images of the Italian scene. Hilda functions as a simultaneously exaggerated and incomplete version of the national artist. As Richard H. Brodhead has stated, Hilda's work as a selfless copyist of Old Masters – a copyist sympathetically attuned to the spirit of canonical works – sacralizes the art she copies and, so, reproduces the cultural hierarchies and forms of authority that such canons serve.[39] Unlike Kenyon, she will not inaugurate new images that connect universal principles to the changing historical conditions of the republic. On the other hand, Miriam Schaefer, as readers have noted, represents the romantic artist: autobiographical, expressive rather than mimetic, revisionist in her handling of biblical themes, and a prolific producer of sketches – examples of a genre which, for writers like Hawthorne, collaborated with the viewer's imagination to suggest greater reaches of aesthetic insight than did completed works.[40] Like Germaine de Staël's poet, Corinne, with whom Miriam compares herself, Miriam is an improvisatrice – but of the visual arts.[41] In addition to representing modern urbanity, as I argued in the previous chapter, with its promise or threat of anti-patriarchal revolution, Miriam functions as a cosmopolitan artist. Her racial/national identity, again like Corinne's, is initially ambiguous ("society" speculates whether she is Jewish, German, or partially African American [21–3]) and then confirmed as indeed international: Jewish/English/Italian (429–30). This sets her apart from the overdetermined national and racial identities of the other major characters and allows her to deconstruct both collective identities and the use of female figures to consolidate those identities. As did Caroline Kirkland's depiction of the French tragic actress Rachel Felix, Hawthorne's depiction of Miriam conflates her gender and her Jewishness to position her as at once icon and artist, at once concerned with issues of republican subjectivity and outside of any possibility of full republican citizenship herself.[42]

Miriam denaturalizes the workings of feminine icons for a visitor who is startled by a glimpse of a manikin in her studio. In doing so, she analyzes the position generally of women as figures, as representational in their function. When the visitor starts at seeing, apparently, "a woman with long dark hair" in a posture of "tragic despair," Miriam assures him,

> "It is a lady of exceedingly pliable disposition; now a heroine of romance, and now a rustic maid: yet all for show, being created . . . to wear rich shawls and other garments in a becoming fashion. This is the true end of her being, although she pretends to assume the most varied duties . . ., while really the poor puppet has nothing on earth to do. Upon my word, I am satirical unawares, and seem to be describing nine women out of ten in the person of my lay-figure!" (41)

In observing the cultural role of women as sliding signifiers, Miriam exposes the fictional nature, to put it redundantly, of the "romance" and of analogous national organizing narratives anchored by female figures. However, Miriam's position as a critic of the workings of romances, whether literary or national, is always threatened and finally engulfed by the very representational role she dissects here. The manikin anticipates Miriam's own appearance, later in the novel, as a dark-haired "heroine" overcome by "tragic despair,"[43] and, in the second half of the romance, as I will argue, Kenyon returns her to the role of an icon – an inspirational aesthetic presence – which, when thoughtfully manipulated by the national artist, can help to mold emerging republican subjectivities.

As national artist, Kenyon must navigate between Hilda's submissive approach to the artistic canon and Miriam's expressivist and deconstructionist orientations, between aesthetic arrest and an awareness of the historical contingency of systems of meaning and identity. These questions of the relationship between transcendent meaning and history become urgent during a midnight tour Hawthorne's artists take of Roman national spaces in the area surrounding the Capitoline Hill. In doing so, they return to the first scenes of the romance; the opening chapters take place in a gallery on the Capitoline Hill, the site of classical Rome's government, rebuilt by Michelangelo, and the source of the name for the U.S. Capitol Building.[44] In the first scene the novel's three artists – Kenyon, Hilda, and Miriam – enact, as Mark Kemp argues, the familiar colonizing gaze of tourists in comparing the fourth, virtually subhuman character, the Italian Donatello, with a statue of a faun, even as Hawthorne sketches the sweeping view of the Forum, with its "threefold antiquity" (6) visible from the gallery's window.[45] The faun, the image of a mythically pre-national, Arcadian Italy, is increasingly brought together with images of republican and imperial nationhood, whose ruins and symbols surround this site, until the area of the Capitoline Hill becomes a palimpsest of possible forms of nationhood.

The later "moonlight ramble" by a larger group of American artists through the Forum, just below, across the Campidoglio (the hill's central square), and to a sheer side of the hill is a tour of the dreamscape of the national imaginary. American identification with Roman history, both republican and imperial, continued unabated from the revolutionary period until the Civil War; American orators repeatedly urged the U.S. to model itself after the Roman Republic, with its mutually enabling virtues of liberty and expansion, while worrying about the nation's possible devolution into the corruption and despotism emblemized by the Roman Empire.[46] Passing from the Coliseum to the Arch of Titus, built to commemorate the conquest of Jerusalem, and into the Forum, Hawthorne's artists imaginatively encounter the violence and confusion of imperial history, a history they simultaneously counter and echo by singing a "thunderous" chorus of "Hail, Columbia!" Given the pervasive identification of the U.S. with classical Rome, their touristic imaginings of Roman history – of "the Roman armies" marching "over the same flag-stones" and through "this Arch of Titus" (159–60) – seem "prophetic visions" of what might be the imperial future of the U.S. Kenyon invokes the legend of Curtius, a fourth-century BCE citizen who leapt into a chasm created by an earthquake in order to close the abyss and save Rome,[47] and asks his fellow artists to imagine this crevice as an opening into the future:

"Imagine the great, dusky gap, impenetrably deep, and with half-shaped monsters and hideous faces looming upward out of it. . . . There, now, is a subject . . . for a grim and ghastly story, . . . with a moral as deep as the gulf itself. Within it, beyond a question, there were prophetic visions – intimations of all the future calamities of Rome – shades of Goths and Gauls, and even of the French soldiers of today. It was a pity to close it up so soon! I would give much for a peep into such a chasm. . . . Doubtless, too, . . . all the blood that the Romans shed, whether on battle-fields, or in the Coliseum, or on the cross . . . ran right into this fatal gulf, and formed a mighty subterranean lake of gore, right beneath our feet." (161, 163)

Kenyon's playful and grisly evocation of the chasm as an opportunity for the artist to engage in national prophecy or to make a romance – an allegorical "story" with a "moral" – out of the confrontation of an honorable citizen with the chaos of a bloody history or future defines the task he is about to take on. The chapter closes with the attempt of Donatello, the Arcadian "faun," to resist the oppressive forces of history by throwing the Model/monk who persecutes Miriam, and who represents her inescapable and perhaps also brutal past, over the side of the Capitoline Hill, thus returning this monstrous figure to a similar abyss. In subsequent chapters, Kenyon obtains, through his allegorical understanding of Donatello's act, his own glimpses into the chasm of history and violence and fashions a narrative and tentative moral out of this event. Just as he uses such historical figures as Cleopatra as allegorical representations of the lessons of history, so he sets out to use Donatello's "Transformation," the title of the first English edition,[48] as an allegory of the emergence of modern consciousness, even as he seeks to direct the emergence of this consciousness and to shape Donatello into a self-sacrificing citizen.

The problem of the relation of the national artist to history, and especially of the artist's role in a nation with imperial ambitions, is posed by a collaborative painting of the Arch of Titus by three American painters, George Healy, Frederic Church, and Jervis McEntee, who have depicted themselves on the right – like Hawthorne's midnight strollers, another group of artists touring the Forum. Standing under the arch are Henry Wadsworth Longfellow and his daughter, Edith, in Rome in 1868. While the painting marks Longfellow's and the painters' claim to the self-culture associated with tourism, it also juxtaposes the U.S. national poet, as Longfellow was then conceived, with images of empire.[49] Predominantly Healy's painting, *The Arch of Titus* (1871, Fig. 5.1) triangulates the concerns of imperial history and literary and visual forms of representation. Healy devised the

Figure 5.1 George Peter Alexander Healy, Frederic Church, and Jervis McEntee, *The Arch of Titus*, 1871. Oil on canvas. Bequest of Dr. J. Ackerman Coles, 1926. Collection of the Newark Museum 26.1260.

painting's structure; he invited the landscape painter Frederic Church to paint in the background of the Coliseum and sky and another landscape painter, Jervis McEntee, to complete the arch, while Healy, a portrait and history painter who had painted Hawthorne's portrait in Boston in 1853, added the figures.[50]

The painting's size (74 x 49 inches) announces its monumental ambitions. On the central ground of Roman power – under the token of territorial conquest and the suppression of rebellion – a team of "national" artists meet: Longfellow, the poet laureate, in effect, author of literary configurations of the American past; Church, the period's predominant national landscape painter, who depicted areas of U.S. territorial, economic, and exploratory expansion, such as the West, South America, and the Polar Sea; and Healy, the painter of statesmen, who in the 1840s and 1850s painted such figures of the emerging political pantheon as Daniel Webster and John Calhoun. The subject of the painting is representation itself:

Church is sketching Longfellow, McEntee points to the sketch and addresses Healy, while Healy looks over Church's shoulder and carries a sketchpad of his own under his arm – thus completing a circle of gazes and gestures which mirror the communal production of a consensus-based art. Longfellow and his daughter, on the other hand, are self-consciously posing and, as passive objects of the painterly gaze, look away from the actively composing group of artists. They strike the awkwardly formal pose of those having their pictures taken; indeed, as Eleanor L. Jones points out, their images are based on a photograph taken in Healy's studio.[51]

The painting addresses historical monuments and the monumentalizing of the national writer. In discussing antebellum monument building – the attempt to construct "'outward types'" of the nation – and the oratorical performances before monuments by such public figures as Webster, Robert H. Byer has observed that the period saw an orator as a "living equivalency" of the monument, also a "type" of the nation.[52] *The Arch of Titus* represents the simultaneous appropriation and transcendence of the monuments of the Roman imperial past and presents Longfellow as a "living equivalency" of the U.S. Like Hawthorne at the time he wrote *The Marble Faun*, as Brodhead has argued, by the 1860s Longfellow is represented and experiences himself as a canonical author.[53]

Nevertheless, Healy represents Longfellow in such terms that his function as type of the nation undermines his monumentality. Healy's national poet is a family man, a republican father, a bourgeois tourist, and this domestic image is at considerable variance with the imperial monument above him. As William L. Vance puts it, this "respected representative of democratic culture" and his daughter seem like "two stiff little dolls"[54] under the massive monument to imperial warfare. But the painting also supports the new construction of imperialism in the mid-century U.S.: the domestic sphere's underwriting of expansionism in what Amy Kaplan has called "manifest domesticity."[55] Healy's work reveals the role of artists and writers in engineering such conjunctions as that of domesticity and empire, even as it shows the awkwardness of articulating emergent national formations in terms of older, classical vocabularies of national space. To return to Hillard's words, the difficulty of reconciling the artist with the "Englishman" may make the past represented by Roman national space and iconography unusable for American artists and citizens. Byer describes Hawthorne's purpose in *The Marble Faun* as a "fragmentation of the monumental sublime," a skepticism toward "monuments as adequate visible embodiments of the politically and morally fractured 'idea of country.'"[56] The artists' tour of the Forum implies that this monumental space cannot be revived for U.S. national purposes. But Hawthorne also documents the continued hunger of republican subjects for such representational adequacies, a longing apparently answered in the iconographical culmination of their tour.

Presidentialist Bodies and Iconoclastic Murder

The images of imperial warfare culminate and are answered, as the artists return to the Capitoline Hill, in an icon and a void: in an image of benign absolute authority in the statue of the emperor Marcus Aurelius (Fig. 5.2) and in the empty space of justice figured by the "precipice" that was the Roman place of execution, the Tarpeian Rock. The image of patriarchal "benediction" and integration into the state offered by the statue of Aurelius is a compensatory fantasy for the previous images of imperial chaos. Hawthorne's description of tourists' responses to the statue traces the effects of what Dana Nelson, drawing on Arend Lijphart, calls "Presidentialism," the "concentration of agency in the body of the president" in the U.S. democratic imaginary. The structure of this imaginary engenders the politically consolidating desire to see the fissures of democracy – and, I would add, of imperial republicanism – healed in the unitary presidential body.[57] While Fuller in describing the proclamation of the Roman Republic shifts the reader's attention from the statue of the "magnificent calm emperor" (one of the "usual" sights in the background) to the anonymous deputy reading the proclamation,[58] Hawthorne makes it the focus of the group of artists as they return to the Campidoglio in their moonlight stroll:

> They stood awhile to contemplate the bronze equestrian statue of Marcus Aurelius. . . . [T]he aspect of dignity was still perfect, clothing the figure as it were with an imperial robe of light. It is the most majestic representation of the kingly character that ever the world has seen. A sight of this old heathen Emperor is enough to create an evanescent sentiment of loyalty even in a democratic bosom; so august does he look, . . . so worthy of man's profoundest homage and obedience, so inevitably attractive of his love! He stretches forth his hand with an air of grand beneficence and unlimited authority, as if uttering a decree from which no appeal was permissible, but in which the obedient subject would find his highest interests consulted; a command that was in itself a benediction. (165–6)

Figure 5.2 Equestrian statue of Marcus Aurelius. Bronze. 11 ft 6 ins. Campidoglio, Rome, second century CE. Scala/Art Resource, New York.

As an artist aspiring to national prominence, Kenyon speaks to the sculptor's role in embodying authority: "'The sculptor of this statue knew what a King should be . . . and knew, likewise, the heart of mankind, and how it craves a true ruler, under whatever title, as a child craves its father!'" (166). The artist's representation of a "command" which is indistinguishable from a "benediction" fulfills the difficult task Hillard set the American cultural elite: the fusion of imperialism and sympathy.

In his *French and Italian Notebooks*, where his own responses to the statue are the source of the above passages, Hawthorne recorded conversations with sculptors about the American project of creating a body of ideal statuary to represent national union. His discussions with Hiram Powers, whose federally commissioned statue *America* (1848–50) Hawthorne saw, particularly reveal his awareness of the ongoing antebellum federal project of decorating the U.S. Capitol Building. In Washington, D.C., the construction of the ideology of Presidentialism was enacted in what one might call the search for Washington's body; as Vivien Green Fryd has demonstrated, Congress repeatedly debated obtaining Washington's remains from Virginia for entombment under the Capitol's Rotunda and planned for decades to commission a sculpture of Washington to be placed over the body. Congress first called (1783) for a "bronze equestrian statue of General Washington clothed in a Roman uniform" and modeled in part on the statue of Aurelius, but the equestrian model proved too monarchical and was rejected.[59] When the Virginia delegation resisted the extradition of Washington's remains, Congress then commissioned another expatriate sculptor living in Italy, Horatio Greenough, to create what Hawthorne disparaged as a "naked respectabilit[y]" (*French and Italian Notebooks*, 432): a seated Washington, modeled on Phidias' lost statue of Zeus in the temple at Olympus, and whose neoclassical vocabulary sought to universalize American republicanism. As Fryd finds in her reading of both the statue and Congressional documents, Greenough's *George Washington* (1832–41) was meant to "'cement the Union'" by "suppressing sectional discord through a self-contained symbol of national strength and unity" and promoting a version of the nation that "transcend[ed] particularism."[60]

In placing Kenyon in front of the Aurelian statue, Hawthorne re-enacts the process by which American artists recuperated Roman (or, in Greenough's case, Greek) images for republican uses. Such "kingly" figures haunt the republican imaginary in this romance less because they represent nostalgia for a "simpler," pre-modern past than because they suggest and shadow modern strategies for ordering disruptive democratic energies by channeling republican allegiances into the "symbolic presidential body," to return to Nelson's formulation, the homogenizing, "strong body" that "blocks imagining democracy as the political and cultural processes of multiple and diverse bodies" (221, 224). Kenyon's role is to mediate between the state and the subject; the national iconographer must know what a republican ruler "should be" – a figure who combines unifying authority with nurturing benevolence – and what the "heart" of the subject "craves." One of his jobs will be to create figural embodiments of the state that are "inevitably attractive" of the subject's "love." The proximity of the functions of religious and national iconography is underscored by Hilda's comment in this scene that real transcendence belongs only to God, a remark which reinforces the putative separation of church and state at just the moment when the slippage between their iconographical programs threatens to become clear.

The dream-tour of national sites ends with the group's view down the side of the Tarpeian Rock. The incorporating promise of the Aurelian statue gives way here to the image of its corollary: the purifying of the state by the literal casting out of traitors. As Kenyon ruminates, "'It was an admirable idea of those stern old fellows, to fling their political criminals down from the very summit on which stood the Senate-House and Jove's temple; emblems of the institutions which they sought to violate.'" That all this represents the dreamwork of nationalism is immediately stated by another artist, who says, "'Come, come; it is midnight. . . . We are literally dreaming on the edge of a precipice. Let us go home!'" (168–9).

These narratives of national order and justice, however, spoken playfully by American tourists, trigger a present historical event: the transformation of Donatello, the (nationally) prelapsarian faun, into what Levine suggests is a republican revolutionary and his murder of the oppressive figure who has been "stalk[ing]" Miriam and the group as a whole.[61] This addition to the "lake" of blood under Rome enables the Italian male's fall into modern consciousness, sexual maturity, and full heteronormative masculinity.[62] The "fierce energy" of the homicide, triggered by his "passion" for Miriam, "kindle[s] him into a man" and "develop[s] within him an intelligence" (172). As readers have noted, the menacing artist's Model emerges, at the scene of his death, from a niche which originally held a statue.[63] If the statue of Aurelius represents the coalescing of political and social power within a figure, Donatello's toppling of this other "figure" (171) represents the dissolution of the tie that binds strands of authority and allegiance together, whether through the medium of the visual arts or through the bodies of powerful political figures. This is an iconoclastic murder, a casting down of an oppressive, patriarchal idol, willed by both Donatello and Miriam. And this is the crime Hilda witnesses and which sends her into the confessional at St. Peter's. These juxtaposed scenes enact a splitting of republican responses to authoritative icons: the desire for a unifying paternal figure and the revulsion against its twin, the oppressive tyrant. Bad icons, it seems, imprison the subject, while good ones reform and liberate; the distinction, however, between oppressive and reforming patriarchal figures is often muddied in *The Marble Faun*.

Incorporating Artists and American Wives

The rest of the novel works to contain the revolutionary rupture signaled by the murder. In the book's second half, Kenyon tests the theories of benevolent incorporation of subjects-in-becoming into the state, under the supervision of the national artist. He manages Donatello's reformation and reintegration into the state, however flawed it appears in the form of despotic Rome. These chapters conjoin the antebellum language of spiritual reform – of introspection, repentance, and growth – with the guidance of an artist, with travel, and with the use of icons as a means of reintegration. In other words, Kenyon shapes the emerging, still "primitive" republican subjectivity of the Italian, Donatello, in just the way U.S. elites wished to shape that of rising lower classes at home. Nancy Bentley has compared Hawthorne's description of the Italian "faun" with his description, in 1862, of escaped American slaves as "natural" men, "wearing . . . a crust of primeval simplicity," "akin to the fauns and rustic deities of olden times."[64] Her reading of the racialized depiction of Donatello illuminates what is at stake for Hawthorne's artist: the reformation of primitive proto-citizens into men in order to harness the "fierce energy" of counter-hegemonic acts. The description of the statue of the faun which Donatello resembles, in the first chapter, is drawn directly from Hawthorne's response to the statue in the notebooks and raises the question of reform immediately; although the faun displays a "lack of moral severity" and is incapable of any "sacrifice . . . for an abstract cause," he is capable of "strong and warm attachment" and "might be educated through the medium of his emotions" (9). And it is through emotions that Kenyon seeks to complete Donatello's development.

Kenyon visits Donatello in his home – moving into his domestic space in his ancestral manor in the Apennines. He first improves the occasion of Donatello's spiritual awakening through his murderous act by modeling his bust, in an attempt to capture the "moral phase through which [he] was now passing"; it is the sculptor's "difficult office" to bring his subject's "characteristics" "out from their depths, and interpret them to all men, showing them what they could not discern for themselves" (270). He guides Donatello through his experience of guilt and growth – "'Believe me, . . . you know not what is requisite for your spiritual growth'" (273) – and recommends travel, that bourgeois strategy of recreation, for his spiritual health. On a journey through the hill towns of central Italy, Donatello augments Kenyon's program of introspection and reincorporation via aesthetic response by praying at roadside shrines. In this leisurely trip, what Richard Millington calls "a cure by tourism,"[65] the language of romance blends into that of spiritual renewal; their "wander[ing]" "like two knights-errant" through "that picturesque . . . region" (289) is also a "penitential pilgrimage" (296) in which the roadside crosses and shrines to the Virgin become "symbols" that, Kenyon hopes, will help Donatello "towards a higher penitence" (299). This chapter is filled with descriptions of the region from Hawthorne's journals, and the discourse of picturesque tourism mingles with those of romance and penitence; the chapter's title, "Scenes by the Way," echoes numerous tourist titles, including N. P. Willis's *Pencillings by the Way* (1835).

The culmination of this redemptive tour is a different national space from Rome: the central square of Perugia. Hawthorne describes this square as the antithesis to the nightmare of imperial history in Rome. This public space holds the essential buildings, both religious and secular, of U.S. republican identity: a church, the "municipal Council-House and Exchange," a market place, and what was once the "Parliament-hall of a nation" in the days of Perugia's independence. Corresponding to the statue of Aurelius is a bronze statue of Pope Julius III, also an image of "patriarchal majesty" offering a "benediction" to citizens (312–14). This site consolidates an idealized and yet, by 1860, archaic image of the nation: a self-contained community (unlike the larger modern nation-state) whose authority emerges through spiritual, that is, cultural, means and where discipline is not enforced by external coercions but is internalized by the citizen. On this site, too, Miriam's role as a redemptive rather than damaging influence on Donatello can emerge. Kenyon has inspired her with his vision of woman's function of offering "intimate help, . . . heart sustenance," and Miriam's answer reveals her full understanding of this aesthetic and integrative role: "'Beauty – if I possess it – shall be one of the instruments by which I shall try to educate and elevate him, to whose good I solely dedicate myself'" (285–6). The square of Perugia, whose space is also an influence on Donatello, is the scene of their chastened reunion and their mutual pledge, as they stand under the outstretched hand of the bronze Pope and its gaze of "grand benignity" (323), to work together, in a nonsexual union, toward the expiation of the crime Miriam wished for and Donatello committed. After this scene, Donatello embraces his own policing and later turns himself in to the authorities for incarceration.

But after this apparently successful exercising of the national artist's power, Kenyon's return to Rome, combined with the temporary loss of Hilda, is marked by revulsion, even nausea, at what now seems to him the "dead and half-rotten city," an emblem of history, understood as the "dark tide of human evil" (412).[66] And his faith in the transformative powers of ideal art falters; separated from Hilda, Kenyon finds that no work of sculpture pleases him and that it has become difficult to work: "he suspected that it was a very cold art to which he had devoted himself. He questioned . . . whether carved marble is anything but limestone, after all" (391). But his revulsion is also informed by his doubts about the role he has just played, about the national artist's right and ability to assist in the "transfiguration" of probational citizens: "The growth of a soul . . . seemed hardly worth the heavy price it had cost . . . A creature of antique healthfulness had vanished from the earth; and, in his stead, there was only one other morbid and remorseful man, among millions that were cast in the same indistinguishable mold" (393). Kenyon's intervention in Donatello's narrative of crime and punishment and his manipulation of the awakening soul of the Italian subject into the self-regulating subjectivity of the modern citizen uneasily echoes the calculated benevolence of Hilda's confessor in St. Peter's and positions the national artist, like the "Jesuitical" priests angling for converted souls, as, in Franchot's words, a "technocrat of the sacred, skilled at its production, distribution, and consumption, . . . [with] technical expertise over the emotions," administering "professionally adroit transactions between the institutional and the individual."[67]

These moral ambiguities of presiding, as an artist, over the emergence of a national subjectivity make Kenyon retreat from this task into the domestic world where the most effective – because most widely and intimately circulated – icon is the middle-class wife, which Hilda eventually becomes. To shore up his own wavering sense of national identity and mission, Kenyon must set up his own domestic icon; he pleads with "Saint Hilda," as he calls her, to "guide me home!" Hilda's final role is to act as the stabilizing, culturally ubiquitous, support to the national project: "enshrined and worshipped as a household Saint" back in New England. There she will manage the relation between individual bodies and the national body, to return to Samuels' terms, through the period's obligatory domesticity and will do so better, Hawthorne implies, than Kenyon can (364, 461).

Hilda's confession in St. Peter's triggers a series of events that illustrates the process of adapting Catholic icons to American uses. Her susceptibility to religious icons and her disclosures in the confessional lead at first to her apparent enslavement by the Church; she is briefly held captive in a convent. But the final result of this experience is not conversion to Catholicism but the conversion of the image of the Madonna into the sentimental image of the American wife, whose policing of the boundary between good and evil will be as effective as St. Michael's in Guido's painting. When installed in every middle-class home, she will shape a virtuous citizenry and attach these citizens to the nation.[68] As will be true of Agnes, Hilda's original nun-like idolatry of religious art and icons is not utterly repudiated but brought into the service of the modern state by her transfiguration into a woman whose capacity for desire makes her a representative modern republican subject, voluntarily moving toward sexual and political union. Hilda's immersion in the visual and ritual culture of Catholicism does not make her a Catholic, as Kenyon at first fears, but instead "soften[s] her out of the chilliness of her virgin pride" (370) and makes her ready to accept her American lover's proposal of marriage.

Kenyon and Hilda complete the romance by marrying and returning not to the U.S. exactly but to New England, where on the eve of the Civil War a collective identity was still imaginable for Hawthorne.[69] Even as it displayed uneasiness about the fragility of the nationalizing project, *The Marble Faun* paradoxically became part of this system of representation when it became a favorite vade mecum of post-war American tourists in Italy, a guide to icons and images and to the fluctuations in the relations of viewing subjects to national icons.[70]

Religious Icons, National Iconography, and Female Bodies in *Agnes of Sorrento*

Stowe sets her historical romance *Agnes of Sorrento* in the late fifteenth century, during the time of the Dominican friar Girolamo Savonarola's revolt against the political repression, luxuries, and art of Medici Florence (when Americans agreed that Italy had had a history), yet the tale moves, as would a nineteenth-century tourist, among the favored aesthetic sites of the Bay of Naples, Rome, and Florence, a route Stowe followed on her third European tour in 1859–60.[71] With its narrative threads of heterosexual love culminating in domesticity, church corruption, and the iconoclastic drive of Savonarola and his followers to purify both church and state, *Agnes* interprets Italian history as a movement toward Protestantism and such modern forms of social and political order as bourgeois marriage and the nation-state. And it replaces an idolatrous aesthetic (the "superstitious" response to religious icons) with a Protestant aesthetic, which substituted naturalized icons, such as landscape images or sentimental genre figures, for Catholic ones.[72] In doing so, it positions the U.S. as the culmination of a progressive line of history and maps the American tourist's route along what it posits as the Italian nation's path toward modernity.

Crucial to this formulation of republican progress is the novel's equivalence, similar to that in *The Marble Faun*, between investing national psychic energy in a charismatic male leader and investing it in the modern wife: between loving Aurelius and loving Hilda. Followers of Savonarola are also those characters who most idealize Agnes. And like Hawthorne's, Stowe's romance, as Annamaria Formichella Elsden observes,[73] replaces male authorities' bodies and voices with female bodies and feelings. On the level of iconographical representation, the male saint's statue whose description opens the book immediately gives way to images of the Virgin, and on the level of plot, the body of Savonarola, who is depicted as both a religious reformer and a national father, is burned, while his vision – one might even say his law – is absorbed into Agnes's emotional being, and her presence becomes the disseminating agent of early Italian nationalism and reform. This partial transference of the nation-binding function from the presidential body to the wife's subjectivity marks the trajectory of Italy's growth as republican, as developing the private and domestic underpinnings of the national consolidation of self-governing citizens. To complete the novel's sequence of increasingly intimate and affective reformation, Stowe's study of an embodied subjectivity in Agnes shifts from Agnes's figuring of religious ideals, visible in parallels between Agnes and religious art, toward her decorporealization, her later description as "a disembodied spirit."[74] Instead of defining Italy as irremediably other, therefore, Stowe defines it as a stage in the gazing American Protestant tourist's subjective genealogy.

But even as Stowe aligns Italy with U.S. definitions of progressive history, nationhood, and aesthetics, she is also using "Italy" as a provisional territory, a spectacle which, in its excess of visual imagery and associations with pre-modern and corporeal aspects of the feminine, cannot be fully recuperated by American understanding. Stowe cordons off these moments of visual and affective excess by coding Italy as a transcendent landscape inhabited by racialized others with access to different modes of seeing; at the same time, she sets the feminine at the center of the successful transition to nationhood. Her vista into cultural memory colonizes the Italian past for American uses. But it also registers, in spite of its central project, the "ambivalence" W. J. T. Mitchell suggests lies in landscape representations, understood as the "dreamwork" of nationalism and imperialism, with their proffering of "both utopian fantasies of the perfected imperial prospect and . . . images of unresolved ambivalence and unsuppressed resistance," a definition I would broaden to include an unrepressed desire for an experience of aesthetic arrest that remains unconvertible to a progressive republican narrative.[75]

As previous chapters have argued, American paintings and illustrations addressed both aspects of tourist responses: the experience of pleasurable excess and a disciplinary reflex. This double response informs a painting of *Agnes*'s setting that foregrounds the role of the female body and subjectivity. The expatriate painter George Loring Brown, whose twenty-year sojourn in Italy and entrepreneurial spirit in marketing his paintings belie Hillard's warning about the enervating effect of Italy on American men, was very successful in the 1850s, especially with U.S. tourists, in a career of reproducing the Italian landscape.[76] Hawthorne visited Brown's studio in Rome and was "delighted" with his "beautiful," even "magical" landscapes (*French and Italian Notebooks*, 176). Brown's popularity was a function of his conservatism;[77] as did the previous generation of artists, he used familiar conventions derived from Claude Lorrain (whose works he had copied as a young man)[78] to idealize and manage the simultaneously pre- and post-national meanings attached to Italy. In his *Sunset, View of Vesuvius and the Bay of Naples* (1864, Fig. 5.3), he creates a supernal coherence in the landscape by using side screens – the tree and the castle – to direct the eye into the vista and a harmonizing light to unify the prospect.

More importantly, the painting reveals associations among religion, nation, and women, as it performs landscape's "dreamwork." The reposing woman in the foreground is at once a model for the tourist's

Figure 5.3 George Loring Brown, *Sunset, View of Vesuvius and the Bay of Naples*, 1864. Oil on canvas. 34¹/₁₆ x 60³/₁₆ ins (86.52 x 152.88 cm). Bowdoin College Museum of Art, Brunswick, Maine. Bequest of Joseph Edward Merrill, Class of 1854, 1909.1.

contemplative submission to the scene of the past and a marker of the scene's difference from the U.S. as a landscape that stimulates aesthetic contemplation; she figures at once the complex subjectivity of the tourist's reverie and the heavily embodied object of that reverie. The religious procession in the left foreground, a staple in American representations of Italy, offers figures that are rooted in the scene by faith and by the force of the past, unlike the geographically and culturally mobile modern traveler. Brown's inscription on the back of the canvas, as described by John W. Coffey, notes the cluster of emblematic images he assembled here that, for Americans, signaled the scene's distance from an active, present history: "'Sunset' / View of *Vesuvius*, & Bay of NAPLES, & City / (taken from *Virgils tomb*) & Old Convent of St Maria / and Religious Procession of the Corpus Domini" [*sic*].[79] The depth of the vista, as we look toward Vesuvius, is an image of past national glory and present feminized passivity but also models the tourist's nostalgic "memory" of a deep pre-national time of "primitive" belief and a combined Arcadian and Christian harmony.[80] The sunset light that bathes the scene signals that this is a dream of social and cultural unity projected into the past.[81] It is the task of *Agnes* to connect this fantasized past, this simultaneously repudiated and attractive pagan/Catholic precursor scene, to the operations of religious and national faith in the U.S. Just as the female figure serves as the threshold to the painting, so Agnes, less sensually portrayed, mediates for other characters and for Stowe's readers between the past and the future.

However, both Brown's and Stowe's subject matter is also a fantasy of visual excess, a sense that the Italian region coded as most childlike and primitive by Americans releases a flood of images that resist social and linguistic orders of discipline.[82] In its treatment of Catholic icons, Stowe's romance folds aesthetic experience easily into the modernizing national project. But its lengthy descriptions of the southern region of the Bay of Naples, drawn from her experiences as a tourist, remain outside of this project, an unassimilated residue of what Stowe also defines as a pagan, childlike, sensual order of experience, left behind by but not subsumed into the plot of the romance. After focusing on its republican narrative, I will return to a consideration of *Agnes*'s visual excess.

Ave Agnes: Incarnating Modern Nations

The plot of *Agnes* fuses Protestantism and nationalism. The title character is one of Stowe's preternaturally pure adolescents who (as does Mary Scudder in *The Minister's Wooing*, 1859) inspires love and piety simultaneously in men. Her suitor, Agostino Sarelli, whom she marries at the end, is a dispossessed nobleman whose estates have been seized by the Borgias, now in power in Rome, who is excommunicated by the corrupt Pope Alexander VI, and who leads a band of equally disaffected men as brigands. Unlike Irving's banditti, Sarelli and his men are unambiguously freedom fighters who may be reincorporated into a reformed church and state. From a follower of Savonarola, Sarelli learns the Protestant gesture of separating the corrupt earthly institution of the Roman Church from the "True Church," while his desire for Agnes permits him to be reconciled to Christianity, and he emerges as a forerunner of nineteenth-century Italian republican revolutionaries; he wishes to rescue "my beautiful Rome" from "under the heel of the tyrant." Savonarola, the novel's major historical figure, is defined as a proto-Protestant, an "Italian Luther," whose proto-nationalist vocabulary – "our Italy" – prefigures the union of the separate Italian states into one nation (312, 98, 293).

In this way, the novel speaks to the American understanding of the Risorgimento as a modernizing, republican movement akin to the emergence of U.S. nationalism and, therefore, participates in what Paola Gemme calls the "invention of America through the discourse on the formation of Italian nationhood" (11). In 1857–60, when Stowe visited Italy twice and began to write *Agnes*, the Risorgimento had actually left its radical republican roots behind and Italy was being politically unified into a modern nation-state – a nation bound by a common language and by a perceived common destiny (a process completed in 1870) – under a monarchy, with limited political freedoms.[83] However, there is no hint in Stowe's romance of this contemporary turn away from a republic as the form national unification was supposed to take; instead, the narrative line of national development continues to be a nineteenth-century American one: the conjoined emergence of Protestantism from Catholicism and republican nationalism from despotism.

For much of this prophetic narrative thrust toward Stowe's U.S., the novel's focus is on Agnes's emotional and cognitive development, the "strange forcing process" that the surrounding characters and environment exert on her "mind" (135). By mapping her eventual growth from an infantile innocence and faith, marked by her desire to become a nun, to a more mature skepticism and adult sexuality, Stowe puts the female subject at the center of modern republican nations. Agnes at once represents the latent Italian nation and, as the emotional and spiritual guide of the promising citizen of the future, Sarelli, provides the affective glue of what will become a progressive, Christian nation. Stowe's sister, Catharine Beecher, famously argued in her *Treatise on Domestic Economy* (1841) that the American wife and mother would through her moral authority in the domestic sphere help to usher in the millennium, the victory, to be achieved first in the U.S., of Christ's kingdom on earth.[84] Given this extraordinary sentimental power, to use Jane Tompkins's phrase,[85] female subjectivity becomes a home not only for the religious imaginary but also for the national imaginary, which it reproduces and nurtures. The reader's tour through Italy and through Agnes's developing consciousness traces the emergence of a national feminine subjectivity in terms of aesthetic and sexual response. As Agnes's preliminary vocation of the bride of Christ gives way to the modern vocation of the angel in the house,[86] Stowe is concerned to retain Agnes's "Catholic" aesthetic response, to purge it of idolatry, and to integrate it into this more modern consciousness. In doing so, Stowe implies that the passive feminine figures in the foreground of tourists' views, such as Brown's painting or the image of an "Italian Flower Girl" in *Godey's*, discussed in the previous chapter, mark the threshold not of an antithesis to nationhood but of its origins. Agnes's transformation must occur at the most intimate and yet most national level of her subjectivity, that of sexuality.

In accord with Stowe's supercessionist treatment of Catholic material, she revises the legend of St. Agnes which serves as the backdrop to her heroine's career. In a discussion of John Keats's reworking of the Agnes legend in his poem "The Eve of St. Agnes," Wendy Steiner sketches the story of this fourth-century Christian martyr in Rome and explains Keats's use of its elements to create the romance's characteristic movement from the viewer's "enthrallment" to the image of the beloved to the reimmersion in time and history figured in romance plots by sexual consummation and marriage. In the legend, Agnes refuses marriage because she has had a vision that she is betrothed to Christ. Punished by the father of a rejected suitor, she is exposed in a brothel (but miraculously protected by a rapid growth of hair and a white garment delivered by an angel), subjected to other trials, and, in a later episode, martyred.[87] On the other hand, Keats imagines his character as exposing herself to the gaze of an earthly lover, after which the pair break the spell of visual/voyeuristic enthrallment through their sexual union. Stowe's revision of the legend links sexual with national union; she replaces Agnes's enthralling dream of becoming the bride of Christ with the vision of purposeful bourgeois marriage, whose "plot" is finally a national one. Stowe's Agnes needs to remain alive and at least somewhat embodied in order to reproduce the reformed subjectivity of the future nation.[88]

This romance plot exists in counterpoint to Stowe's Protestant subplot of the dangers of seduction within the confessional; Agnes's purity attracts the spiritual and then the sexual attention of her father confessor. In her characterization of this priest, Father Francesco, another disciple of Savonarola, Stowe emphasizes the same conjunction of sexual and transcendent (whether spiritual or national) desires that she highlights in her depiction of Sarelli's desire for Agnes and of Agnes's learned desire for Sarelli. The tragedy of Francesco's fate is that he cannot participate in the social structures that would legitimate this "natural" conjunction; "There was a moment when his whole being vibrated with a perception of what a marriage bond might have been that was indeed a sacrament" (49), but his vows of celibacy condemn him instead to vigils of penance in the "sulphurous" region of Vesuvius's crater (256).[89] While marriage is naturalized as a method of integrating citizens into the nation, Father Francesco's attempts to unite Agnes to the Church and to discipline the desiring body become grotesque and are implicitly written out of the national narrative. Like Hilda's scene in the confessional, Agnes's confessional scenes are informed by the paranoid view of priests that pervaded antebellum Protestant culture. But Stowe repeatedly separates Catholic images from their institutional environment; confessing to Father Francesco may be risky, but the operation of images – of art, statues, emblems – is benign.[90]

Agnes's reproductive capacities, her destiny as wife and mother, emerge not in tension with Catholic religious iconography but out of it. Like Hilda, Agnes is repeatedly associated with the Madonna; she has a shrine to the Madonna and Child in her garden in Sorrento. But Stowe compares her most specifically to the Virgin at the moment of the annunciation.[91] At a crucial moment in her courtship Agnes becomes a "metonym[. . .] for art," as Gail Smith has said.[92] Her great-uncle, Father Antonio, is an artist and member of Savonarola's convent in Florence, San Marco's, and is influenced by the frescoes left there by Fra Angelico; during a visit to Sorrento, he decides that Agnes is the perfect model for an image of the annunciation he plans for a breviary (106). As he and his great-niece sit in her garden, which overhangs a ravine – a gorge described in sensual, pagan terms as an abyss opening into pre-Catholic Italy – talking of this project, the scene of the annunciation suddenly becomes literalized and sexualized. Sarelli emerges

from the side of the gorge . . . and stood in the moonlight before
Agnes. He bore in his hand a stalk of white lily . . ., such as one sees
in . . . pictures of the Annunciation. The moonlight fell full upon his
face, revealing his haughty yet beautiful features, agitated by some
profound emotion. . . . [H]e kneeled, and kissing the hem of her robe,
and laying the lily in her lap, "Holiest and dearest," he said, "oh,
forget not to pray for me!" He rose again . . . sprang over the garden
wall, and . . . rapidly descend[ed] into the shadows of the gorge. (107)

That night Agnes has an erotic dream in which her suitor becomes
explicitly the angel of the annunciation, complete with white gar-
ments and wings. Sarelli's face seems "elevated and etherealized,
glowing with a kind of interior ecstasy"; he floats toward her with
an equally transfigured, "radiant," lily, with which he touches her
forehead, inspiring in her "a delicious tranquility, a calm ecstasy,"
and she hears the words, "The Lord hath sealed thee for his own!"
The dream, however, ends with Sarelli changed back into his usual
appearance, as he pleads, "'Oh, Agnes! . . . little lamb of Christ,
love me and lead me!' – and in her sleep it seemed to her that her
heart stirred . . . with a strange new movement . . . and thereafter her
dream became more troubled" (123–4).

These erotically charged scenes depict the redemptive possibilities of the modern wife in terms of a Pre-Raphaelite and Ruskinian
aesthetic, most influential in the 1850s and early 1860s.[93] Echoing
American adherents of the English art critic John Ruskin, Stowe
asserts that the best and only truly original Italian art was Christian,
represented by such painters as Fra Angelico, and that with Michelangelo and Raphael this art at once reached its highest technical per-
fection and began to decline. With the loss of Christian piety in art
came the loss of "Italian nationality" and "national development"
(127). Stowe's Pre-Raphaelite-inflected conflation of Italian piety, art,
and nationalism makes sense in the context of mid-nineteenth-century Anglo-American perceptions of the Risorgimento. The English
Pre-Raphaelite Brotherhood (P.R.B.) was founded in the revolutionary year of 1848 by, among others, the Anglo-Italian artist Dante
Gabriel Rossetti, whose father, an exiled Italian liberal, was a poet
and a Dante scholar.[94] Pro-republican in Italian politics in their early
years, the group included the painter William Holman Hunt, whose
Rienzi (1849), mentioned in the previous chapter, brought medieval
subject matter to the support of the Roman Revolution.[95] Champi-
oned by Ruskin, who befriended Stowe in Europe,[96] the Brotherhood
rejected the conventions of British academic art, advocated for the

"primitive" and apparently less mediated works of Italian painters before Raphael, and practiced a devotional, *plein-air* approach to painting nature.[97] As Elizabeth Prettejohn explains, the P.R.B.'s commitment to "'truth-in-nature'" meant that "[t]he unit of 'truth' in Pre-Raphaelite painting is the detail, the smallest element that can be given its own distinctive identity"; this principle was articulated in Ruskin's often-quoted directive that painters "'should go to nature in all singleness of heart, . . . having no other thought but how best to penetrate her meaning; rejecting nothing, selecting nothing, scorning nothing.'"[98] The Pre-Raphaelites connected this "primitive" literalism in depicting nature, according to Prettejohn, with the "religious sincerity" of late medieval and early Renaissance Italian painters.[99]

The Pre-Raphaelite elevation of Fra Angelico as an ideal Christian painter who combined an allegiance to "truth-in-nature" with piety and Italian national identity informs Stowe's description not only of Father Antonio's love for Fra Angelico but also of his own practice.[100] The rhetoric Stowe gives Father Antonio matches the Pre-Raphaelite emphasis on discovering "meaning" through meticulous observations of nature. As he explains to Agnes, painting the details of nature is a form of worship; "'not a twig rustles, not a bird flies, nor a flower blossoms,'" but he is inspired – as he "'walk[s] the earth in a dream of bliss'" – to draw God's "'sweet handiwork'" (103). As art historians have documented, this emphasis resonated with a younger generation of American artists and critics, who promoted both Ruskin's and the P.R.B.'s claims for art in two art journals – *The Crayon* (1855–61) and *The New Path* (1863–5) – and who welcomed a traveling exhibition of English P.R.B. art in 1857–8.[101]

Americans were less interested in the P.R.B.'s preoccupation with medieval art and subject matter;[102] however, this preoccupation, together with the connection between a detailed representation of natural forms and religious insight, appears in *Agnes*. Naomi Sofer argues that Stowe's new attention to religious art in the novel preceding *Agnes* accords with the art criticism in *The Crayon* in the late 1850s and with the writings of the American art critic James Jackson Jarves, who was strongly influenced by Ruskin.[103] In Father Antonio's perceptions, Stowe makes plain the connection between the P.R.B. aesthetic of worshipful representations of nature and their interest in late medieval depictions of the annunciation; both concern themselves with incarnation, the word made flesh.[104] As an itinerant friar wandering through the Italian countryside, Antonio's perception of natural forms as divine expressions impels him to "'fall on

my face before the humblest flower'" (103). His decision to paint
Agnes as the Virgin at the moment of the annunciation emerges out
of a similar perception of "grace" in the "peasant-girl" (104, 107),
and the literalized episode of the annunciation, when Sarelli appears
with his lily stalk, comes after a conversation between Antonio and
Agnes about the flora in their surroundings and Antonio's insight
that Agnes embodies the characteristics of the Virgin. Antonio's art
documents, in effect, a series of incarnations.

Stowe casts the moment that Agnes moves in her desires from celibacy to marriage in terms of a Pre-Raphaelite fusion of the annunciation and the sexual dreaming associated with the Eve of St. Agnes. In
a discussion of women's bodies and art in *Agnes*, Gail Smith points
out that Agnes's dream echoes the tradition that young women
dream of their future husbands on the Eve of St. Agnes and suggests that Stowe is thinking of Keats's poem (a subject, I would add,
also painted by William Holman Hunt) here and elsewhere in the
romance.[105] Stowe conflates sexual union and its associated escape
from the paralysis of idolatry with the incarnation of modern nations
through consensual marriage; as she transfers her desires from the
convent to marriage, Agnes repeats the Virgin's lines at the annunciation: "'Behold the handmaid of the Lord! be it unto me according
to His word!'" (221). Such scenes imply that the heir of fifteenth-
century Italian piety is U.S. republicanism and its theory of marriage
as the process by which citizenship is reproduced. To put this another
way, as Jenny Franchot has argued, "The Protestant cult of domesticity . . . enabled a partial recovery of a [Catholic] incarnational and
intercessory 'aesthetic'" through art historical "celebrations of the
Madonna" (253).

Linda Dowling explains that for the Victorians "the past constituted an open vocabulary of politics – in the case of . . . the Pre-
Raphaelites, an allegiance to republicanism," as the republics in
the "age of Giotto and Dante" served as models for the "struggle
for republicanism . . . in Italy."[106] Agnes becomes in her physical
and subjective identity the most national form of Italian art and
a nationalizing agent. And she does so by existing at the nexus of
bodily and spiritual influences; Smith argues that her function is that
of a sacrament, at once "an earthly sign and a spiritual grace."[107]
Stowe invokes a favorite Pre-Raphaelite reference at this juncture.
She compares Agnes's "'great grace of a beauty,'" as her great-
uncle says, "'which draws the soul upward to the angels, instead of
downward to sensual things,'" with the beauty of Dante's "'holy

Beatrice'"; she adds in a footnote Charles Eliot Norton's translation
of Dante's sonnet on Beatrice (which ends, ". . . saying to the soul,
'Aspire!'") and follows this with a similar sonnet Sarelli writes, in
which he compares the redemptive possibilities of Agnes's love with
the "'blessed Mary['s]'" capacity to "'Receive the love of sinners'":
"'Let thine acceptance be like that on high!'" (108, 114).[108] As
Father Antonio wisely notes, "'Beauty is the Lord's arrow'" (109).
Beauty in this romance is also a reforming nationalism's arrow;
Agnes's sacramental function, together with Savonarola's oratory,
transmutes Sarelli's inchoate "sense of personal wrong into a fixed
principle of moral indignation," a conflation of revived piety and
"patriotism" (349).

Taken frequently by her grandmother to a convent dedicated to
St. Agnes, where the nuns provide her with childcare and an education, Agnes is formed by an environment which offers a continuous line of development from pagan to Christian images. Built on
the foundations of a temple to Venus, the convent houses frescoes
of the life and martyrdom of St. Agnes but easily subsumes earlier
images of womanhood, including a classical statue of a nymph pouring water into a fountain, whom the nuns have "baptized" and rede-
fined as St. Agnes herself, "dispensing the waters of purity to the
convent" (62).[109] Agnes resembles St. Agnes, at first, in her aspirations but also resembles the nymph in her pensive expression and in
the posture of her body, poised at the threshold of "the development
of womanhood" (74). Rather than repudiate the temple of Venus,
the convent of St. Agnes sublimates it and prompts Agnes's development along a string of images and icons: marble nymph to St. Agnes
to pre-Raphaelite Virgin to modern wife. Her piety is a forerunner
of American forms of belief – "The Christian faith we now hold,
who boast our enlightened Protestantism, has been transmitted to us
through the hearts and hands of such" (150–1) – while her image is
"the fair symbol" (122) of a faith whose "renewal" blends the secular and the pious, the "Roman" and the "Christian" (118), in Sarelli
and thus leads to emerging forms of nationalism. Her picture, drawn
by Father Antonio, becomes the currency of religious and national
salvation as it passes between her great-uncle and her would-be husband, an emblem of both "earthly" and "heavenly love," a "sacrament" leading the faithful toward redemption (179).

Stowe recasts Italian women's figures in landscape and genre
scenes as transformative catalysts instead of as signs of modern
Italy's powerlessness and emphasizes the power of Italian women

to inspire change rather than act as signs of stasis.[110] In Agnes the pious woman's sexuality transmutes the primal energies symbolized by the gorge from which Sarelli rises into politically and religiously constructive ones; she serves as the disciplinary agent that transforms Sarelli from outlaw to proto-republican citizen. Instead of enervating her suitor, she modernizes him. Or, to return to Steiner's analysis of the romance genre, Agnes learns, through her dream of Sarelli-as-Gabriel, to transfer her idolatry of religious icons and her desire for Christ to an earthly attachment to Sarelli, and both of them move through their earlier idolatrous enthrallments, including Sarelli's worship of Agnes, to historical agency.

Sublimating Agnes

The process of Agnes's development is completed when she makes a pilgrimage to Rome and is jolted out of her lingering tendency to idolatry, her belief that Rome is the "earthly image of her Saviour's home above" and that the Pope is "the real image of her Redeemer" (370). Abducted by one of the Pope's lecherous Borgia relatives but rescued from his "impure den" by her vigilant lover, Agnes suffers a conversion experience to a more Protestant gaze, which recognizes a metaphor when it sees one and does not confuse earthly institutions or theatrical displays with spiritual realities; a "veil [is] torn from her eyes" and she joins Savonarola's party just in time to witness his execution (393, 397–8). Her exposure to the corruption of Rome triggers "a change in her whole nature," a growth in self-possession and agency; as they leave Rome, Sarelli puts the reins of her horse "in her hand" and notes a new resolve: "a flash from her eye, and an heroic expression on her face, such as he had never remarked before" (397). Agnes speaks "firmly" and expresses a willingness to die with her great-uncle in defense of the "'honor of the true faith'" (396, 398). Sarelli deflects this archaic urge toward martyrdom, the original Agnes's end, into the nineteenth-century wife's instructional mission: "'[L]ive,'" he says, "'to teach it [the true faith] to me!'" (398). If female subjectivity is central to the nation, then Agnes's development into a conscious and willing partner with Sarelli in the redemption of faith and nation, as well as her geographical movement from the infantility of Sorrento through the decadence of Rome to reformist Florence, recapitulates Italy's religious history, ensures modern Italy's future, and validates the modern Christian reformist nation that is Stowe's United States.

Agnes arrives in Rome during Holy Week, the week memorializing Christ's arrival in Jerusalem, his initial popular acclaim, and his crucifixion and resurrection; this defining moment in the liturgical calendar was the most popular week for tourists to visit.[111] American depictions of Rome at Holy Week emphasized Protestant strategies of viewing the spectacle of Catholicism. Characteristic are James Jackson Jarves's iconoclastic and anti-Catholic essays on Italy, which were first serialized in *Harper's* magazine and then published as a travel book: *Italian Sights and Papal Principles, Seen Through American Spectacles* (1856). An art critic, an advocate of Ruskin's ideas, an expatriate living in Florence, and an early collector of Italian painting before Raphael, Jarves enabled his Protestant readers "to drain medieval art of its specifically Catholic meaning" and to see the uses of art to revive religious faith and democratic nationalism.[112] As Roger Stein has shown, fifteenth-century Florence was for Jarves a model for the nineteenth-century U.S.: a "vigorous republic" whose "artistic pre-eminence" derived from the democratic and Christian basis of its art. Like Stowe, Jarves turned such "great Catholic figures" as Savonarola "into evangelicals and puritans" (Stein, 142–4). And, like Stowe, Jarves contrasted a republican and reformist Florence with a papal Rome, whose "debasing shows" both veil and reveal the papacy's political oppression and "decrepitude" (Jarves, 251, 303): "Romanism and republicanism are antagonistic powers" (342).

While advocating for early Italian art, *Italian Sights* inoculates readers against the contagion of "idolatry" (Jarves, 302), that is, of papal principles; the text and the accompanying engravings work together to train tourists to view Catholic images without succumbing to Catholic idolatry.[113] The numerous illustrations in Jarves's three chapters on Holy Week in Rome emphasize the "theatrical spectacle" (239) generated by the papacy; they include twenty pictures of the "costume[s]" that set apart various levels of Church "hierarchy" (238), from the Pope to papal chair bearers, as well as pictures of responses to church ritual and of the effects of papal rule on Italian character. One engraving of figures of banditti juxtaposed with monks is titled "Brigands – Armed and Unarmed" (338). Americans are taught to recognize the varieties of clerical figures in papal Rome, to see excessive emotion and abjection in the popular response to processions and even in the time-honored and hitherto tranquil image of the woman praying before the shrine, and to see the results of the papal governance of Rome in poverty, theft by outlaws and by the church, "idleness" (284), and thoughtless pleasure.

Figure 5.4 *A Roman Procession*, in James Jackson Jarves, *Italian Sights and Papal Principles, Seen Through American Spectacles* (New York: Harper and Brothers, 1856). Harvard College Library, President and Fellows of Harvard College. Digitized by Google. Accessed through Google Books.

The engraving *A Roman Procession* (Fig. 5.4; 287) highlights the traditional difference between Italy and the U.S. in tourist views by conjoining idolatry, women's emotion, and the feminization of Italian men;[114] a kneeling man and two women in traditional dress implore the aid of the saint whose statue is being carried by priests and monks through the street to cure a sick woman they are supporting. The picture follows a passage in which Jarves states that "the absurd spectacles of the Church ... cultivate credulity and ignorance among the people, and teach them to rely more upon the ... supernatural care of deceased saints than upon their own exertions" (286). Unlike the procession in Brown's view of the Bay of Naples, which invokes a reverie of an imagined archaic harmony, this representation of a religious procession is critical and anthropological in its detail, as it focuses on the contemporary institution of "Romanism" as modernity's other. Jarves's emphasis on excessive demonstrations of dependency and affect in women's bodies addresses the link between women, the reception of icons, and the formation of a religious or national subjectivity; American women, one infers, must inhabit this mediating position in a more disciplined fashion.

Similarly, Stowe depicts Rome as the spectacular center of a corrupt papacy and Florence as a proto-Protestant and republican religious and civic space. When Agnes arrives in Rome, she attends Palm Sunday observances and witnesses the procession of the pope, a procession that Stowe describes in much the same theatrical terms as Jarves. After noting that Rome is "a forest of . . . costumes, a pantomime of shifting scenic effects of religious ceremonies," Stowe observes the implicit "satire of the contrast" between Christ's arrival in Jerusalem, "meek and lowly, riding on an ass," and the "gorgeous ceremonial" of the pope's Palm Sunday procession, filled with "all that could dazzle and bewilder" and in which Alexander VI is carried "on high, like an enthroned God" (382, 384–5). Agnes's kidnappers come out of those who make up the procession; after the service, a "servant in a gorgeous scarlet livery" abducts her in "the finest of the equipages, where she was lost to view" (386). If Hawthorne's Rome is national and imperial, Stowe's is ecclesiastical; the central structure in *Agnes*'s Rome is neither the Forum nor the Capitoline Hill but St. John Lateran, the cathedral of Rome and the seat of the pope.[115]

More relevant to Stowe's political purposes is Florence, which she lauds as a medieval haven of "liberty," religious art and "republican simplicity" – characteristics Savonarola is trying to revive. Influenced by what Sofer calls the "proliferation of . . . writing about Savonarola and his role in resisting Medici-inspired paganism" in the 1850s,[116] Stowe continues to link religion, art, and republicanism. In her descriptions of medieval Florence as a pious polity "pervaded by one spirit," she inserts Catholic Italy – as aesthetic territory – into the direct line of spiritual descent from Israel to New England, a familiar trajectory for New England Protestants but now one that incorporates its traditional other: "The men of Florence in its best days were men of a large, grave, earnest mould. What the Puritans of New England wrought out with severest earnestness in their reasonings . . . these early Puritans of Italy embodied in poetry, sculpture, and painting. They built their Cathedral . . ., as the Jews of old built their Temple, with awe and religious fear" (283–4).

The two crucial spaces in the novel's action are the monastery of San Marco and the "grand square" (408): on the one hand, the religious and artistic and, on the other, the civic center of the city. In his own lengthy treatment of Florence and Savonarola in *Italian Sights*, Jarves represents the Piazza del Gran Duca as the epicenter of the struggle between "the rule of the people" and "the tyranny of princes" (74) and Savonarola as both a "prophet" predicting the Reformation and a "zealous . . . republican" (76, 78) who attempted to restore democracy in Florence.[117] Similarly, Stowe highlights the square as the scene of Savonarola's martyrdom to both political and religious principles. His execution represents the turning point of Florentine history from "the era of her artists, her statesmen, . . . and her scholars" to "the era of her disgrace and subjugation," as well as the re-enactment of Pilate's and Herod's agreement to sacrifice Christ (408–9), a more authentic replaying of the events of Holy Week, for Stowe, than the rituals in Rome. As does Agnes, Savonarola mediates between secular history and the spiritual realm of typology.

As both Savonarola, the burner of blasphemous art, and Jarves are in different senses iconoclasts, it is useful to see how Stowe, whose Savonarola is unambiguously Christ-like (unlike George Eliot's ambivalently rendered Savonarola in *Romola*, 1863),[118] negotiates this aspect of Protestantism. It is helpful here to remember W. J. T. Mitchell's discussion of the nineteenth-century "rhetoric of iconoclasm," quoted in the analysis of Kirkland above; the iconoclast defines the idolator as someone "who has 'forgotten' something – his own act of projection" of value into the fetishized object, while the iconoclast "sees himself at a historical distance from the idolator, working at a more 'advanced' . . . stage in human evolution, therefore in a position to provide a . . . historicizing interpretation of myths taken literally by the idolator."[119] Stowe does indeed interpret fifteenth-century (and nineteenth-century) Italian responses to religious iconography as characteristic of that earlier "stage in human evolution," but, rather than drain the icons of Catholicism completely of meaning, Stowe also sees the modern reader as having forgotten something: the use of aesthetic response in the development of faith. In part because of her ongoing migration from her father's Calvinism to Episcopalianism,[120] which accommodated the sacramental more fully, she uses the "word" less to discipline the visual than to complement it. She represents Savonarola as a Puritan preacher who meditates on Fra Angelico's *Crucifixion*, and she defines Pre-Raphaelite Florentine art as parallel to the textual works of New England Puritans: "eloquent picture-writing by which burning religious souls sought to preach the truths of the invisible world to the eye of the multitude" (283). Giotto's paintings are like the sermons of Jonathan Edwards (284).[121]

Like Jarves she is trying to train the tourist's eye. However, Stowe defines the tourist gaze as disengaged and overly mediated by language; "In our day," she notes, paintings such as the *Crucifixion* in San Marco's "are visited by tourists with red guide-books in their hands, who survey them in the intervals of careless conversation" (291). She identifies two passionate all-consuming gazes in late medieval and early Renaissance Italy from which Baedeker-carrying tourists and readers at home may learn how and how not to see. The ideal gaze is shared by the religious artist, in this case Fra Angelico, who painted the *Crucifixion* "on his knees, weeping and praying as he worked," and by "simple-hearted Christians" who experienced such images "as a perpetual sacrament of the eye, by which they received Christ into their souls" (291).[122] The other gaze is an intensely secular, urban, predatory gaze, to which Agnes is subjected in Rome and which Stowe defines more explicitly in a chapter on Milan as the gaze of ruthless consumption; "the great, vain, wicked city," whose streets feature the "gay costumes and brilliant trappings" that characterize a "passion for personal adornment," is "all alive with the lust of the flesh, the lust of the eye, and the pride of life" (304, 301). This is the gaze of power, of "upper classes" sheltered by the Church (303). Stowe turns her mitigated iconoclasm on the false idols of corrupt belief and of a rising tide of consumerism; she evangelizes the tourist's eye, to divert it toward the pious images of a true national art, such as the image of Agnes. By doing so, she is using the primitive Catholic gaze to revive the Protestant, republican gaze.

Indeed, in the scene in which Savonarola meditates on Fra Angelico's *Crucifixion*, in anticipation of his own approaching fate, the monk's gaze becomes a model of the way to look at art. Stowe describes the painting's inclusion of the "company of saints of all ages" who witness Christ's death, a company whose presence "express[es] the unity of the Church Universal," and she depicts Savonarola as so "absorbed in pensive contemplation" that he does not hear visitors approaching (291). Her language here and elsewhere draws on the discourse of spiritualism, the mid-century religious movement that promised communication with the spirit world through mediums put into mesmeric trances.[123] By evoking this discourse, Stowe implies that spiritualism is the modern form of the

Catholic religious response she validates in Agnes, Father Antonio, and Savonarola – and, therefore, that it can re-enchant the Protestant religious imaginary. Like many reformers, Stowe was sympathetic to spiritualism.[124] As P. Gabrielle Foreman and Reginald H. Pitts have said, this "important, . . . radical movement" drew progressives, from abolitionists to women's rights advocates, and "appropriated space for women's expression and leadership in religious, political, social, and medical reform."[125] Similarly, the art historian Charles Colbert documents Jarves's attraction to the movement's "humane agenda," together with its appeal as a "bulwark against the . . . materialism and atheism in the modern world," and notes that Jarves himself became a medium in Florence in 1855, as he was beginning his influential career as an art historian.

Colbert argues that Jarves's spiritualism shaped his understanding of the relationship of the gazing viewer to art. Spiritualists felt traces of past lives on objects the dead had handled; sensitivity to such traces opened up communication with the dead. Hence, according to Colbert, Jarves's emphasis on collecting original paintings, rather than the copies with which many antebellum collectors were content. Spiritualist belief informed art appreciation; original art offered, as Jarves said, "'the spiritual communion with generations gone, through the medium of what they have left behind visible to our senses.'" Jarves's "advocacy of the extended gaze," which created the possibility of spiritualist communion with the painter, became normative, a "contribution made by spiritualism to American visual culture." It is this "colloquy of spirits" in which Savonarola participates.[126]

Stowe emphasizes a sustained gaze that opens the viewer to communion with the artist's spirit and, through him, with a larger spiritual world of welcoming presences. She highlights Savonarola's "mesmeric glance," "large, deep . . . eyes" (288), and visual capacities that indicate both a medium's sensitivity to the spirit world and his ability to "'electrify'" others:[127] "His eye had a wonderful dilating power" (293). His ability to become "absorbed," via the beatific Fra Angelico's painting, in communion with the saints reinforces his implied connection with Agnes, who feels around her the invisible world of the saints and the dead:

> To the mind of the really spiritual Christian of those ages the air of
> this lower world was not as it is to us, . . . a blank, empty space from
> which all spiritual sympathy and life have fled, but, like the atmo-
> sphere with which Raphael has surrounded the Sistine Madonna, it

was full of sympathizing faces, a great "cloud of witnesses." The holy dead were not gone from earth; the Church visible and invisible were in close, loving, and constant sympathy, – still loving, praying, and watching together, though with a veil between. (83)

Stowe's language here is informed by spiritualism's promise of communication with the loving, still-present dead, by a reassuring sense of an invisible community that filled the "blank, empty space" of modernity with "sympathy." In her 1855 essay "The Ministration of Our Departed Friends," Stowe states that "one of the deepest . . . cravings of the human heart, as it follows its beloved ones beyond the veil, is for some assurance that they still love and care for us"; loss is compensated by the spiritualist encounter with the beloved dead: "We are encompassed about by a cloud of witnesses, whose hearts throb in sympathy with every effort and struggle" (198, 202). Referring in both texts to the biblical verse Hebrews 12: 1, "Wherefore, seeing we also are compassed about with so great a cloud of witnesses, let us lay aside every weight . . .," Stowe compares the personal dead with the "holy dead," the family of the faithful.[128] The spiritualist gaze assuages modern isolation and "reenchant[s] the world"[129] both for modern mourners and for Protestant spectators of Italian art.

Stowe's depiction of Savonarola's death, as he and two of his disciples are burned at the stake, combines aspects of this spiritualist vision with the trope of benediction that Hawthorne invokes with the statues of Aurelius and Pope Julius III: "To the last, that benignant right hand which had so often pointed the way of life to that faithless city was stretched out over the crowd in an attitude of blessing; and so loving, . . . the souls of the martyrs ascended to the great cloud of witnesses above" (410). This figure of benign authority is less a figure of the state – a presidentialist body – than a prophet of the future consolidation of a Protestant, republican Italy. Indeed, his body is incinerated, sublimated, as he departs the visible for the invisible Church. Savonarola joins the world of art as well; Stowe notes that Raphael later painted him "among the Apostles and Saints" (412) in one of the Vatican's halls. Savonarola connects imminent and transcendent worlds, the dead with the living and with future generations; as a medium, in effect, he unites them, just as he anticipates the political union of the divergent Italian states. American spiritualists, as Bret E. Carroll has demonstrated, connected their religious with their political beliefs in what he has called "spiritualist republicanism."[130] Stowe's Savonarola seems to embody this religious/ideological formation.

While also mediating between the secular and the transcendent, Agnes remains in the corporeal world. However, her physicality as a character dissolves in the last pages of the novel, as she, too, is sublimated into a more generalized function. One of the curious parallels between Stowe's and Hawthorne's romances is that both Agnes and Hilda disappear toward the end of the novels in mini captivity narratives; Hilda is held in a convent and released in exchange for Donatello's surrender to the law, and Agnes is abducted into the brothel-like quarters of one of the emblematically bad Borgias. Of course, as vessels carrying the national spirit, they must be recovered. Both emerge from their captivities ready to marry, to embrace their roles as saviors of their husbands and, presumably, as mothers of future citizens. Their psychological transformation into wives happens off-stage, as do the subsequent weddings; this transmutation remains at once necessary and mystified, "lost to view" (386). The narrator describes Agnes in great physical detail in Sorrento, where the opening description features hair and eye color, the shapes of nose and forehead, "long eyelashes" that "lie softly down on the pale, smooth cheek," and where her responses manifest themselves corporeally: "a bright color flushing into her smooth brown cheeks, and her large dreamy eyes suddenly upraised with a flutter" (8, 10). Such descriptions culminate in Rome, where her "enthusiastic imagination" responds to ecclesiastical spectacle through a heightened bodily beauty that attracts her kidnappers: "she seemed to burn and brighten like an altar-coal, her figure seemed to dilate, her eyes grew deeper and shone with a starry light, and the color of her cheeks flushed up with a vivid glow" (385). This is the last physical description; after her recapture, Agnes's thoughts, words, and situation appear, but not her body. Paradoxically enough, at the point of sexual maturation, Agnes's body disappears from the text as she moves toward the miracle of marriage, the sacrament whereby female sexuality is simultaneously enacted and vanishes from view.[131]

The decorporealization of women in the "public" realm of the novels' descriptions and the relegation of their bodily selves to the "private" realm of undepicted married life, to which the reader is not privy, indicates the route by which they become effective reproducers of national ideology; both disappear into marriage at the end. That Agnes's disembodiment has a national function is related to John

Carlos Rowe's insight that "Kenyon and Hilda develop an aesthetic of sublimation," as opposed to the "transnational," "cosmopolitan," and racialized identity and "aesthetic of unsublimated expression" Miriam represents.[132] No longer an enthralling visual idol or even a picture exchanged between pious men, Agnes gets married on the last page of the novel and blends into history, acting as an invisible leaven within the body of the emerging nation.

The Visual Excess of Sorrento's Gorge

Nevertheless, in her writing of *Agnes* Stowe lingered longest on the body of Italy, the primitive landscape of Sorrento, with its attractive, pagan, sensual gorge. Her biographer, Joan Hedrick, says that readers found the description of the gorge alone worth the cost of the *Atlantic*, where *Agnes* was serialized.[133] Stowe merges the perspective of "the present traveller" with that of fifteenth-century inhabitants who stand on the bridge leading into the town and look down into the two-hundred-foot depths of the "Gorge of Sorrento" and out to the "shimmer[ing]" Mediterranean through an atmosphere that, as in a George Loring Brown painting, is "a glorifying medium, rich in prismatic hues of enchantment" (16–17).[134]

The cottage Agnes shares with her grandmother hangs on a side of this ravine and offers a privileged perspective into its depths:

> One could look down into the gloomy depths of the gorge, as into some mysterious underworld. Strange and weird it seemed, with its fathomless shadows and its wild grottoes, over which hung . . . long pendants of ivy, while dusky gray aloes uplifted their horned heads from great rock-rifts, like elfin spirits struggling upward out of the shade. Nor was wanting the usual gentle poetry of flowers; for white iris leaned its fairy pavilion over the black void like a pale-cheeked princess from the window of some dark enchanted castle, and scarlet geranium and golden broom and crimson gladiolus waved and glowed in the shifting beams of the sunlight. Also there was in this little spot what forms the charm of Italian gardens always, – the sweet song and prattle of waters. A clear mountain-spring burst through the rock . . . and fell with a lulling noise into a quaint moss-grown water-trough, which had been in former times the sarcophagus of some old Roman sepulchre . . .; while a veil of ferns and maiden's hair, studded with tremulous silver drops, vibrated to its soothing murmur. (17–18)

This opening into the realm of the preconscious, of inchoate desires, and of the pagan past becomes a touchstone throughout the first half of the romance. Just as Sarelli rises from the gorge and the "elfin spirits" of the aloes "struggl[e] upward out of the shade," so do other signals emanate from this realm. Agnes's "favorite place" is a "moss-grown marble parapet" overlooking the ravine; the sight plunges her into reveries that involve these emanations, which "stimulated her impressible imagination" (21–2). Pagan myths, "sculptural fragments," a "prodigal Nature" (18), and sexual desire – in the form of a love song from Sarelli – well up from the gorge: "ancient Italian tradition made it the home of fauns and dryads, wild woodland creatures, intermediate links between vegetable life and that of sentient and reasoning humanity" (21). It is at once beautifully innocent and "haunted by evil spirits" left over from "old heathen times," whose singing is said to attract and tempt Christians (173, 76, 74). In one such twilight reverie, a "white mist . . . slowly rising, wavering, undulating, and creeping its slow way up the sides of the gorge . . . seem[s] like the goblin robe of some strange, supernatural being" (22). Pleasurably uncanny, this ravine constitutes the prehistory of and establishes the conditions for Agnes's growth and influence.

Agnes is highly responsive to the gorge. She also wishes to discipline it, by having a shrine put up that will disperse the old heathen spirits, but Stowe emphasizes her early, pubescent affinity with this territory. As they walk through it on the way to town, her grandmother calls her a "wild girl!"; Agnes is at home within it, moving among its grottoes and rocks, gathering flowers: "Out of her apron were hanging festoons of golden broom, crimson gladiolus, and long, trailing sprays of ivy; while she held aloft in triumph a handful of the most superb cyclamen, whose rosy crowns rise so beautifully above their dark quaint leaves in moist and shady places" (56). Although Agnes's destiny is a sublimated state of cultural influence through marital erasure, her roots are in the gorge. Stowe's imaginative lingering in the vicinity of this primal space of vegetative abundance and undisciplined exuberance works at cross purposes with the novel's trajectory.

In a recent book, Dorri Beam analyzes a neglected aspect of nineteenth-century American women's prose, what reviewers called a "highly wrought style," as a rhetoric of excess with both "aesthetic and feminist rationale[s]" that featured "voluptuously turned language, the textured layering of sensual detail and image, and a syntax of endless accrual as the occasion for twinned aesthetic delight and (equally pleasing) aggression toward any aesthetic experience figured as transcendence of the feminine or material." Although Beam draws her examples from other writers, Stowe, I would argue, invokes this style here to underscore Sorrento's association with the feminine, the visual, the fluid, and the material and to entangle her reader in its fruitful pull away from the transcendent. Beam notes that "Fruits and flowers are featured prominently" in women's highly wrought texts and are linked to their "meditations on their aesthetic strategies"; "'formlessness' or overdevelopment takes the shape of possibilities – of resistance to the containment of women's desire by narrative shape or social structure. . . . Theirs is a strategy of increase, . . . stylistic profusion, . . . elaboration that elongates."[135] Stowe's cascading descriptions of flora in these and other passages (there are eight species in the long quotation alone), her detailing of sensual images, her lists of participles (as in the sentence on the rising mist) that prolong the present moment and resist narrative closure, and her "syntax of endless accrual" constantly defer the novel's departure from Sorrento and what it represents.

Although the arc of Stowe's romance is from the formless, profuse, and feminine world, embedded in the material and figured by Sorrento, toward the religious and political forms of transcendence represented by Florence, the weight of the novel is with the former: the undisciplined portions of the matter of "Italy." Stowe connects Agnes's heightened receptivity to the gorge with her receptivity to religious rituals and art; both indicate the "mediïstic" power of Italian women. As so many U.S. writers do, Stowe uses "English" obtuseness as a warning to Americans not to let an emphasis on the masculine word blind them to the feminine, visual, and – here – spiritualist aspects of "Italy":

> Certain English writers, looking entirely from a worldly and philosophical stand-point, are utterly at a loss to account for the power which certain Italian women of obscure birth came to exercise in the councils of nations merely by the force of a mystical piety; but the Northern mind of Europe is entirely unfitted to . . . appreciate the psychological religious phenomena of Southern races. The temperament which in our modern days has been called the mediïstic, and which with us is only exceptional, is more or less a race-peculiarity of Southern climates, and gives that objectiveness to the conception of spiritual things from which grew up a . . . whole world of religious Art. (112–13)

Savonarola draws the novel's characters out of the warm bath of preconscious southern Italy to Florence, with its associations, for U.S. and British readers, of modernity and republicanism. But if one function of the romance is to move Agnes from the gorge to Florence, another function is to reimmerse the reader in the gorge, to afford the modern subject contact with the pre-modern, feminine, racialized, and mystical territory that breeds mediums.

At the moment Agnes accepts her sexuality as part of her identity – and accepts that this identity entails marriage and domestic life – she lets go of the memory of the gorge and of her childhood landscape of Sorrento (399). The extraordinary lushness of possibility embodied in the language associated with the gorge vanishes from the book, replaced by the distanced, sober, hearsay description of the married Agnes as a pious "princess." Savonarola gets the last word after all; in the final paragraph, in a rhetorical gesture in which Stowe fuses floral language (or perhaps co-opts it) with that of reform and nationhood, his "living words" become the "seeds of immortal flowers which blossomed in secret dells . . . of his beautiful Italy" (412). But readers loved the gorge, not so much the martyr. In readers' responses, Stowe's highly wrought descriptions of the territory of unformed possibility triumph over the narrative reassertion of word, marriage, self-sacrifice, and history. The trance-like, mesmeric state that the gorge induces in Agnes and that its descriptions offer to induce in the reader accords with Beam's assertion that women writers who use a highly wrought style "refuse," in such passages, "any instrumentalizing of language or a working through matter toward a notion of transcendent spirit" (26). It is the prerogative of the romance form to linger in such enthrallments before the return to narrative; however, it is also Stowe's feminist resistance to the devaluation of the cluster of traits assigned to the feminine that prolongs the reader's tour of the fertile area of Sorrento.

Italian Abysses

It is striking that both Hawthorne and Stowe center their romances on "chasm[s]" opening up beneath the feet of tourists – that is, on a real or imagined geography where the endless recesses of tourists' dreams are figured as a "gulf," "gorge," or "underworld." These spots – the "great, dusky gap, immeasurably deep" that myth places below the Forum and the "gloomy depths . . . strange and weird" of Sorrento's gorge – powerfully attract modern travelers: Kenyon, who "would give much for a peep into such a chasm," and the tourists who stand on Sorrento's bridge.[136]

The dreams welling up out of these "depths" are strongly gendered. Under the national and imperial monuments of Hawthorne's

Forum lies the nightmare of masculine violence, a blood-filled "gulf" "with half-shaped monsters ... looking upward out of it." The national union promised and seemingly elicited by the monumental iconography of the Arch of Titus and the patriarchal statue of Aurelius is haunted by the chaos and "gore" of armies throughout history, from early Rome to the contemporaneous French occupiers. The monstrous figures of the "chasm" give the lie to the consolidating "dignity" of the Aurelian statue and cast doubt on the ability of "majestic representation[s]" to produce voluntary union.[137]

If Hawthorne's Italian abyss offers a vision of masculine violence, Stowe's, as I have argued, offers a vision of a different, positively rendered chaos: that of unbound feminine potential, a fantasy of the primal landscape of the mother before the ordering forces of the word, the law, and the father arrive. Too inchoate to supply icons, the fertile gorge nevertheless is the generative energy behind them, sending up hints of "elfin spirits" and "fauns and dryads." It is on the verge of this gorge that Sarelli, the violent outlaw, acts as annunciating angel to Agnes and triggers her transformation into a mother of modern Italy.

Both romances figure the incarnation of modern Italy through the arrival of adult masculinity into a primitive, fertile space inhabited by "fauns," "intermediate links between vegetable life and ... reasoning humanity" (Stowe's words, but also Hawthorne's point). Therefore, both trace "transformations" in their title characters, archaic Italians who become disenchanted and fall into modernity. Hawthorne's pastoral "faun," Donatello, whose ancestors talked to animals, must murder a tyrant to achieve maturity, while Stowe's Agnes must give up her enchanted gorge to become Sarelli's wife. Of these endings, Stowe's is the more optimistic; Agnes's new duties will eventuate in the self-disciplined man and woman of the future – a future that will take the shape of a republican and Protestant nation. And her "mediïstic" piety will continue to connect her, however tenuously, with "Southern climates." Hawthorne's faun also moves into history, but history here is less progressive than cyclical. The chasm under the Forum reveals not merely the past but also the future – it is "prophetic" – and implies that the route into adult male nation-building will always lie through bloodshed. Modernity seems merely to signify alienation, and a disciplinary society leads the faun to prison.

Inevitably, both romances end by privileging marriage, with its forward narrative movement, over art as the principal means of unifying the body of a republic. Hawthorne shifts his focus to Kenyon and Hilda, who escape from Italy and its history lessons into American marriage, which may diminish the need for violence in composing the nation. And Stowe's marriage plot gives narrative shape to Sarelli's otherwise chaotic predatory activity even as it brings originary feminine, pagan energies into the present through Agnes's aesthetic sensibilities. Italian resources will continue to be accessible to the modern male citizen via the Protestant wife. All in all, marriage is the most fitting way to exit "Italy" and go home to the U.S.

Conclusion: Gender and Genre

Friday, Christmas Day [1857]. Went to Boston at seven, 'twas bitter cold. . . . Went to the Fair, and saw many beautiful articles; the most beautiful was a set of photographs of the different ruins of Rome executed by Mrs. Jam[i]eson's son-in-law and sent by her from Rome to the Bazaar. The explanations were written by her and accompanied by her autograph.

Charlotte Forten Grimké[1]

As the twenty-year-old Charlotte Forten describes her visit to the annual Boston Anti-Slavery Fair, she highlights two experiences: seeing some of the famous men associated with the movement (Wendell Phillips, Charles Sumner, and Ralph Waldo Emerson – "it was *glorious* to see such a trio" [274]) and seeing the items on sale at the fund-raising Bazaar. Of the "many beautiful articles" contributed by supporters of abolition she singles out a cluster of tourist materials, a package sent by a famous British writer on travel, art, and aesthetic perception: Anna Jameson, author of *The Diary of an Ennuyée* and books on literature, women's work, and Italian art. The photos she includes are by Robert Macpherson, who in 1857 was at the peak of his popularity as the expatriate Scottish photographer of Roman ruins, buildings, and landscapes.[2] In subsequent years photographs would quickly become a familiar part of the ritual of tourism; post-Civil War tourists in Rome bought unbound copies of Hawthorne's *Marble Faun* and personalized them by having them bound with their own selections of photos of famous sites, sites described in the romance.[3] But at this moment Macpherson's photos were new, "exquisite" (274), and even startling. Jameson's "explanations" of the sites her niece's husband (not her son-in-law, as Forten supposes) had photographed added value because of her status as an art historian and as the author of a popular fictionalized travel book which combined aesthetic perception with emotional response. The buyer would have received classic views of the major tourist sites of Rome in a cutting-edge medium by an innovative photographer and an informed commentary that mediated the visual impact of the pictures; in addition, the signature of a celebrity, in the autograph-hungry culture of the period, would have lent a personal connection and (unlike the photos) a singular, unreproducible, and authentic touch to the cluster.

This journal entry shows the reach of visual and textual representations of tourist sites into American culture, even as it rehearses the familiar tourist's triangulation of Britain, Italy, and the U.S. The juxtaposition of the cultures of tourism and reform makes more sense than it initially might. As Lisa A. Long observes, Forten repeatedly idealizes Italy, especially Rome, in her journals as the place of "'genius'" and "'beauty'" and as the site where she could imagine her own intellectual achievement and personal fulfillment, away from the multiple pressures and constraints of her status as an educated but impoverished black woman in the antebellum U.S.[4] Like many young women, Forten found reading Elizabeth Barrett Browning's *Aurora Leigh* (1856), the narrative poem and *Bildungsroman* in which the title character finally reconciles her English and Italian traits, spellbinding; she is "completely fascinated with 'Aurora'" and feels an intimacy with Barrett Browning: "I feel that she is indeed my *friend*" (200). During the Civil War, while Forten is teaching emancipated slaves in the South Carolina Sea Islands, the poem remains a touchstone: "This eve. devoured 'Aurora Leigh' for the *very manyth* time" (408).[5] Not only a highly literary education but also texts associated with tourism and especially with travel to Italy hold the promise of a cultivated interiority, a subjectivity that in turn authorizes the task of shaping future citizens.[6] *Aurora Leigh* is both an escape from the difficult contexts of race and gender oppressions and of war in the U.S. and a support for doing cultural, nation-shaping work there.

This conclusion suggests some final implications of the connection between a gendered Italy and a form of writing – tourist writing – defined by its openness to visual images, a connection especially meaningful in the context of nineteenth-century national identities. And it argues that this link proceeds out of the ability of both the gendered image and the appropriate textual form of its representation to engage tourists' and readers' emotions, to provide a geographical and textual space for pleasurably working through the combination of desires, attachments, and separations that mark the development of a modern U.S. subjectivity.

The insistence on Italy as feminine has significant and enduring implications for the transatlantic construction of U.S. identity. This trope persisted throughout the nineteenth century, even after Italy became a unified nation-state in 1870 and entered the modern world of development – of trade and railroads. As Henry James says in 1877, in "Italy Revisited," "Young Italy, preoccupied with its economical and political future, must be heartily tired of being admired for its eyelashes." Indeed, James's essay puts this explicitly feminized Italy – "the Italy of your desire" – in tension with "her" contemporary, masculine, "enterprising" inhabitants: the generic "youth" who has built "tram-cars in Rome" and who may well "begin to resent our insufferable aesthetic patronage." The juxtaposition of "old" and "new" Italy leads to incongruities that ambush the tourist; when James "reverent[ly]" approaches a traditional "wayside shrine" to the Madonna "in the soft twilight" with its "little votive lamp," he smells "an incongruous odour . . . that of petroleum; the votive taper was nourished with the essence of Pennsylvania." His response disrupts the dream state of aesthetic tourism: "I burst out laughing." James repeats the phrase "young Italy" as he describes the drive to modernize the nation; by doing so, he traces Giuseppe Mazzini's political movement, "Young Italy," to unify and democratize Italy into the present, when unification has been achieved but progress toward democracy has been stalled by monarchy. This generation of Young Italy is embodied in a "young man" who at first appears as a "figure" to "set off the landscape" surrounding a "picturesque old city" and who approaches James singing and "with his coat slung over his shoulder . . . in the manner of a cavalier in an opera." However, the young man turns out to be "unemployed," "a brooding young radical and communist, filled with hatred of the present Italian government," and longing for a revolution which would "chop off the heads of the king and his family." James acknowledges the "absurd[ity]" of his initial tourist's construction of the scene, but he concludes his essay with a return to aesthetic response: he leaves behind the "express train" – the "puffing indiscretion" – that has taken him to the hill town of Orvieto and climbs up to see the "high concert of colour" of Orvieto's medieval cathedral.[7] There were exceptions, some Americans who, like Fuller, immersed themselves in political, literary, or social movements. The literary critic Etta Madden is currently researching a group of later nineteenth-century expatriate women who entered into such Italian movements and contexts.[8] Nevertheless, most tourists, including James, went to Italy for the eyelashes.

The persistence of this approach to Italy is related to colonial or similar practices of feminizing and aestheticizing the other in order to reinforce racial, economic, social, or political forms of dominance. However, studying this version in the context of tourism extends our understanding of such practices. Because this trope draws on nineteenth-century images of women as sliding signifiers, "Italy" is able to mirror back to the tourist gaze different, even contradictory, aspects of traits associated with the feminine and defined as both outside and integral – if supplemental – to national life. Romantic British writers influencing Americans, for example, often define Italy as a seductress, pulling travelers away from productive, national life; Stowe, on the other hand, describes the gorge at Sorrento as in some ways maternal, an extravagant, primal uterine space from which not-yet-disciplined or even fully formed energies emerge. Cooper's pronouncement that Italy is "like another wife" at one stroke domesticates the British image, turns the possibly threatening force of non-American visual experience into a comfortably subordinate life partner, and emphasizes its provisional status – after all, in the northeast U.S. the concept of "another wife" is necessarily fictional. Defined as female, Italy is an elastic symbol, reusable for several generations of Americans engaged in the ongoing cultural work of defining "American" qualities as both the opposite of and in intimate relation with the qualities of "Italy." Taking a final look at this trope sheds light on nineteenth-century uses of gender in the transatlantic process of defining nations.

The above chapters trace repetitive, habitual links among concepts of the feminine, the visual, and the pre-modern and argue that tourists bundle these concepts into the image of Italy to solidify a still-fluid U.S. national subjectivity through a dialectical engagement with this image. But this analysis also uncovers a sustained language of affect; tourists, both male and female, "love" Italy. Aesthetic tourism offers U.S. travelers the chance to engage barely articulated attachments: to embrace values subordinated at home, to reside in temporary intimacy with aspects of experience that seem to have no place in the rapidly developing U.S., and to mourn imagined – or perhaps real enough – losses in the psyche caused by modernity. The Italian tour entails visual work, but it also entails emotional work, and it renders both forms of labor pleasurable. The play of dialectics, of binaries, in the transatlantic construction of nationhood skates across the surface of a deeper emotional give and take between attachment and release, cathexis and mourning, subjection and dominance. These processes have little to do with the return to ancestral homelands described in other tourist accounts.[9] None of the tourists discussed here have Italian ancestry. Instead, the feminization of Italy allows for this broad range of emotional activity, which in turn underwrites the complex construction of the modern U.S.

Transatlantic perspectives ask us to pay a different kind of attention to the genres that characterized antebellum writing. The preceding chapters analyze travel books but also discuss the ways in which tourist writing pervades other forms, such as journalism, poetry, or fiction. Tourist writing pops up frequently in this era and in various genres and venues; new scholarly attention to periodicals reveals that travel writings appear regularly in magazines and newspapers throughout the century. Scholars have begun to read these pieces and their subsequent collection into books, as, for example, Leslie Eckel does in her discussion of Grace Greenwood.[10]

The fluidity of tourists' projections of gender is related to the pervasiveness of the genre of tourist writing. Although I often use "travel writing" and "tourist writing" interchangeably (indeed, the influential sociologist Dean MacCannell deconstructed any opposition between "travel" and "tourism"), this study does highlight the particular functions of writing coming out of what we would see as a conventional European tour. If nineteenth-century tourism focused on the cultivation of the (nationally defined) self, then tourist writing, as an insistently first-person genre, illuminates the process of that cultivation – the cultural significance of conventional aesthetic responses to conventional sights. The analysis in the chapters above defines the markers of tourist writing and argues for its importance in understanding the period's print culture. These markers all underscore the profoundly anti-narrative nature of this genre. They include: the ritual performance of aesthetic arrest, the inundation of language by images, the momentary ceding of control of the eye from the subject to the object of the gaze, and the simultaneous validation of this apparent loss of authority and its recuperation through conventions of framing and ordering the visual field – conventions often projected onto the image itself and understood as originating there, rather than in the spectator. Tourist writing, therefore, transforms what could be an occasion (travel) for a strongly linear narrative describing movement through space into a series of halts, standstills, where motion and time are suspended.

By doing so, it opens the tourist's and reader's perceptions to an excess of meaning in the foreign scene, that is, meaning which escapes linguistic definition. The overwhelming feeling of psychological safety in tourism and tourist writing, in spite of such exposure to foreign scenes, derives from the force of the visual conventions that structure and mediate this exposure. Given the origin of some of these conventions in Italian works of art, tourists experienced an epitome of this process in Italy. The dialectic of motion and arrest, word and image, disembodied eye and excessively embodied landscapes and peoples, results in a form of writing that escapes nineteenth-century definitions of rational and purposeful rhetoric and that tries to approximate visual response, especially its power to realign the less conscious aspects of subjectivity.

In making these arguments, this book aims to highlight the promise of studying the intersections of textual and visual culture for articulating formations of class, gender, and national subjectivities – especially in the case of tourism and its expressions, which existed at the juncture of visual experience and written communication. European tourism, in its modern middle-class form, began for Americans in the antebellum era. The writers and artists discussed here fashioned the normative gaze that would inform the experience of participants in the post-Civil War era of mass tourism, as well as influence the growing investment in national iconography in the last third of the century. Tourism – as the nexus of visual work, transatlantic travel, national imagining, and print culture – remains a capacious field for research.

Notes

Introduction

1. B. Taylor, 15. Subsequent page numbers are given in the text. As many of his books were on Middle Eastern or Far Eastern travel and his translations were often from German authors, much of the scholarship on Taylor focuses on his Orientalist depictions or on his relationship with Germany.
2. See Corley's biography on Taylor's career and on the "canny rapprochement" his first travel book achieves "between the cultural refinement associated with aristocratic leisure and a lusty egalitarianism associated with democratic liberty and the dignity of labor." Corley adds, "Since Taylor's precedent-setting account in *Views Afoot* of backpacking across Europe on less than a dollar per day, travel literature has presented the fruits of foreign travel as a commodity available for purchase by nearly every class of society" (47).
3. In the poetic conventions Taylor observed, the archaic "thee" flagged a heightened intimacy.
4. Wright found that "In the nineteenth century at least a hundred professional American writers travelled to that country and . . . published works concerning it, and at least as many other Americans published accounts of their visits there" (*American Novelists in Italy*, 20).
5. Stebbins et al. describe the eighteenth-century context of English touring and artistic training in Italy that American artists entered (*Lure of Italy*, 29–39). Soria identifies "over 300 American artists" who "lived and worked" in Italy, 1760–1914 (16).
6. On republican Rome and the Arcadian landscape, see Vance, I, 1–30, 81–90. For examples of the Gothic uses of Italy in English fiction, see Radcliffe's novels of the 1790s.
7. Following Anderson's *Imagined Communities*, critics have studied the novel and the newspaper as the forms that most fully imagined nineteenth-century nations into being; A. Miller argues that U.S. landscape painting had the same function.
8. A. Miller, 21. On transatlantic approaches to Cole and other antebellum artists and writers, see Hemingway and Wallach.
9. See, for example, Kohn et al.

10. This period marks a turn from primarily coerced to voluntary migration in the Atlantic world; O'Reilly notes that before 1850 "only 10 percent of migrants" to the Americas were free, as most were enslaved and some were imprisoned or indentured (307, 318).
11. Child, 63.
12. Sedgwick, *Letters from Abroad*, II, 121–2.
13. Fuller, *"These Sad But Glorious Days"*, 98–9, 51.
14. Brown, 132, 176, 113.
15. Dorr, 162.
16. For the literary consequences of these exchanges, see Eckel and Elliott; Giles's "Introduction" (1–14) makes this point.
17. See Capper, *Margaret Fuller: An American Romantic Life*, II, 258, on Fuller's interaction with foreign-language newspapers in New York.
18. See Fagg, Pethers, and Vandome on periodical publishing and network theory. On the international practice of reprinting, see McGill.
19. See, for example, Blackett and McFadden. For transatlantic literary expressions of reform, see P. Cole, *The American Writer and the Condition of England*, and Claybaugh.
20. Buzard, for example, who otherwise focuses on British writers, devotes a substantial section to James.
21. See Brooks, *Dream of Arcadia* (1958); Baker, *Fortunate Pilgrims* (1964); and Wright, *American Novelists in Italy* (1965).
22. Urry, *Tourist Gaze*.
23. See Riall's introduction to Italian history in this period and to its historiography. On the resumption of English tourism to Italy after Napoleon's defeat, see C. P. Brand.
24. See, for example, Howe and N. Harris.
25. See L. Reynolds, *European Revolutions*, and Berthold, *American Risorgimento*.
26. See C. P. Brand.
27. See P. Cole's work, such as "The Nineteenth-Century Women's Rights Movement and the Canonization of Margaret Fuller" and "Fuller's Lawsuit and Feminist History"; see also essays in Argersinger and Cole.
28. Capper makes this point in his introduction to Capper and Giorcelli, eds, *Margaret Fuller: Transatlantic Crossings*.
29. See Zwarg for this argument.
30. The definitive discussion of antebellum genre painting is Johns'.
31. Franchot has documented the dynamics of this polarization.
32. Urry, 2.

Chapter 1

1. Gilpin, 47.
2. Myers, 74, 59.

3. Similarly, Buzard defines tourism as "an exemplary practice of modern liberal democracies" in its claim to popular accessibility and its simultaneous masking of the material inequalities of class, gender, and national identities (6–7).

4. Irving refers to his association with Allston in Rome in his *Journals and Notebooks*, 262, 268, 270, 276. Callow discusses Irving's relationships with artists, especially Allston (38–44).

5. This is Eagleton's term; in eighteenth-century British aesthetics, the function of the aesthetic is to "convert . . . ethical ideology" into "spontaneous social practice" (40).

6. Stanley Williams, 3, but see chapter 1 in general.

7. D. P. Nord, 115. Nord juxtaposes the contents (aimed at an "elite audience") of the *New-York Magazine* (begun 1790) with its subscriber list, made up half of professionals and merchants and half of shopkeepers and artisans, to argue for this "social function of reading" in the late eighteenth-century U.S.

8. See Burstein, chapter 1, for a similar depiction of the Irving family's activity.

9. Irving, *History, Tales and Sketches*, 49. Stanley Williams discusses the creation of *Salmagundi* in chapter 4.

10. Stanley Williams, 79; Wright, "Introduction," in Irving, *Journals*, xxxiii; Hedges, 45–7.

11. Burstein adds that the Irving brothers were active in the literary "club tradition" in New York, modeled on British club culture (24–5).

12. Stanley Williams, 118–19. Hedges discusses Irving's venture into parody before his tour in the "letters" of "Jonathan Oldstyle" (17–33).

13. Travel writing was one of the genres parodied in *Salmagundi*, which included excerpts from a fictional travel journal: "Left Princeton – country finely diversified with sheep and haystacks" (*History, Tales and Sketches*, 98). Hedges points out *Salmagundi*'s "interest in travel and travel writing" (52–3). Lueck (*American Writers and the Picturesque Tour*) discusses Paulding's enacting and satirizing the picturesque tour in his subsequent travel writings.

14. Wright, "Introduction to Volume I," xxx, xxxiv.

15. Trease, 3.

16. Hibbert, 20. Hibbert says that this rigorous program was often ignored; tourists tended to exercise their other aristocratic prerogative – leisure – rather than management. Eighteenth-century Americans echoed this link between presiding over landscapes visually and managing them economically or socially; Jefferson advises prospective tourists to gather economic and agricultural information and to look for improvements to bring home – "useful . . . animals" or "lighter mechanical arts"; a tourist's first step in a city should be to buy a map and to "go to the top of a steeple to have a view of the town and its environs" (147–8).

17. In this respect the tourist can mimic the view from the center of the "panoptic establishment" – can play at exercising the disciplinary gaze which he may (or may not) expect to assume in earnest when he returns home (Foucault, 205).
18. Batten, 29, 97, 114.
19. Bermingham, 14–21. Eagleton also discusses implications of the middle-class preoccupation with manners in this period (41–2).
20. Stanley Willams, 65–6.
21. Irving, *Journals*, 59, 248. I follow Irving's spelling etc. in these quotations without comment.
22. Fabricant, 56; I am indebted for the reference to Fabricant's article to Alan Wallach.
23. The best example of an eighteenth-century American version of the prospect is Timothy Dwight's *Greenfield Hill* (1794), especially "Part I: The Prospect," where he adapts the form to New England political and social ideals (139–55).
24. See Addison's statements on landscape and on the function of sight in the series of essays "The Pleasures of the Imagination" (numbers 411–21 of *The Spectator*).
25. Wright, "Introduction to Volume I," xxxiii.
26. Andrews discusses the shared vocabulary of landscape aesthetics and stage design and notes that some landscape painters also worked as set designers (29–30).
27. Sample titles of Gilpin's work include: *Observations on the River Wye and Several Parts of South Wales, &c. Relative Chiefly to Picturesque Beauty: Made in the Summer of the Year 1770* (1782) and *Remarks on Forest Scenery, and Other Woodland Views (Relative Chiefly to Picturesque Beauty)* (1791).
28. Hedges, 40; Wright, *American Novelists in Italy*, 55–6. Lueck analyzes Gilpin's picturesque aesthetics in the "American Grand Tour" (*American Writers and the Picturesque Tour*, 16) in the northeastern U.S. in the 1820s to 1830s. See Dekker (*Fictions of Romantic Tourism*) on Radcliffe's use of Gilpin (73–4) and on her *Mysteries of Udolpho* and *The Italian* (113–23).
29. In addition to several sources cited below, see G. Levine. Interest in literary theory in the 1980s–1990s renewed interest in eighteenth-century aesthetic theory.
30. Conron argues that all mid-nineteenth-century American arts are "invested with a grammar of picturesque forms" (9); Lueck, *American Writers and the Picturesque Tour*; Bunn, 127, and see 129–31.
31. Gilpin emphasizes tone as a tool to unify a composition: "blend thy tints, . . . Harmonious, till one general glow prevail / Unbroken by abrupt and hostile glare" (113).
32. Robinson, 143; he is quoting Donald Lowe, *History of Bourgeois Perception*.

33. Quoted in Andrews, 65. The passage is from Price's *An Essay on the Picturesque* (1794).
34. Addison, *Remarks on Italy*, 285.
35. Addison, "Letter from Italy," *Works*, I, 166, 161.
36. Mason, note to Thomas Gray's *Journal* of a visit to the Lake District, quoted in Hussey, 109. Also see Gilpin, 106–7, for a statement that echoes Mason's.
37. Andrews, 240. See Conron. Bermingham notes the commodifying of the picturesque and its adaptation to "democratic" values in the nineteenth century (83–5). For a related point, see R. Williams's summary of Antonio Gramsci's definition of hegemony (109).
38. Quoted in Bermingham, 69.
39. Andrews, 59.
40. For a related discussion, see Barrell on the positioning of the rural poor in late eighteenth-century English landscape paintings, which represent landscape as an analogy of society and "combine" laboring and leisured rural classes in "a harmonious whole" (22).
41. Churchill, 1–3.
42. Andrews, 81. He says that "appropriate" is Gilpin's word.
43. Hedges makes this comment in discussing the following passage (40).
44. Irving first makes this lament in a breezy letter soon after arriving in Europe: "the sea has much degenerated since ancient days, for then one could hardly sail out of sight of land without meeting Neptune and his suite in full gallop, whereas I have passed across the wide Atlantic without seeing even a mermaid" (quoted in Stanley Williams, 48).
45. In doing so, Irving touches on the debate among English theorists on the origin of aesthetic impressions: in nature or in the observer. Cahill remarks on "the phenomenological gap between aesthetic subjects and aesthetic objects whose uncertain topography was the persistent dilemma of eighteenth-century theorists. In connecting beauty and sublimity with the formal qualities of objects, . . . writers gain the moral assurance of the imagination's universality but at the cost of the specificity of the perceiving subject. Conversely, in locating the source of beauty and sublimity in the imagination of the perceiver, they elevate the moral status of aesthetic perception and invention while leaving the imagination vulnerable to the moral hazard of its radical autonomy" (4).
46. Cahill, 9, 5.
47. Hedges, 227; Rubin-Dorsky, 191; M. D. Bell, 80.
48. Anthony, 42, 43, 57, 63–5. Kopec, 717, 710–11. Kopec links Irving's decision to write for money with his use of the picturesque, which Kopec suggests is a "speculative" mode (720).
49. Kerber studies the associations among Federalist writers, including Irving, between "Democracy" and "violence and chaos" (174–6). Burstein calls Irving's youthful political orientation a "mild Federalist" one (19).

50. Irving, *Tales of a Traveller*, ed. Haig, 49–50.
51. According to Reichart, Schiller – author of the popular bandit play *Die Räuber* (1781) – was Irving's "favorite German author" (181).
52. See Honour (240–4) and Hobsbawm (19–23) on the brigand in romanticism.
53. In this reading, I ignore a tale, "The Belated Travellers," Irving inserted between "The Little Antiquary" and "The Popkins Family" to fill up the pages needed for the first English edition (Haig, "Introduction," xx). The tale differs from Part III's other indirectly narrated tales; it features aristocratic characters, successful romantic love, and a defeat of the banditti. Irving retreats in this addition from the implications of the unaltered set of tales; "The Belated Travellers" offsets the accounts of assaults on women with an image of idealized sexual interaction. I have tried to use passages present in the first, U.S. edition and to avoid other (minor) insertions as well. For the *Tales*' tangled textual history, see Haig, "Textual Commentary," 281–6.
54. Irving, *Journals*, 127–31, 148–52.
55. In a letter to his English publisher Irving says that his character "is not meant for that of an English *Nobleman* specifically; but as one of the general Run of English travelling gentlemen" (Haig, "Textual Commentary," 310).
56. Irving, *Tales of a Traveller*, 1st American edn, III, 10.
57. Hedges, 109, 122. Irving apparently read Burke in 1810 and was reading Gilpin's *Remarks on Forest Scenery* while working on the *Tales*.
58. Hussey, 83.
59. Quoted in Novak, 228. She gives no note on her source.
60. Hedges makes this point in discussing the frame narrative's comic tone (219–20).
61. See the first U.S. edition, 49. Irving omitted the mention of Byron and Scott in the English edition.
62. Hedges summarizes the critical opinion on Irving's letter to Henry Brevoort (193–4).
63. Irving, *Letters*, II, 90–1.
64. Haig summarizes the reviews ("Introduction," xxi–xxiv). Stanley Williams says, "never was a book of Irving's so damned," and gives excerpts from reviews that charged Irving with obscenity, plagiarism, and flattering the aristocracy (276–8).
65. Thanks to Sandhya Shetty for calling my attention to the emphasis on property in the Popkins episode.
66. As Churchill notes (2), such neoclassical travelers as Addison looked for classical Rome in modern Italy and concluded that they, rather than the Italians, inherited the disciplined life of imperial Rome.
67. He adapts his description of Rome from a line he quotes from Pope's "Epistle to Mr. Addison" in his Italian journal (*Journals*, 261): " – Rome her own sad sepulchre appears."

68. Burke, 51.
69. Ruskin complained about it in the 1840s (41); Gerdts and Thistlethwaite describe the genre's popularity in the U.S.
70. Rosen and Zerner, 39.
71. Honour reproduces this painting (242); see also Lacambre, 594–5. Hobsbawm reproduces a similar English painting: Charles Eastlake's *Bandit of the Apennines* (1824) (following 104).
72. Lacambre, 595; Honour, 241.
73. Parry summarizes this model of history and its depictions by Cole (141–4); see also Wallach, "Thomas Cole: Landscape and the Course of American Empire" (90–5).
74. Novak, 228.
75. Irving comments on seeing Claude's works there in his journal; Wright notes that he probably saw "The Mill" (another title for *Landscape with Dancing Figures*): Irving, *Journals*, 289.
76. In this other landscape, the artist again begins with a view of the Campagna and ends with the bandits in the "foreground," which reminds him of "those savage scenes of Salvator Rosa" (193).
77. Irving, *Miscellaneous Writings 1803–1859*, 174.
78. Bjelajac, *Washington Allston*, 3, 40, 35, 37, 41, 46, 167. See Bjelajac on Allston's embrace of George Field's "mystical," alchemical, and "trinitarian" 1817 treatise, *Chromatics or An Essay on the Analogy and Harmony of Colours* (43–5). Bjelajac asserts not that Allston was a Mason but that many of his acquaintances and patrons were.
79. Quoted by E. P. Richardson, 60.
80. Gerdts and Stebbins juxtapose two such paintings that may date from his Italian period: the serene *Morning in Italy* (ca. 1805–8) and the rockily picturesque *Italian Landscape* (ca. 1805), 179, discussed on 47, 49.
81. Allston, *Monaldi*; see the author's note, 5.
82. Irving may have read Allston's manuscript of *Monaldi* and drawn on it in writing this story (Clark, 111–14).
83. Gerdts, "Paintings of Washington Allston," 19–20. Gerdts notes Allston's increasing reliance on Claude (58, 98, 146–8).
84. Gerdts, "Paintings of Washington Allston," 38–9, 42, 47; Bjelajac, *Washington Allston*, 20–1, 176 n. 32. Lüth discusses Wilhelm von Humboldt's earlier stay in Paris and his interest in French educational theories, theories sometimes at odds with his Kantian concepts of *Bildung* (263–6). See Bjelajac, *Millennial Desire*, for the German art colony's turn toward prophetic, Christian themes (69).
85. Monk, "Introduction," *The Sublime*.
86. Kant, *Critique of Judgment*, 100, 97. The German terms are "ein Vermögen zu widerstehen" and "unsere übersinnliche Bestimmung," in Kant, *Kritik der Urteilskraft*, 101, 97.
87. Wolf, 205, 202. Wolf analyzes the structure of Cole's painting in Freudian and Lacanian terms.

88. See A. Miller (150, 154–60), on the place of Durand's painting in the "invention" of a U.S. national landscape.
89. Weiskel analyzes the experience of "excess on the part of an object" or "excess on the plane of the signifiers" (103) in oedipal and structuralist terms.
90. Gerdts, "Paintings of Washington Allston," 146. Gilpin adapts this principle in advising sketchers to harmonize their drawings with a series of washes (*Three Essays*, 80–1).
91. Allston, *Lectures on Art*, 70, 60, 74. I pass here over his definitions of the sublime that connect this response more closely with his history paintings than with his landscapes. But Allston's emphasis throughout the "Introductory Discourse" (where he defines his terms) is on the ideal as the goal of aesthetic response. He subsumes the beautiful into the sublime at the end of this essay; all modes of harmony point to the transcendent destiny of the "disembodied" soul, which hopes to find its "true correlative" not in physical objects but in God (73–4).
92. Bjelajac, *Washington Allston*, 157; Bjelajac, *Millennial Desire*, 80, 6–7, 82.
93. Quoted by Vance, I, 106.
94. Stebbins finds that the painting is based on a sketch Allston composed from nature in Italy in 1804–5: "Drawings of Washington Allston," 214. See also Wallace, 84–6.
95. Gerdts, "Paintings of Washington Allston," 146.
96. Wolf, 60.
97. Bjelajac, *Washington Allston*, 30, 55; these insights are suggested by his discussion of the moon in Allston's *The Angel Releasing St. Peter from Prison* (1814–16).
98. Bjelajac, *Millennial Desire*, 78, 145–6. Bjelajac expands on this point in *Washington Allston*.
99. Michasiw, 84, 94. Similarly, in speaking of his historical writings, Hedges says, "Irving did not see through the physiognomy or phenomenology of experience to a permanent reality" (261).
100. Vivien Jones observes: "a set of flexibly analogous signifiers – woman/estate/nature/nation – underlies" eighteenth-century picturesque theories, in which "anxieties about private property and national identity are articulated in terms of voyeurism and sexual possession" (121). This logic informs Irving's tale of theft and rape, as does the association of whiteness with the middle class.
101. Quoted by Rubin-Dorsky, 181. See Haig's summary of reviews ("Introduction," xxi–xxiv).
102. M. D. Bell argues that Irving depicts the painter as "idiotic" and comic (79); because of the evidence of the early journal, I take the painter more seriously as an aspect of Irving's own perspective.
103. For accounts of this transition, see Hedges, 236–8, and Stanley Williams, chapter 13. See Stanley Williams (302–8) and Burstein (196, 302, 309–11) for the reception of the *Life* and for Irving's life as a diplomat.

104. M. D. Bell's discussion of the breakdown of associationism in the *Tales* (73–7) informs my understanding of the various dissociations Irving enacts in the *Tales* and *The Alhambra*.
105. Stanley Williams, 373.
106. As Hedges notes, Irving issued the book first in Crayon's name but in later editions in his own name, even as he kept "Crayon" on the title pages of *The Sketch Book, Bracebridge Hall*, and the *Tales* (265). Rubin-Dorsky notes Crayon's disappearance (249) and discusses the architecture of the Alhambra as structurally consonant with the needs of Irving's imagination (234–41). On the other hand, Scraba argues that in the first edition Irving uses Crayon to create a tension between "Crayon's Romantic experiences" and "Irving's Romantic irony" (278).
107. See Almeida on Spain in English Romantic writings.
108. Lenehan and Myers note that one reviewer compared Irving to "contemporary painters like Wilkie, Leslie, and Turner" (xxxiv).
109. Irving's interest in the imaginative possibilities of this landscape emerges in the journal of his first trip to Granada in 1828, where he comments on Edenic valleys of fertility in a harsh mountainous landscape: see *Journal of Washington Irving, 1828*.
110. Bjelajac sees Allston's 1830s paintings of women in reverie as a part of the movement of Boston elites "away from fraternal ritual toward the feminine, familial cult of domesticity" in their pursuit of "social harmony through spiritual alchemy or individual self-refinement" (*Washington Allston*, 159). For many antebellum male travelers the Italian tour is connected with this project.
111. Scraba documents Irving's pervasive presence even now at the Alhambra and on its website (275–6, 280). Rubin-Dorsky argues that Irving's writings spoke to the "anxiety about the breakdown . . . of community" that existed "below the surface bravado" of an expanding U.S. (5).

Chapter 2

1. Emerson, *Journals*, 78.
2. Baker, 20–1. Soria notes that after Allston's visit (the first decade of the century) American artists did not really return to Italy until 1825 (31).
3. C. P. Brand, 3, 228. Brand mentions that the publication of travel books and articles on Italy was at its greatest volume from 1819 to 1828 (23) and that "a crowd of . . . English painters" copied Old Masters and sketched landscapes in this period (141, 168). See Dekker, *Fictions of Romantic Tourism*, on English Romantic tourists and writers, such as Byron and Mary Shelley, in Italy (221–53).
4. This is Emerson's title for one of his own exercises in implied national self-definition: *English Traits*.

5. Studies of the American process of developing a literary voice both in terms of and in opposition to the British voice include Weisbuch's *Atlantic Double-Cross* and Giles's *Transatlantic Insurrections*.

6. See R. Richardson for a discussion of Emerson's turn toward the visual in his Italian tour – "the confirmation of the importance of the eye" (125) – and for a discussion of his reading of Goethe's *Italiensiche Reise* in Italy.

7. Kasson carries this critical assumption, present in most works on Cole and Cooper, into her study of their European phases; the "running subtheme" of Cooper's travel books is "the definition of an American national character" (*Artistic Voyagers*, 144). See Callow on their association in New York.

8. For chronologies see Parry, 375–8, and Conron and Denne's introduction to Cooper's *Gleanings in Europe: Italy*, xviii.

9. Hillard, *Six Months in Italy*, 11–12.

10. Goethe's conclusion that Rome is not a "supplement" to the tourist's identity but instead a catalyst for its transformation influences such later travelers as Fuller (*Italian Journey*, 412; *Italienische Reise*, 400). Another way of suggesting the risk that Italian travel poses to identity appears in such Gothic fiction as Radcliffe's *Mysteries of Udolpho* (1794). English perceptions of north/south polarities reflect northern attitudes generally. For similar French and German approaches see Stendhal's *Rome, Naples et Florence* (1826) and the third and fourth volumes (1830–1) of Heine's *Reisebilder*.

11. W. J. T. Mitchell, *Iconology*, 110.

12. Baker, 27–8, 200; C. P. Brand, 3; Brooks, *Dream of Arcadia*, 15, 31; Wright, *American Novelists in Italy*, 31.

13. Wallach, "Cole, Byron, and *The Course of Empire*," 375–9.

14. Cole included verses from Byron in advertisements and exhibition catalogues (Wallach, "Cole, Byron," 377–8). Cooper began two novels inspired by Italy – *The Bravo* and *The Wing-and-Wing* – with quotations from *Childe Harold* and included lines from other poems by Byron as epigraphs for later chapters.

15. For Cooper's admiration for Staël's daughter, whom he met in Paris, and for his father's legal efforts on behalf of Staël in New York, see *Letters and Journals*, I, 199–200, 204. For his irritation with French discussions of *Corinne*, see *Gleanings in Europe: France*, 184. Of Byron, whose works he knows well, Cooper says he disliked his "character," although "he was certainly a man of great genius": *Letters and Journals*, I, 405.

16. Byron, 233, 237.

17. See Vance, I, 4–5, 184–8, on the ways in which Michelangelo's Capitol and the Capitoline Hill in general, with its views and sculpture galleries, prompted both historical and aesthetic associations in American visitors.

18. Staël, *Corinne, or Italy*, 19–22; *Corinne, ou l'Italie*, 49–52.

19. Staël, *Corinne, or Italy*, 315; *Corinne, ou l'Italie*, 447–8.
20. Churchill, 3, 23.
21. Eagleton, 27–8, 116, 40–1, 28, 118.
22. Staël, *Corinne, or Italy*, 394, 396; *Corinne, ou l'Italie*, 557.
23. N. Harris, 146, 159, 168.
24. Scudder, "Introduction," in Longfellow, *Outre-Mer and Drift-Wood*, 9.
25. Johnston, "Samuel F. B. Morse's *Gallery of the Louvre*," 42, 56, 42–3, 56, 57. Johnston sets Morse's "emphasis on the primacy of the aesthetic" (57) in the context of his virulently anti-Catholic public positions in the U.S. later in the 1830s (59).
26. I am adapting Eagleton's use of these terms in his discussion of Schiller's aesthetics, 115.
27. Hazlitt, *Complete Works*, X, 207. See Wu for a description of Hazlitt's tour of Italy (364–76).
28. Wallach, "Cole, Byron, and *The Course of Empire*," 377. On Cole's reactions to Turner, see Costello.
29. Powell, 166, 170.
30. For a study of Turner's sustained engagement with Claude, see Warrell.
31. Novak mentions this prevalence of "Claudian conventions" in depictions of the Italian landscape, 214.
32. MacCannell, 77, 82–4.
33. Jameson, 321–2, 324–5. This book moved Allston to write a poem celebrating her ability to recall "Italy" to his mind: "To the Author of 'The Diary of an Ennuyée,'" in *Lectures on Art, and Poems*, 377–80. See Moine on Jameson's uses of Byron and Staël.
34. Willis, 67. For a survey of Willis's writings on Italy, see Wright (*American Novelists in Italy*, 71–8), who also discusses this passage.
35. Hillard, *Six Months in Italy*, quoted in Novak, 209.
36. Hazlitt, "On Going a Journey," 303.
37. See, for example, the engraving of Allston's *Moonlight* by George B. Ellis in *The Atlantic Souvenir* of 1828, printed along with a poem inspired by the painting: "Moonlight. An Italian Scene," by Henry Pickering, 210–13. An annual devoted to images and texts inspired by travel in Italy (and by English conventions) is Thomas Roscoe's *The Landscape Annual*, of which three out of four issues were subtitled *The Tourist in Italy*.
38. For information on *Italy* and its publication history, see Hale. On his collaboration with Turner, see Powell, 131–6, and Holcomb, "A Neglected Classical Phase of Turner's Art," 405–10. In some of the cheaper editions, Turner's landscapes disappeared and only Stothard's figures remained. All three mention *Italy*'s influence on Ruskin.
39. Holcomb studies Rogers' awareness of other British works on Italy in the 1820s and his collaboration with Turner in creating the illustrated 1830 edition of *Italy*; in doing so, she notes the shift toward the visual in encountering Italy in this decade, the "new circumstance

that Italian travel . . . could not be treated successfully without a compelling appeal to visual experience" ("Turner and Rogers' 'Italy' Revisited," 94).

40. Twain, 158. My guess is that Twain copies this passage from a guide-book rather than consulting Rogers directly.
41. Cooper, *Letters and Journals*, I, 263–4; quoted in Parry, 100, 103.
42. Cooper, *Letters and Journals*, II, 178. Cooper quoted Rogers extensively in the epigraphs of his chapters in *The Bravo*. Cole used a passage from Rogers in a catalogue description of *Landscape Composition, Italian Scenery* (1833); see Craven, 1021.
43. Rogers, 35–9.
44. Wright, *American Novelists in Italy*, 142.
45. This is Gilbert's language: "female Italy neither contains nor condones the super-egoistic repressions that characterize patriarchal England" (196).
46. Cole adds, "I found myself a nameless, noteless individual, in the midst of an immense selfish multitude." Quoted in Parry, 102.
47. Sedgwick, *Letters from Abroad*, I, 111–12. C. Mulvey analyzes American reactions to the British class system, 147–61.
48. Cooper, *Gleanings in Europe: England*, 259.
49. Emerson, *English Traits*, 60.
50. Fuller, *"These Sad But Glorious Days"*, 294.
51. Franklin discusses Cooper's friendship with and patronage of Greenough, 148–51.
52. *Letters and Journals*, II, 371.
53. Willis exemplifies the tourist's tendency to intensify this conflation of the visual and the erotic the further he travels from England. Constantinople, near the easternmost extent of his trip, makes him say, "If we could compel all our senses into one, and live by the pleasure of the eye, it were a Paradise untranscended" (302); the 1842 edition includes as its only illustration an engraving of a bare-chested gypsy girl, one of the "more interesting object[s]" (305) Willis saw near Constantinople and, by implication, a representative image.
54. Noble, 103.
55. Cooper, *Italy*, 21.
56. See, for example, the middle-class couple in Albert Bierstadt's *The Arch of Octavia (Roman Fish Market)* (1858). For discussions of this and similar paintings, see Richardson and Wittmann.
57. For the aesthetic and historical meanings which the Coliseum had for Americans, see Vance, I, 43–67.
58. Peale, 189.
59. See Kasson on Cole's movement from the alienating environment of the English art world to the revitalizing influence of Horatio Greenough's "circle" in Florence (*Artistic Voyagers*, 98, 101–6).
60. Cole, letter to William Dunlap, quoted in Noble, 125.

61. Mitchell, *Iconology*, 112.
62. Salomone, 1364, 1360, 1369. C. P. Brand notices a similar lapse of "serious" historical writings on either past or present Italy in England between the efforts of Gibbon and Roscoe in the late eighteenth century and the resumption of "conscientious" research in the 1840s (187, 195).
63. Wittmann, 553. Greenhouse notes that art is here in the service of Christianity, as the sketch book "leads our gaze from the artist's hand upwards to the church spire" ("Huntington and Christian Art," 109).
64. Several scholars, including Salomone, set Fuller's projected "History of Italian Liberation" apart from other writings on Italy; the notes for this work, along with Fuller herself, were lost in the shipwreck off New York in 1850. Douglas also connects Fuller's hopes for the Roman Republic with her feminism (284).
65. See Butler. Thanks to Michael Ferber for this reference. American tourists read the English Romantic poets selectively and emphasized texts that would help them to retain the distancing and depoliticizing effect of nostalgia.
66. Hamilton (*America's Sketchbook*) discusses this literary form in the U.S.
67. Conron and Denne, "Historical Introduction", in Cooper, *Italy*, xxxix. See Ringe for another approach to Cooper's visual habits. Cooper avoids not only historical reveries and sentimental stories in his sketches but also any engagement with the banditti tradition, which he dismisses, ascribing any anxiety about "Italian banditti" to "busy fancy" (*Italy*, 13–14).
68. Spiller, chapter 12.
69. McWilliams, 183. See also his discussion of *The Bravo*, 154–66.
70. Kennedy, 111, 115. He calls the *Gleanings* series "the most ambitious effort by an antebellum American author to scrutinize the new nation from a critical transnational perspective" (91).
71. Ringe, "Introduction" to *The Bravo*; Ringe summarizes several critical readings of the political debate in which the novel is involved (8–9). An analysis of *The Bravo* that establishes its American political and social context in greater detail is R. Levine's chapter 2 in *Conspiracy and Romance*.
72. Cooper, *England*, 103, 107. Kasson also finds this "disjunction between appearance and reality" in *The Bravo* (*Artistic Voyagers*, 153).
73. McKinsey, 111. Like many Italian landscapes, Weir's portrait of Red Jacket also entered popular culture via the medium of the gift annual; an engraving of it, together with an anonymous poem inspired by it, appears in *The Talisman* of 1829 (Bryant et al.). These publications indicate that the heroic American portrait and the feminized Italian landscape were understood as representative and contrasting images within the ongoing dialogue over U.S. cultural identity.
74. Reproduced in *Antiques*, 101 (June 1972), 981. See also Eldredge and Novak, item no. 43.

75. Eldredge uses this phrase to describe American impressions of Italy in general (vi).

76. For a dissenting view, see Bryant's remarks on Florence in 1834. He confirms the truth of Cole's depiction of Italy's transfiguring light in a painting of the Arno but critiques the deforestation of the area; "the hand of man" has both "embellish[ed]" and "deform[ed]" Tuscany in an imperfect marriage: *Picturesque Souvenir*, 24–6.

77. Ourusoff, 17, 18.

78. *The Amulet*, ed. S. C. Hall. The first stanza of the accompanying poem, "Florence," by Laman Blanchard, reads as follows:

> A dream of love, a dream of light –
> > A glimpse, a gleam of fairy-land –
> A haunt of glory, meets the sight;
> > 'Tis some enchanted strand!
> A circle where sorrow entereth not –
> The home of beauty – a golden spot!

79. Women tourists sometimes shift between an identification with Italy and an identification with the male voice. See Jameson for an English example of a negotiation between these two positions, although sometimes her borrowing the masculine terms of tourist desire seems forced; as she describes a landscape near Perugia, she says: the "mist sank gradually to the earth, like a veil dropped from the form of a beautiful woman, and nature stood disclosed in all her loveliness" (121).

80. Bachelard, 167.

81. Allston, *Lectures on Art, and Poems*, 70, 60, 74.

82. Cole's entry of September 1847 appears in Noble, 281–2.

83. Cooper, *Gleanings in Europe: The Rhine*, 157–8.

84. An example of discussions of the ideological implications of Burke's gendered aesthetics appears in W. J. T. Mitchell, *Iconology*, 129–30.

85. Emerson, *English Traits*, 21.

86. See Nevius's reading of this and the next scene I discuss, 49–55.

87. I adapt this phrase from Conron and Denne's discussion of Cooper's landscape aesthetics in their "Historical Introduction" to *Italy*, xxxv.

88. Baigell, *Thomas Cole*, 46. In thinking about Cole's Italian work, I have also consulted Jaffe.

89. See Cole's comments on this site in Erwin, 9.

90. Chambers, 11–12.

91. *Friendship's Offering* (ed. Waterman), drawn by P. Williams, engraved by G. B. Ellis; the issue includes an accompanying prose piece, "Shrines," by William Howitt (234–41). See also John Kensett's painting *The Shrine – A Scene in Italy* (1847), in Coffey, 28, 84.

92. Kloss, 121–2.

93. Clarke includes Cole's preparatory sketches of the landscape, the shrine, and the figure (116–20).

94. Wallach, "Making a Picture," 83–4. See discussion at the end of Chapter 1.
95. Baigell, *Thomas Cole*, 70.
96. On the stationary panorama, see Oettermann and Comment; Huhtamo discusses the moving panorama.
97. Comment, 7.
98. See Oettermann's suggestive point, i.e., that the circular panorama shifted away from painting's traditional "central" perspective – which assigned one vanishing point and, therefore, one viewer to a picture – to a more "democratic" "multiperspective" that accommodated many simultaneous viewers looking at different parts of the 360° image surrounding them (31–2).
99. Wallach ("Making a Picture," 83), Novak (18–26), and Parry (124–5) consider the panorama's influence on landscape painting. Parry discusses Cole's *Mount Etna* (292–4).
100. Wallach, "Thomas Cole: Landscape and the Course of American Empire," 77.
101. T. Cole, 46–9.
102. Stansell and Wilentz, 18. See also A. Miller on Cole's proximity to the Whig party's anti-Jacksonian anxiety over the unleashed growth and possible moral and financial disintegration of the U.S. (25–39).
103. Hussey, 85; also quoted in Nevius, 53.
104. Robinson, 73, 79, 88–9, 143.
105. Comment, Huhtamo, and Oettermann document the history of the panorama. Oettermann observes that the related forms of the panorama and the panopticon emerged concurrently; Robert Barker began trying to paint his first panorama in 1787, the year Jeremy Bentham began publicizing his ideas for the panopticon (40).
106. Madison has traced Cooper's sources for Yvard in Byron's *The Corsair* and *Lara*, sources which he argues connects Yvard to French revolutionary struggles against tyranny; however, he also points out Cooper's condemnation, in his *History of the Navy* (1839), of privateering as an occupation whose "'aim is to turn the waste and destruction of war, to the benefit of avarice'" (128–9).
107. Cooper is probably drawing on Robert Southey's biography of Nelson for his idealization of Caraccioli, his critique of Nelson, and his mistaken implication of Lady Hamilton in the intrigues surrounding the execution, and, of course, he is inventing a granddaughter for Caraccioli in the character of Ghita. Thanks to Hugh C. MacDougall for this reference.
108. See McKinsey's discussion of similar attempts to see Niagara Falls as though for the first time (189–247).
109. Cooper, *Wing-and-Wing*, 196–8.
110. Cooper, *Wing-and-Wing*, 196–8.
111. See Becker on this villa and on a panoramic description of the Bay of Naples from this site in Cooper's novel *Water Witch* (1830).

112. MacDougall, 1–3. See MacDougall for a record of this screen and another screen (with fewer visual and more textual artifacts) of mementos from Europe.
113. McWilliams, 217. McWilliams analyzes *Home as Found* in terms of this loss of power and Cooper's resistance to shifting class lines and the changing basis of wealth, 216–37.
114. Nevius, 61–2.
115. See McWilliams, chapter 4; on Sedgwick, see Kelley, "Negotiating a Self," 392–3.
116. Cooper, *American Democrat*, 110–14.
117. Pudaloff, 278.
118. Cooper is aware of the function of the two forms of what Anderson called "the technical means for 're-presenting' the *kind* of imagined community that is the nation" – the press and the novel – in shaping the national consciousness of the citizen (25).
119. McWilliams, 222–7, 232.
120. Cooper, *Home as Found*, 113–14.
121. McWilliams, 235.
122. Vance, I, 94.
123. L. Mulvey, 19.
124. See Bjelajac's description of the New England clerisy's attempt to control social change through art and other institutions in *Millennial Desire*, 148. This attempt is similar to the American Tract Society's (and other benevolent and evangelical groups') flooding of the nation with illustrated tracts throughout this period; as Morgan demonstrates, the ATS discovered the mass-produced image as a "new moral technology" that could enhance the "Protestant apparatus of conversion." His finding that the "mass-produced images of the benevolent associations" were meant to shape not only the "'other'" – i.e. "the immigrant, the urban worker, and the poor" – but also the middle-class self is related to my argument that the visual experience of Italy (either through tourism or through consuming images and travel writing in U.S. print culture) was meant both to shape the self and to manage such others: "every effort at influence was directed inwardly as well as outwardly" (5, 108).
125. I discuss all these forms except for children's literature elsewhere in this book. For examples of juvenile works, see Barbara H. Channing's *The Sisters Abroad; or, An Italian Journey* (1857) or one of Samuel G. Goodrich's Peter Parley books: *The Travels, Voyages, and Adventures of Gilbert Go-Ahead: In Foreign Parts* (1856). See also Eckel's discussion of Grace Greenwood's inclusion of European travel accounts in her children's magazine *The Little Pilgrim* (1853–68) (129).
126. But see Eckel's reading of Longfellow's tour as a preparation for a much less conservative, even "radical," program of promoting "multilingual learning to a wider audience" at home; she argues that this is part of Longfellow's effort to reinvent the university in the U.S.

along the lines of German universities: "the work of the professor in an open, European-style university is a form of inherently progressive political action that has larger implications for a nation's cultural development" (28).

Chapter 3

1. Kirkland, *Holidays Abroad*, I, 195.
2. Eagleton, 59.
3. Kelley, "Introduction," *Power of Her Sympathy*, 32.
4. For discussions of American, English, and German women tourists and their writings, see Schriber, Gilbert, Elsden, K. Siegel, Frawley, and Felden.
5. Armstrong, 8.
6. Sommer, 6. See also her chapter on Cooper and Sarmiento (52–82).
7. Berlant, 28.
8. Zwarg, 125.
9. See Mills for a similar discussion of later nineteenth-century British women travel writers, "pulled . . . in different textual directions" by the "discourses of imperialism and femininity," a "textual unease" apparent in their texts (3). Homestead defines a perhaps related strategy for women of navigating literary property issues; Sedgwick's republican model of authorship, located between the gender-inflected modes of "commercially interested proprietary authorship and authorial oblivion," "powerfully positioned" her in the marketplace (69).
10. Kelley, "Introduction", *Hope Leslie*, 11; Damon-Bach and Clements, xxiii–xxv.
11. Susan Williams ("Authors and Literary Authorship," 111) explains that "depictions of women authors" in this period "were part of a larger national project of defining and civilizing the new nation, especially through normative depictions of white womanhood." See her discussion of an engraving in *Graham's Magazine*, in 1843, that "subsumes" portraits of women writers including Sedgwick "into the nationalist iconography of the whole."
12. Belasco, 269, 261.
13. Lupfer, 253. See Lupfer on the growth and practices of such magazines, and of their courting of U.S. authors.
14. Capper, *Margaret Fuller: An American Romantic Life*, II, 196.
15. In addition to C. Mitchell, and Bean and Myerson's introduction to Fuller's *Tribune* writings (*Fuller, Critic*), see Nerone's discussion of the *Tribune* in the context of mid-century newspaper publishing in the U.S. (233, 238).
16. Bohls, 3, 19. See also Fish's definition of women's "mobile subjectivity" – "a fluid and provisional . . . subject position" – in women's texts that combine travel and work (6).

17. Gilbert, 196.
18. Elsden, x–xi.
19. E. Ann Kaplan, 3, 9. In her book on film, Kaplan differentiates between the gaze and look, which, she argues, characterizes reciprocal relations rather than the dominance associated with the gaze.
20. Cherry, 114.
21. G. Pollock contrasts women's domestic gazes with the masculine, urban gaze of the flaneur. In her study of Victorian women painters, Cherry adds the "philanthropic" and "metropolitan" gazes to Pollock's analysis (118). Ryan finds that the emerging construction of middle-class women as consumers in the mid-century U.S. gave women access to urban areas increasingly set aside as shopping districts, districts which solicited women's looks (76–7).
22. Kasson, *Marble Queens*, 38–9, 69–72.
23. Cherry, 115–16. Urry makes a similar point when he emphasizes that "There is no single tourist gaze as such. It varies by society, by social group and by historical period" (1).
24. See Kelley, *Private Woman, Public Stage*, for the classic discussion of women writers moving across public and private lines; for more recent critiques and reassessments of scholars' reliance on the "separate spheres" model of analyzing gender practices in the nineteenth century, see Davidson's special issue of *American Literature*, "No More Separate Spheres!," and Elbert's *Separate Spheres No More*.
25. Ryan, 86–7. For a related reading, see D. E. Nord on Victorian urban women writers' "split identifications" (12).
26. Elsden, xiv.
27. Ryan, 82–3. See Bruce Mills's "Introduction" to Child's *Letters from New-York* and Karcher (299, 302–5) on Child's urban excursions.
28. Sedgwick, *Letters from Abroad*, II, 126, 296–7. Subsequent references appear in the text.
29. Kirkland, *Holidays Abroad*, vi. Subsequent references appear in the text.
30. Fuller, *"These Sad But Glorious Days"*, 135–6.
31. See Buzard on Italy as feminized – cast as seductive woman – in English and American male tourist writing (132–9); Churchill on the pattern of attraction and disappointment, "enervation" and even death, in English and American literary treatments of Italy (3, 23, 58, 159); and J. Siegel on the genre linked to this pattern: the "art romance."
32. The name, "Murray," may be a joke about her character's degree of immersion in tourism; John Murray of London published a popular series of guidebooks, a series the Sedgwicks used and to which Sedgwick refers in her travel book.
33. Sedgwick, "Incident at Rome," 104–8. Subsequent references are cited parenthetically in the text. At this point *Graham's* was called *Graham's Lady's and Gentleman's Magazine*. Periodical names fluctuated.

34. See Urry for a discussion of "the tourist gaze," a "socially organized" gaze "constructed through difference" that reinforces the normative identities of tourists (1–2).
35. Buzard, 134.
36. Gilman, 23.
37. In discussing the ideological relationship between word and image in the nineteenth century, I draw on Gilman's "Interart Studies" and Mitchell's historical discussion of this relationship in aesthetic theory in *Iconology*.
38. Bohls, 16.
39. N. Harris, 146–8.
40. A. Kaplan has argued for "the relationship of domesticity to nationalism and imperialism" (582) in antebellum culture. See her article for readings which illustrate the mutual reinforcement of the "separate spheres" in these projects.
41. Franchot, 19. Periodicals also juxtaposed U.S. frontier and Italian sites; see the inclusion of the poems "The Last of His Race" (on the suicide of a "warrior chief") and "Decay and Rome" on the same page of *Graham's* (April 1848, 220).
42. Titles indicating this double focus include: Irving's *The Sketch Book* (1819–20) and *A Tour on the Prairies* (1835); Cooper's Leatherstocking novels and his series of travel books, *Gleanings in Europe* (1836–8); Kirkland's *A New Home, Who'll Follow? or, Glimpses of Western Life* (1839) and *Holidays Abroad; or, Europe from the West* (1849); Hawthorne's *The Scarlet Letter* (1850) and *The Marble Faun* (1860); Fuller's *Summer on the Lakes* (1844) and her dispatches from Europe to the *New-York Tribune* (1846–50); Greenwood's *A Forest Tragedy; or, The Oneida Sisters* (1855) and *Haps and Mishaps of a Tour in Europe* (1854).
43. See Fetterley's analysis of race, "Republican sisterhood," and brotherhood in *Hope Leslie*.
44. See Chielens's discussion of the reputation and popularity of *Graham's* in the 1840s (157).
45. Sedgwick quotes here from Wordsworth's *The Excursion*, Book Fourth, ll. 735–7.
46. Mellor, 156–66; Kelley, "Introduction," *Power of Her Sympathy*, 26–7.
47. Kelley, "Introduction," *Power of Her Sympathy*, 32.
48. Melissa Homestead has, in conversation, pointed out Sedgwick's allusions to Staël's novel *Corinne* (1807), influential for tourists (W. Stowe, 14), in Sedgwick's novel *Clarence* (1830). Sedgwick tends to identify Staël and her heroine, an *improvisatrice*, with the socially disruptive egotism of another female character and to characterize her own heroine, Gertrude Clarence, as facilitating, by contrast, male aesthetic response in cultivated conversations, much as Sedgwick defines the feminine role in her letter to Charles. But the novel may also suggest,

more surreptitiously, parallels between Gertrude and Corinne in their capacity for connoisseurship.

49. I am thinking here of E. Sedgwick's classic discussion of women as the medium of exchange between men in the formation of homosocial bonds and the maintenance of patriarchal power.

50. Kelley, "Introduction," *Power of Her Sympathy*, 17–18, 24–31.

51. Avallone illuminates Sedgwick's participation in the inter-gender nineteenth-century conventions of cultural discussions, in "Catharine Sedgwick and the 'Art' of Conversation."

52. Elsden discusses Sedgwick's feminist commentary on European women's positions (16–19).

53. Gemme, 110.

54. See, for example, her description of meetings with Milanese contacts: *Letters from Abroad*, II, 31–68.

55. I draw here on E. Ann Kaplan's discussion of "looking relations," shaped by gender, race, and national identity, in films about travel. But see also Damon-Bach on Sedgwick's description of her visits to literary women in Britain, earlier in her travel book, where she recounts meeting Mary Russell Mitford and Joanna Baillie, and where she – interestingly, as Damon-Bach demonstrates – recounts excursions with Anna Jameson, whose name she omits in an effort to ensure Jameson's privacy ("Sedgwick Tours England," 32–9).

56. See L. Reynolds, *European Revolutions*, and Gemme for U.S. responses to the Risorgimento, and Vance for a reading of Sedgwick's responses to the social inequalities of Rome (II, 116–17, 169–70).

57. Sedgwick extrapolates a national masculine political agency from the example of the Italian revolutionaries imprisoned by the Austrians following a failed 1821 revolt: "I wish that those who ignorantly think lightly and speak disparagingly of 'Italians' could know these men. . . . We honour our fathers for the few years of difficulty through which they struggled; and can we refuse our homage to these men, who sacrificed everything . . . that man holds most dear, to the sacred cause of freedom and truth? and let me ask, what should we in reason infer of the nation whence they came? surely that there are many ready 'to go and do likewise'" (*Letters from Abroad*, II, 31–2).

58. See Schriber for a discussion of the relationships of separation and identification, "difference and doubling," in U.S. women's travel narratives between the narrators and the women they see in other countries (81–9).

59. See Addison's *Remarks on Italy* (1705), Goethe's *Italienische Reise* (1829), and James's *Italian Hours* (1909).

60. As in the writings of most American tourists (W. Stowe, 13), another English poet, Byron (especially *Childe Harold*), was Sedgwick's frequent touchstone in her responses to Italy.

61. Johns, 8–10, 83–4.

62. Franchot discusses a "Protestant gaze on Rome, a gaze that . . . celebrated Catholicism as a spectacle, and fantasized the consumption of this foreign substance rather than conversion to it" (234).

63. Vance, I, 94.

64. On the anti-Jacksonian leanings of many of Cole's Whig patrons, see A. Miller, 21–39; Stansell and Wilentz, 18–19; and Wallach, "Thomas Cole," 67, 70, 94.

65. See Chambers on the significance of medieval ruins in Cole's Italian compositions.

66. As Wallach points out ("Thomas Cole," 38), the patron, Luman Reed, who commissioned *Italian Scene* from Cole was a "self-made m[a]n," a merchant whose "art collection was his entrée to a higher level of respectability." Parry also discusses this painting (136–8).

67. A. Miller, 148, 150.

68. See the discussion of *Mount Etna* in Chapter 2.

69. Wallach has discussed the ways in which Cole's American landscape paintings, when viewed as a group and in the context of his series *The Course of Empire*, are situated along a timeline of national history and can often "be read as episodes or fragments of a mythic-historical narrative" ("Thomas Cole," 64).

70. Thanks to Mary Rhiel and Rachel Trubowitz for this point.

71. Mills, 106.

72. Elsden also discusses this episode (19–20).

73. L. Reynolds documents American response to the revolutions of 1848 in periodicals and by canonical writers; see his summary of the first outpouring of support and of the belief that these revolutions followed in the tradition of the American Revolution (*European Revolutions*, 10–14). One of his quotations emphasizes the American support for the iconoclastic aspect of the French revolution; as Thomas Buchanan Read wrote, "the people" seize the monarchical throne, "dash it to earth, and trample it down, / Shivered to dust, with the Orleans crown."

74. Warner, 120.

75. L. Reynolds, "American Cultural Iconography," 385–7. Antebellum culture produced both public icons (see Abrams, and Greenhouse, "Imperiled Ideals," on the murals commissioned for the Capitol Building) and private forms of consuming collective fantasies of nationhood, such as tourism and fiction (see Warner, following Anderson, on the shift toward a more fully "imagined community" in early nineteenth-century novels).

76. Osborne describes Kirkland's editing of and contributions to the *Union* (87–107). As Fink notes, "antebellum magazines" participated in "the project of universal education, in building informed and virtuous citizens of the republic, . . . [and] in cultivating the tastes of an emerging middle class" (214).

77. Lehuu examines, for example, the mutual constitution of the middle-class female subject and the public sphere of print in her study of illustrations and fashion plates in the antebellum periodical *Godey's Lady's Book*.

78. Leverenz refers to "authorship as a feminized profession" (14) in his discussion of the ways in which tensions between patrician and Jacksonian masculinities shaped men's writings. I also draw here on Douglas. Okker makes a similar point about the ways in which women periodical editors used the rhetoric of separate spheres (even as their practice belied it) to claim belles-lettres as their province; she quotes one editor, Ann Stephens: "'poetry, fiction, and the lighter branches of the sciences are woman's appropriate sphere, as much as the flower-garden, the drawing-room, and the nursery'" (18).

79. Osborne, 88–9.

80. Zagarell, xxi.

81. See A. Kaplan for an overview of "separate spheres" scholarship and connections between antebellum women's cultural work and U.S. national expansion. In referring to women as "emblems," I quote Schriber, who argues that even as travel and travel writing became increasingly common practices for women in the nineteenth century, women's cultural status as such icons made them "symbol[s] of the republic" abroad (33–7).

82. Steele, *Transfiguring America*, 114.

83. Franchot, 12, 6.

84. See my discussion in Chapter 2 of Longfellow's typical response to religious art in his sketch book *Outre-Mer*.

85. Vance, I, 207–10.

86. Halttunen, 57–60.

87. Kirkland prefers the American sculptor Hiram Powers' *Greek Slave* (1844) (I, 204, 235). See Kasson on mid-century audience responses to ideal sculpture (*Marble Queens*, 21–45) and especially to *The Greek Slave* (46–72).

88. Zagarell, xix–xx.

89. Zagarell, xxi; Osborne, 91, 104.

90. Schriber, 23–4.

91. Bellows was an influential Unitarian clergyman in New York and a frequent spokesperson on issues of social reform and education; he published and at times edited the *Christian Inquirer*, a periodical he asked first William Kirkland and then, at William's death, Caroline Kirkland to edit until her assumption of the editorship of the *Union*. See Eliot, "Henry Whitney Bellows"; Osborne, 87; Zagarell, xx–xxi; and Roberts.

92. As Lawrence says, travel elicited "questions concerning women as both subjectivities and semiotic signs" (156).

93. U.S. tourist accounts emphasized other nationally motivated stereotypes of elite Italian women, in contrast with American women; Jarves is typical in commenting on their supposed "immoral" nature in taking a lover after an arranged marriage (126–7).
94. See Jenkins for a somewhat different approach to the problem of women travelers gazing at "other" women.
95. For accounts of Rachel's associations with all three forms of government in France during her life (monarchy, republic, empire), of her appeal for both reactionaries and a popular and republican audience, of her performances of the Marseillaise, and of her later tour of the U.S., see Brownstein's biography and Stokes.
96. Brownstein, 172–7.
97. Brownstein, 174, 181, 189–91.
98. See Ryan and G. Pollock for the urban elite assumptions that associated the direct gaze with lower-class, sexually available, or even threatening women; they argue that the modern city, both New York and Paris, became a territory defined by the flaneur, whose commodifying and erotic gaze created what Ryan calls a "gender geography" (68) in which "woman" figures as a principal object, a "sign" which consolidated the identity of bourgeois male citizens (G. Pollock, 67, 71).
99. G. Pollock, 69.
100. Wallach, "Making a Picture," 84; Crary, 19.
101. W. J. T. Mitchell, *Iconology*, 193–205.
102. K. Siegel also finds that women's "presenting themselves as subjects" in public resulted in "textual turbulence" in their travel writing (5).
103. W. Stowe, 27.
104. Buzard, 115–18.
105. Byron, 237.
106. W. J. T. Mitchell, *Landscape and Power*, 7.
107. Crary, 136.
108. Wallach, "Making a Picture," 83–4; see Chapter 1 for a discussion of the term "panoptic sublime." For an example of a prospect view that reveals the continuity between eighteenth- and nineteenth-century prospect viewing, see Greene's "Letters from Rome: Letter First," whose first line – "The first view of Rome should be taken from the tower of the Capitol" – is followed by a comprehensive survey.
109. Crary, 16.
110. Berlant, 24.
111. For a reading of Kirkland's insights into the political situation in Rome in the spring of 1848 and for her mixed assessment of the Pope, as well as for a summary of the historical moment in Rome, see Vance (II, 122–5).
112. For a sequence of events and documents of the Second Republic, see Price.

113. Gemme, on the other hand, reads the boys' figures as standard representations of a politically infantilized, irrational Italy (46–9). Manoguerra also reads the use of boyish figures as representing Italy's condition of tutelage in the ways of democracy ("This Cause Is Ours," 45–6). While this approach makes sense, I think that the U.S. connotations of newsboys together with the denial of vista in the scene pull its implications in a different direction.
114. Johns, 190–3.
115. Stebbins notes that Heade, a landscape and botanical artist, painted only two genre scenes in his career, both products of his stay in Italy: the now-lost *The Goat-Herd* (1850), which may have been a standard genre image, given its title, and the innovative *Roman Newsboys* ("Martin Johnson Heade," 201).
116. Manoguerra, "This Cause Is Ours," 44; Vance, II, 124, 126; Stebbins, "Martin Johnson Heade," 201.
117. Stebbins says that the shadow on the left indicates a buyer's approach ("Martin Johnson Heade," 201). But Manoguerra notes the "broad hat" of the shadow and argues persuasively that it marks the Jesuit threat to the revolution, from Protestant and *Il Don Pirlone*'s perspectives ("This Cause Is Ours," 46).
118. Stebbins, "Martin Johnson Heade," 201.
119. Vance, II, 126.
120. Ferguson, 8, 12–13, 37.
121. L. Reynolds, *European Revolutions*, 23.

Chapter 4

1. Fuller, *"These Sad But Glorious Days"*, 256–7. Subsequent references are cited in the text.
2. Capper, "Getting from Here to There," 9; see Eckel on Fuller's sense of the relationship between the transnational pursuit of democracy and "journalism's role in the unceasing effort of building a nation" (50).
3. Zwarg, 125, 175–7.
4. See also A. Taylor on Fuller's "strategy of dialogic encounter" (116) in her European dispatches.
5. Steele, *Transfiguring America*, 3–11.
6. Capper, *Margaret Fuller: An American Romantic Life* II, 196.
7. A. Taylor, 123, 118. The array of discourses in antebellum newspapers is related, I think, to McGill's argument about the period's "culture of reprinting": that a "republican understanding of print culture as public property" – which encouraged the uncompensated reprinting of British and U.S. texts and held international copyright agreements at bay – saw the "decentralization of the literary marketplace"

as supporting "democratic institutions" through the dissemination of knowledge (14, 3).

8. Avallone, "Margaret Fuller and 'the best living prose writer,' George Sand."

9. T. Mitchell, 220–55.

10. A number of biographers and literary critics have discussed these final years in her life, as well as the lost manuscript. Biographers who treat this period and the manuscript include: von Mehren, *Minerva and the Muse*, 230–339; Capper, *Margaret Fuller*, II, 320–497; Murray, 306–404; Marshall, *Margaret Fuller*, 288–371; Matteson, 333–413. See Capper for the political and historical stages of the European and Italian revolutions of 1847–9, as Fuller experienced them, and for an assessment of her lost manuscript.

11. Capper, *Margaret Fuller*, II, 346–50, 365–7, 395–401, 438. For research supporting the evidence of Fuller's marriage, see von Mehren, "Establishing the Facts on the Ossoli Family." See Murray (359–62) for an opposing argument.

12. Mellow, 425–515; Wineapple, 271–316.

13. P. Cole, "The Nineteenth-Century Women's Rights Movement"; L. Reynolds, *Righteous Violence*, 38–55.

14. Byer, 163. Susan Williams, "Manufacturing Intellectual Equipment," 118.

15. See, for example, Levin; Dekker, *American Historical Romance*; A. Miller.

16. See, for example, L. Reynolds and Smith, "Introduction," in Fuller, *"These Sad But Glorious Days"*, 164, 230, 320; see also Bean and Myerson, "Introduction," in *Margaret Fuller, Critic*, on Fuller's recognition of her work at the *Tribune* as "shaping" "national political programs" (xv). See her New Year's Day letter to the *Tribune* on 1 January 1846, on the eve of the Mexican War and before her European sojourn. Here she attempts to recall Americans from their immersion in money-getting to the ideals of the Revolution; she notes the ominous facts of slavery, the annexation of Texas, and oppression in Europe, but she prophesies that there is "a great time" coming, that it will be characterized by "Democracy," and that "Our country will play a ruling part" (*Margaret Fuller, Critic*, 332). L. Reynolds, in *European Revolutions and the American Literary Renaissance*, discusses the "prophetic" voice she increasingly assumed in the Roman dispatches, where she predicts future, successful revolutions even as the European ones fail in 1848–9 (64, 72). Fuller uses the prophetic voice to attempt to call nations into being or, as in the case of the U.S., into fuller being. Gemme reads Fuller's dispatches as jeremiads, critiques whose purpose is to recall citizens to the U.S.'s "original promise" and which thus affirm "American republican exceptionalism" (91).

17. Fuller, "Peale's *Court of Death*," in *Margaret Fuller, Critic*, 295–7. In her review of Allston, Fuller says that his "genius" is not in "the

grand historical style" but in the province of "the Beautiful" (Fuller, "A Record of Impressions," in *Papers on Literature and Art*, 115). For an introduction to the genre of history painting, see Mitnick.

18. As Anderson famously argued, the newspaper, consumed by citizens daily in a "mass ceremony," became a crucial instrument for creating and verifying the "imagined community" of the modern nation (35–6).

19. Berthold, *American Risorgimento*, 45. For another account of the response of the U.S. press to the 1848 revolutions in Europe, see L. Reynolds, *European Revolutions*, 1–24. Reynolds and Smith describe the enthusiastic support of the American public in their "Introduction" to *"These Sad But Glorious Days"*, 1. My own survey of periodicals in this period supports their findings.

20. The *Tribune* habitually ran travel letters (together with book reviews, occasionally fiction, and notices of the arts) on its front page and did not separate "cultural" and political news, as papers would do later. Fuller's letters from Europe, even before they became a strictly political account of events in Italy, usually appeared on the first page (see Reynolds and Smith's notes to individual dispatches). The *Tribune* also ran Taylor's travel letters from California on p. 1; see issues in late 1849 and early 1850. The *Tribune* included very few illustrations in this period.

21. Tuckerman, *Italian Sketch Book*, 3rd edn, 16. See also the first edition of *Italian Sketch Book*, "By an American".

22. Bean and Myerson, "Introduction," in *Margaret Fuller, Critic*, xxiv–xxv; Capper, *Margaret Fuller*, II, 215, 236. As Steele argues, the editor of the *Democratic Review*, John O'Sullivan, and Fuller shared the conviction that "mass-market publications like the *Democratic Review* and the *New-York Tribune* would play a major role in shaping the national imaginary" (*Transfiguring America*, 249). The *Democratic Review* reprinted Fuller's final dispatches to the *Tribune*.

23. Laura Jehn Menides and Bruce I. Weiner describe the combination of party politics and literary ambitions in the *Whig Review* and the *Democratic Review* as well as their adversarial relationship (in Chielens, 29–34, 425–32).

24. Marvel, 456; Casali, 449. For the antebellum "tradition of bachelor fiction" (139) in which Marvel worked in his best-known book, *Reveries of a Bachelor* (1850), see d'Amore; this persona is similar to the one he employs in his travel sketches. For Casali's career as a journalist in New York, see Ridinger.

25. Anon., "Arts and Artists in America," 658–63.

26. Anon., "Revolutionary Secret Societies of Modern Italy," 260–76; [William Gillespie], "A Day in Pisa," 112–15.

27. Gemme, 13, 17, 35.

28. Zwarg, 211–15.

29. Johns, xi–23, 82–9.

30. Greenhouse, "Landing of the Fathers." Other analyses of mid-century history painting include: Abrams; Husch; Truettner; Gerdts and Thistlethwaite; B. Gaehtgens; and Groseclose, "American Genesis."

31. See Levin. Reynolds and Smith, "Introduction," in Fuller, *"These Sad But Glorious Days"*, 27.

32. Some art historians, such as Greenhouse, also discuss a blurring of the boundaries between history and genre painting, especially in genre scenes from the lives of the Founding Fathers. In this case, genre painting served to "humanize" such figures as Washington and to represent them as typifying the national character (Greenhouse, "Landing of the Fathers," 58). However, this other use of genre did not enter into U.S. depictions of Italy, and I find the distinctions between these two modes most useful for studying the American gaze abroad.

33. In the other form of painting they used in depicting Italy – landscape – U.S. artists, as I noted in Chapter 2, favored serene pastoral compositions populated sparsely with such timeless rural and religious figures as goatherds, peasant women, and monks. As Fuller's dispatches focus on urban Rome and the crowds and central actors of the Roman Revolution, she is less concerned with negotiating the conventions of landscape than with examining those of genre and history painting.

34. For connections between portraiture and history paintings of contemporary events, see Voss.

35. For an exception, see L. Reynolds's inclusion of illustrations of Garibaldi and one battle from the *Illustrated London News* (*European Revolutions*, 70, 73).

36. A. Kaplan, 582.

37. In *Godey's Lady's Book*, for example, Italy is a frequent subject for fiction, poetry, travel notes, and illustrations throughout the 1840s. This frequency drops off in the early 1850s; by the second half of the decade, Italy almost disappears from the pages of *Godey's*.

38. Lee, 375–6.

39. I take the concept of the culturally designated "bearer" of the social gaze from L. Mulvey.

40. Gemme, 60.

41. Buonomo, 15. Buonomo says that redemptive ethnography assumes that "'what matters'" in the other culture is its past, which needs to be saved on paper; the representing viewer is not invested in its present or future.

42. Anon., "The Italian Peasant Boy," 229.

43. Anon., "Modern Rome," 297; modern Rome is defined, characteristically for the period, architecturally as Renaissance and baroque and socially as consisting of a "very mixed race" that possesses "little of the ancient Roman blood," is superstitious, and reveals "a picture of distressing immorality." George H. [*sic*] Curtis, 22–6; E. Pollock, 52–4. The Curtis of the second piece may be George W. Curtis, a friend of

Fuller's who was in Italy at the same time; see von Mehren, *Minerva and the Muse*, 269, 322. Other examples include the artist Christopher Cranch's "Ode to Southern Italy," which depicts Italy's "enchanted sleep" and asks this "land of golden light" to "Shake off the unmanly trance / Of slavish ignorance" (*Putnam's Magazine*, July 1853, 23–4); the poem is published anonymously, but Soria identifies the author as Cranch, who traveled and painted in Italy in the late 1840s (97).

44. For a discussion of Morse's painting and the "popular" nature of this subject for American artists, see Ricci, "Morse." For Kensett, see Coffey, 84; for an account of Kensett's European sojourn in the 1840s, in association with other American painters, see Simon.

45. Carlton was a genre painter active in Boston in the 1840s and 1850s; see Groce and Wallace, 110. *Italian Scene* hangs in the National Museum of American Art in Washington. Thomas Hicks, one of Fuller's friends in Rome, painted a similar scene: *Fountain a la Palestrina* (1850). See Ricci, "Hicks."

46. In her analysis of this scene, Ellison argues that Fuller, worried about the similarity of her responses to those of conventional tourists, differentiates between her own and others' responses by emphasizing the "interdependence of political spectacle, sympathetic witness, aesthetic sensation, and ideological understanding"; "For Fuller, aesthetic pleasure has to be earned by the ability to read correctly the power relations represented in the scene before her" (292–3). See also Chevigny, "To the Edges of Ideology," 191.

47. Mena Marqués.

48. For a discussion of Hunt's interest in Rienzi, see Landow, 22–5; Landow notes that the painting was inspired by Edward Bulwer-Lytton's historical novel *Rienzi* (1835), a novel that also inspired Richard Wagner's opera *Rienzi* (Honour, 175). See also Reynolds and Smith's note on Rienzi in *"These Sad But Glorious Days"*, 257.

49. The artist's blindness is significant because he was probably her close friend Thomas Hicks, as Reynolds and Smith point out (257–8), and her lover, Giovanni Ossoli, belonged to the Civic Guard, although perhaps not a part of the unit attending the proclamation. Her judgment of Hicks, if that is who the artist is, underscores the difficulty of revising her reader's aesthetic responses; as she notes elsewhere, Hicks was "deeply penetrated by the idea of social reform, and especially by the hopes of the Associationists" (*Letters*, IV, 307). Ellison also notes the artist's "failure to see 'soldiers' as 'the people'" (294).

50. See another translation of this proclamation in D. Smith, 162. Other documents Fuller translates include an anonymous revolutionary pamphlet (228–9), Pope Pius IX's letter of excommunication of those participating in Rome's republican government (251–3), and letters between republican leaders and the French besiegers of Rome (295–8). Her work as a translator on behalf of U.S. readers seems to be an

extension of what W. Stowe argues is Fuller's exploitation of "the poly-
vocality of travel writing" (121).

51. Fleischmann, "Cultural Translation as Cultural Critique," 2, and
Zwarg, as quoted in Fleischmann, 7. See also Zwarg (59–96) and Boggs
on the significance of translation for Fuller; as Boggs notes, Fuller, for
whom "cultural identity" was "relational," "practiced translation as a
social ethics" (91–2).

52. Vance, II, 132–5. Capper defines Fuller's understanding of "the people" as including "the masses," in addition to the "artisan, middle-
class, and professional" classes organizing in political clubs (*Margaret
Fuller*, II, 382).

53. L. Reynolds, *European Revolutions*, 76. Thanks also to Larry Reynolds for a conversation in which he elaborated on Fuller's doubts about
the "People." Gemme argues that Fuller's letters home constituted a
"private history" of the revolution and echoed American doubts about
the republican fitness of "the people," while her *Tribune* dispatches
"praised" "Italian liberalism" (99, 97). Fuller's conscious construction
of, for example, Garibaldi's troops as heroic patriots in the description
discussed below is clarified by a previous personal letter, to Ossoli,
where she depicts some of his soldiers as murderous "desperados"
(*Letters*, V, 223).

54. Chevigny, "To the Edges of Ideology," 189, 191.

55. Buonomo notes that Fuller wished for America to regain its Revolutionary politics and to "assume leadership of the international democratic movement" (34).

56. Ellison, 292.

57. Fuller is certainly aware of these conventions. See her *Tribune* letter on
American artists in Rome, where she mentions the difficulty of being
a "historical painter" in the U.S. (266). See also Reynolds and Smith's
introduction, where they discuss Fuller's painterly strategies of writing
history (27–9).

58. L. Reynolds, in *European Revolutions* (72), remarks that Fuller creates such scenes "to endow her material with epic grandeur." See also
Ellison, 294–5.

59. Berthold, "Melville, Garibaldi, and the Medusa of Revolution," 105,
111.

60. Capper, *Margaret Fuller*, II, 456.

61. See Dekker, *American Historical Romance*, for a consideration of
Scott, the historical romance, and nineteenth-century forms of nationalism – and for Scott's influence on American writers. L. Reynolds links
Fuller's evoking of Scott in this passage and in her book on the U.S.
frontier, *Summer on the Lakes* (1844), with such romantic historians
as Bancroft: "Subjective Vision," 4, 9.

62. Greenhouse, "Imperiled Ideals," 263, 275.

63. Fuller, *"These Sad But Glorious Days"*, 132–4.

64. Gerdts, "'Good Tidings,'" 58, 62.
65. Thistlethwaite, "Most Important Themes," 8. The phrase is from Diderot.
66. Gerdts, "Düsseldorf Connection," 154.
67. See Groseclose, *Emanuel Leutze*, 31–8.
68. Burnham and Giese, 11.
69. Douglas argues that Fuller was most interested in writing history (286). In analyzing Fuller's monumentalizing description of Garibaldi's departure from Rome, I emphasize her use of aesthetic conventions to create a coherent Italian nationhood in the U.S. imagination. However, Steele illuminates another, more eruptive, aspect of Fuller's depictions of revolution: her use of "the aesthetics of the sublime," which were characteristic of late eighteenth- and early nineteenth-century "moments of revolutionary upheaval." Fuller's "political sublime" conveys "the awe of democratic political transgression and the exaltation of transcending the limits of individuality through connection to the revolutionary spirit of the people," or to what Mazzini called "'the collective life'" (*Transfiguring America*, 274, 277).
70. L. Reynolds's discussion of U.S. responses to the 1848 revolutions in *European Revolutions* emphasizes the American focus on Paris and Rome. See also Ferguson.
71. Hudspeth, 180.
72. Anderson, *Imagined Communities*. For a characteristic treatment of the relations between literary forms and the nation, see Brennan, who argues that novels were a "practical means of *creating* a people" (50). Warner distinguishes between an earlier role of print culture in elaborating a public sphere and the function of the novel and argues that "although the nation-state was the product of the eighteenth century, the national imaginary was a product of the nineteenth" (120). For a challenge to the Anderson model, see Loughran, who argues that early U.S. print culture was local, regional, and fragmented.
73. E. Jones notes that the Pincian Hill was a "popular" site with "artists, photographers, and other travelers" in the antebellum and post-Civil War periods ("Sanford Robinson Gifford", 230).
74. Hawthorne, *Marble Faun*, 106–7. Subsequent citations appear in parentheses. Page numbers refer to both the Centenary Edition of 1968 and Brodhead's Penguin edition, which is based on the Centenary Edition.
75. During, 142–3.
76. See Machor, 121–2; Scobey.
77. Benjamin's articulation of Baudelaire's figure of the flaneur as the characteristic figure of modernity has informed art-historical accounts and literary criticism of the period. In this section I draw on G. Pollock's discussion of gender and the gaze in nineteenth-century French painting and D. Brand's reading of antebellum American male writers as flaneurs. Historical studies informing my thinking are Ryan's investigation of women

and public space in nineteenth-century U.S. cities and Stansell's study of women in antebellum New York.

78. Bean and Myerson, "Introduction," in *Margaret Fuller, Critic*, xxi–xxii. See also Capper on Fuller's coverage of New York: *Margaret Fuller*, II, 202–13, 256–61.

79. Von Mehren, *Minerva and the Muse*, 218.

80. C. Mitchell, 16–17.

81. These examples are from Mitchell's edition of Fuller's New York journalism. The complete edition of Fuller's journalism in New York is Bean and Myerson's *Margaret Fuller, Critic*.

82. See Klimasmith for a related discussion of the relationship between domestic space and the "networked spaces of the industrial city" in *The Blithedale Romance*, where Hawthorne "imagine[s] what kind of subject might emerge from an urban landscape dominated by hotels, boarding houses, and tenements" (18).

83. C. Mitchell notes that in the mid 1840s, in its early days, the *Tribune* was a relatively small newspaper competing with two other papers for predominance in New York and not the nationally influential paper it became in the 1850s (10, 13).

84. D. Brand, 123. Cain's edition of *Blithedale Romance* incorporates period documents on social reform, utopian communal experiments, and related issues.

85. D. Brand, 124–7. My thinking about *Blithedale* as an urban text has also benefited from Von Rosk and Klimasmith.

86. G. Pollock, 67.

87. Benjamin, 58.

88. Bremer, 30.

89. W. Stowe, 48.

90. Bremer, 13.

91. See Steele, "Reconfiguring 'Public Attention,'" on the ways in which Fuller's New York writings moved beyond the visual conventions of the flaneur to a "demystification of urban spectacle" and drew her readers' "attention" to the ideological "fault-lines fracturing urban society" (127, 125).

92. See von Mehren, *Minerva and the Muse*, 13; Capper, *Margaret Fuller*, I, 10–13.

93. Eckel, 63–4.

94. On the constitution of this subjectivity, see Nelson.

95. See Habermas on the eighteenth-century public sphere.

96. Ferguson, 68–9.

97. See Rigal's chapter 1, "Raising the Roof: Authors, Architects, and Artisans in the Grand Federal Procession of 1788," for a discussion of parades in the early Republic as synecdoches of the new nation.

98. See Gemme on Fuller's dispatches as nationalist jeremiads (92–6).

99. See von Mehren on Fuller's Fourierist friends in New York (*Minerva and the Muse*, 224) and Capper for Fourier's influence on Transcendentalist and reformist circles (*Margaret Fuller*, II, 109, 133–4). For Fourier's influence on Fuller's feminism, see Zwarg (24–8, 52–5) and Steele, *Transfiguring America* (228–31). For discussions of Fuller's engagement with the various socialisms of the 1840s, see Tuchinsky and Fleischmann, "Margaret Fuller's Socialism."

100. Fuller usually sees British interests as reactionary; of the *London Times* she says, "There exists not in Europe a paper more violently opposed to the cause of freedom" (*"These Sad But Glorious Days"*, 294).

101. See Brodhead's "Introduction," in *Marble Faun*, xvii–xviii. Hawthorne, *French and Italian Notebooks*. As Thomas Woodson, the editor of these journals, says, "the romance is pervasively indebted to the notebooks" ("Historical Commentary," *French and Italian Notebooks*, 920).

102. Brodhead, *School of Hawthorne*, 73–5.

103. R. Levine, "'Antebellum Rome' in *The Marble Faun*," 31, 25.

104. Ryan, 61–8, 75.

105. Herbert, 215–72.

106. T. Mitchell, 227.

107. Franchot discusses Hilda's disappearance in terms of the conventions of the American Protestant "convent captivity narrative" (357).

108. Such characters are also staples of the "mysteries of the city" fiction by authors such as George Lippard, who focused their novels on New York and Philadelphia in the 1840s and 1850s. See D. Reynolds, 82–4.

109. Buonomo, 52–3.

110. Child, *Letters from New-York*. See Karcher (299, 302–4); Mills, "Introduction" to Child's *Letters from New-York*; Ryan (82–3), for discussions of Child's urban explorations. For Fern's career, see Kelley, *Private Woman, Public Stage*.

111. Herbert, 215.

112. Barrett Browning, *Aurora Leigh*, ed. Reynolds.

113. Lewis, "Introduction," in *The Education of Fanny Lewald*, xviii; V. R. Jones, 128–33; Ricorda, 107, 116–19.

114. Dabakis, 10. See both Dabakis and Culkin for connections among women writers and artists in Rome.

115. See R. Levine on the carnivalesque energies released by these figures and then suppressed ("'Antebellum Rome' in *The Marble Faun*," 29–30).

116. I draw here on W. J. T. Mitchell's discussion of landscape representations as the "'dreamwork' of imperialism," in "Imperial Landscape," *Landscape and Power*, 10.

117. Gollin and Idol describe Hawthorne's response to Hosmer's statue (96).

118. Culkin, 58–60; Dabakis, 134.

119. Dabakis, 132–5, 54. In a related fashion, the anonymous poet of "Zenobia" in the March 1855 *Democratic Review* (219–21) imagines that Zenobia foresees the fall of Rome.
120. Kasson, *Marble Queens*, 151.
121. Dabakis argues that given its political context – the imminent union of Italy in 1860 – and its similarity to an ancient statue of Minerva in the Capitoline Museum, *Zenobia* hinted at support for the Risorgimento, as Minerva signaled a "once powerful Rome" (134–5).
122. L. Reynolds, *European Revolutions*, 74–6. Elbert, in "Striking a Historical Pose," connects antebellum tableaux vivants and Fuller's representations of historical, mythological, and allegorical women in her Boston Conversations for women and in *Woman in the Nineteenth Century*. In addition, like Kirkland, Fuller was fascinated with the tragic actress Rachel's performances in Paris (although she did not see Rachel's later rendition of the Marseillaise); she attended seven or eight performances of this "true genius" (*"These Sad But Glorious Days"*, 104–6).

Chapter 5

1. Hillard, *Relation of the Poet to His Age*, 50.
2. H. Stowe, *Agnes of Sorrento*, 17–18.
3. Hedrick, 232–45. See Kohn et al., xi–xxxi.
4. Both traveled in Europe extensively in the 1850s: Hawthorne as U.S. consul to Liverpool and then as a resident in England and Italy (1853–60) and Stowe as a three-time traveler, in 1853, 1856, and 1859 (Hedrick, 266; Wineapple, 269–327). Wright notes that Stowe wrote "travel letters" for a periodical, letters she reworked in *Agnes* (*American Novelists in Italy*, 90, 92). This chapter has benefitted from two collections of essays on Hawthorne and Stowe abroad: Martin and Person (eds), *Roman Holidays*, and Kohn et al. (eds), *Transatlantic Stowe*.
5. Commentators on the romance as different as Steiner (48–9) and Dryden (xi) generally base their readings of the romance on Frye's association of romance, archetype, and dream. See also Gollin on *The Marble Faun* as a dreamscape (176–94).
6. Steiner, 1, 3, 13, 48, 57, 91. Steiner argues that the romance narrativizes and implicitly analyzes these moments of ekphrasis in poetry; see her discussion of Keats.
7. Hawthorne, *Marble Faun*, introduction by Brodhead, 3. Subsequent citations will appear in the text.
8. Steiner, 55.
9. See M. D. Bell's treatment of writers who found an "affinity" between the romance and the new nation (160–2). The most useful summary of the long history of criticism on the American romance for my purposes

is R. Levine's *Conspiracy and Romance*. See also Thompson and Link's discussion of the romance and its criticism.

10. Geertz, "Thick Description."
11. Samuels, *Romances of the Republic*, 12.
12. Sommer, 6, 35.
13. Sofer, 23–4, 30. Sofer is analyzing Stowe's chapter "Which Treats of Romance," from her novel *The Minister's Wooing*, published serially in the *Atlantic Monthly* in 1858–9. Wright says that *The Minister's Wooing* "is in many ways an early version" of *Agnes* (*American Novelists in Italy*, 101).
14. Dekker, *American Historical Romance*, 73–5, 87. Sommer, 56.
15. M. D. Bell, 162, 172. R. Levine, *Conspiracy and Romance*, 4.
16. Stowe began sending installments of *Agnes* to the *Atlantic* for serialization in January 1861 (Hedrick, 298).
17. On the planning of New York and its implications, see Upton, 8–9.
18. On Washington's design, see Luria, 3–25.
19. On the Capitol Building and its art, see Fryd and Abrams. Vance notes that Twain compared St. Peter's to the Capitol Building, to the advantage of the Capitol (II, 97).
20. *The American Magazine of Useful and Entertaining Knowledge* (Boston, 1836).
21. I refer here back to the art historians who have informed previous chapters' arguments about the nature of, respectively, history painting, genre painting, and landscape painting as modes of representing history, peoples, and territory: Ayres, Johns, and A. Miller.
22. N. Harris, chapters 8, 10, 11; A. Miller, chapter 2.
23. Franchot, 16–17, 234. See also Vance, II, 3–40.
24. See Armstrong on women as representative modern subjects. Anderson, *Imagined Communities*. Samuels, "Introduction," in *Culture of Sentiment*, 4–5; Samuels quotes Stowe's phrase, "feel right," from *Uncle Tom's Cabin*.
25. Given the Hawthornes' association in Rome with expatriate women sculptors, Proctor argues that the romance is "shadowed by the all-too-present absence of the Woman sculptor" (61).
26. See Franchot on the confessional as the site of sexual seduction in the U.S. Protestant imagination (121–6).
27. Franchot, 100.
28. R. Levine argues that for American elites the Catholic Church seemed "an institutional model of hierarchical control during a decade ... that saw an increasing realization of such control in prisons, factories, and plantations," but that its "advocacy of hierarchy, in the context of the European revolutions of 1848–9, smacked of reactionary priest-craft" (*Conspiracy and Romance*, 163). For political analyses of *The Marble Faun*, see R. Levine, "'Antebellum Rome' in *The Marble Faun*," 19–38; Kemp, 209–36.

29. Hillard, *Relation of the Poet to His Age*, 50. See listing on Hillard by "G.H.G." in *Dictionary of American Biography*. For his friendship with Hawthorne, see Wineapple, *passim*.
30. Franchot, 240.
31. Franchot, 235–6. See Gollin and Idol for Hawthorne's responses, in both his journals and the novel, to these and other works of art.
32. Myers, 59.
33. Kemp, 224.
34. Kasson discusses Story's *Cleopatra*, his career, and the statue's depiction and promotion in *The Marble Faun* (*Marble Queens*, 208–17).
35. Hawthorne, *Marble Faun*, 4. I mention Hosmer's *Zenobia* in reference to Miriam at the end of Chapter 4.
36. "G.H.G," listing on Hillard, *Dictionary of American Biography*. For a reading of Hillard's *Six Months in Italy* and a comparison of Hillard with Fuller, whom he knew, see Russo.
37. For an account of the political uses of sentiment and sympathy in the early republic and the antebellum U.S., see Barnes; the quotation is from p. 2. See also Anderson.
38. See Gollin and Idol on his visits to American artists' studios (93–6). As Brodhead notes, Kenyon's studio had also been Antonio Canova's, but Hawthorne experienced it as Lander's (*Marble Faun*, 474 n.1). See Dabakis for the sexual anxiety that marked the expatriate American community's response to Lander (as a single woman artist), and for her interactions with Hawthorne (67–81).
39. Brodhead, *School of Hawthorne*, 73–5.
40. For a reading of Hawthorne's interest in the sketch, see Hamilton, "Hawthorne, Modernity, and the Literary Sketch."
41. See Rodier for connections between these novels.
42. See Greenwald for a reading of the function of Miriam's Jewish identity in the novel. See also Kolich for an analysis of Miriam as the nineteenth-century figure of "the secret Jew," whose family has been coerced into conversion by papal policies and who embodies the period's association of Jews with republicanism and the Risorgimento.
43. D. Reynolds associates Miriam with popular American representations of "dark female stereotypes" (382) and argues that the manikin's "'gesture of tragic despair'" reveals Miriam's "real self" (384).
44. Fryd, 10.
45. Kemp, 219–30.
46. Vance summarizes the scholarly consensus on American political identification with Rome and examines the ways in which tourist encounters with Rome by the intellectual and political elite were shaped by this identification (I, 7–15).
47. See Brodhead's note on Curtius, *Marble Faun*, 478 n.1.
48. On the process of giving *The Marble Faun* a title, see Claude M. Simpson, "Introduction," Centenary Edition of *The Marble Faun*, xxv–xxviii.

49. Still valuable in assessing Longfellow's position as a national "public poet" are Charvat's chapters on Longfellow. For a transatlantic approach, see Eckel on Longfellow.
50. See Baigell for a list of the public figures Healy painted: *Dictionary of American Art*, 160. See Mellow (423) and Wineapple (265) for Hawthorne's sitting for Healy. See Voss for Healy's aspirations as a history painter.
51. E. Jones, "George Peter Alexander Healy", 244–6.
52. Byer, 164–5.
53. See Brodhead's discussion of James T. Fields as the creator of the canon of American literature in the 1850s, which included Hawthorne and Longfellow (*School of Hawthorne*, 56), and his analysis of the paralyzing effect this status may have had on Hawthorne's later career as a writer, a paralysis which, Brodhead argues, is both manifested in and examined in *The Marble Faun* (67–80). I am also struck by the similarity of the reference to "'the Roman arch'" Berthold finds in Melville's lecture on "Statues in Rome" (1857), after his trip to Italy, an architectural form that mirrors the "Roman spirit," which "'support[s] whatever is soundest in societies and states'"; as Berthold argues, Melville infers that "a dividing America . . . sorely needs triumphal arches to validate its faltering republican experiment" and "ponders the function of art in an insecure nation" (*American Risorgimento*, 185).
54. Vance, I, 57.
55. See A. Kaplan.
56. Byer, 164, 169.
57. See Kemp's related argument that the novel is an "unstable national narrative that both worries over the demise of the nation-state – the United States – and endorses the imperial vision that will sustain it" (210).
58. Fuller, *"These Sad But Glorious Days"*, 256–7.
59. But see Fuller's support for "an equestrian statue of Washington" (*"These Sad But Glorious Days"*, 269), as she writes from revolutionary Rome in 1849.
60. Fryd, 62, 65, 68, 86.
61. Kemp, 222.
62. See Person for a discussion of this "traumatic scene" in which Donatello's "polymorphously perverse," "effervescent sexuality is heterosexualized with a vengeance via the triangulation that Miriam's gaze enforces" (119–21).
63. See, for example, Auerbach, 104.
64. Bentley, 901. See Riss for a further comparison of these two racialized images in *The Marble Faun* and in "Chiefly About War Matters."
65. Millington, "Where Is Hawthorne's Rome?," 21.
66. Also shedding light on Kenyon's response is Franchot's discussion of *The Marble Faun* and other Protestant texts as "endow[ing] the Eternal City . . . with an obdurate material excess"; Italy "is not a

'fairy precinct' but the opposite: a region of excessive representation, of gorgeous, decadent, or even morbid representations of the body that clog the romance's efforts to distill . . . them" (352).

67. Franchot, 239.

68. Tellefsen argues that Hilda will also ensure a white citizenry, especially in her repudiation of Miriam, whose character draws on the figure of the tragic mulatta; Hilda "demonstrates the vulnerability of white, Protestant-American identity to the influence of other ethnic, religious, and racial identities" and her "reclaiming of the freedom and integrity of the white Puritan American is based upon *reconciling* with the Catholic Other (represented here by the Church and the Roman law) and *rejecting* the Africanist Other" (464, 459, 471).

69. See Wineapple's quotation of Hawthorne's letter to Henry Bight (334) and her discussion of "Chiefly About War Matters" (349–51). See also R. Levine, "'Antebellum Rome' in *The Marble Faun*," 32.

70. Susan Williams describes the popular practice among American and English tourists of having their copies of *The Marble Faun* rebound with photographs (often fifty to a hundred photos) of the sites and works of art Hawthorne mentions and thus transformed into a "personalized souvenir" ("Manufacturing Intellectual Equipment," 124–8).

71. Hedrick, 266, 292.

72. This Protestant aesthetic approximates what Stowe calls for in *Sunny Memories*, as Sofer says: "'a new school of [American] art, based upon Protestant principles'" (quoted in Sofer, 20).

73. Elsden, 59.

74. Stowe, *Agnes of Sorrento*, 350. Subsequent citations will appear in the text.

75. W. J. T. Mitchell, *Landscape and Power*, 9–10.

76. *George Loring Brown*, 13, 20.

77. Like Brown, Hawthorne is retrospective in his embrace of idealist aesthetics, with its rhetoric of depth and its search for the imagination's transcendence of the mundane. His anonymous review of the first installments of Dickens's *Pictures from Italy*, serialized in 1846 under the title *Traveling Letters, Written on the Road*, reveals his awareness of other approaches to sketching Italy, as he showers a deprecating praise on Dickens's emphasis on "surface" descriptions and the more trivial operations of the "fancy": "nothing from the author's pen . . . has ever surpassed the richly grotesque surface of life which he here flings off to us. There seems to be no intellect employed in this operation – . . . everything being effected by a quick pair of eyes, a sunny fancy, and a most genial heart" (review of Calvert and Dickens, 331).

78. Brown started his career by copying the works of Claude Lorrain, the seventeenth-century painter of the Roman countryside whose works seemed to Americans archetypal visions of Italy, so well that he was called "Claude Brown" (Leavitt and Barry, 11).

79. Coffey, 81.
80. The conservative implications of these conventions of structure and lighting are clear to a number of writers. See Lynch's poem, reprinted in the Associationist paper the *Harbinger*, where she contrasts the "sunset glow" projected by the tourist's gaze ("Italia! . . . Memory's sunset glow / Its radiance o'er thee cast") with the liberating and "future"-oriented light of dawn in the revolutionary year of 1848. Brown's painting captures the oppressive nostalgia of that "sunset glow."
81. Brown executed a series of etchings which played more intimate variations on these motifs, as in the combination of the ruins of history and the genre scene of peasants in the foreground in his *View Near Rome* (1854), in the collection of the Museum of Fine Arts, Boston.
82. See my discussions of Cooper's, Sedgwick's, and Curtis's treatments of this area in Chapters 2, 3, and 4.
83. See Gemme for a description of this historical process (10–11). For a set of maps illustrating "the progress of Italian unification" from July 1859 to October 1860, see D'Agostino, 22.
84. C. Beecher, 36–8. See Morgan, who examines the visual culture emanating from the belief of many evangelicals, including Lyman Beecher (Catharine and Harriet's father), that "the millennium would commence in America" and that it was not "merely the product of divine intervention into history but . . . [a] result of the progressive development of human society led by the [U.S.] republic" (49, 48).
85. Tompkins, 122. Tompkins cites Beecher (143).
86. Gilbert and Gubar discuss such connections, cited by Adams, 5.
87. Steiner, 62–5.
88. Thanks to Rachel Trubowitz for this insight, and for other thoughts that inform this section.
89. See Franchot on the Calvinist and Dantesque inflections of Stowe's description of Francecso's "scorched soliloquies from the pit of the volcano" (254–5).
90. Sofer notes that in both *The Minister's Wooing* and *Agnes of Sorrento* Stowe "attempts to balance her admiration for Italian religious art with her suspicion of Catholicism" (31).
91. Elsden also notes Agnes's association with the Madonna (50). For a discussion of nineteenth-century representations of the Virgin in English and American women's texts, see Adams.
92. G. Smith, 169.
93. Stein, especially chapters 4 to 7. Sofer cites Stein and argues that Stowe drew on "the Ruskin-inspired discussion of the visual arts" to affirm the integration of literary and religious expression and so to resist the emerging "redefinition of literary art as secular and masculine" (25).
94. McLaughlin, 22.
95. For a discussion of Hunt's *Rienzi*, see Harrison, 13–14.
96. Kohn et al., xvi.

97. For an important assessment of the Pre-Raphaelites, see Prettejohn. See Harrison and Newall (3–9) for an overview of the relationship between Ruskin and the P.R.B.
98. Prettejohn, 171, 172.
99. Prettejohn, 61. She analyzes this connection in a discussion of Charles Allston Collins's *Convent Thoughts* (1850–1) (63).
100. See, for example, Harrison and Newall's discussion of Rossetti's sketch *Fra Angelico Painting* (c. 1853), which depicts the artist kneeling as he paints (49).
101. Ferber, "'Determined Realists.'" See Casteras's chapter "The 1857–58 Exhibition of English Art in America" on periodical reviews and audience responses to this exhibition (43–68).
102. Indeed, as Gerdts says, "American Pre-Raphaelite painters, unlike their . . . English counterparts, whose subjects were primarily figurative, specialized in landscape, still life, and the 'nature study'" ("Through a Glass Brightly," 39).
103. Sofer finds that "Stowe's ideas" in *The Minister's Wooing* (1859) "resona[t]e with the writings in *The Crayon* – a magazine devoted to Ruskin's ideas that was published between 1855 and 1861 – and with James Jackson Jarves's *Art-Hints* (1855), the first work of original art criticism by an American" (28).
104. See Prettejohn's discussion of Rossetti's famous painting of the annunciation, *Ecce Ancilla Domini!* (1849–50) (51). Stowe claims an incarnational aesthetic for the writer retelling biblical narratives in her "Introductory Essay" to her brother Charles Beecher's 1849 book *The Incarnation: or, Pictures of the Virgin and her Son*, when she posits an inherent drive of the "faculty of the imagination" to create "some image" in accord with read narratives and argues for the informed writer's ability to transmute the "blank, cold, vague, misty images of an uninstructed mind" into vivid images which are "more like truth" (1323–4). As Hochman says in her introduction to Stowe's essay in the journal *PMLA*, such a writer can "mak[e] elusive realities palpable" (1320).
105. G. Smith, 181. See Prettejohn for a reproduction of Hunt's rendition of Keats's poem in *The Eve of St. Agnes* (1848) (33).
106. Dowling, 21.
107. G. Smith, 173. Greenhouse makes a similar point about Huntington's paintings, which represent the "mutually ameliorating association of Christianity and art, of spiritual and material, linked through the symbolic agency of the ideal female form" ("Huntington and Christian Art," 109–10).
108. In documenting the Pre-Raphaelite engagement with Dante, McLaughlin notes both their preoccupation with his account of Beatrice in *La Vita Nuova* and Dante's status at mid-century as the "bard" of a "unified Italy"; the Victorian figure of Dante blended republican, sexual,

and religious aspirations (34). Dowling discusses the founding decade of the P.R.B., Ruskin's early volumes of *Modern Painters* and defense of the P.R.B., and their influence on such younger New England intellectuals and reformers as Charles Eliot Norton, who came to know Ruskin and Rossetti in the 1850s and translated Dante's *La Vita Nuova* at about the same time that Stowe was writing *Agnes* (13–35).

109. G. Smith emphasizes that Stowe's Italy is a "palimpsest," a "blending of pagan and Christian," where "one cannot erase the substrate" (171–2).

110. Elsden argues that Stowe emphasizes Catholicism's "matrifocal traditions" (60).

111. See Baker (46) on the standard route of the antebellum tour of Italy.

112. On Jarves and Ruskin, see Casteras (25–7) and Stein (especially 124–46; the quotation is on 142).

113. See Morgan on the relationship between images and language in antebellum religious publications: "When left unanchored by words . . . or authoritative texts, images are capable of an autonomy and a polyvalence that alarmed Protestants." In discussing U.S. Protestants' anti-Catholic iconoclasm (some of it violent), Morgan notes their association of Catholic imagery with "idolatry" and adds that "Iconoclasm, literacy, and proselytism bolstered one another. . . . Redemption and idolatry were very much about race and nationhood" (217, 219–20).

114. Jarves comments on the pernicious effects of Catholicism and repressive government on Italian gender formations. Because they are educated in convents and lack "good home educations," women are ignorant, "untidy," and neglect both homes and children; Italian "political history" creates a "general effeminacy and want of energy [in] the male sex" (315).

115. The sixteenth-century basilica of St. Peter's was, of course, not available for Stowe to describe in her late fifteenth-century plot.

116. Sofer, 60; Sofer summarizes this body of nineteenth-century historical scholarship on Savonarola (241). Stein summarizes Jarves's and Norton's association of the peak of Florentine art and faith with Savonarola (143).

117. Jarves defines Savonarola as at once allied to the leaders of the Reformation and different from them in his racially based "enthusiasm" and "ardent temperament": "Had his mind been tempered with the sound reason that guided the German reformers, the energy and courage that was common to both would have made him a Calvin for Italy" (77).

118. See Sheets.

119. W. J. T. Mitchell, *Iconology*, 197.

120. Gatta documents Stowe's denominational shift and, by the mid 1860s, her formal membership in the Episcopal Church, and he traces the aesthetic ramifications in her novels.

121. Stowe quotes Ruskin here: "'the earlier efforts of Giotto and Cimabue are the burning messages of prophecy delivered by the stammering lips of infants'" (284). The unattributed passage is from Ruskin's *Modern Painters*, I, 10.
122. Stowe shared this popular view of Fra Angelico as kneeling as he painted with the Pre-Raphaelites; see note 100, above.
123. The most useful source on spiritualism in the U.S. is Carroll.
124. Hedrick describes Stowe's participation in séances (339, 367, 391).
125. Foreman and Pitts, xxxix; the context is their discussion of Harriet Wilson's post-Civil War career as a lecturer on behalf of spiritualism. See Carroll, 4, for a similar connection between spiritualism and reform.
126. Colbert, 22, 21–3, 23, 26.
127. Jarves, quoted in Colbert, 23.
128. *The Holy Bible*, authorized King James Version (Cleveland and New York: Meridian Books, The World Publishing Co.). Thanks to the Reverend Theodore H. Bailey for help in locating this chapter and verse.
129. Colbert, 28.
130. See Carroll's chapter "Spiritualist Republicanism" in *Spiritualism in Antebellum America*, 35–59.
131. This seems in accord with Alexis de Tocqueville's famous comment that American women, unlike their French counterparts, disappear from society once they are married (II, 212).
132. Rowe, 100–3.
133. Hedrick, 293. Elsden also notes that Sorrento is a "dream space," although she is interested in Stowe's "fantasies of ideal community" (64).
134. Other descriptive passages also include an excess of visual matter, especially descriptions in which Rome itself, the center of decadence, is suffused with floods of light that transfigure it. Stowe embraces P.R.B. theory without embracing its aesthetic of utter clarity of atmosphere and of detail; she's still drawn to Brown et al.'s aesthetic, with its atmospheric veil that acts as a "glorifying medium." As a writer, Stowe draws selectively on various aesthetics and sees no contradiction between them.
135. Beam, 2, 21.
136. Thanks to Sarah Sherman, who suggested I bring these depths together and whose insights enrich this section. As I refer to passages previously quoted in this chapter, I have not supplied page numbers with the quotations in this section.
137. Hawthorne uses the word "abyss" (461) to indicate another mystified gap – the unbridgeable separation between Miriam and Hilda at the end of the romance.

Conclusion

1. Grimké, 273. Thanks to David Watters for suggesting I read her journal.
2. For information on Macpherson and a study of his career and photographs, see Munsterberg.
3. See Susan Williams, "Manufacturing Intellectual Equipment," 124–8.
4. Long, 42.
5. Forten also reads Staël's *Corinne* but is less enthusiastic, perhaps because it is a French translation exercise (275–8).
6. Also see Long on Forten's complex positioning with regard to class.
7. James, "Italy Revisited," *Italian Hours*, 392, 389, 393, 396–7, 411–12.
8. See, for example, Madden. Thanks to Professor Madden for allowing me to read her forthcoming article.
9. See Hawthorne's *American Claimant Manuscripts*, in *Centenary Edition of the Works*, vol. 12.
10. Eckel discusses Greenwood's travel letters to the *National Era* and the *Saturday Evening Post* and their gathering into her successful book *Haps and Mishaps of a Tour in Europe* (128–9, 135–42).

Bibliography

Primary Sources

Addison, Joseph. "The Pleasures of the Imagination." Numbers 411–21 of *The Spectator*, vol. III. Ed. Donald Bond. Oxford: Oxford University Press, 1965. 535–82.

—. *Remarks on Italy*. London, 1718.

—. *Works*, vol. I. Ed. George Washington Greene. New York: Putnam, 1854.

Allston, Washington. *Lectures on Art, and Poems*. Ed. Richard Henry Dana, Jr. New York: Baker and Scribner, 1850.

—. *Monaldi*. Boston: Little and Brown, 1841.

Anon. "Arts and Artists in America." *American Whig Review* (December 1845): 658–63.

—. "The Festa di Pie di Grotta." *Godey's Lady's Book* (January 1841): 1.

—. "The Italian Peasant Boy." *Godey's Lady's Book* (December 1845): 229.

—. "Modern Rome." *Sartain's Union Magazine* (October 1852): 297.

—. "The Revolutionary Secret Societies of Modern Italy." *United States Magazine and Democratic Review* (September 1841): 260–76.

Barrett Browning, Elizabeth. *Aurora Leigh*. Ed. Margaret Reynolds. New York: Norton, 1996.

—. *Casa Guidi Windows*. Ed. Julia Markus. New York: Browning Institute, 1977.

Beecher, Catharine E. *A Treatise on Domestic Economy: For the Use of Young Ladies at Home, and at School*. Boston: Marsh, Capen, Lyon, and Webb, 1841.

Blanchard, Laman. "Florence." *The Amulet*. Ed. S. C. Hall. London: Westley and Davis, 1831. 251–2.

Brown, William Wells. *The American Fugitive in Europe: Sketches of Places and People Abroad*. Boston: Jewett, 1855.

Bryant, William Cullen. *The Picturesque Souvenir: Letters of a Traveller*. New York: Putnam, 1851.

Bryant, W. C., R. C. Sands, and G. C. Verplanck, eds. *The Talisman*. New York: Elam Blass, 1829.

Burke, Edmund. *A Philosophical Enquiry into the Origin of Our Ideas of the Sublime and Beautiful.* Ed. James T. Boulton. Notre Dame: University of Notre Dame Press, 1968.

Byron, George Gordon (Lord). *Poetical Works.* Ed. Frederick Page and John Jump. Oxford: Oxford University Press, 1970.

Casali, G. F. Secchi de. "Italy in 1846." *American Whig Review* 5 (April 1847): 357–70.

Channing, Barbara H. *The Sisters Abroad; or, An Italian Journey.* Boston: Whittemore, Niles, and Hall, 1857.

Child, Lydia Maria. *Letters from New-York.* Ed. Bruce Mills. Athens: University of Georgia Press, 1998.

Cole, Thomas. "Sicilian Scenery and Antiquities: Number Two." *The Collected Essays and Prose Sketches.* Ed. Marshall Tymn. St. Paul: John Colet Press, 1980. 37–50.

Cooper, James Fenimore. *The American Democrat.* Introduction by H. L. Mencken. Indianapolis: Liberty Fund, 1981.

—. *The Bravo.* Ed. Donald A. Ringe. New Haven: College and University Press, 1963.

—. *Gleanings in Europe: England.* Ed. Donald A. Ringe, Kenneth W. Staggs, James P. Elliott, and Robert D. Madison. Albany: State University of New York Press, 1982.

—. *Gleanings in Europe: France.* Ed. Thomas Philbrick and Constance Ayers Denne. Albany: State University of New York Press, 1983.

—. *Gleanings in Europe: Italy.* Ed. John Conron and Constance Ayers Denne. Albany: State University of New York Press, 1981.

—. *Gleanings in Europe: The Rhine.* Ed. Ernst Redekop, Maurice Geracht, and Thomas Philbrick. Albany: State University of New York Press, 1986.

—. *Gleanings in Europe: Switzerland.* Ed. Robert E. Spiller, James F. Beard, Kenneth W. Staggs, and James P. Elliott. Albany: State University of New York Press, 1980.

—. *Home as Found.* Introduction by Lewis Leary. New York: Capricorn Books, 1961.

—. *The Last of the Mohicans.* Introduction by Richard Slotkin. New York: Viking Penguin, 1986.

—. *The Letters and Journals of James Fenimore Cooper*, vols. I–II. Ed. James Franklin Beard. Cambridge, MA: Harvard University Press, 1960–4.

—. *The Wing-and-Wing.* New York: Hurd and Houghton, 1876.

Curtis, George H. [*sic*]. "Southern Italy." *Sartain's Union Magazine* (July 1848): 22–6.

Dickens, Charles. *Pictures from Italy, and American Notes. The Complete Works of Charles Dickens*, vol. XXIV. New York: Society of English and French Literature, n.d.

Dorr, David. *A Colored Man Round the World.* Cleveland, 1858.

Dwight, Timothy. *Greenfield Hill*. In *Early American Poetry*. Ed. Jane Dona-
  hue Eberwein. Madison: University of Wisconsin Press, 1978. 139–89.
Eliot, George. *Romola*. London: J. M. Dent and Sons, 1965.
Emerson, Ralph Waldo. *English Traits*. Ed. Howard Mumford Jones.
  Cambridge, MA: Harvard University Press, 1966.
—. *Journals*, vol. IV. Ed. Alfred R. Ferguson. Cambridge, MA: Harvard
  University Press, 1964.
Fuller, Margaret. *The Letters of Margaret Fuller*, vols. IV–V. Ed. Robert N.
  Hudspeth. Ithaca and London: Cornell University Press, 1987–8.
—. *Margaret Fuller, Critic: Writings from the New-York Tribune, 1844–1846*.
  Ed. Judith Mattson Bean and Joel Myerson. New York: Columbia Univer-
  sity Press, 2000.
—. *Papers on Literature and Art*. London: Wiley and Putnam, 1846.
—. *Summer on the Lakes, in 1843*. Introduction by Susan Belasco Smith.
  Urbana and Chicago: University of Illinois Press, 1991.
—. *"These Sad But Glorious Days": Dispatches from Europe, 1846–1850*.
  Ed. Larry J. Reynolds and Susan Belasco Smith. New Haven: Yale Univer-
  sity Press, 1991.
—. *Woman in the Nineteenth Century*. In *The Essential Margaret Fuller*.
  Ed. Jeffrey Steele. New Brunswick, NJ: Rutgers University Press, 1992.
  243–378.
[Gillespie, William]. "A Day in Pisa." *United States Magazine and Democratic
  Review* (August 1845): 112–15.
Gilpin, William. *Three Essays: On Picturesque Beauty; on Picturesque
  Travel; and on Sketching Landscape*, 2nd edn. Westmead, England:
  Gregg International, 1972.
Goethe, Johann Wolfgang von. *Italian Journey*. Trans. W. H. Auden and
  Elizabeth Mayer. San Francisco: North Point Press, 1982.
—. *Italienische Reise*. Ed. Herbert von Einem and with commentary by
  Peter Sprengel. Munich: Goldmann, 1986.
Greene, George Washington. "Letters from Rome: Letter First." *Knickerbocker*
  (November 1841): 371–4.
Greenwood, Grace [Sara Jane Lippincott]. *A Forest Tragedy; or, The Oneida
  Sisters*. 1855.
—. *Haps and Mishaps of a Tour in Europe*. Boston: Ticknor, Reed, and
  Fields, 1854.
Grimké, Charlotte Forten. *The Journals of Charlotte Forten Grimké*. Ed.
  Brenda Stevenson. New York and Oxford: Oxford University Press,
  1988.
Hawthorne, Nathaniel. *The American Claimant Manuscripts*. In *The
  Centenary Edition of the Works of Nathaniel Hawthorne*, vol. 12.
  Ed. L. Neal Smith, Claude M. Simpson, and Edward H. Davidson.
  Columbus: Ohio State University Press, 1977.
—. *The Blithedale Romance*. Ed. William E. Cain. Boston: Bedford Books,
  1996.

—. *The French and Italian Notebooks*. Ed. Thomas Woodson. Columbus: Ohio State University Press, 1980.

—. *The Marble Faun: Or, The Romance of Monte Beni*. Centenary edition. Ed. William Charvat, Roy Harvey Pearce, Claude M. Simpson, Matthew Bruccoli, Fredson Bowers, and L. Neal Smith. Columbus: Ohio State University Press, 1968.

—. *The Marble Faun: Or, The Romance of Monte Beni*. Introduction by Richard Brodhead. New York: Penguin, 1990.

—. *The Scarlet Letter*. Ed. Rita K. Gollin. Boston: Houghton Mifflin, 2002.

[Hawthorne, Nathaniel]. Review of *Scenes and Thoughts in Europe*, by George H. Calvert, and *Traveling Letters*, by Charles Dickens, *Salem Advertiser* (29 April 1846). Rpt. Randall Stewart, "Hawthorne's Contributions to the *Salem Advertiser*," *American Literature* 5 (1933–4): 330–1.

Hazlitt, William. *Complete Works*, vol. X. Ed. P. P. Howe. London: J. M. Dent and Sons, 1932.

—. "On Going a Journey" (1822). In *Prose of the Romantic Period*. Ed. Carl Woodring. Boston: Houghton Mifflin, 1961. 295–303.

Heine, Heinrich. *Reisebilder*. "Nachwort" by Joseph A. Kruse. Frankfurt: Insel, 1980.

Hillard, George Stillman. *The Political Duties of the Educated Classes: A Discourse Delivered Before the Phi Beta Kappa Society of Amherst College*. Boston: Ticknor and Fields, 1866.

—. *The Relation of the Poet to His Age: A Discourse Delivered Before the Phi Beta Kappa Society of Harvard University*. Boston: Charles C. Little and James Brown, 1843.

—. *Six Months in Italy*, 3rd edn, 2 vols. Boston: Ticknor, Reed, and Fields, 1854.

Howitt, William. "Shrines." *Friendship's Offering*. Philadelphia: Marshall, Williams, and Butler, 1841. 234–41.

Irving, Washington. *The Alhambra*. Ed. William T. Lenehan and Andrew B. Myers. Boston: Twayne, 1983.

—. *History, Tales and Sketches*. New York: Library of America, 1983.

—. *Journal of Washington Irving, 1828*. Ed. Stanley T. Williams. New York: American Book Co., 1937.

—. *Journals and Notebooks*, vol. I, 1803–1806. Ed. Nathalia Wright. Madison: University of Wisconsin Press, 1969.

—. *Letters*, vol. II. Ed. Ralph M. Aderman et al. Boston: Twayne, 1979.

—. *Miscellaneous Writings 1803–1859*. Ed. Wayne R. Kime. Boston: Twayne, 1981.

—. *The Sketch-Book*. Ed. Susan Manning. Oxford: Oxford University Press, 1996.

—. *Tales of a Traveller*. 1st American edn. Philadelphia: H. C. Carey and I. Lea, 1824.

—. *Tales of a Traveller*. Ed. Judith Giblin Haig. Boston: Twayne, 1987.

—. *A Tour on the Prairies*. Introduction by John Francis McDermott. Norman: University of Oklahoma Press, 1956.

James, Henry. *Italian Hours*. In *Collected Travel Writings: The Continent*. Notes by Richard Howard. New York: The Library of America, 1993.

Jameson, Anna. *The Diary of an Ennuyée*. Boston: Ticknor and Fields, 1857.

Jarves, James Jackson. *Italian Sights and Papal Principles, Seen Through American Spectacles*. New York: Harper and Brothers, 1856.

Jefferson, Thomas. *The Life and Selected Writings of Thomas Jefferson*. Ed. Adrienne Koch and William Peden. New York: Random House, 1972.

Kant, Immanuel. *Critique of Judgment*. Trans. J. H. Bernard. London: Hafner Press, 1951.

—. *Kritik der Urteilskraft*. Ed. Heinrich Schmidt. Leipzig: Alfred Kröner, 1925.

[Kemble, Fanny] Mrs. Butler. *A Year of Consolation*. New York: Wiley and Putnam, 1847.

Kirkland, Mrs. [Caroline]. *Holidays Abroad; or Europe from the West*, 2 vols. New York: Baker and Scribner, 1849.

—. *A New Home, Who'll Follow?* Ed. Sandra A. Zagarell. New Brunswick and London: Rutgers University Press, 1990.

Lee, Henry G. "The Italian Flower Girl." *Godey's Lady's Book* (June 1849): 375–6.

Lewald, Fanny. *The Education of Fanny Lewald: An Autobiography*. Trans. and ed. Hanna Ballin Lewis. Albany: State University of New York Press, 1992.

Longfellow, Henry Wadsworth. *Outre-Mer and Drift-Wood*. Introduction by Horace E. Scudder. Boston: Houghton Mifflin, 1886.

Lynch, Anne C. "Day-Dawn in Italy." *Harbinger* (15 January 1848).

Magoon, E. L., et al. *The Home Book of the Picturesque, or, American Scenery, Art, and Literature*. New York: Putnam, 1852.

Marvel, Ik [Donald Grant Mitchell]. "A Glimpse of the Appenines." *American Whig Review* 4 (November 1846): 449–58.

Noble, Louis B. *The Life and Works of Thomas Cole*. Ed. Elliot S. Vesell. Cambridge, MA: Harvard University Press, 1964.

Peale, Rembrandt. *Notes on Italy*. Philadelphia: Carey and Lea, 1831.

Pickering, Henry. "Moonlight. An Italian Scene." *The Atlantic Souvenir*. Philadelphia: Carey, Lea, and Carey, 1828. 210–13.

Pollock, Edward. "Italy." *Sartain's Union Magazine* (January 1852): 52–4.

Radcliffe, Ann. *The Italian, or the Confessional of the Black Penitents: A Romance* (1797). Ed. Frederick Garber. Oxford: Oxford University Press, 1971.

—. *The Mysteries of Udolpho* (1794). Ed. Bonamy Dobrée. Oxford: Oxford University Press, 1970.

Rogers, Samuel. *Italy*. London: Cadell and Moxon, 1830.

Roscoe, Thomas, ed. *The Landscape Annual*. London: Jennings and Chaplin, 1830–3.

Ruskin, John. *Modern Painters*, vol. I. London: Smith, Elder, 1843.

Sand, George. *Lettres d'un Voyageur*. Trans. Sacha Rabinovitch and Patricia Thomson. New York and London: Penguin, 1987.

Sedgwick, Catharine Maria. *Clarence: Or, A Tale of our Own Times*, rev. edn. New York: Putnam, 1852.

—. *Hope Leslie; or, Early Times in the Massachusetts*. Ed. Mary Kelley. New Brunswick, NJ: Rutgers University Press, 1987.

Sedgwick, Miss C. M. "An Incident at Rome." *Graham's Lady's and Gentleman's Magazine* 27 (1845): 104–8.

[Sedgwick, Catharine Maria]. *Letters from Abroad to Kindred at Home*, 2 vols. New York: Harper and Brothers, 1845 [1841].

de Staël, Germaine. *Corinne, or Italy*. Trans. and ed. Avriel H. Goldberger. New Brunswick, NJ: Rutgers University Press, 1987.

—. *Corinne, ou l'Italie*. Ed. Simone Balayé. Paris: Gallimard, 1985.

Stendhal [Marie Henri Beyle]. *Rome, Naples, and Florence*. Trans. Richard N. Coe. London: John Calder, 1959.

—. *Rome, Naples et Florence*. Ed. Pierre Brunel. Paris: Gallimard, 1987.

Story, William Wetmore. *Roba di Roma*, 2 vols. Boston: Houghton, Mifflin, 1889.

Stowe, Harriet Beecher. *Agnes of Sorrento*, 21st edn. Boston: Houghton, Mifflin, n.d.

—. "Introductory Essay." Intro. by Barbara Hochman. *PMLA* 118.5 (2003): 1320–4.

—. *The Minister's Wooing*. In *Uncle Tom's Cabin, or, Life among the Lowly; The Minister's Wooing; Oldtown Folks*. New York: Literary Classics of the United States: Viking, 1982. 521–876.

—. "The Ministration of Our Departed Friends: A New Year's Revery." *The Mayflower, and Miscellaneous Writings*. Boston: Phillips, Sampson, 1855. 197–203.

—. *Sunny Memories of Foreign Lands*. Boston: Phillips, Sampson; New York: J. C. Derby, 1854.

—. *Uncle Tom's Cabin: Authoritative Text, Backgrounds and Contexts, Criticism*, 2nd edn. Ed. Elizabeth Ammons. New York: Norton, 2010.

Taylor, J. Bayard. *Views A-Foot; or, Europe seen with Knapsack and Staff*, rpt of 1848 edn. Philadelphia: David McKay, 1890.

Tocqueville, Alexis de. *Democracy in America*, 2 vols. Trans. Henry Reeve and Francis Bowen, ed. Phillips Bradley. New York: Knopf, 1945.

Tuckerman, Henry T. *The Italian Sketch Book*, 1st edn, "By an American." Philadelphia: Key and Biddle, 1835.

—. *The Italian Sketch Book*, 3rd edn. New York: J. C. Riker, 1848.

Twain, Mark. *The Innocents Abroad*. Afterword by Leslie Fiedler. New York: New American Library, 1980.

Waterman, Catherine H., ed. *Friendship's Offering*. Philadelphia: Marshall, Williams, and Butler, 1841.

Willis, N. P. *Pencillings by the Way*, 2nd edn. London: George Virtue, 1842.

Secondary Sources

Abrams, Ann Uhry. "National Paintings and American Character: Historical Murals in the Capitol Rotunda." In Ayres. 65–79.

Adams, Kimberly VanEsveld. *Our Lady of Victorian Feminism: The Madonna in the Work of Anna Jameson, Margaret Fuller, and George Eliot*. Athens: Ohio University Press, 2001.

Almeida, Joselyn M. *Romanticism and the Anglo-Hispanic Imaginary*. Amsterdam and New York: Rodopi, 2010.

Anderson, Benedict. *Imagined Communities: Reflections on the Origin and Spread of Nationalism*, rev. edn. London: Verso, 1991.

Andrews, Malcolm. *The Search for the Picturesque: Landscape Aesthetics and Tourism in Britain, 1760–1800*. Stanford: Stanford University Press, 1989.

Anthony, David. *Paper Money Men: Commerce, Manhood, and the Sensational Public Sphere in Antebellum America*. Columbus: Ohio State University Press, 2009.

Argersinger, Jana L., and Phyllis Cole, eds. *Toward a Female Genealogy of Transcendentalism*. Athens and London: University of Georgia Press, 2014.

Armstrong, Nancy. *Desire and Domestic Fiction: A Political History of the Novel*. Oxford: Oxford University Press, 1987.

Auerbach, Jonathan. "Executing the Model: Painting, Sculpture, and Romance-Writing in Hawthorne's *The Marble Faun*." *English Literary History* 47 (1980): 103–20.

Avallone, Charlene. "Catharine Sedgwick and the 'Art' of Conversation." In Damon-Bach and Clements. 192–208.

—. "Margaret Fuller and 'the best living prose writer,' George Sand: A Revisionist Account." *Nineteenth-Century Prose* 42.2 (2015): 93–124.

Ayres, William, ed. *Picturing History: American Painting 1770–1930*. New York: Rizzoli, 1993.

Bachelard, Gaston. *The Poetics of Reverie*. Trans. Daniel Russell. Boston: Grossman Publishers, 1969.

Baigell, Matthew. *Dictionary of American Art*. New York: Harper and Row, 1982.

—. *Thomas Cole*. New York: Watson-Guptill Publications, 1981.

Bailey, Brigitte, Katheryn P. Viens, and Conrad Edick Wright, eds. *Margaret Fuller and her Circles*. Durham: University of New Hampshire Press, published in association with the Massachusetts Historical Society, 2013.

Baker, Paul R. *The Fortunate Pilgrims: Americans in Italy, 1800–1860*. Cambridge, MA: Harvard University Press, 1964.

Barnes, Elizabeth. *States of Sympathy: Seduction and Democracy in the American Novel.* New York: Columbia University Press, 1997.

Barrell, John. *The Dark Side of the Landscape: The Rural Poor in English Painting 1730–1840.* Cambridge: Cambridge University Press, 1998.

Bate, W. J. *From Classic to Romantic: Premises of Taste in Eighteenth-Century England.* New York: Harper and Row, 1961.

Batten, Charles L. *Pleasurable Instruction: Form and Convention in Eighteenth-Century Travel Literature.* Berkeley: University of California Press, 1978.

Beam, Dorri. *Style, Gender, and Fantasy in Nineteenth-Century American Women's Writing.* Cambridge: Cambridge University Press, 2010.

Becker, Robert. "Fenimore Cooper in Sorrento: Tasso's House; Experiences Today." *The James Fenimore Cooper Society Newsletter* 25.3 (2014): 1, 5–7.

Belasco, Susan. "The Cultural Work of National Magazines." In Casper et al. 258–70.

Bell, Michael Davitt. *The Development of American Romance: The Sacrifice of Relation.* Chicago: Chicago University Press, 1980.

Bell, Millicent, ed. *Hawthorne and the Real: Bicentennial Essays.* Columbus: Ohio State University Press, 2005.

Benjamin, Walter. *Charles Baudelaire: A Lyric Poet in the Era of High Capitalism.* Trans. Harry Zohn. London: New Left Books, 1973.

Bentley, Nancy. "Slaves and Fauns: Hawthorne and the Uses of Primitivism." *English Literary History* 57 (1990): 901–37.

Berlant, Lauren. *The Anatomy of National Fantasy: Hawthorne, Utopia, and Everyday Life.* Chicago: University of Chicago Press, 1991.

Bermingham, Ann. *Landscape and Ideology: The English Rustic Tradition, 1740–1860.* Berkeley: University of California Press, 1986.

Berthold, Dennis. *American Risorgimento: Herman Melville and the Cultural Politics of Italy.* Columbus: Ohio State University Press, 2009.

—. "Melville, Garibaldi, and the Medusa of Revolution." In Reynolds and Hutner. 104–37.

—. "Response to 'Subjective Vision, Romantic History, and the Return of the "Real": The Case of Margaret Fuller and the Roman Republic.'" *South Central Review* 21 (2004): 18–21.

Bhabha, Homi K., ed. *Nation and Narration.* London and New York: Routledge, 1990.

Bjelajac, David. *Millennial Desire and the Apocalyptic Vision of Washington Allston.* Washington, DC: Smithsonian Institution Press, 1988.

—. *Washington Allston, Secret Societies, and the Alchemy of Anglo-American Painting.* Cambridge: Cambridge University Press, 1997.

Blackett, R. J. M. *Building an Antislavery Wall: Black Americans in the Atlantic Abolitionist Movement, 1830–1860.* Baton Rouge: Louisiana State University Press, 1983.

Boggs, Colleen Glenney. *Transnationalism and American Literature: Literary Translation 1773–1892.* New York: Routledge, 2007.

Bohls, Elizabeth A. *Women Travel Writers and the Language of Aesthetics, 1716–1818*. Cambridge: Cambridge University Press, 1995.

Bramen, Carrie Tirado. "A Transatlantic History of the Picturesque: An Introductory Essay." *Nineteenth-Century Prose* 29.2 (2002): 1–19.

Brand, C. P. *Italy and the English Romantics: The Italianate Fashion in Early Nineteenth-Century England*. Cambridge: Cambridge University Press, 1957.

Brand, Dana. *The Spectator and the City in Nineteenth-Century American Literature*. Cambridge: Cambridge University Press, 1991.

Bremer, Sidney H. *Urban Intersections: Meetings of Life and Literature in United States Cities*. Urbana: University of Illinois Press, 1992.

Brennan, Timothy. "The National Longing for Form." In Bhabha. 44–71.

Brodhead, Richard H. *Cultures of Letters: Scenes of Reading and Writing in Nineteenth-Century America*. Chicago: University of Chicago Press, 1993.

—. *The School of Hawthorne*. New York: Oxford University Press, 1986.

Brooks, Van Wyck. *The Dream of Arcadia: American Writers and Artists in Italy 1760–1915*. New York: E. P. Dutton, 1958.

George Loring Brown: Landscapes of Europe and America 1834–1880. Exhibition catalogue. Essays by Thomas W. Leavitt and William David Barry. Burlington, VT: Robert Hull Fleming Museum, 1973.

Brownstein, Rachel M. *Tragic Muse: Rachel of the Comédie-Française*. New York: Knopf, 1993.

Bunn, David. "'Our Wattled Cot': Mercantile and Domestic Space in Thomas Pringle's African Landscapes." In W. J. T. Mitchell, ed. 127–73.

Buonomo, Leonardo. *Backward Glances: Exploring Italy, Reinterpreting America (1831–1866)*. London: Associated University Presses, 1996.

Burnham, Patricia M., and Lucretia Hoover Giese, eds. *Redefining American History Painting*. Cambridge: Cambridge University Press, 1995.

Burstein, Andrew. *The Original Knickerbocker: The Life of Washington Irving*. New York: Basic Books, 2007.

Butler, Marilyn. "The Cult of the South: The Shelley Circle, its Creed and its Influence." *Romantics, Rebels and Reactionaries: English Literature and its Background, 1760–1830*. Oxford: Oxford University Press, 1982. 113–37.

Buzard, James. *The Beaten Track: European Tourism, Literature, and the Ways to "Culture," 1800–1918*. Oxford: Oxford University Press, 1993.

Byer, Robert H. "Words, Monuments, Beholders: The Visual Arts in Hawthorne's *The Marble Faun*." In D. Miller. 163–85.

Caesar, Terry. *Forgiving the Boundaries: Home as Abroad in American Travel Writing*. Athens: University of Georgia Press, 1995.

Cahill, Edward. *Liberty of the Imagination: Aesthetic Theory, Literary Form, and Politics in the Early United States*. Philadelphia: University of Pennsylvania Press, 2012.

Callow, James T. *Kindred Spirits: Knickerbocker Writers and American Artists, 1807–1855*. Chapel Hill: University of North Carolina Press, 1967.

Capper, Charles. "Getting from Here to There." In Capper and Giorcelli. 3–26.

—. *Margaret Fuller: An American Romantic Life*, 2 vols. New York and Oxford: Oxford University Press, 1992, 2007.

Capper, Charles, and Cristina Giorcelli, eds. *Margaret Fuller: Transatlantic Crossings in a Revolutionary Age*. Madison: University of Wisconsin Press, 2007.

Carroll, Bret E. *Spiritualism in Antebellum America*. Bloomington and Indianapolis: Indiana University Press, 1997.

Casper, Scott E., Jeffrey D. Groves, Stephen W. Nissenbaum, and Michael Winship, eds. *A History of the Book in America*, vol. III: *The Industrial Book, 1840–1880*. Chapel Hill: University of North Carolina Press, published in association with the American Antiquarian Society, 2007.

Casteras, Susan P. *English Pre-Raphaelitism and Its Reception in America in the Nineteenth Century*. London and Toronto: Associated University Presses, 1990.

Chambers, Bruce. "Thomas Cole and the Ruined Tower." *Currier Gallery of Art Bulletin* (Fall 1983): 2–32.

Charvat, William. *The Profession of Authorship in America 1800–1870*. Ed. Matthew J. Bruccoli. New York: Columbia University Press, 1992.

Cherry, Deborah. *Painting Women: Victorian Women Artists*. London: Routledge, 1993.

Chevigny, Bell Gale. "To the Edges of Ideology: Margaret Fuller's Centrifugal Evolution." *American Quarterly* 38.2 (1986): 173–201.

—. *The Woman and the Myth: Margaret Fuller's Life and Writings*, rev. edn. Boston: Northeastern University Press, 1994.

Chielens, Edward E., ed. *American Literary Magazines: The Eighteenth and Nineteenth Centuries*. Westport, CT: Greenwood Press, 1986.

Churchill, Kenneth. *Italy and English Literature, 1764–1930*. New York: Palgrave Macmillan, 1980.

Clark, Michael. "A Source for Irving's 'The Young Italian.'" *American Literature* 52 (1980): 111–14.

Clarke, John R. "An Italian Landscape by Thomas Cole." *Arts Magazine* 54.5 (1980): 116–20.

Claybaugh, Amanda. *The Novel of Purpose: Literature and Social Reform in the Anglo-American World*. Ithaca: Cornell University Press, 2007.

Coffey, John W. *Twilight of Arcadia: American Landscape Painters in Rome, 1830–1880*. Exhibition catalogue. Brunswick, ME: Bowdoin College Museum of Art, 1987.

Colbert, Charles. "A Critical Medium: James Jackson Jarves's Vision of Art History." *American Art* 16 (2002): 19–35.

Cole, Phyllis. *The American Writer and the Condition of England, 1815–1860*. New York: Garland Publishing, 1987.

—. "Fuller's Lawsuit and Feminist History." In Bailey et al. 11–31.

—. "The Nineteenth-Century Women's Rights Movement and the Canonization of Margaret Fuller." *ESQ: A Journal of the American Renaissance* 44.1–2 (1998): 1–33.

Comment, Bernard. *The Painted Panorama*. Trans. Anne-Marie Glasheen. New York: H. N. Abrams, 2000.

Conron, John. *American Picturesque*. University Park: Pennsylvania State University Press, 2000.

Copley, Stephen, and Peter Garside, eds. *The Politics of the Picturesque: Literature, Landscape, and Aesthetics since 1770*. Cambridge: Cambridge University Press, 1994.

Corley, Liam. *Bayard Taylor: Determined Dreamer of America's Rise, 1825–1878*. Lewisburg, PA: Bucknell University Press, 2014.

Costello, Leo. "'Gorgeous, but altogether false': Turner, Cole, and Transatlantic Ideas of Decline." In Hemingway and Wallach. 183–205.

Crary, Jonathan. *Techniques of the Observer: On Vision and Modernity in the Nineteenth Century*. Cambridge, MA: MIT Press, 1990.

Craven, Wayne. "Thomas Cole and Italy." *The Magazine Antiques* 114 (1978): 1016–27.

Culkin, Kate. *Harriet Hosmer: A Cultural Biography*. Amherst: University of Massachusetts Press, 2010.

Dabakis, Melissa. *A Sisterhood of Sculptors: American Artists in Nineteenth-Century Rome*. University Park: Pennsylvania State University Press, 2014.

D'Agostino, Peter R. *Rome in America: Transnational Catholic Ideology from the Risorgimento to Fascism*. Chapel Hill: University of North Carolina Press, 2003.

Damon-Bach, Lucinda. "Catharine Maria Sedgwick Tours England: Private Letters, Public Account." In Lueck et al. 21–48.

Damon-Bach, Lucinda, and Victoria Clements, eds. *Catharine Maria Sedgwick: Critical Perspectives*. Boston: Northeastern University Press, 2003.

D'Amore, Maura. "'A Man's Sense of Domesticity': Donald Grant Mitchell's Suburban Vision." *ESQ: A Journal of the American Renaissance* 56.2 (2010): 135–61.

Davidson, Cathy, ed. "No More Separate Spheres!" Special issue of *American Literature* 70 (1998).

Dekker, George. *The American Historical Romance*. Cambridge: Cambridge University Press, 1987.

—. *Fictions of Romantic Tourism: Radcliffe, Scott, and Mary Shelley*. Stanford: Stanford University Press, 2005.

Dictionary of American Biography. New York: Charles Scribner's Sons, 1932.

Douglas, Ann. *The Feminization of American Culture*. New York: Doubleday, 1988.

Dowling, Linda. *Charles Eliot Norton: The Art of Reform in Nineteenth-Century America*. Hanover and London: University of New Hampshire Press, 2007.

Dryden, Edgar A. *The Form of American Romance*. Baltimore: Johns Hopkins University Press, 1988.

During, Simon. "Literature—Nationalism's Other? The Case for Revision." In Bhabha. 138–53.

Eagleton, Terry. *The Ideology of the Aesthetic*. Oxford: Blackwell, 1990.

Eckel, Leslie Elizabeth. *Atlantic Citizens: Nineteenth-Century American Writers at Work in the World*. Edinburgh: Edinburgh University Press, 2013.

Eckel, Leslie Elizabeth, and Clare Frances Elliott, eds. *The Edinburgh Companion to Atlantic Literary Studies*. Edinburgh: Edinburgh University Press, 2016.

Elbert, Monika M. "Striking a Historical Pose: Antebellum Tableaux Vivants, *Godey's* Illustrations, and Margaret Fuller's Heroines." *New England Quarterly* 75 (2002): 235–76.

—, ed. *Separate Spheres No More: Gender Convergence in American Literature, 1830–1930*. Tuscaloosa: University of Alabama Press, 2000.

Eldredge, Charles C., and Barbara Novak. *The Arcadian Landscape: Nineteenth-Century American Painters in Italy*. Exhibition catalogue. University of Kansas Museum of Art, 1972.

Eliot, Samuel Atkins. "Henry Whitney Bellows." *Dictionary of American Biography*, vol. II. Ed. Allen Johnson. New York: Charles Scribner's Sons, 1929. 169.

Ellis, Kate Ferguson. *The Contested Castle: Gothic Novels and the Subversion of Domestic Ideology*. Urbana and Chicago: University of Illinois Press, 1989.

Ellison, Julie. *Delicate Subjects: Romanticism, Gender, and the Ethics of Understanding*. Ithaca: Cornell University Press, 1990.

Elsden, Annamaria Formichella. *Roman Fever: Domesticity and Nationalism in Nineteenth-Century American Women's Writing*. Columbus: Ohio State University Press, 2004.

Erwin, Kathleen. *Fair Scenes and Glorious Works: Thomas Cole in Italy, Switzerland, and England*. Exhibition catalogue. Detroit: Detroit Institute of Arts, 1991.

Fabricant, Carole. "The Aesthetics and Politics of Landscape in the Eighteenth Century." In *Studies in Eighteenth-Century British Art and Aesthetics*. Ed. Ralph Cohen. Berkeley: University of California Press, 1985. 49–81.

Fagg, John, Matthew Pethers, and Robin Vandome. "Introduction: Networks and the Nineteenth-Century Periodical." *American Periodicals: A Journal of History and Criticism* 23 (2013): 93–104.

Felden, Tamara. *Frauen Reisen: Zur literarischen Repräsentation weiblicher Geschlechterrollenerfahrung im 19. Jahrhundert*. New York: Peter Lang, 1993.

Ferber, Linda S. "'Determined Realists': The American Pre-Raphaelistes and the Association for the Advancement of Truth." In Ferber and Gerdts. 11–37.

Ferber, Linda S., and William H. Gerdts. *The New Path: Ruskin and the American Pre-Raphaelites*. New York: Brooklyn Museum and Schocken Books, 1985.

Ferguson, Priscilla Parkhurst. *Paris as Revolution: Writing the Nineteenth-Century City*. Berkeley: University of California Press, 1994.

Fetterley, Judith. "'My Sister! My Sister!': The Rhetoric of Catharine Sedgwick's *Hope Leslie*." *American Literature* 70 (1998): 491–516.

Fink, Steven. "Antebellum Lady Editors and the Language of Authority." In S. Harris. 205–21.

Fish, Cheryl J. *Black and White Women's Travel Narratives: Antebellum Explorations*. Gainesville: University Press of Florida, 2004.

Fleischmann, Fritz. "Cultural Translation as Cultural Critique." In Fleischmann, ed. 1–24.

—. "Margaret Fuller's Socialism." In Bailey et al. 181–210.

—, ed. *Margaret Fuller's Cultural Critique: Her Age and Legacy*. New York: Peter Lang, 2000.

Foreman, P. Gabrielle, and Reginald H. Pitts. "Introduction." In Harriet E. Wilson, *Our Nig: Or, Sketches from the Life of a Free Black*. New York: Penguin, 2005. ix–xxx.

Foucault, Michel. *Discipline and Punish*. Trans. Alan Sheridan. New York: Random House, 1979.

Franchot, Jenny. *Roads to Rome: The Antebellum Protestant Encounter with Catholicism*. Berkeley: University of California Press, 1994.

Franklin, Wayne. "James Fenimore Cooper and American Artists in Europe." In Hemingway and Wallach. 144–67.

Frawley, Maria H. *A Wider Range: Travel Writing by Women in Victorian England*. London and Toronto: Associated University Presses, 1994.

Fryd, Vivien Green. *Art and Empire: The Politics of Ethnicity in the U.S. Capitol, 1815–1860*. New Haven: Yale University Press, 1992.

Frye, Northrop. *Anatomy of Criticism: Four Essays*. Princeton: Princeton University Press, 1957.

"G.H.G." "George Stillman Hillard." *Dictionary of American Biography*, vol. IX. Ed. Allen Johnson. New York: Charles Scribner's Sons, 1932. 49–50.

Gaehtgens, Barbara. "Fictions of Nationhood: Leutze's Pursuit of an American History Painting in Düsseldorf." In Gaehtgens and Ickstadt. 147–82.

Gaehtgens, Thomas W., and Heinz Ickstadt, eds. *American Icons: Transatlantic Perspectives on Eighteenth- and Nineteenth-Century American Art*. Santa Monica: Getty Center for the History of Art and the Humanities, 1992.

Gatta, John. "The Anglican Aspect of Harriet Beecher Stowe." *The New England Quarterly* 73 (2000): 412–33.

Geertz, Clifford. "Thick Description: Toward an Interpretive Theory of Culture." *The Interpretation of Cultures: Selected Essays*. New York: Basic Books, 1973. 3–30.

Gemme, Paola. *Domesticating Foreign Struggles: The Italian Risorgimento and Antebellum American Identity*. Athens: University of Georgia Press, 2005.

Gerdts, William H. "The Düsseldorf Connection." In Gerdts and Thistlethwaite. 125–68.

—. "'"Good Tidings" to the Lovers of the Beautiful': New York's Düsseldorf Gallery, 1849–1862." *American Art Journal* 30 (1999): 50–81.

—. "The Paintings of Washington Allston." In Gerdts and Stebbins. 9–174.

—. "Through a Glass Brightly: The American Pre-Raphaelites and Their Still Lifes and Nature Studies." In Ferber and Gerdts. 39–77.

Gerdts, William H., and Theodore E. Stebbins, Jr. *"A Man of Genius": The Art of Washington Allston (1779–1843)*. Boston: Museum of Fine Arts, 1979.

Gerdts, William H., and Mark Thistlethwaite. *Grand Illusions: History Painting in America*. Fort Worth: Amon Carter Museum, 1988.

Gilbert, Sandra. "From *Patria* to *Matria*: Elizabeth Barrett Browning's Risorgimento." *PMLA* 99.2 (1984): 194–211.

Gilbert, Sandra M., and Susan Gubar. *The Madwoman in the Attic: The Woman Writer and the Nineteenth-Century Literary Imagination*. New Haven: Yale University Press, 1979.

Giles, Paul. "Introduction: The New Atlantic Literary Studies." In Eckel and Elliott. 1–14.

—. *Transatlantic Insurrections: British Culture and the Formation of American Literature, 1730–1860*. Philadelphia: University of Pennsylvania Press, 2001.

Gilman, Ernest B. "Interart Studies and the 'Imperialism' of Language." *Poetics Today* 10 (1989): 5–30.

Gollin, Rita K. *Nathaniel Hawthorne and the Truth of Dreams*. Baton Rouge: Louisiana State University Press, 1979.

Gollin, Rita K., and John L. Idol, Jr. *Prophetic Pictures: Nathaniel Hawthorne's Uses of the Visual Arts*. Westport, CT: Greenwood Press, 1991.

Greenhouse, Wendy. "Daniel Huntington and the Ideal of Christian Art." *Winterthur Portfolio* 31 (1996): 103–40.

—. "Imperiled Ideals: British Historical Heroines in Antebellum American History Painting." In Burnham and Giese. 263–76.

—. "The Landing of the Fathers: Representing the National Past in American History Painting, 1770–1865." In Ayres. 45–63.

Greenwald, Elissa. "Hawthorne and Judaism: Otherness and Identity in *The Marble Faun*." *Studies in the Novel* 23 (1991): 128–38.

Groce, George C., and David H. Wallace. *The New-York Historical Society's Dictionary of Artists in America, 1564–1860*. New Haven: Yale University Press, 1957.

Groseclose, Barbara S. "American Genesis: The Landing of Christopher Columbus." In Gaehtgens and Ickstadt. 11–32.

—. *Emanuel Leutze, 1816–1868: Freedom Is the Only King*. Washington, DC: Smithsonian Institution Press, 1975.

Habermas, Jürgen. "The Public Sphere." In *Rethinking Popular Culture: Contemporary Perspectives in Cultural Studies*. Ed. Chandra Mukerji and Michael Schudson. Berkeley: University of California Press, 1991. 398–404.

Haig, Judith Giblin. "Introduction." In Irving, *Tales of a Traveller*. xiii–xxvi.

—. "Textual Commentary." In Irving, *Tales of a Traveller*. 281–317.

Hale, J. R. "Introduction." In *The Italian Journal of Samuel Rogers*. London: Faber and Faber, 1956. 9–115.

Halttunen, Karen. *Confidence Men and Painted Women: A Study of Middle-Class Culture in America, 1830–1870*. New Haven: Yale University Press, 1982.

Hamilton, Kristie. *America's Sketchbook: The Cultural Life of a Nineteenth-Century Literary Genre*. Athens: Ohio University Press, 1998.

—. "Hawthorne, Modernity, and the Literary Sketch." In Millington, ed. 99–120.

Harris, Neil. *The Artist in American Society: The Formative Years, 1790–1860*. Chicago: Chicago University Press, 1982.

Harris, Sharon M., ed., with Ellen Gruber Garvey. *Blue Pencils and Hidden Hands: Women Editing Periodicals, 1830–1910*. Boston: Northeastern University Press, 2004.

Harrison, Colin. "The Pre-Raphaelites and Italian Art before and after Raphael." In Harrison and Newall. 10–21.

Harrison, Colin, and Christopher Newall. *The Pre-Raphaelites and Italy*. Farnham and Burlington: The Ashmolean Museum, Oxford University, 2010.

Hedges, William L. *Washington Irving: An American Study, 1802–1832*. Baltimore: Johns Hopkins University Press, 1965.

Hedrick, Joan D. *Harriet Beecher Stowe: A Life*. Oxford: Oxford University Press, 1994.

Hemingway, Andrew, and Alan Wallach, eds. *Transatlantic Romanticism: British and American Art and Literature, 1790–1860*. Amherst and Boston: University of Massachusetts Press, 2015.

Herbert, T. Walter. *Dearest Beloved: The Hawthornes and the Making of the Middle-Class Family*. Berkeley: University of California Press, 1993.

Hibbert, Christopher. *The Grand Tour*. London: Weidenfeld and Nicolson, 1969.

Hobsbawm, E. J. *Bandits*. London: Weidenfeld and Nicolson, 1969.

Holcomb, Adele M. "A Neglected Classical Phase of Turner's Art: His Vignettes to Rogers's *Italy*." *Journal of the Warburg and Courtauld Institutes* 32 (1969): 405–10.

—. "Turner and Rogers' 'Italy' Revisited." *Studies in Romanticism* 27.1 (1988): 63–95.

Hollington, Michael, Catherine Watts, and John Jordan, eds. *Imagining Italy: Victorian Writers and Travellers*. Newcastle upon Tyne: Cambridge Scholars Publishing, 2010.

Homestead, Melissa J. *American Women Authors and Literary Property, 1822–1869*. Cambridge: Cambridge University Press, 2005.

Honour, Hugh. *Romanticism*. New York: Harper and Row, 1979.

Howe, Daniel Walker. *What Hath God Wrought: The Transformation of America, 1815–1848*. New York: Oxford University Press, 2007.

Hudspeth, Robert N. "Margaret Fuller and Urban Life." In Bailey et al. 179–205.

Huhtamo, Erkki. *Illusions in Motion: A Media Archaeology of the Moving Panorama and Related Spectacles*. Cambridge, MA: MIT Press, 2013.

Hunt, John Dixon. *The Figure in the Landscape: Poetry, Painting, and Landscape Gardening during the Eighteenth Century*. Baltimore: Johns Hopkins University Press, 1976.

Husch, Gail E. "'Freedom's Holy Cause': History, Religious, and Genre Painting in America, 1840–1860." In Ayres. 81–99.

Hussey, Christopher. *The Picturesque: Studies in a Point of View*. London: Frank Cass, 1967.

Jaffe, Irma B., ed. *The Italian Presence in American Art 1760–1860*. New York: Fordham University Press, 1989.

Jenkins, Ruth Y. "The Gaze of the Victorian Woman Traveler: Spectacles and Phenomena." In K. Siegel. 15–30.

Johns, Elizabeth. *American Genre Painting: The Politics of Everyday Life*. New Haven: Yale University Press, 1991.

Johnston, Patricia. "Samuel F. B. Morse's *Gallery of the Louvre*: Social Tensions in an Ideal World." In Johnston, ed. 42–65.

—, ed. *Seeing High and Low: Representing Social Conflict in American Visual Culture*. Berkeley: University of California Press, 2006.

Jones, Eleanor L. "George Peter Alexander Healy." In Stebbins et al. 244–6.

—. "Sanford Robinson Gifford." In Stebbins et al. 229–30.

Jones, Verina R. "Journalism, 1750–1850." In Panizza and Wood. 120–34.

Jones, Vivien. "'The Coquetry of Nature': Politics and the Picturesque in Women's Fiction." In Copley and Garside. 120–44.

Kaplan, Amy. "Manifest Domesticity." *American Literature* 70 (1998): 581–606.

Kaplan, E. Ann. *Looking for the Other: Feminism, Film, and the Imperial Gaze*. New York: Routledge, 1997.

Karcher, Carolyn L. *The First Woman in the Republic: A Cultural Biography of Lydia Maria Child*. Durham, NC: Duke University Press, 1994.

Kasson, Joy S. *Artistic Voyagers: Europe and the American Imagination in the Works of Irving, Allston, Cole, Cooper, and Hawthorne*. Westport, CT: Greenwood Press, 1982.

—. *Marble Queens and Captives: Women in Nineteenth-Century American Sculpture.* New Haven: Yale University Press, 1990.

Kelley, Mary. "Introduction." In Catharine Maria Sedgwick, *Hope Leslie; Or, Early Times in the Massachusetts.* New Brunswick, NJ: Rutgers University Press, 1987. ix–xxxix.

—. "Introduction." In *The Power of Her Sympathy: The Autobiography and Journal of Catharine Maria Sedgwick.* Boston: Massachusetts Historical Society, 1993. 3–41.

—. "Negotiating a Self: The Autobiography and Journals of Catharine Maria Sedgwick." *New England Quarterly* 66.3 (1993): 366–98.

—. *Private Woman, Public Stage: Literary Domesticity in Nineteenth-Century America.* Oxford: Oxford University Press, 1984.

Kemp, Mark A. R. "*The Marble Faun* and American Postcolonial Ambivalence." *Modern Fiction Studies* 43 (1997): 209–36.

Kennedy, J. Gerald. "Cooper's Europe and His Quarrel with America." In *A Historical Guide to James Fenimore Cooper.* Ed. Leland S. Person. Oxford: Oxford University Press, 2007. 91–122.

Kerber, Linda. *Federalists in Dissent: Imagery and Ideology in Jeffersonian America.* Ithaca and London: Cornell University Press, 1970.

Klimasmith, Betsy. *At Home in the City: Urban Domesticity in American Literature and Culture, 1850–1930.* Durham: University of New Hampshire Press, 2005.

Kloss, William. *Samuel F. B. Morse.* New York: Harry N. Abrams, 1988.

Kohn, Denise, Sarah Meer, and Emily B. Todd, eds. *Transatlantic Stowe: Harriet Beecher Stowe and European Culture.* Iowa City: University of Iowa Press, 2006.

Kolich, Augustus M. "Miriam and the Conversion of the Jews in Nathaniel Hawthorne's *The Marble Faun.*" *Studies in the Novel* 33 (2001): 430–43.

Kopec, Andrew. "Irving, Ruin, and Risk." *Early American Literature* 48.3 (2013): 709–35.

Lacambre, Jean. "Léopold Robert." *French Painting 1774–1830: The Age of Revolution.* Exhibition catalogue. Detroit and New York: Detroit Institute of Arts and Metropolitan Museum of Art, 1975.

Landow, George P. *William Holman Hunt and Typological Symbolism.* New Haven: Yale University Press, 1979.

Lawrence, Karen. *Penelope Voyages: Women and Travel in the British Tradition.* Ithaca and London: Cornell University Press, 1994.

Leavitt, Thomas W., and William David Barry. *George Loring Brown: Landscapes of Europe and America, 1834–1880.* Exhibition catalogue. Burlington, VT: Robert Hull Fleming Museum, 1973.

Lehuu, Isabelle. "Sentimental Figures: Reading *Godey's Lady's Book* in Antebellum America." In *The Culture of Sentiment: Race, Gender, and Sentimentality in Nineteenth-Century America.* Ed. Shirley Samuels. Oxford: Oxford University Press, 1992. 73–91.

Lenehan, William T., and Andrew B. Myers. "Introduction." In Irving, *The Alhambra*. xi–lv.

Leverenz, David. *Manhood and the American Renaissance*. Ithaca: Cornell University Press, 1989.

Levin, David. *History as Romantic Art: Bancroft, Prescott, Motley, and Parkman*. Stanford: Stanford University Press, 1959.

Levine, George, ed. *Aesthetics and Ideology*. New Brunswick, NJ: Rutgers University Press, 1994.

Levine, Robert S. "'Antebellum Rome' in *The Marble Faun*." *American Literary History* 2 (1990): 19–38.

—. *Conspiracy and Romance: Studies in Brockden Brown, Cooper, Hawthorne, and Melville*. Cambridge: Cambridge University Press, 1989.

Long, Lisa A. "Charlotte Forten's Civil War Journals and the Quest for 'Genius, Beauty, and Deathless Fame.'" *Legacy* 16.1 (1999): 37–48.

Loughran, Trish. *The Republic in Print: Print Culture in the Age of U.S. Nation Building, 1770–1870*. New York: Columbia University Press, 2007.

Lueck, Beth L. *American Writers and the Picturesque Tour: The Search for National Identity, 1790–1860*. New York: Garland, 1997.

Lueck, Beth L., Brigitte Bailey, and Lucinda L. Damon-Bach, eds. *Transatlantic Women: Nineteenth-Century American Women Writers and Great Britain*. Durham: University of New Hampshire Press, 2012.

Lupfer, Eric. "The Business of American Magazines." In Casper et al. 248–58.

Luria, Sarah. *Capital Speculations: Writing and Building Washington, D.C.* Durham: University of New Hampshire Press, 2006.

Lüth, Christoph. "Wilhelm von Humboldts Netzwerk mit Intellektuellen und Politikern in Paris: Annäherung und Distanz." *Paedagogica Historica* 43.2 (2007): 257–69.

MacCannell, Dean. *The Tourist: A New Theory of the Leisure Class*. New York: Schocken Books, 1976.

MacDougall, Hugh C. "The Cooper Screens: An Inventory." *James Fenimore Cooper Society Miscellaneous Papers* no. 8. Cooperstown: James Fenimore Cooper Society, 1996.

McFadden, Margaret H. *Golden Cables of Sympathy: The Transatlantic Sources of Nineteenth-Century Feminism*. Lexington: University Press of Kentucky, 1999.

McGill, Meredith. *American Literature and the Culture of Reprinting, 1834–1853*. Philadelphia: University of Pennsylvania Press, 2003.

Machor, James L. *Pastoral Cities: Urban Ideals and the Symbolic Landscape of America*. Madison: University of Wisconsin Press, 1987.

McKinsey, Elizabeth. *Niagara Falls: Icon of the American Sublime*. Cambridge: Cambridge University Press, 1985.

McLaughlin, Martin. "The Pre-Raphaelites and Italian Literature." In Harrison and Newall. 22–35.

McWilliams, John, Jr. *Political Justice in a Republic: James Fenimore Cooper's America*. Berkeley: University of California Press, 1972.

Madden, Etta. "American Anne Hampton Brewster's Social Circles: Bagni di Lucca, 1873, and Roman Rodolfo Lanciani." In *Questioni di Genere: Femminilità e Effeminatezza nella Cultura Vittoriana*. Ed. Roberta Ferrari and Laura Giovannelli. Bologna: Bononia University Press, 2016. 117–44.

Madison, Robert D. "Cooper's *The Wing-and-Wing* and the Concept of the Byronic Pirate." In *Literature and Lore of the Sea*. Ed. Patricia Ann Carlson. Amsterdam: Rodopi, 1986. 119–32.

Manoguerra, Paul A. "This Cause Is Ours: Martin Johnson Heade's *Roman Newsboys* and the American Reaction to the Roman Republic of 1848–49." In Manoguerra. 35–49.

Manoguerra, Paul A., with an essay by Janice Simon. *Classic Ground: Mid-Nineteenth-Century American Painting and the Italian Encounter*. Athens: Georgia Museum of Art, 2004.

Marshall, Megan. *Margaret Fuller: A New American Life*. Boston: Houghton Mifflin Harcourt, 2013.

—. *The Peabody Sisters: Three Women Who Ignited American Romanticism*. Boston: Houghton Mifflin, 2005.

Martin, Robert K., and Leland S. Person, eds. *Roman Holidays: American Writers and Artists in Nineteenth-Century Italy*. Iowa City: University of Iowa Press, 2002.

Matteson, John. *The Lives of Margaret Fuller*. New York: Norton, 2012.

Mellor, Anne K. *Romanticism and Gender*. New York: Routledge, 1993.

Mellow, James R. *Nathaniel Hawthorne in His Times*. Boston: Houghton Mifflin, 1980.

Mena Marqués, Manuela B. "Murillo, Bartolomé Esteban." *Oxford Art Online*. <http://www.oxfordartonline.com/subscriber/article/grove/art/T060472?q=Murillo%2C+Bartolom%C3%A9+Esteban&search=quick&pos=1&_start=1#firsthit> (accessed 17 June 2016).

Michasiw, Kim Ian. "Nine Revisionist Theses on the Picturesque." *Representations* 38 (1992): 76–100.

Miller, Angela. *The Empire of the Eye: Landscape Representation and American Cultural Politics, 1825–1875*. Ithaca: Cornell University Press, 1993.

Miller, David C., ed. *American Iconology: New Approaches to Nineteenth-Century Art and Literature*. New Haven: Yale University Press, 1993.

Millington, Richard. "Where Is Hawthorne's Rome? *The Marble Faun* and the Cultural Space of Middle-Class Leisure." In Martin and Person. 9–27.

—, ed. *The Cambridge Companion to Nathaniel Hawthorne*. Cambridge: Cambridge University Press, 2004.

Mills, Sara. *Discourses of Difference: An Analysis of Women's Travel Writing and Colonialism*. London: Routledge, 1991.

Mitchell, Catherine C., ed. *Margaret Fuller's New York Journalism: A Biographical Essay and Key Writings*. Knoxville: University of Tennessee Press, 1995.

Mitchell, Thomas R. *Hawthorne's Fuller Mystery*. Amherst: University of Massachusetts Press, 1998.

Mitchell, W. J. T. *Iconology: Image, Text, Ideology*. Chicago: University of Chicago Press, 1986.

—, ed. *Landscape and Power*. Chicago: University of Chicago Press, 1994.

Mitnick, Barbara J. "The History of History Painting." In Ayres. 29–43.

Moine, Fabienne. "*The Diary of an Ennuyée*: Anna Jameson's Sentimental Journey to Italy or the Exile of a Fragmented Heart." In *Exiles, Emigrés and Intermediaries: Anglo-Italian Cultural Transactions*. Ed. Barbara Schaff. Amsterdam: Editions Rodopi, 2010. 289–300.

Monk, Samuel H. *The Sublime: A Study of Critical Theories in Eighteenth-Century England*. Ann Arbor: University of Michigan Press, 1960.

Morgan, David. *Protestants and Pictures: Religion, Visual Culture and the Age of American Mass Production*. New York: Oxford University Press, 1999.

Mulvey, Christopher. *Transatlantic Manners: Social Patterns in Nineteenth-Century Anglo-American Travel Literature*. Cambridge: Cambridge University Press, 1990.

Mulvey, Laura. "Visual Pleasure and Narrative Cinema." *Visual and Other Pleasures*. Bloomington and Indianapolis: Indiana University Press, 1989. 14–28.

Munsterberg, Marjorie. "A Biographical Sketch of Robert Macpherson." *Art Bulletin* 68 (1986): 142–53.

Murray, Meg McGavran. *Margaret Fuller: Wandering Pilgrim*. Athens: University of Georgia Press, 2008.

Myers, Kenneth John. "On the Cultural Construction of Landscape Experience: Contact to 1850." In D. Miller. 58–79.

Nelson, Dana D. *National Manhood: Capitalist Citizenship and the Imagined Fraternity of White Men*. Durham, NC: Duke University Press, 1998.

Nerone, John. "Newspapers and the Public Sphere." In Casper et al. 230–48.

Nevius, Blake. *Cooper's Landscapes: An Essay on the Picturesque Vision*. Berkeley: University of California Press, 1976.

Nord, David Paul. "A Republican Literature: Magazine Reading and Readers in Late-Eighteenth-Century New York." In *Reading in America: Literature and Social History*. Ed. Cathy N. Davidson. Baltimore: Johns Hopkins University Press, 1989. 114–39.

Nord, Deborah Epstein. *Walking the Victorian Streets: Women, Representation, and the City*. Ithaca: Cornell University Press, 1995.

Novak, Barbara. *Nature and Culture: American Landscape and Painting, 1825–1875*. New York: Oxford University Press, 1980.

Oettermann, Stephan. *The Panorama: History of a Mass Medium*. Trans. Deborah Lucas Schneider. New York: Zone Books, 1997.

Okker, Patricia. *Our Sister Editors: Sarah J. Hale and the Tradition of Nineteenth-Century American Women Editors*. Athens and London: University of Georgia Press, 1995.

O'Reilly, William. "Movements in the Atlantic World, 1450–1850." In *The Oxford Handbook of The Atlantic World 1450–1850*. Ed. Nicholas Canny and Philip Morgan. Oxford: Oxford University Press, 2011. 305–23.

Osborne, William S. *Caroline M. Kirkland*. New York: Twayne Publishers, 1972.

Ourusoff, Elizabeth. "*View of Florence from San Miniato.*" *The Bulletin of the Cleveland Museum of Art* 49 (1962).

Panizza, Letizia, and Sharon Wood, eds. *A History of Women's Writing in Italy*. Cambridge: Cambridge University Press, 2000.

Parry, Ellwood C., III. *The Art of Thomas Cole: Ambition and Imagination*. Newark and London: University of Delaware Press and Associated University Presses, 1988.

Person, Leland S. "Falling into Heterosexuality: Sculpting Male Bodies in *The Marble Faun* and *Roderick Hudson*." In Martin and Person. 107–39.

Pollock, Griselda. *Vision and Difference: Femininity, Feminism, and the Histories of Art*. London and New York: Routledge, 1988.

Powell, Cecilia. *Turner in the South: Rome, Naples, Florence*. New Haven: Yale University Press, 1987.

Pratt, Mary Louise. *Imperial Eyes: Travel Writing and Transculturation*. London and New York: Routledge, 1992.

Prettejohn, Elizabeth. *The Art of the Pre-Raphaelites*. Princeton: Princeton University Press, 2000.

Price, Roger, ed. *1848 in France*. Ithaca: Cornell University Press, 1975.

Proctor, Nancy. "The Purloined Studio: The Woman Sculptor as Phallic Ghost in Hawthorne's *The Marble Faun*." In Martin and Person. 60–72.

Pudaloff, Ross. "The Gaze of Power: Cooper's Revision of the Domestic Novel, 1835–1850." *Genre* 17 (1984): 275–95.

Reichart, Walter A. "Some Sources of Irving's 'Italian Banditti' Stories." *Festschrift für Walther Fischer*. Heidelberg: Carl Winter, 1959.

Reynolds, David S. *Beneath the American Renaissance: The Subversive Imagination in the Age of Emerson and Melville*. New York: Knopf, 1988.

Reynolds, Larry J. "American Cultural Iconography: Vision, History, and the Real." *American Literary History* 9 (1997): 381–95.

—. *European Revolutions and the American Literary Renaissance*. New Haven: Yale University Press, 1988.

—. *Righteous Violence: Revolution, Slavery, and the American Renaissance*. Athens and London: University of Georgia Press, 2011.

—. "Subjective Vision, Romantic History, and the Return of the 'Real': The Case of Margaret Fuller and the Roman Republic." *South Central Review* 21 (2004): 1–17.

Reynolds, Larry J., and Gordon Hutner. *National Imaginaries, American Identities: The Cultural Work of American Iconography*. Princeton: Princeton University Press, 2000.

Riall, Lucy. *The Italian Risorgimento: State, Society, and National Unification*. London and New York: Routledge, 1994.

Ricci, Susan C. "Thomas Hicks." In Stebbins et al. 198–200.

—. "Samuel F. B. Morse." In Stebbins et al. 282–6.

Richardson, E. P. *Washington Allston: A Study of the Romantic Artist in America*. Chicago: University of Chicago Press, 1948.

Richardson, E. P., and Otto Wittmann, Jr. *Travelers in Arcadia: American Artists in Italy 1830–1875*. Exhibition catalogue. Detroit and Toledo: The Detroit Institute of Arts and the Toledo Museum of Art, 1951.

Richardson, Robert D., Jr. "Emerson's Italian Journey." *Browning Institute Studies* 12 (1984): 121–31.

Ricorda, Ricciarda. "Travel Writing, 1750–1860." Trans. Sharon Wood. In Panizza and Wood. 107–19.

Ridinger, Gayle. "A Short Biography of Francesco Secchi de Casali." The Secret Price of History, <http://www.secretpriceofhistory.com/francesco-secchi-de-casali.html> (accessed 24 March 2017).

Rigal, Laura. *The American Manufactory: Art, Labor, and the World of Things in the Early Republic*. Princeton: Princeton University Press, 1998.

Ringe, Donald A. *The Pictorial Mode: Space and Time in the Art of Bryant, Irving and Cooper*. Lexington: University Press of Kentucky, 1971.

Riss, Arthur. *Race, Slavery, and Liberalism in Nineteenth-Century American Literature*. Cambridge: Cambridge University Press, 2006.

Roberts, Audrey J. "New Light on Caroline Kirkland's New York Years." *American Literary Realism* 36 (2004): 269–76.

Robinson, Sidney K. *Inquiry into the Picturesque*. Chicago: University of Chicago Press, 1991.

Rodier, Katharine. "Nathaniel Hawthorne and *The Marble Faun*: Textual and Contextual Reflections of *Corinne, or Italy*." In *The Novel's Seductions: Staël's* Corinne *in Critical Inquiry*. Ed. Karyna Szmurlo. Lewisburg, PA: Bucknell University Press; London: Associated University Presses, 1999. 221–42.

Rosen, Charles, and Henri Zerner. *Romanticism and Realism: The Mythology of Nineteenth-Century Art*. New York: Norton, 1985.

Rowe, John Carlos. "Nathaniel Hawthorne and Transnationality." In Millicent Bell. 88–106.

Rubin-Dorsky, Jeffrey. *Adrift in the Old World: The Psychological Pilgrimage of Washington Irving*. Chicago: University of Chicago Press, 1988.

Russo, John Paul. "The Unbroken Charm: Margaret Fuller, G. S. Hillard, and the American Tradition of Travel Writing." In Capper and Giorcelli. 124–55.

Ryan, Mary P. *Women in Public: Between Banners and Ballots, 1825–1880.* Baltimore: Johns Hopkins University Press, 1990.

Salomone, A. William. "The Nineteenth-Century Discovery of Italy: An Essay in American Cultural History. Prolegomena to a Historiographical Problem." *The American Historical Review* 73.5 (1968): 1359–91.

Samuels, Shirley. "Introduction." In *The Culture of Sentiment: Race, Gender, and Sentimentality in Nineteenth-Century America.* Ed. Samuels. Oxford: Oxford University Press, 1992. 3–8.

—. *Romances of the Republic: Women, the Family, and Violence in the Literature of the Early American Nation.* Oxford: Oxford University Press, 1996.

Schriber, Mary Suzanne. *Writing Home: American Women Abroad, 1830–1920.* Charlottesville: University Press of Virginia, 1997.

Scobey, David M. *Empire City: The Making and Meaning of the New York City Landscape.* Philadelphia: Temple University Press, 2002.

Scraba, Jeffrey. "'Dear Old Romantic Spain': Washington Irving Imagines Andalucía." In Almeida. 275–96.

Sedgwick, Eve Kosofsky. *Between Men: English Literature and Male Homosocial Desire.* New York: Columbia University Press, 1985.

Sheets, Robin. "History and Romance: Harriet Beecher Stowe's *Agnes of Sorrento* and George Eliot's *Romola*." *Clio* 26 (1997): 323–46.

Siegel, Jonah. *Haunted Museum: Longing, Travel and the Art-Romance Tradition.* Princeton: Princeton University Press, 2005.

Siegel, Kristi, ed. *Gender, Genre, and Identity in Women's Travel Writing.* New York: Peter Lang, 2004.

Simon, Janice. "'Impressed in Memory': John Frederick Kensett's *Italian Scene*." In Manoguerra, *Classic Ground*. 51–70.

Smith, Denis Mack, ed. *The Making of Italy, 1796–1870.* New York: Walker and Co., 1968.

Smith, Gail K. "Art and the Body in *Agnes of Sorrento*." In Kohn et al. 167–86.

Sofer, Naomi Z. *Making the "America of Art": Cultural Nationalism and Nineteenth-Century Women Writers.* Columbus: Ohio State University Press, 2005.

Sommer, Doris. *Foundational Fictions: The National Romances of Latin America.* Berkeley: University of California Press, 1991.

Soria, Regina. *Dictionary of Nineteenth-Century American Artists in Italy, 1760–1914.* London: Associated University Presses, 1982.

Spiller, Robert E. *Fenimore Cooper: Critic of His Times.* New York: Minton, Balch, 1931.

Stansell, Christine. *City of Women: Sex and Class in New York, 1789–1860.* New York: Knopf, 1986.

Stansell, Christine, and Sean Wilentz. "Cole's America." In Truettner and Wallach. 3–21.

Stebbins, Theodore E., Jr. "The Drawings of Washington Allston." In Gerdts and Stebbins. 203–42.

—. "Martin Johnson Heade." In Stebbins et al. 201–3.

Stebbins, Theodore E., Jr., et al. *The Lure of Italy: American Artists and the Italian Experience 1760–1914*. Boston and New York: Museum of Fine Arts, Boston, and Harry N. Abrams, Inc., 1992.

Steele, Jeffrey. "Reconfiguring 'Public Attention': Margaret Fuller in New York City." *Nineteenth-Century Prose* 42.2 (2015): 125–54.

—. *Transfiguring America: Myth, Ideology, and Mourning in Margaret Fuller's Writing*. Columbia: University of Missouri Press, 2001.

Stein, Roger B. *John Ruskin and Aesthetic Thought in America, 1840–1900*. Cambridge, MA: Harvard University Press, 1967.

Steiner, Wendy. *Pictures of Romance: Form Against Context in Painting and Literature*. Chicago: University of Chicago Press, 1988.

Stokes, John. "Rachel Felix." In Michael R. Booth, John Stokes, and Susan Bassnet, *Three Tragic Actresses: Siddons, Rachel, Ristori*. Cambridge: Cambridge University Press, 1996. 66–116.

Stowe, William W. *Going Abroad: European Travel in Nineteenth-Century American Culture*. Princeton: Princeton University Press, 1994.

Tamarkin, Elisa. *Anglophilia: Deference, Devotion, and Antebellum America*. Chicago: University of Chicago Press, 2008.

Taylor, Andrew. *Thinking America: New England Intellectuals and the Varieties of American Identity*. Durham: University of New Hampshire Press, 2010.

Tebbel, John, and Mary Ellen Zuckerman. *The Magazine in America, 1741–1990*. Oxford: Oxford University Press, 1991.

Tellefsen, Blythe Ann. "'The Case with My Dear Native Land': Nathaniel Hawthorne's Vision of America in *The Marble Faun*." *Nineteenth-Century Literature* 54 (2000): 455–79.

Thistlethwaite, Mark. "The Most Important Themes: History Painting and Its Place in American Art." In Gerdts and Thistlethwaite. 7–58.

Thompson, G. R., and Eric Carl Link. *Neutral Ground: New Traditionalism and the American Romance Controversy*. Baton Rouge: Louisiana State University Press, 1999.

Tompkins, Jane. *Sensational Designs: The Cultural Work of American Fiction 1790–1860*. Oxford: Oxford University Press, 1985.

Trease, Geoffrey. *The Grand Tour*. New York: Holt, Rinehart and Winston, 1967.

Truettner, William H. "The Art of History: American Exploration and Discovery Scenes, 1840–1860." *American Art Journal* 14 (1982): 4–31.

Truettner, William H., and Alan Wallach, eds. *Thomas Cole: Landscape into History*. New Haven and Washington, DC: Yale University Press and the National Museum of American Art, 1994.

Tuchinsky, Adam-Max. "'More Anon': American Socialism and Margaret Fuller's 1848." In Bailey et al. 100–27.

Upton, Dell. "Inventing the Metropolis: Civilization and Urbanity in Antebellum New York." In *Art and the Empire City: New York, 1825–1861.* Exhibition catalogue. Ed. Catherine Hoover Voorsanger and John K. Howat. New York: Metropolitan Museum of Art, 2000. 3–45.

Urry, John. *The Tourist Gaze: Leisure and Travel in Contemporary Societies.* London: Sage Publications, 1990.

Vance, William L. *America's Rome,* 2 vols. New Haven: Yale University Press, 1989.

Von Frank, Albert. *The Sacred Game: Provincialism and Frontier Consciousness in American Literature, 1630–1860.* Cambridge: Cambridge University Press, 1985.

Von Mehren, Joan. "Establishing the Facts on the Ossoli Family: An Experiment in E-Mail Research." *Margaret Fuller Society Newsletter* 9 (2001): 2–3.

—. *Minerva and the Muse: A Life of Margaret Fuller.* Amherst: University of Massachusetts Press, 1994.

Von Rosk, Nancy. "Domestic Visions and Shifting Identities: The Urban Novel and the Rise of a Consumer Culture in America, 1852–1925." Dissertation, University of New Hampshire, 1999.

Voss, Frederick. "Webster Replying to Hayne: George Healy and the Economics of History Painting." *American Art* 15 (2001): 34–53.

Wallace, Marcia Briggs. "Washington Allston's *Moonlit Landscape.*" In Jaffe. 82–94.

Wallach, Alan. "Cole, Byron, and *The Course of Empire.*" *Art Bulletin* 50.4 (1968): 375–9.

—. "Making a Picture of the View from Mount Holyoke." In D. Miller. 80–91.

—. "Thomas Cole: Landscape and the Course of American Empire." In Truettner and Wallach. 23–111.

Warner, Michael. *The Letters of the Republic: Publication and the Public Sphere in Eighteenth-Century America.* Cambridge, MA: Harvard University Press, 1990.

Warrell, Ian. *Turner Inspired: In the Light of Claude.* Exhibition catalogue. London: National Gallery Company, 2012.

Weisbuch, Robert. *Atlantic Double-Cross: American Literature and British Influence in the Age of Emerson.* Chicago: University of Chicago Press, 1986.

Weiskel, Thomas. *The Romantic Sublime: Studies in the Structure and Psychology of Transcendence.* Baltimore: Johns Hopkins University Press, 1976.

Williams, Raymond. *Marxism and Literature.* Oxford: Oxford University Press, 1977.

Williams, Stanley T. *The Life of Washington Irving*, vol. I. New York: Oxford University Press, 1935.

Williams, Susan S. "Authors and Literary Authorship." In Casper et al. 90–116.

—. "Manufacturing Intellectual Equipment: The Tauchnitz Edition of *The Marble Faun*." In *Reading Books: Essays on the Material Text and Literature in America*. Ed. Michele Moylan and Lane Stiles. Amherst: University of Massachusetts Press, 1996. 117–50.

Wineapple, Brenda. *Hawthorne: A Life*. New York: Knopf, 2003.

Wittmann, Otto. "The Attraction of Italy for American Painters." *Antiques* (May 1964): 552–6.

Wolf, Bryan Jay. *Romantic Re-Vision: Culture and Consciousness in Nineteenth-Century American Painting and Literature*. Chicago: University of Chicago Press, 1982.

Wright, Nathalia. *American Novelists in Italy. The Discoverers: Allston to James*. Philadelphia: University of Pennsylvania Press, 1965.

—. "Introduction to Volume I." In Irving, *Journals and Notebooks*, vol. I, 1803–1806. xxvii–xxxvi.

Wu, Duncan. *William Hazlitt: The First Modern Man*. Oxford and New York: Oxford University Press, 2008.

Zagarell, Sandra A. "Introduction." In Caroline Kirkland, *A New Home, Who'll Follow?* New Brunswick, NJ: Rutgers University Press, 1990. xi–xlvi.

Zwarg, Christina. *Feminist Conversations: Fuller, Emerson, and the Play of Reading*. Ithaca and London: Cornell University Press, 1995.

Index

References to images are in *italics*; references to notes are indicated by n.